Management Development

In organizational development, the effectiveness of management is recognized as one of the determinants of organizational success. Therefore, investment in management development can be of direct economic benefit to the organization. This volume provides a comprehensive and up-to-date account of the state of research and practice in management development.

Although existing knowledge in this field is acknowledged as being relatively extensive, the book recognizes a need continually to update this current body of knowledge with the latest innovations in high-quality research and practice. By disseminating new empirical research, the book aims to inform teaching and learning and provide examples to stimulate future research and encourage the use of research-based practice in organizations.

With contributions from a host of respected thinkers – including, for example, Geoff Chivers, Richard Thorpe and Jonathan Winterton – this book will be a highly valuable research and learning tool for all those students and researchers with an interest in this area.

Rosemary Hill is a visiting research fellow in the Nottingham Business School and an independent HR consultant specializing in individual and organization development. **Jim Stewart** is Professor of HRD at Nottingham Business School.

Routledge studies in human resource development
Edited by Monica Lee
Lancaster University, UK

HRD theory is changing rapidly. Recent advances in theory and practice, how we conceive of organizations and of the world of knowledge, have led to the need to reinterpret the field. This series aims to reflect and foster the development of HRD as an emergent discipline.

Encompassing a range of different international, organizational, methodological and theoretical perspectives, the series promotes theoretical controversy and reflective practice.

Management Development

Perspectives from research and
practice

**Edited by Rosemary Hill
and Jim Stewart**

LONDON AND NEW YORK

First published 2007
by Routledge
2 Park Square, Milton Park, Abingdon, Oxon OX14 4RN

Simultaneously published in the USA and Canada
by Routledge
270 Madison Ave, New York, NY 10016

Routledge is an imprint of the Taylor & Francis Group, an informa business

© 2007 selection and editorial matter Rosemary Hill and Jim Stewart;
individual chapters, the contributors

Typeset in Baskerville by Wearset Ltd, Boldon, Tyne and Wear
Printed and bound in Great Britain by TJI Digital, Padstow, Cornwall

British Library Cataloguing in Publication Data
A catalogue record for this book is available from the British Library

Library of Congress Cataloging in Publication Data
A catalog record for this book has been requested

ISBN10: 0-415-39602-6 (hbk)

ISBN13: 978-0-415-39602-8 (hbk)

Contents

Figures

Tables

Notes on contributors

Graham Borley has extensive and practical business experience spanning a 20-year period, which includes senior developmental roles for three blue-chip organizations. At the time of writing his chapter he was the Talent Development Manager at Panasonic UK. Graham is currently the Practice Head for Change and Strategic Human Capital Improvement at the Blue Edge Consulting group.

Dr Nadine Bristow has had a 19-year career working within the HRD/HRM field. She specializes in action learning facilitation and became a DBA in 2001 with her research in this field. Through her organization, Acorn Training & Consultancy Services Ltd, her goal is to make action learning 'the development tool of choice'.

Dr Paul Brown is a Senior Lecturer in Strategic Management at the University of Northampton, where he was previously Director of Sunley Management Centre, a residential management development and training centre. His teaching is mostly on postgraduate programmes, and his research areas are management development and business strategy.

Geoff Chivers is Emeritus Professor of Professional Development in the Professional and Management Development Centre of the Business School at Loughborough University. Previously Professor of Continuing Education at the University of Sheffield, Geoff has a career-long interest in adult education and training, with a particular focus on continuing professional development.

Norma D'Annunzio-Green is a Senior Lecturer in HRM at Napier University, Edinburgh. Current research centres on HRM in the service sector. She has published in a number of HRM journals, co-edited a textbook on *HRM in Tourism and Hospitality*, and is on the Editorial Board of *The International Journal of Contemporary Hospitality Management*.

Karin Derksen is HRD consultant at EMC Learning in Company. As a consultant she focuses on management development, especially in combination with business development. She tries to stimulate organizations to learn more at the workplace, during day-to-day work. A visible effect of learning interventions at the workplace is her goal.

Annie Dutech teaches Human Resource Management at Toulouse Business School, where she coordinates the HR Department. Her research interests include management development and human resource strategy.

Tim Finch-Lees has spent the bulk of his managerial career with Diageo PLC, occupying a variety of senior positions in the UK, France and South America. Before this, he worked for Allied-Signal in France and the USA, and for Booz Allen and Hamilton in London. Currently, he is a doctoral researcher and associate teaching fellow at Birkbeck, University of London.

Helen Francis is a Senior Lecturer in HRM and Fellow of the CIPD. Having published in a wide range of HRM and management journals, her current research interests include investigations into the future roles of HR practitioners, management learning, and application of discourse theory in management research.

Dr Hans-Werner Franz is a social scientist (also translator, interpreter, journalist) and senior researcher and consultant at Sozial-forschungsstelle Dortmund. His fields of expertise include development of vocational training systems; organization development; cooperative work systems; organizational quality (focus on EFQM); labour market; and regional development with a focus on old industrial regions.

Dr Thomas Garavan is a Senior Lecturer in HRD at the University of Limerick, Ireland. He is currently the editor of the *Journal of European Industrial Training*. His research interests include training design, management development processes, stakeholders' approaches to training management, and management development centre processes. He has published widely in the areas of employee training and development, and is the co-author of the leading Irish training and development textbook.

Jeff Gold is Principal Lecturer in Organisation Learning at Leeds Business School. The fourth edition of his textbook on *Human Resource Management* (with John Bratton) was published by Palgrave Macmillan in 2006, and a book on *Management Development* (with Alan Mumford) was published in January, 2004.

Bob Hamlin is Emeritus Professor of Human Resource Development at the University of Wolverhampton, and a management and organization development consultant. His research is focused mainly on managerial and leadership effectiveness within public and private sector organizations, the results of which have been published widely both nationally and internationally.

Dr Rosemary Hill is a visiting research fellow in the Nottingham Business School, and an independent HR consultant specializing in individual and organization development across a range of industry sectors. She works closely with the UK National School of Government on projects and MD programmes aligned to civil service HR modernization. She is also a key associate of the Leadership Foundation for Higher Education, and an external moderator of CIPD professional programmes. Rosemary has contributed chapters to other books in the Routledge 'Studies in HRD' series.

Robin Holt is Roberts University Fellow at Leeds University Business School. He received his PhD in Government from the LSE. His work involves the investigation of the social and moral rules and purposes informing economic and organizational activity. He has published in a number of fields, but mainly that of organization studies.

Paul Keursten is a partner in Kessels & Smit, The Learning Company, and director of the Foundation for Corporate Education. His consultancy, teaching and research work focuses on learning in a knowledge economy; learning for innovation; work-based learning; and combining learning and organizational development. Currently he is also leading a research programme on knowledge productivity.

Alain Klarsfeld teaches European Human Resource Management in the Toulouse Business School international programmes, and is responsible for a specialized Masters degree for HR managers. He has published extensively on the management of competence, having edited *Gérer les compétences: Des instruments aux processus* (Vuibert, 2003) with Ewan Oiry.

Françoise Le Deist teaches Human Resource Management and Organizational Behaviour at Toulouse Business School, where she is responsible for specialized Masters degrees for managers in the health and pharmaceutical sectors. She is currently researching European approaches to competence development and the management of competence in the hospitals sector.

Chris Mabey has worked as an occupational psychologist for British Telecom, and headed up management training for Rank Xerox UK. He is Professor of Human Resource Management at Birmingham University Business School, where he teaches International HRM on the Masters programmes and leads a European project on management development. For further details, see: www.business.bham.ac.uk/bbs.

Dr Alma McCarthy is a Lecturer in HRD at the J.E. Cairnes Graduate school of Business and Public Policy at NUI, Galway, Ireland. She has published nationally and internationally on multisource feedback, management training and development, and work–life balance. Her research interests include management development, 360-degree feedback, and work–life balance.

Jill Palmer is a solicitor, HR professional PRINCE2 practitioner. After eight years leading change at DaimlerChrysler UK Limited as Customer Operations Director, General Counsel and HK Director, Jill now runs Proleader Limited, the change management advisor, which undertakes strategic reviews, change implementation and coaching for its clients.

Claire Ponsford was a placement student at Panasonic, completing research for her dissertation at the same time as co-authoring the chapter with Graham Borley. She has since graduated from Plymouth University, in 2005, with a degree in Personnel Management. Claire is a graduate member of the CIPD and is currently working as an HR adviser for a global pharmaceutical organization. An HR generalist who is involved at every stage of the employee life cycle, aiming to deliver tactical solutions to support business strategies, Claire aspires to become an HR manager.

Dr Clare Rigg is Senior Lecturer in the School of Business and Social Studies at the Institute of Technology, Tralee, Ireland. Her early work was in local government and the voluntary sector, working on urban regeneration. For many years she has worked with practitioners from all sectors, integrating action learning and action research with issues of organization development, leadership and management development, and with improving inter-agency working. She has researched and written on action learning, critical action learning, management learning and human resource development.

Rod Shelton is Course Director of the MSc in Leadership and Change Management at UCE Birmingham Business School. His approach uses action research to enable participation and ensure innovation and effective growth. Rod is currently working with leaders in several sectors and organizations, including health, housing, the voluntary sector, distribution and automotive. He has contributed to BSi and European Commission projects on knowledge and culture.

Lynda (Lyn) Stansfield is an academic, Chartered HR practitioner and executive coach with over 30 years' management and leadership development experience across public and private sectors. She has directed MBA programmes and taught at several business schools, including Cranfield and Bradford. Lyn is currently a Development Adviser for the National Senior Careers Advisory Service, Home Office.

Jim Stewart is Professor of HRD at Nottingham Business School, where he is also Joint Course Leader of the highly successful NBS Doctorate in

Business Administration. He is Chair of the UFHRD and active in national roles with the CIPD. Jim is co-editor of four other books in the Routledge Studies in HRD Series

Jan N. Streumer is a Professor at Rotterdam University, The Netherlands. He has specialized in Vocational Education and Human Resource Development. His teaching, research and consulting interests include school-to-work transition, transfer of training, on-the-job training and work-related learning. He serves on the editorial board of several scientific journals (for example, *International Journal of Human Resource Development and Management*, *International Journal of Vocational Education and Training*, and *Human Resource Development International*). He has served as board member of the Academy of HRD.

Richard Thorpe is Professor of Management Development at Leeds University Business School. Following a period working in industry, he joined the Pay and Reward Research Centre at Strathclyde University. More recently, his teaching and research have focused on management learning and organizational development. He is a member of the ESRC Training and Development Board, and on the Council of the British Academy of Management.

Kiran Trehan is Head of Department of Management at the University of Central England, where she undertakes research, teaching and consultancy with a variety of public and private sector organizations in the area of human resource/organizational development. Her fields of interest include critical approaches to HRD, management learning, power and emotions in organizational development. Her current research interests include critical thinking in HRD, critical reflection and action learning in practice, with particular reference to leadership development, power relations and group dynamics.

Jaap Voeten is a development economist who has worked for years in small business and women's entrepreneurship promotion. As resident Senior Adviser to research and training projects of the Vietnam Women's Union, he gained hands-on experience in qualitative and quantitative impact assessment studies. Current research focuses on institutions in small business, and management development.

Jonathan Winterton is Professor of Human Resource Development and Director of Research and International Development at Toulouse Business School. Researching management development, vocational training and social dialogue, he co-authored *Developing Managerial Competence* (Routledge, 1999) with Ruth Winterton and is currently editing *Trade Union Approaches to Competence Development* with Lars Magnusson.

Foreword

Management development (MD) is a large and complex field with fuzzy boundaries and many perspectives. Trying to get to grips with it must be rather like wrestling an octopus – I have never tried to do this, but I imagine octopus wrestlers might well have a strong need for a good net in which to capture the thing. I was therefore delighted to be asked to provide a foreword to this book, which not only provides the net but also does so in a scholarly and accessible manner.

Both the editors and each of the contributing authors is well respected in the field and has something unique to say. This is important, as the field of MD is littered with toolkits of how to do it – often demonstrating little thought about what 'it' is or whether the tools are fit for purpose. That is not the case here. Each writer takes a key issue in the field, and explores it in the light of the theories and practices that surround it. Some focus more in one way, and others in another, but in essence each writer is providing a detailed, up-to-date snapshot of his or her area of interest.

This is important, as the theory and practice of MD are not easily bounded notions. Not only do 'theory' and 'practice' influence each other; not only is the area to which they are applied contentious (for example, is MD 'really' about developing people or organizations?); not only is there debate about what is meant by 'development' (Lee, 1997) and by 'management'; not only are there differences between different types of organization, levels within an organization, and cultural approaches; but also there are major ethical, economic and political questions about what the outcome of such development should be.

Essentially, each of us experiences management development in our own way, limited and enhanced by our own circumstances and understanding. What I find to be helpful, you might hate; what I hate now might, with time, turn out to be a key point in my development as a manager (Lee, 2002). Taking a step back – as a management educator, how do I know what is 'best' at this instant for each of those that I am educating? (Lee, 1996). What right do I have to determine this? A further step back – and more questions. What is the unique nature of the organization, and how, and should, I be influencing this? Indeed – can developing the managers actually change the organization? Or is 'management develop-ment' just a way of keeping 'management developers' in a job?... and so on.

Many questions can be asked, but should we expect answers? In a con-stantly changing complex and situated area like this, detailed answers to specific questions often don't help much – instead, what is needed is information and understanding. We need to know what is happening else-where, how others have done things in particular situations, what the implications have been, how others conceptualize what is happening, and how this contributes to the bigger picture. With that information, we can at least start to determine our own view of the 'practice' of management development, and locate our preferred 'theory' within the spread of the field.

This book helps to address the need for information. Chapters in the first section look at some of the fundamental issues in MD – should it focus on the individual or the organization? – at ethical concerns, and its impact and contribution to strategy. The second part of the book looks at comparative aspects, seeking insight from organizations and practice in different contexts and countries, including European nations and a Japan-ese multinational. Practice in the Netherlands and Vietnam is also explored in the third section. This looks at the impact of MD in different circumstances, including the health and retail sectors, SMEs, and the impact upon individuals and women. The final section examines the effects of different MD interventions, including multi-source feedback, and issues around commitment, constructionist approaches, critical leadership development and action learning.

Taken separately, each writer provides a snapshot of a particular area of interest, but together the writers are also providing us with a treasure map – showing the paths for those who wish to engage in the specific debates raised by the authors. The treasure map, or overview, is achieved by the way in which Rosemary and Jim have worked with the authors and their contributions to provide a wide-ranging and integrated picture of the field – joined-up snapshots, perhaps? Whilst the content and import of each chapter varies, the authors address their topic from a questioning stance that is located (and so locates the area) within a wider perspective that is grounded in empirical research.

Perhaps the octopus-catching net could be better described as a nexus of questions that, in coming together, help delineate the field (theoretic-ally and in practice), and in doing so move it on.

I am delighted to be associated with this book, and recommend it to you.

Monica Lee
Lancaster University and Northumbria University

References

Lee, M.M. (1996) 'Competence and the new manager', in Lee, M.M., Letiche, H., Crawshaw, R. and Thomas, M. (eds), *Management Education in the New Europe: Boundaries and Complexity*, London: Routledge, pp. 101–17.

Lee, M.M. (1997) 'The developmental approach: a critical reconsideration', in Burgoyne, J. and Reynolds, M. (eds), *Management Learning*, London: Sage.

Lee, M.M. (2002) 'Who am I? An introduction to self development in organisations', in Pearn, M. (ed.), *Individual Differences and Development in Organisations*, Chichester: Wiley, pp. 17–34.

Acknowledgements

We would like to thank our contributors for the chapters in this book. The staff at Routledge, especially Terry Clague and Katherine Carpenter, also deserve our thanks, and we appreciate the support and encouragement of Monica Lee, who edits this series and has written the foreword for the book. We also both thank our partners and families for their support and understanding during the preparation of the book.

Professor Jim Stewart
Dr Rosemary Hill
Nottingham Business School
The Nottingham Trent University

1 Researching and practising management development

Jim Stewart and Rosemary Hill

Introduction

This book is an edited volume of original chapters, all of which have been specifically written for it. The idea for the book originated in the supervision of a number of Doctor of Business Administration (DBA) research projects into management development (MD), three of which feature as chapters in the book (Chapters 2, 4 and 18).

In common with the other volumes in the Studies in HRD Series, the overall purpose of the book is to advance knowledge and understanding of the concept of HRD and its professional practice. Whilst confident in the assertion that MD is intrinsic to HRD theory and practice, we do not adopt a singular or consistent understanding in the book of what MD might be. The book does, however, address a number of questions about the conceptualization, scope, impact and delivery of MD. These are:

- What are the parameters of MD?
- What can we learn from comparative insights of MD?
- What is the impact of MD?
- What aspects of MD (techniques and approaches) are being engaged in MD research and practice?

In the conclusion to this book, at Chapter 19, we explore our response to these questions through an analysis of the key arguments and themes presented in the individual chapters.

'Leadership' and 'management'

The terms 'leadership' and 'leadership development' add a further level of interest to the 'management development' debate. There is a wealth of diverse perspective concerning 'management' and 'leadership' and their application in organizational management and leadership studies and practices (see, for example, Bennis, 1994; Kotter, 1996). Some commentators will favour one of two polarized positions: those who perceive 'management' and 'leadership' as being distinctly different from each other in both concept and practice; and those who assign them as one and the same. In the literature, too, there is a plethora of opinion that presents neither polarized position but rather argues a blend of perspectives from both (see Aditya *et al.*, 2000).

There is also diverse opinion regarding the conceptualization and applicability of 'management' development and 'manager' development. Again, some make little or no distinction, whilst others perceive the former as being primarily concerned with the creation and enhancement of 'management' as an organizational capability or competence, and the latter more about the enabling of individuals in the organization to be more effective managers of people, projects and processes (Stewart, 2004).

The contributors in this book also have wide and diverse views in these matters, and individuals' chapters will inevitably be representative of their own management/leadership paradigm and experiences – either explicitly or implicitly applied. The 'management–leadership' nexus provides fertile ground for discussion, and in our concluding chapter we also explore the nature and extent of contributors' engagement with the notions of 'management' and/or 'leadership'.

Aims

The book is intended to provide a comprehensive and up-to-date work on the state of research and practice in management development. Although existing knowledge in this field is acknowledged as being relatively extensive, the book recognizes a significant need continually to update the current body of knowledge on MD with the latest innovations in high-quality research and practice in various geographical and organizational contexts. The overall aim of the book, therefore, is two-fold: first, to disseminate the results of a wide range of MD research and practice, both in the UK and overseas, in order to inform teaching and learning; second, to provide examples of both MD research and practice to inform and stimulate future research, and to encourage the use of research-informed or evidence-based practice in organizations. A number of subsidiary aims flow from these two main aims. These are:

- to describe and analyse the current context of MD research and practice;
- to evaluate a range of current approaches both in and outside of the UK;
- to provide a resource to academics and students researching management development practice;
- to provide a range of examples of research and practice to inform and support the teaching of management development as a subject;

- to provide a resource to HR practitioners and line managers to develop research-based and critically analysed management development interventions.

Readership

The latter three items in the list of subsidiary aims, above, give an indication of our intended readership. The book, and its constituent contributions, may be considered to fall into the publishing category of research monograph, meaning that the content will be of relevance and interest to academic researchers and policy-makers and advisers. That said, the category of the book will vary according to the market, and may well be conceived of as a 'textbook' – a publication intended to support what is now referred to as learning and teaching – for advanced students of HRD, including those on specialist Masters and Doctoral programmes. The book also contains a wealth of discussion, analysis and technique of interest to the HR 'practitioner-scholar' – primarily those concerned with the development and delivery of research-informed or evidence-based HRD/HRM practice.

A final point needs to be made about intended and potential readership. The book draws upon MD research and practice both in the UK and overseas, and so will be of interest to students of international HRD/HRM. The book will also be of relevance to policy-makers, managers and HR professionals who work in, or associate with, international organizations and bodies.

Structure and organization

The overall structure of the book reflects its main and subsidiary aims, and is also representative of the speculation about MD introduced at the beginning of this chapter. For these reasons, individual chapters are grouped into five parts:

- Part I: Parameters of management development
- Part II: Comparative insights
- Part III: Impact of management development
- Part IV: Aspects of management development
- Part V: Editors' conclusion.

Part I contains four chapters. Whilst each discusses a distinct and separate MD theme, feature or concept, collectively these chapters provide a rudimentary characterization and scoping of MD and its territory. Part II then offers further insight by means of four chapters each of which draws upon some form of comparative MD study or practice. The main aim of each of the four chapters in Part III is to report on the impact of a particular MD or leadership programme. Part IV contains five chapters, and is concerned with different aspects of MD conceptualization, design and delivery. Finally, in Part V, Chapter 19 provides the editors' conclusion.

Each of the book parts is preceded with a brief introduction and summary in order to integrate and strengthen key arguments across the range of individual chapters in the particular part. Individual chapters adopt a similar structure and a common content, which may include the following items:

- objectives
- theoretical context
- research context
- findings/results
- interpretation
- conclusions
- key learning points.

It is intended that this common structure will enable the reader to make cross-chapter comparisons against a particular activity, theme, or phenomenon – for example, to determine what MD literature or theory seems prevalent, or to compare and contrast the range of research methods and MD practices presented in the book.

The book has a number of other defining characteristics. Each contribution includes and draws upon research projects and/or organizational practice conducted by the authors. As well as reporting the results of research or practice, the contributors also provide accounts of the process adopted to achieve these results – that is, either the research methodology or the practice intervention – in order to support the design of future research projects and management development interventions. Finally, the editors and contributors are all established and published researchers and/or seasoned practitioners in the field of management development and/or human resource development in organizations.

References

Aditya, R., House, R.J. and Kerr, S. (2000) 'Theory and practice of leadership: into the new millennium', in Cooper, C.L. and Locke, E.A. (eds), *Industrial and Organizational Psychology*, Oxford: Blackwell Business.

Bennis, W. (1994) *On Becoming A Leader*, New York: Perseus Books.

Kotter, J. (1996) *Leading Change*, Boston, MA: Harvard Business.

Stewart, J. (2004) 'Developing managers and managerial capability', in Leopold, J., Harris, L. and Watson, T. (eds), *The Strategic Managing of Human Resources*, Harlow: FT Prentice Hall.

Part I

Parameters of management development

Introduction

Each part of the book has an introduction similar to this one. These serve the purpose of setting the scene for the chapters that follow in each part. Some attempt is made in the part introductions to identify emerging themes and arguments. However, readers will soon realize that the content of individual chapters is capable of multiple interpretations and does, therefore, provide a rich source of debate. We have no wish as editors to close off that debate or to present ourselves as arbiters of what are the 'correct' or most 'useful' interpretations to be taken from chapters and book parts. The introduction to each part is, therefore, again intended simply as an aid to understanding and further analysis, and to perhaps inform subsequent debate. Such analysis and debate will themselves be the key to learning from the book rather than didactic expositions from the Editors.

We have named this first part of the book 'Parameters of management development'. It contains four chapters, each of which discusses a distinct and separate MD theme, feature or concept. Collectively, these chapters provide a useful lens through which a rudimentary characterization and scoping of MD and its territory can be viewed and examined. A brief analysis of the main themes from the chapters is presented at the end of this introduction. We do not contend that this is in any way a definitive or exhaustive representation of what the 'parameters' of MD might be; the four chapters here merely provide a foundation upon which subsequent parts and chapters in the book will inevitably build.

In Chapter 2, Clare Rigg offers a fundamental challenge to the purpose of management development. She argues that although within MD there have long been inherent tensions regarding its focus (for example, whether it is concerned with developing the resourcefulness of managers, or with developing the capacity of the organization), a further and perhaps more significant challenge comes from questioning whether the world can sustain organizational practices. The title of this chapter ('Corporate technocrats or world stewards – what's the point of management development?') is formed in a growing body of concern amongst management development practitioners over the wider consequences of their work – a concern that questions whether MD is refining individual skills and organizational capabilities to continue operating in ways that have serious human and ecological consequences. The chapter explores comparative influences of critical management and technicist management learning on managers' practice at work, and highlights the notion of the 'ethics of managing' and, by association, the ethics of developing managers and the management capacity of organizations.

The theme of ethics in management development can also be traced in Chapter 3 by Tim Finch-Lees and Chris Mabey – albeit posited in an individual rather than a global context. They argue that traditional research perspectives essentially take the 'M' in MD for granted, seeing 'the manager' as a self-evident entity that needs only to be improved upon, or in other words 'developed'. Instead they offer a critical discursive perspective to the analysis of MD, a perspective where the theoretical component considers language (and more generally semiosis) to be *constitutive* of social reality as opposed to being merely a means by which reality is *represented*. Research findings illustrate how MD can be as implicated in the constitution/regulation of managerial identity as it is in the actual development of managers. The research presented in the chapter is drawn from a wider study of MD practices across seven European countries (see Chapter 6 in Part II of this volume for a discussion of the French strand of this pan-European study).

In Chapter 4, Paul Brown develops a specific strand of MD. The chapter provides, from the literature, an overview of conceptual frameworks and best practice in strategic management development (SMD), and reports findings of the author's doctoral research into SMD. The research broadly aimed to synthesize and test conceptual frameworks which could contribute to a more developed theoretical basis for SMD, and to provide an understanding of some contingent aspects of SMD programme design. The author uses a case-study methodology to explore barriers and drivers in SMD, the causal influences on strategic capability and the effect of the commitment to strategic management on the design and evolution of SMD programmes. Findings are mapped against a hypothesis founded in the literature review, and a preliminary pilot case-study investigation. The chapter concludes by commenting on the contingent nature of effective SMD programme design and models this contingent relationship in a four-stage typology.

The final chapter in Part I of the book (Chapter 5), by Geoff Chivers, addresses the challenge of responding to the development needs of large numbers of senior and middle managers who become suddenly unemployed as a result of major industrial collapse. Based on a retraining programme initiated by the author in the coal-mining, steel-making and associated engineering industries in northern England in the late 1980s, the chapter outlines the thinking behind the development of this 'Management Update' programme, discusses the strengths and weaknesses of its funding mechanism, and reports on the known outcomes for individuals. Personal reflections on the author's own learning from the programme lead into a contemporary discussion of ways in which development for managers in employment sectors in decline should be addressed, both before and after job loss occurs.

Summary

We now briefly examine what the four chapters in this first part of the book might be telling us about the 'parameters of management development'. Along with themes from other parts of the book, these ideas are further explored in our conclusion in Chapter 19. But first, how are we using the term 'parameter'? The Concise Oxford dictionary indicates three broad explanations:

1   A quantity consistent in the case considered but varying in different cases
2   A characteristic or feature
3   A constant element or factor, especially serving as a boundary.

Together these are helpful to the analysis of MD 'parameters', as, drawing upon the constant elements or features of MD in their varying forms across the four chapters, we do begin to see a rudimentary framework – or boundary – emerging. The overall message of this part of the book might, therefore, be summarized as something like this:

* Ultimately, MD is globally bounded, as it has the potential to be impacted by, and to impact upon, critical global issues.
* At the other end of the scale, MD is bounded by a responsibility towards managers as individuals, as it has the potential to be impacted by, and to impact upon, the subjective perspectives and uniqueness of people.
* MD has the potential to construct itself as a practical intervention in response to the negative consequences of change within a nation's socio-economic environment.
* When conceived of as 'strategic', by implication, MD has the potential to position itself as an effective and ethical force for change and improvement in organizations, in individuals and in the external environment.

To restate a point already made, this brief introduction suggests some lines of thought for readers to follow when reading the subsequent chapters. These ideas are by no means exclusive nor exhaustive, and we would encourage readers both to build upon our analysis and to identify additional themes within the wealth of detail and insight contained in the chapters in this part and the other three parts of the book.

2 Corporate technocrats or world stewards?

What's the point of management development?

Clare Rigg

Rationale

There is a growing body of concern amongst management development practitioners regarding the wider consequences of our work. Whilst we might describe our interventions with people in benign terms, such as enabling, developing potential, empowerment and such like, are we failing to see a bigger picture of our work? Might our work in fact have the consequence of refining individual skills and developing organizational capabilities to continue operating in ways that have serious human and ecological consequences? Corporate scandals such as Enron,[1] Arthur Andersen,[2] WorldCom,[3] ImClone Systems,[4] and mis-selling of financial products such as endowments,[5] have focused attention on the ethics of managing. Events as far afield as Cancun, or even the UK Hutton Inquiry, have directed critical attention on the social relations of work organizations, and the impact of business on people's lives. Such events provide accumulating impetus for those who argue for management education and development to integrate consideration of social and environmental terms of business.

In management development there have long been inherent tensions within competing rationales regarding whether the focus is developing the resourcefulness of managers, or developing the capacity of the organization. But a further challenge comes from critiques of the purpose of business which question whether the world can sustain organizational practices that do not incorporate wider societal responsibilities. Is it good enough simply to be concerned with the production of corporate technocrats, or should the rationale be managers as world stewards? Hence it is timely to pose the question, what is the purpose of management development?

Objectives

This chapter offers a discourse perspective to the question through four stages: first, it presents an argument of management learning as discursive encounter; second, it compares critical management learning and technicist management education as offering different discursive resources to enable managers to construct their working worlds; third, using the concept of emergence (Watson and Harris, 1999) it illustrates how managers actively construct their own realities; and finally, it concludes that as management developers we should be concerned with discursive closure (Bryman, 1999) – namely that we set boundaries on managers' practice by the discursive resources we either introduce or restrict them from encountering.

The chapter draws illustrations from a three-year comparative study of managers who have participated in a critical management postgraduate course with others who participated in technicist management courses. Research methods combined an ethnographic approach with content analysis of postgraduate management students' reflective texts.

Theoretical context

Approaches to management development – technicist and critical compared

In the latter decades of the twentieth century, development of management capability received increasing attention around the world as a route to enhance organization performance. Britain has seen various exhortations to improve the development of managers since the mid-1980s, notably with such reports as those by Constable and McCormick (1987), Handy (1988), Storey et al. (1997) and Thomson et al. (1997). Invariably, the rationale for management development has been presented as being to better pursue competitive advantage; to 'meet the changing character of market conditions' (Storey et al., 1997: 207); or to fulfil the needs of business strategy – as Woodall and Winstanley (1998: 3) put it, 'organizational management is a vital ingredient in securing improved business performance'. The focus of such 'technicist' management development conceives of managers as technocrats who, through acquiring knowledge about the range of business functions (such as operations, finance or human resources) and better skills in reading the environment and thinking strategically, will become more effective at extracting value from those resources and delivering benefits for the customer and shareholder.

There has been very little consideration of the role management development might play in either preventing or sustaining such corporate behaviour as the scandals above exemplify. There is rarely consideration of the non-financial costs across a value chain in technicist management development, and where there is it is bundled into a separate subject termed 'business ethics' or 'corporate social responsibility'. So, by a technicist management discourse I refer to ideas of management in which performativity is emphasized and managing is presented as a value-neutral activity that strives for rationality, seeking to control, predict and search for efficiency. The social relations of managerial work (Whittington, 1992), the emotional (Fineman, 1999) and psychosocial dynamics of organizations have no place, and there is little space for raising questions regarding the environmental and international consequences of business activity. Questions of business standards, or the role of business in society, receive no priority. As Alvesson and Willmott (1996: 17) put it, 'the functional rhetoric of technical rationality' denies or mystifies the moral basis of management practice.

Of critique and being critical

In contrast, a critical management discourse is grounded in:

> an appreciation of the pressures that lead managerial work to become so deeply implicated in the unremitting exploitation of nature and human beings, national and international extremes of wealth and poverty, the creation of global pollution, the promotion of 'needs' for consumer products etc.
>
> (Alvesson and Willmott, 1996: 39)

In this sense critical management learning is not only about critique, in the Watson (1999) sense of thinking and arguing or questioning of convention, but also encompasses 'critical pedagogy' in that it 'not only offers a challenging view of management as a social, political and economic practice, but does so in a way that stimulates student involvement of a kind that is rare in other forms of management education' (Grey *et al.*, 1996: 109). Reynolds (1997) describes this as a combination of content radical (subject matter that raises questions of power, social relations, environmental consequences, etc.) and process radical (pedagogical relations that are likely to include some of action learning sets, learning community, and critical reflection).

My argument is that critical management learning, although not a homogenous, uncontested or unproblematic territory, offers an encounter with discursive resources that are differentiated from the dominant technicist discourse of management. To engage in critical management learning is to encounter a coherent, though not watertight, system of meanings which encompasses language, ideas and philosophies. The encounter introduces particular discursive resources – ideas or words which in themselves have no inevitable meaning, but coalesce together to give the discourse its logic and apparent coherence. So the concepts power, control or performance have different meanings within technicist and critical management discourses.

Through process radical pedagogy, critical management learning also exposes managers to the ways in which discursive practices are deployed to express dominant values, beliefs and ideas, to convey meaning (Van Dijk, 1997). For Michel Foucault, discursive practices '*position* us in relations of power' (cited by Ian Parker, 1999: 6), or as Ian Parker defines it, they are an act or practice which 'reproduces the material basis of the institution' (Parker, 1999: 17). Discursive practices[6] encompass a range of communicative acts, both verbal and non-verbal, including stories, narratives, rituals (such as making the tea or the format of meetings), rhetoric, language games such as names, conversations, sense-making, signs and architecture – the physical organization of space and bodies. As such, critical management learning offers managers different resources on which to draw to make sense of and to enact their practice. The significance is to address discursive closure – how, as Francis and D'Annunzio-Green (2004) describe it, 'orders of discourses set boundaries upon managers' construction of meaning'.

Research context

The research this chapter draws on was a three-year comparative study of managers who participated in a critical management postgraduate course with others who participated in technicist postgraduate management education/development.

Critical management learning in practice

The critical management post-graduate course was a three-year part-time post-graduate Diploma in Management/Masters in Organization Development based at a UK university. Several features of this programme combined to give it a critical management learning approach, in terms of the above definition. Critical management was experienced primarily in the course of the learning process, through action learning sets, process facilitation, action research, and the idea of a learning community, and to a lesser extent in content. There were some lecture inputs, but students spent two-thirds of their time working collectively in an action learning set (ALS) of about six to eight members, facilitated by a tutor. The ALS fulfilled a number of functions. It undertook group consultancy tasks, and in doing this participants were encouraged to reflect on how they worked together and to confront process issues in some depth. Participants were also encouraged to exchange their experiences, within the ALS, of doing their dissertations and preparing their individual papers. In this sense, students' dialogue and social support were seen as fundamental to the course. The ALS was also frequently a source of diversity, where issues mirrored some of the patterns of power and inequality within organizations and society. Students were encouraged, through reflective assignments and facilitator questioning, to work constructively with that diversity and to reflect on and learn from their feelings and experiences of doing so. As such, emotion and lived experience in general were valued as sources of management learning.

An action research methodology was deployed for the Masters dissertation during which students were encouraged to explore the epistemological basis of action research. Action research has a long history of use for radical community action, and this led many to engage with some of the critical theory that it implies (Carr and Kemmis, 1986). A further element of critical learning was a critical self-reflection paper, an autobiographical reflection on the manager's development, which each individual wrote. In this, participants were encouraged to identify core assumptions, to understand some of their patterns and the contextual influences on them. Depending on their particular focus, individuals were thus introduced to critical concepts derived from such areas as feminism, post-colonialism, social constructionism and critical pedagogy.

Throughout this management development programme, the question of who owned the learning, the diagnosis of issues or problems, and the solutions to the issues or problems, was central to the staff roles. Tutors took two basic, mutually supportive consultancy roles: Task Consultant, offering information, models, or reading relating to the task, and Process Consultant, making the participant/group aware of group processes.

Research design

Research methods combined an ethnographic approach of micro-ethnography (Czarniawska, 1998) through shadowing eight managers at work and using ethnographic and narrative interviews with them and other organization members, with a content analysis of the language used within 49 postgraduate management students' reflective texts. The aim of the research was to study the influence of formal learning on management practice by researching microprocesses of managing employed in the everyday social interactions that company members engaged in as they undertook their work. The underlying research question was, 'How do managers talk about themselves, their managing, and their organizations?' The study used Foucault's thought/action perspective to explore whether managers who had encountered critical management discourse made sense of their practice in ways that differed from those who engaged in technicist management development.

The next section gives outline details of five managers from the study, who will be drawn upon to illustrate the ensuing discussion.

Analysis and evaluation of research material

Illustrative cases[7]

1 *Sam – 'Metal Tubes'*
   Sam completed a critical management Diploma in Management Studies and an MSc in Organization Development. He was co-founder

of Metal Tubes, a small company of ten people who work across Britain to project manage the design and installation of air-conditioning systems.

2   *Dale – 'Feeding the Stars'*
Dale was the owner-manager of Feeding the Stars, another small company, fluctuating between ten and 15 people, which services actors on film locations around Britain, providing mobile accommodation, catering, shopping and other services. She was near the end of a critical management Masters programme.

3   *Caroline – 'Holistic Housing'*
Caroline was a director of a medium-sized organization (200 employees) which began as a Housing Association, but over the past three years had been redefined as a social investment agency. She had recently completed an MBA, a technicist management development programme.

4   *Rod – 'Retention'*
Rod was in the process of trying to establish himself as a management consultant focusing on staff retention, since he had completed his MBA, a technicist management development programme.

5   *Jack – 'Market ReDesign'*
Jack was Brand Consultant in a company of 30 people, Market ReDesign, which had been created as a design agency over ten years previously. Jack joined the company as an Account Manager about six years ago, having trained as a graphic designer and run his own design business, both in Britain and in Italy. He had recently completed a postgraduate course in Marketing, a technicist management development programme.

The following discussion is presented under three themes: first, it will show that managers actively construct their own realities, drawing on discourse (concepts, language, communicative practices) as a resource to help make sense of and shape action in their organizational practice. Second, the illustrations will be used to show how, whilst there is no simplistic linear relationship between new language and new practice, the consequence of exposure to critical management learning is it that it centralizes existence of competing discourses, of power and conflict – which thereby provide differing and more extensive resources for managers to draw on to make sense of their organizational world compared to those in a discourse of technicist management development. Third, the discussion will use the concept of emergence (Watson and Harris, 1999) to explore how managers learn to make sense of rival discourses and actively reconstruct their realities.

Resources to construct new meaning

A thought–action perspective implies that introduction to new thought and language can contribute to individuals reconstituting themselves, which could produce changed managerial action. In exploring whether and when learning produced new discourses, the study was interested in whether the focal managers' course-acquired language had become a language of action in their managing and organizing.

All five managers introduced above referred to having acquired a specific language through their management course, and three (Caroline, Rod and Dale) explicitly described how they could use their knowledge as marking out a boundary that excluded those not in the know. Rod described the language he had encountered through his MBA as a 'language of thought' which helped him look at things in different perspectives. Caroline explicitly described how some of the managerial concepts she had encountered had enabled her to re-conceptualize the whole purpose of what she does. Jack agreed that his Diploma in Marketing gave him new ways of thinking and phrasing his work. He said it gave him both a business language that helped him talk to clients as well as a new language of thought that gave him a different way of thinking about graphic design, and of enacting his role. He said:

> I mean marketing is a consumer-friendly approach to business, and design has a critical part to play in that. It's meant that I've been able to filter business-talk into design language.

He outlined how his course learning had affected his entire perception of his own role and of his company's business. He gave an account of what he and his colleagues aimed to do with clients, describing the 'customer journey' that takes the customer through a 'brand journey'. He talked of 'creating a play'; of 'choreographing the customer experience'; using 'visual language' to build a brand. Since the course he has reconstructed himself replacing his old titles of graphic designer and account manager with Brand Consultant. He related how he drew from his course:

> my whole job is about building personalities around companies, so I can actually define the right design visual language, the right visual tone to suit the personality that they need against their competitors, either future ones or current ones. So I'm designing something that's got a lot more longevity to it, than if, historically, whereas if I hadn't done the Marketing Diploma it would have been very much now-and-then, without a picture, a broader picture, the horizons of what was coming up, therefore, we're actually able to sort of embed it in. I mean, that's a shorthand version of it.

In this he could be said to be drawing on a range of discursive resources from marketing to reframe the company discourse.

Sam's narratives convey an interweaving between his company's development and his views of his course, that runs deeply through his sense of thinking and managing:

> Well I think it was something Don and I got so much from and changed our thinking and our perspective on how we were to run our business.

Sam also described a particular way of running meetings, which ended with what he termed a 'workout' in which members gave and received feedback from each other, in a kind of verbal 360-degree appraisal:

> We have a Communications Forum which was designed from my paper, funnily enough, that was one of the outputs of my paper (over 6 years ago) . . . because we do try to do the good and the bad, and that is one way of sharing information.

Some aspects of his course appeared to have become integral to the ways Sam thought about his work, particularly the action research approach of his MSc:

> then from the DMS point of view, and certainly the Action Research MSc. point of view, that is very much something you are doing in action research, you are finding out a piece of information, applying it, checking it out and then going back to the literature or your peers or some other area to find out some more information and gradually rack it up, how you improve the company. . . . You can overlay action research on to the sort of company that we wanted to be, that was a company that knew very little to start with but wanted to improve ourselves through the methods that we were getting from the DMS and MSc.

His emphasis on learning as an organization practice was echoed by other organization members. It seemed a discursive resource that was integral to their accounts of the company. For example, one of the project managers described the company ethos:

> Metal Tubes is good because I know in a lot of companies, larger companies, you are under a lot of pressure to meet budgets or, you know, do things on programme. Here we are still under pressure but we don't get, you know, we know we are not going to get the sack if we don't meet that budget but we know that we can learn from that. I mean on Cardiff I produced a cost of quality and we kind of went through it in the meeting and Sam would say – okay, why haven't we made – I don't know – X amount of pounds there, and you know you just have to explain why: our supplier let me down so I had to order it

from somewhere else, it was more expensive, and then it will be – Well, why didn't you order it six weeks ago? Well because I was too busy doing it because I didn't get the support, and it – we just talk about it really. I think, because you are not under that pressure, you learn more effectively I suppose.

Critical management practice

Critical management writers suggest that managers with a critical aware-ness are not only conscious, but also concerned that their choices and actions have political consequences on the environment, on exploitation of people, or on extremes of wealth and poverty (e.g. Alvesson and Will-mott, 1996; Guba and Lincoln, 1994). So, one of the interesting aspects of this study was to see whether there were differences in critical manage-ment practice between those managers who engaged in a critical manage-ment programme compared to those from a technicist course.

Overall, the research study illustrated how any expectation that a crit-ical management programme produces critical managers and a technicist programme does not is highly simplistic. For example, the manager dis-playing the most critical perspective, Caroline, did a technicist MBA. Overall, she was already 'critical' in many perspectives, and the course challenged some of this in the Watson (1999) sense of critical-thinking and arguing, making her more receptive to practical uses of ideas from marketing and mission statements, to the extent they could help her in her work. Dale, who did a critical programme, acknowledged that it heightened her political awareness, making her conscious of her employees' power. For Rod, from a technicist MBA, avoiding exploitation of people in the ways they are managed was a major concern, but articu-lated within a humanist discourse rather than a critical, politicized perspective. These were values he deemed to precede his MBA. In Sam's discursive practice there were elements of egalitarianism: he made the coffee; he shared a cramped open-plan office; he espoused a desire for openness and honesty within the company's Communications Forum; and he had self-consciously tried to recruit and train women into a predomi-nantly male industry.

In Market ReDesign, Jack was critical in his use of course content, in the sense of questioning or critique (Watson, 1999), but there was no evid-ence of being critical in the sense of critical management as explicated above. At one point in the interview Jack described how he had been working with a nationalized company, Communications Y, to re-brand itself:

The way it was done, because I'd worked with them for a year, of asking questions, I knew about their business. But what we did, our job was to have a vision for what Communications Y was all about, so the work that we did last year, was having this vision, not of Communications Y today, but where Communications Y will be in 5–10 years time. And that was the strategic work that we got paid £½ million to do. Out of that, having that vision in mind, then it was, how does the internet strategy fit into that? How best deliver it. So I didn't have to ask any questions. I just had to map it out. But I had to map it out to enable the current business structure to fit into it. For it to grow into the next phase.

He went on to describe how the sticking point in implementing the re-branding plans was that the company 'needed a new culture', new employee behaviours, but the employees were a blockage to such change.

There was no acknowledgement of the implications for social relations of Market ReDesign using their expertise to reach such judgements, and no self-questioning from Jack. This could be interpreted as an absence of critical thinking.

There were also contrasts in the discursive practices and resources of Sam and Jack which could be traced to the management discourses of their courses: Jack's had no content on wider management functions, or critical management questions. And he openly admitted he lacked understanding of people issues, in terms, for example, of understanding 'cultural' issues or people's responses to change, nor had he any interest in organization politics. He appeared to ask no wider questions about the implications of his work on brands, for example, for employees or the environment, and he seemed to adopt unquestioningly the marketing discourse of the primacy of customer needs. Yet he was clearly a very ethical person. For example, he said the main reason he chose to remain disengaged from line-managing any staff was that he wanted to be able to go home at night feeling 'morally comfortable', by which he said he meant he did not want to be involved with activities such as misleading or manipulating staff, or laying them off.

Sam's espoused beliefs of sharing, review, learning and criticism, which he attributed to his management learning course, could indeed have been resources inspired by the process critical nature of the course, and indeed the Communication Forum workout process is a discursive practice directly modelled on the DMS/MSc action learning sets.

More widely, the study did not disprove a link between encounter with critical management discourse and critical management practice. However, as these illustrations show, it reinforced Clegg and Hardy's (1999) caution against implying a simple linear link between new talk, new meaning, different thinking and new action, and lent weight to the existence of emergence.

Emergence

Watson and Harris (1999: 238) describe managers as emergent in the sense that they are

> *making their worlds at the same time as their worlds are making them.* Managers are seen as involved in 'emergence' both in shaping their personal sense of 'self' and in shaping organizational work activities through 'organizing'.

All the managers I interviewed and shadowed could be described as emergent in that they drew from their formal management learning to shape their work activities and sense of self. For example, Sam's world became one of project management, consultancy and constant improvement through learning; Jack reconstructed himself as a brand consultant; Caroline wove managerialist ideas into her social justice driven activities.

One of Jack's statements sums up the process of emergence:

> And equally just as much as I've learnt from it, I think I could feed back into Marketing. I'd question some of the things that they've set up because they grab too quickly at formulas which they think have worked. So in a way it's not purely a question of me taking what's there. I take some and I learn some. Then I adapt it.

Emergence can be conceived as if individuals are each on their own journey, working out what they are doing, defining their path, constantly modifying their perspectives, if only infinitesimally through every day micro-experiences. Emergence accords with Bryman's thinking on interpretive autonomy (Bryman, 1999: 36), in which he argues that even with discursive closure, when 'orders of discourses set boundaries upon managers' construction of meaning' … they also create ambiguities that provide them with space to carve out their own spheres of 'interpretive autonomy' (Francis and D'Annunzio-Green, 2004: 13).

Conclusions and key learning points for management development

In summary, the illustrations above show how, for these managers, their course-acquired language had become a language of action in their managing and organizing. They developed their working practices, their definitions of what they did, through this language, and gave the language meaning through their actions. As such, they demonstrated the potential relationship between discursive practices of managing and formal management learning. In other words, they had been provided with new discursive resources. In Metal Tubes, there was a strong sense in which the organization of the company, the company discourse itself, had been informed by and reflected on in the course of Sam's formal learning. However, this is not a linear or uncritical transmission of learning, rather a constant process of reviewing experience, seeking out ideas from elsewhere, experimenting, and ongoing learning. For Jack, at Market ReDesign, it could be said that the course introduced him to a wider managerial (marketing) discourse, which provoked him both personally to employ new discursive resources, and to try to change those of his organization colleagues. Jack, like Sam, also did not apply course content uncritically, but modified ideas and made them his own. The gaps are as interesting. The absence of wider organization or management discourse within his course presented him with frustrations when he did not understand or know what to attempt when clients faced challenges to their branding plans from employees – what he termed a 'culture block'. This can be understood as him saying he did not have the language, or the discursive resources, with which to conceptualize and act on these problems; his Marketing course did not provide these.

A key rationale within the literature on critical management learning, for encouraging managers to be critical, lies in the realization of how powerful managers now are in the world, yet how poorly traditional management education has prepared them for considering questions of power and responsibility. Porter and colleagues (1989: 71) suggest that the purpose of critical management thinking is to develop in managers 'habits of critical thinking . . . that prepare them for responsible citizenship and personally and socially rewarding lives and careers'. For Hugh Willmott (1997: 175) the challenge for critical management learning is:

> to envision and advance the development of discourses and practices that can facilitate the development of 'management' from a divisive technology of control into a collective means of emancipation.

In evaluating the potential of critical management learning to deliver this, it is important to be cautious regarding any inevitable direction of flow. It could well be that a critical management awareness, in heightening the managers' awareness of power, merely enhances their ability to influence more effectively. The consequence may or may not be emancipatory for anyone.

The research study did not find a unitary acceptance and adoption of critical management ideas amongst those who engaged with critical management learning, and nor did it reveal a corresponding absence amongst those from a technicist course. This would have been too simplistic a relationship between new language and changed practice. Rather, what the illustrations demonstrate is how managers actively construct their own realities, drawing on discourse (concepts, language, communicative practices) as a resource to help make sense of and shape action in their organizational practice. Learning offers new discursive resources which may be employed in new actions and may be interlinked into a coherent new discourse, but may also be interwoven with resources a person draws from other discourses, and not necessarily in non-contradictory ways.

Managers learn to make sense of rival discourses and actively reconstruct their realities. The challenge for management development is that they cannot do this if not exposed to rival discourses. That is the route to discursive closure. Hence the value of critical management learning is it makes central the existence of competing discourses; of power and conflict. In doing so, the encounter provides differing and more extensive resources for managers to draw on to make sense of their organizational world, compared to a discourse of technicist management development that privileges performativity and presents managing as a value-neutral activity that strives for rationality, seeking to control, predict, and search for efficiency.

No management development programme, critical or otherwise, can guarantee the production of managers who conceive of themselves as world stewards rather than corporate technocrats. However, the point of management development should be to have tried; to have enabled managers to encounter rival discourses, and then let emergence take its course.

Notes

1 Enron, the US energy company that collapsed amid scandal in late 2001, evaded billions of dollars in tax with the help of 'some of the nation's finest' accountants, investment banks and lawyers, as reported by Bateson Report, February 2003, commissioned by the US Senate Finance Committee.
2 In 2002, a jury in the United States found accountancy firm Arthur Andersen guilty of obstructing justice by shredding documents relating to the failed energy giant Enron.
3 WorldCom, the telecom firm, filed for bankruptcy in 2002 after uncovering $11bn in alleged accounting fraud. In 2003, the company itself and six former employees, including the ex-chief executive and former chief financial officer, were charged with 'executing a scheme to artificially inflate bond and stock prices by intentionally filing false information with the Securities & Exchange Commission' (Source: Accountancy Age.com 28–08–2003).
4 In 2002, the former president and founder of biotechnology firm ImClone Systems was indicted for fraud in an alleged insider trading scandal, accused of providing information to family members that enabled them to sell shares before the price fell.
5 Millions of people in the UK are thought to have been mis-sold mortgage endowment policies during the 1980s and 1990s, meaning that the policy was inappropriate for them and advisers who sold the product did not fully explain how the endowment worked, the market risks or its suitability for the individual's circumstances.
6 'Discursive act' and 'discursive practice' will be used interchangeably.
7 Names of individuals and companies have been fictionalized to protect anonymity.

References

Alvesson, M. and Willmott, H. (eds) (1996) *Making Sense of Management*, London: Sage.

Bryman, A. (1999) 'Leadership in organizations' in Clegg, S., Hardy, C. and Nord, W.R. (eds), *Managing Organizations: Current Issues*, London: Sage.

Carr, W. and Kemmis, S. (1986) *Becoming Critical: Education Knowledge and Action Research*, London: Falmer Press.

Clegg, S.R. and Hardy, C. (eds) (1999) *Studying Organization*, London: Sage.

Constable, J. and McCormick, R. (1987) *The Making of British Managers*, London: British Institute of Management/Confederation of British Industry.

Czarniawska, B. (1998) *A Narrative Approach to Organization Studies*, Qualitative Research Methods Series 43, London: Sage.

Fineman, S. (1999) 'Emotion and organizing', in Clegg, S.R. and Hardy, C. (eds), *Studying Organization*, London: Sage.

Francis, H. and D'Annunzio-Green, N. (2004) 'A discourse perspective on change and management learning', *Fifth International Conference on HRD Research and Practice Across Europe*, Limerick, Ireland, 27–28 May.

Foucault, M. (1980) *Power/Knowledge*, New York, NY: Pantheon.

Grey, C., Knights, D. and Willmott, H. (1996) 'Is a critical pedagogy of management possible?', in French, R. and Grey, C. (eds), *Rethinking Management Education*, London: Sage.

Guba, E. and Lincoln, Y. (1994) 'Computing paradigms in qualitative research', in Denzin, N.K. and Lincoln, Y.S. (eds), *Handbook of Qualitative Research*, Thousand Oaks, CA: Sage.

Handy, C. (1988) *The Making of Managers*, London: MSC/NEDC/BIM.

Parker, I. (1999) *Critical Textwork: An Introduction to Varieties of Discourse and Analysis*, Buckingham: Open University Press.

Porter, L.W., Muller, H.J. and Rehder, R.R. (1989) 'The making of managers: an American perspective', *Journal of General Management*, 14(4): 62–76.

Reynolds, M. (1997) 'Towards a critical pedagogy', in Burgoyne, J. and Reynolds, M. (eds), *Management Learning: Integrating Perspectives in Theory and Practice*, London: Sage.

Storey, J., Edwards, P. and Sissons, K. (1997) *Managers and Their Making*, London: Sage.

Thomson, A., Storey, J., Mabey, C., Gray, C., Farmer, E. and Thomson, R. (1997) *A Portrait of Management Development*, London: Institute of Management.

Van Dijk, T.A. (ed.) (1997) *Discourse as Structure and Process*, Vol. 1, London: Sage.

Watson, T. (1999) 'Beyond Managism: negotiated narratives and critical management education in practice'. Paper presented to the First International Conference on Critical Management Studies University of Manchester, 14–16 July.

Watson, T. and Harris, P. (1999) *The Emergent Manager*, London: Sage.

Whittington, R. (1992) *What is Strategy – and Does it Matter?* London: Routledge.

Willmott, H. (1997) 'Critical management learning', in Burgoyne, J. and Reynolds, M. (eds), *Management Learning*, London: Sage.

Woodall, J. and Winstanley, D. (1998) *Management Development – Strategy and Practice*, Oxford: Blackwell.

3   Management development

A critical discursive approach

Tim Finch-Lees and Chris Mabey

Objectives

In this chapter we take a 'critical discursive' approach to the study and evaluation of management development (MD). Having first explained what this implies, we draw on both theory and our own empirical research to illustrate how such an approach can add to our understanding of the functioning and effects of MD. Whilst our exposition of the approach will be necessarily brief, we provide further sources of information for readers who may wish to deepen their knowledge of the approach. We also suggest areas where the approach might be usefully employed for the analysis of MD, both from a research perspective and from that of the practitioner or policy-maker.

Theoretical context: being 'critical' and being 'discursive'

The traditional or mainstream treatment of MD has been to understand it as an activity that exists primarily to build the knowledge, skills and abilities of managers. Usually this is with a view to ultimately enhancing 'performance' at the organizational and even the macro-economic levels of analysis (see, for example, Winterton and Winterton, 1999; DTI, 2001). Whilst acknowledging the value of this functionalist perspective to the study of MD, we would nevertheless argue that it tends to take the 'M' in MD for granted. It does so by considering the manager to be a largely self-evident entity, needing only to be improved upon (or 'developed') to the mutual interests of both the individual and the organization. A critical discursive perspective to MD provides a stark contrast to this by focusing much more on the 'M' than the 'D'. In other words, it is a perspective which seeks to understand the ways in which MD can be instrumental in constituting the very subjectivities (or senses of self) upon which notions of 'development' might actually depend. Seeing MD in this way opens up avenues for research that go beyond issues of functional effectiveness by delving into the broader and often conflicting interests that MD might be serving. But what do we mean when we describe our approach as both *critical* and *discursive*?

The approach can be described as *discursive* inasmuch as it acknowledges the centrality of *discourse* in terms of how regimes of knowledge and corresponding social practices come to be produced, taken for granted and part of everyday common sense (Mama, 1995; cited in Dick and Cassell, 2002). Discourses can themselves be understood as semiotic resources[1] (Fairclough, 2001) on which we can draw in order to construct representations of our own selves and also the social practices/institutions with which we interact. There are normally different and often competing discourses available to us in constructing such representations (Wodak and Meyer, 2001) although some are likely to be more available to us than others. As such, certain discourses can be described as dominant, hegemonic (Fairclough, 1992) or indeed institutionalized whenever they become so taken for granted as to effectively rule out plausible alternatives (Phillips *et al.*, 2004). This is, therefore, a perspective which sees language as not just a form of representation, but also a powerful form of action, with discourse analysis (DA) providing a means of gaining insight into such matters. DA comes in many different forms, both critical and non-critical. It can be understood to take on a *critical* form when it seeks to focus on the processes that give rise to instances of dominance, hegemony and institutionalization, and when it seeks to assess the interests that such processes might be either serving or neglecting. We would argue that MD is a particularly rich context for the use of critical discursive research, since it typically involves language-intensive interventions through which managerial identities are often shaped, negotiated, regulated and transformed (Fairclough and Hardy, 1997; Alvesson and Willmott, 2002).

We should at this stage point out that there are several different forms of and techniques for critical discursive research (Meyer, 2001). Our approach in this chapter is to present one relatively accessible form and to demonstrate how and to what effect we have used this in researching MD. The approach in question is Norman Fairclough's version of critical discourse analysis (CDA), and we will spend the next couple of paragraphs outlining some of CDA's basic characteristics, terminology and theoretical underpinnings. Space precludes anything more than a very simplified account of CDA. A more detailed synopsis can be found in Fairclough (2001), with fuller expositions in Fairclough (1992, 1995, 2003).

In terms of its theoretical underpinnings, CDA is partially grounded in the work of Michel Foucault, who used the concept of discourse to refer to the differing ways in which areas of knowledge are produced, structured and linked to social practices and power relations. The Foucauldian view is that discourses do not just reflect social entities and relations (including social subjects such as 'managers'), but actively construct or constitute them (Fairclough, 1992). However, Foucault's treatment of discourse did not extend to a concern for the detailed analysis of individual texts (Fairclough, 2003). As such, Foucauldian forms of discourse analysis have been criticized for their inability adequately to theorize or indeed analyse processes of human agency (Newton, 1998; Reed, 2000). Partly in order to address such concerns, CDA draws upon a range of more textually oriented forms of DA, such as critical linguistics (Fowler and Kress, 1979), in order to equip itself with a range of techniques for close up textual analysis. By combining Foucauldian insights with a close-up textual orientation, CDA can be considered a 'middle range' perspective (Alvesson and Karreman, 2000) that permits the researcher to avoid focusing on macro-structural issues at the expense of micro-processes of agency, or vice versa (Fairclough, 2003). It does this by allowing the researcher to focus on the constant interactions between structure and agency and to understand how each can be mutually constitutive of the other (Phillips *et al.*, 2004). CDA can be described as 'realist' (Reed, 2000; Fairclough, 2003) in that it sees processes and relations as being ontologically prior to objects and entities whilst recognizing the latter as socially produced 'permanences' (Harvey, 1996; cited in Fairclough, 2005). These permanences can be understood as becoming sufficiently 'real' so as to constrain and set limits around possibilities for agency. Epistemologically, priority is given neither to structures nor (agential) processes, but rather to the relationships between them and to the tensions that arise in their mutual constitution. In summary, this realist form of CDA permits the researcher to pay better attention to processes of and constraints to agency compared with other, more purely constructivist, forms of DA.

In terms of its practicalities, CDA offers a three-dimensional framework that encompasses and links: pieces of text;[2] instances of discursive practice; and forms of social practice. At the textual level, CDA draws attention to how any part of a text will be simultaneously accomplishing three things, namely: (1) representing and constructing a particular reality; (2) projecting and negotiating social relationships; and (3) setting up links with other parts of the text and with the overall context. These accomplishments are achieved respectively via 'ideational', 'interpersonal' and 'textual' functions (Halliday, 1978). At the level of discursive practice, CDA's primary focus of attention lies in the processes by which texts are produced, distributed and consumed, with activities of interpretation playing a key role in all of these. A particular focus of attention at this level relates to the notion of intertextuality (Bakhtin, 1986), which addresses the historically situated nature of discourse by highlighting the way in which any text will typically incorporate elements from prior texts. Finally, at the level of social practice, CDA draws on Althusser (1971) in order to analyse the ideological aspect of discourse and Gramsci (1971) in order to examine processes of hegemonic struggle and social change.

In addition to the terminology set out above, the approach encompasses a wealth of further terms each with its own CDA-specific significance. Several of these will be employed in the presentation of our data in a later section. For ease of reference, the first use hereafter of any such term is shown in ***bold/italics***, and a brief explanation thereof can be found in the glossary included as Appendix 3.1.

Research context

The research that we present in this chapter is drawn from a wider study of MD practices across seven European countries (Mabey and Ramirez, 2004; Finch-Lees *et al.*, 2005a, 2005b; Mabey and Gooderham, 2005).[3] One of the aims of the overall study was to cast light on some of the less obvious interests being served by MD, with particular attention being paid to issues of power and control. Here we show how CDA was used to understand some of these interests. Due to space restrictions, we will illustrate the approach using just a few 'vignettes' from a single case-study organization which we shall refer to under the pseudonym of CapCo. CapCo is a major UK-headquartered multinational, manufacturing and distributing a range of premium-branded consumer goods to around 180 countries. It has approximately 25,000 employees worldwide. The company employs a programme of capability-based MD (CBMD) focused around an internally developed framework of leadership capabilities. See Figure 3.1 for an explanation of how the framework is structured.

The main research question we set ourselves was the intentionally broad one of:

> Which interests are being served by the company's capability-based approach to management development?

In attempting to address such a broad question, we also set ourselves a number of more focused, supporting questions, as follows:

- What are the discourses, the taken-for-granted assumptions and the ideological themes contained within the company's CBMD documentation?
- How do stakeholders account for their experiences of the capability approach itself and the related development initiatives? To what extent do such accounts contain themes of unity, disruption, ambiguity or contradiction (both in their own right and/or with reference to the ideological themes and assumptions espoused by the company documentation)? How do these aspects manifest themselves in stakeholders' language use?
- How do these accounts and the analysis thereof help us understand which stakeholder interests are being served/neglected by CBMD in CapCo?

There were two distinct phases of data construction.[4] The first of these was the gathering of relevant company documentation regarding CapCo's

CapCo's leadership capabilities are subdivided into the following categories: Ideas; Emotional energy; People performance; Edge; and Living the values. Each of these is supported by a general descriptive statement, before then being broken down into a more detailed set of behavioural, skill or knowledge attributes. Each of these attributes is supported by descriptive criteria, progressively graded as: Baseline; Developing; Experienced; Mastery.

The above can best be illustrated by taking an actual example from the company documentation. Edge, for example, is described in overall terms as:

'The ability to face reality and take tough decisions about products, costs and people to deliver sustainable results'.

This is then supported by the more detailed attributes of: Anticipation; Tenacity; Prioritization; Urgency; Courage. Each of these is broken down into graded descriptive statements. Taking *Prioritization* as an example, the graded statements read as follows:

(1) Baseline	(2) Developing
Operates in purposeful manner against agreed priorities	Operates in determined and purposeful manner. Organises actions around key goals

(3) Experienced	(4) Mastery
Drives business area performance against clearly defined priorities	Ruthlessly prioritises, highly focused approach to driving total business achievement

Figure 3.1 CapCo's capability framework.

CBMD programme. Such documentation included the capability frameworks themselves, an initial briefing pack sent out to the organization's 'leadership' population along with a broader array of presentational and briefing materials setting out the nature and overt intent of each specific development intervention (e.g. learning workshops, assessment programmes, appraisal formalities, etc.) within the overall programme.

A second phase of data construction involved nine managers taking part in one-to-one interviews, each lasting around an hour. Participants consisted of both HR and line managers, with a mix of grades, nationalities and geographical (including overseas) remits. The sample size reflects the study's aim of facilitating explanation at the level of discursive expression, rather than any attempt to generalize based on statistically representative populations (Kamoche, 2000). All interviews were loosely structured (Alvesson and Deetz, 2000), the overall aim being to elicit participants' personal and subjective evaluations of CapCo's CBMD activities. The interviews were tape-recorded and transcribed. All extracts herein are presented according to a simplified Jeffersonian convention (included as Appendix 3.2) adapted from Potter and Wetherell (1987).

Analysis and evaluation of data

In this section we begin by drawing upon CDA to highlight some of the ideological features and assumptions of the MD programme, as reflected in the company documentation. We will then go on to contrast these with our analysis of the interview data.

Company documentation

We start with an extract from an address by the company CEO contained in the company's main briefing pack supporting the programme:

> The first phase of CapCo's evolution is behind us [...] Recent results are encouraging but our *investors* are not yet convinced that our strategies will deliver the *value improvement they require*. We must now execute the next phase of CapCo's evolution and speed is critical. [...] CapCo *needs* swift market based execution that will drive profitable growth. This in turn requires *empowered, energized management teams who are passionate* about growing our brands by continually satisfying the needs of our consumers. However, to leverage the intellectual capital of *the organization*, those teams must be bound together by common values, behaviours and leading-edge business processes. [...] *The CapCo Way* is about those beliefs, behaviours and processes and is an important first step in ensuring that decentralized operating units operate in a way that will *maximize the value* of the enterprise; [...] The CapCo Way, coupled with the aggressive business strategies already in place can and will *drive CapCo to greatness*.

From a CDA angle, the **interpersonal** features of the above text demonstrate a highly declarative **mood** with strong and frequently obligational forms of **modality**. The predominant **ideational functioning** is passive and relational with little agency. All in all, the audience is being 'told', without any kind of equivocation, about how things 'are' and, as such, all statements are represented as facts rather than opinions. CDA encourages us to scrutinize the truth status of such statements, certainly for example in terms of: what the 'organization' (itself a **nominalization** that removes any sense of agency from activities of 'organizing') might actually 'need'; how we might know when 'value' is likely to have been 'maximized'; what 'greatness' might actually mean; and exactly how or why the CapCo Way[5] might be instrumental in bringing all this about. By glossing over such issues, the text presupposes a high degree of understanding on the part of the audience thus making available a **subject position** of 'knowledgeable reader' along with the more explicit position of 'empowered, energized, passionate team member and manager'. All this, along with a very simplified form of **textual functioning**, serves to protect the various truth claims from critical attention. Indeed, the text can itself be understood as an exercise of power on behalf of its author, who implicitly lays claim to a subject position of 'objective truth teller'. However, from the CDA perspective such statements are to be regarded as inherently ideological inasmuch as they could, in practical terms, never really be proved or indeed disproved.

The above extract gives a flavour for the way in which the overall rationale and context for the company's CBMD programme is discursively constructed. We supplement this below with an extract taken from the company's briefing document on its 'Benchmarking for Development' initiative. This is an initiative which involves selected managers being invited to work with a firm of external consultants, using various assessment tools (including 360-degree feedback) to establish their own capability profiles and development plans:

> The CapCo Way is *designed* to ensure we focus on the keys to our business success [...] by putting in place the processes and behaviours that will *guarantee* consistent and sustainable excellence across CapCo.
> [...]
> To get the most out of the [Benchmarking for Development] experience you will need to be open-minded and be prepared to *open up* and take a *few risks*. This won't always be easy or comfortable but is likely to enhance the quality of feedback and learning you gain.
> [...]
> The first session will focus on *mapping out* your experience and functional skill base and your leadership capabilities. Where psychological assessments are used they will be fully explained. The second session, which will take place shortly after the first, will focus on *drawing out* your strengths and development needs
> [...]
> The process outlined above allows *effective diagnosis* of the factors that underpin capabilities and development needs. We believe that this is essential if individuals are to be helped in a detailed manner to build on their strengths, to address areas for improvement and fulfil their potential.

The above passages display a revealing blend of **genre**. In the first paragraph, the genre of advertising is drawn upon with the CapCo Way and its related development programmes being presented as a form of commodity (Fairclough, 1992) that has been specifically 'designed' to 'guarantee' success. Commodifying development in this way casts the employee into the subject position of consumer, thus reinforcing an image of free choice, materialism and enterprise (Fournier, 1998). The next paragraphs draw much more upon a technical/medical/scientific genre that conjures up images of a prospective patient needing to be reassured about an impending 'diagnosis'. All in all, *metaphor* and genre combine to portray capabilities as being innate properties of the individual that simply need to be uncovered (or 'drawn out') with the help of expert techniques, combined with self-exploration and the 'opening up' of oneself in front of others. In terms of further reading, Townley (1994) illustrates the objectifying/subjectifying potential of such 'developmental' processes by characterizing them as Foucauldian techniques of 'examination' and 'confession'.

The above extract finishes with a reference to CBMD as being a way of allowing each and every member of the organization to 'fulfil their potential'. This discourse of self-actualization is drawn upon extensively throughout the documentation, for example, by making it clear that every employee is expected to establish their own 'Be the Best Development Plan', the purpose of which is to:

> Drive professional development and enhance every individual's contribution to the achievement of personal and business goals [. . .] to ensure that everyone has the opportunity to become the brightest star they can be.

In this passage, CDA helps draw attention to a *presupposition* in the very naming of the development plan itself, i.e. that it is natural that 'everyone in the company' should strive to 'be the best' they possibly can be in the work context and that this happily fulfils both 'personal *and* business goals'. Statements such as these can be understood to both marginalize and de-legitimize inherent conflicts and trade-offs between work and non-work identities. Furthermore, using the word 'opportunity' to imply choice belies the fact that these 'Be the Best Development Plans' are in fact a mandatory element of the CapCo performance management system.

One prominent way in which this discourse of self-actualization is further reinforced in the documentation is via a mix of metaphorical language drawn from the worlds of accounting and competitive sport, for example by representing CBMD as a form of 'investment' in the managerial self that then leads to a form of payback in terms of personal 'growth'. Such growth is typically expressed in terms of ever-increasing levels of performance via a continual 'raising of the bar' linked ostensibly to consequent progression in career, status and salary. The overall effect is to promote a discourse whereby employees are encouraged to think of themselves as mini-enterprises (du Gay *et al.*, 1996; Covaleski *et al.*, 1998; Fournier, 1998), but whose value is to be measured not in terms of share price, but in ever-increasing levels of capability and performance. Accounting metaphor is taken even further in the following passage, which speaks of aggregating or consolidating people, capability-wise, in much the same way as a corporate enterprise would consolidate the balance sheets of its individual entities:

> [The CBMD programme] provides the organisation with an excellent opportunity to look at the aggregate outputs and review its overall capabilities against world class benchmarks. This will enable us to plan and take action to address organisation capability gaps and enhance organisational performance for the future.

Our analysis of the company documentation has remained necessarily brief. However, our aim is to show how such documentation draws upon discourses of scientific objectivity, accounting and competitive sports to construct an image of capability that resides within the individual, needing only to be 'drawn out' in order to then be measured, quantified, recorded and consolidated. As part of this process, the genre of advertising is utilized to commodify the related development programmes, portraying them as a voluntaristic means to 'guarantee' success for both employee and organization. This discourse of unitarism, where development and performance become almost synonymous (Antonacopoulou and Fitzgerald, 1996), combines with those of accounting, enterprise, consumerism and the career to conjure up an ideological image of the employee as an enterprising project of the self (du Gay *et al.*, 1996; Covaleski *et al.*, 1998; Fournier, 1998). The image is one in which it becomes as natural for the employee to self-actualize in the service of the organization as it is for the organization to maximize its own value in the service of the shareholder.

We now turn our attention to an analysis of our interview data. Our aim is to demonstrate how and to what effect participants both buy into and resist (sometimes almost simultaneously) the ideological stance of the company documentation. We will achieve this primarily by exploring some of the contrasting subject positions taken up by the participants.

Interview data

A relatively frequent dynamic that arose during the interviews was one of stakeholders both adopting and resisting the subject positions made available by the company documentation. In the following extract, we can see how one stakeholder (Participant 2) initially aligns himself unproblematically with the careerist and entrepreneurial discourses running through the company documentation:

> [The capabilities] are important to me because they're part of my development plan [...] and it's there that they become <u>vitally</u> important to me ... I don't move on unless I can demonstrate ... performance and development against those particular things.

However, rather than continuing with this careerist and entrepreneurial self-maximizing subject position, later in the interview this same stakeholder began to reflect on the enduring politics of the career system within CapCo. In doing so, he adopted a starkly contrasting subject position which might be aptly described as 'materially satisficing cynic':

> Are the capabilities [...] really valued...? Umm ... they will be ... and they can be if we make them work ... I just don't ... [...] and you might think I'm a little cynical about it ... yeah there is a cynical ... tag on me ... um about this stuff but er ... what they don't show is that there might be some glass barriers, some glass ceilings which you can't see ... and they're the bits of ... around personal development which ... if there are <u>unwritten</u> rules ... and unwritten things which well ... if you want to progress you <u>have</u> to go out and spend time ... going and flogging <u>yourself</u> ... constantly ... um ... otherwise individuals naively assume that by performing against ... capabilities and objectives they will get recognized and seen. [...] I can ... be <u>mastery</u> on everything ... but still be in the wrong flavour of the month department ... and er ... [chuckles] if your face doesn't fit you know then ... um ... then <u>yeah</u> you have to realize it and make ... be big enough to say OK I'm gonna make a big change and go somewhere else ... and people know this place is quite comfortable ... um ... financially and when you've been in as long as I have it takes quite a step to jump out and find something else to do.

In these extracts, we see how the stakeholder switches between an initial subject position that buys into the unitarist, objectivist and apolitical ideology of the company documentation and a later, resistant one that represents such ideology as a deceptive illusion that only the 'naive' should believe in. With regard to this, we should state that our use of CDA does not extend to any attempt to ascertain what the participant might be 'really' thinking or feeling, but more to examine what the stakeholder might be accomplishing via such talk. As such, contradictions like the one set out above do not present 'problems' to be ironed out via further interview probing, but rather opportunities for critical insight. For example, this simultaneous adoption of opposing subject positions provides an indication of how employees might knowingly participate in activities of mutual deception or 'calculative compliance' (Willmott, 1993) vis-à-vis the organization. And as we can see from the above, they may do this if nothing else for the sake of financial satisficing or indeed their very survival within the organization.

Although space precludes a detailed analysis, similar dynamics of ambivalence were observed during several other of our CapCo interviews and we present two further examples, from culture and gender perspectives respectively. In relation to (national) culture, one manager on secondment to the UK from a developing nation (Participant 8) expressed initial appreciation at the way in which his participation in CBMD helped him feel part of the CapCo 'family' whilst also providing him with an understanding of the expectations that he needed to live up to in order to progress career-wise (Kamoche, 2000). However, later in the same interview he expressed frustration at the fact that his identity within the organization (at least for career purposes) had been reduced to little more than an expression of standardized capability against an Anglo-Saxon norm. The situation was rendered all the more oppressive by the fact that he was under constant scrutiny against the capabilities via 360-degree feedback, to the extent that he was even being assessed by an *external* service provider with whom he was closely working. Participant 8 had therefore resigned himself to a certain degree of 'surface acting' (Clarke, 1999) simply to demonstrate 'development' or 'performance' against the capabilities for career purposes:

> The ... capability development process [...] in my view needs not be ... [...] brought across as ... 'this is the only path through which you know you can progress in the organization...' (mm right) ... because if you do that then human beings are only human ... then people come across differently, they will behave differently ... or you may actually end up identifying the wrong development areas.

Elsewhere in the interview the stakeholder also expressed ambivalence about the degree to which conformity to this Anglo-Saxon model of capability would serve his career interests once he had returned to his home-country organization, with its own distinct behavioural norms.

Our final (and gender-related) example comes from a female HR manager (Participant 3) who initially expressed almost evangelical enthusiasm for the capabilities, especially in terms of the subject position they permitted her to take up – i.e. that of 'selfless developer of others':

> You <u>tend</u> to be just quite <u>selfless</u> about it [i.e. CBMD]. You tend to want to do all of the <u>good</u> work for the groups of people that you <u>support</u> ... rather than focus on, you know, what does it mean for you.

However, later in the same interview she began to express a degree of unease at the way in which 'Edge' (the label for one of the capability clusters) was being given an apparently masculine/competitive interpretation by the exclusively male executive board. She also felt that 'Edge' was being arbitrarily singled out by the board as being more important than the other, arguably less masculine, capabilities. This left Participant 3 questioning the degree to which she felt willing or indeed able to adopt a certain (i.e. masculine) self for the sake of career progression that she felt was at odds with her 'true' (i.e. more feminine) self:

> So there was a kind of a <u>tension</u> in myself in … thinking through my <u>own</u> development [...] around well … am I gonna have to <u>change</u> myself so <u>fundamentally</u> as a human being kind of thing … [...] in trying to <u>address</u> this behaviour that's kind of expected within CapCo [...] and er I actually came to the conclusion that actually what I need to do is to be true to myself.

Interpretation and conclusions

Our presentation of the data has been necessarily selective and brief. However, the aim has been to demonstrate the use of CDA in helping to appreciate how and to what effect CapCo's CBMD programme can be understood to be inherently implicated in processes of identity construction and, consequently, in those of identity regulation. In the first section of our data analysis, we saw how the company documentation appears to be actively encouraging employees to adopt a managerial self that is unproblematically knowable, calculable, measurable, discussible (Townley, 1994) and thus 'developable' in standardized capability terms. This in turn purports to provide a means by which individuals can achieve a certain form of entrepreneurial and careerist self-actualization for the mutual benefit of both individual and organization. In the second section, we saw how employee stakeholders tended to oscillate between an embracement of such ideals and a certain questioning thereof. Our point here is not to pass judgement on CBMD activities (or those of MD more generally) as being inherently and unilaterally negative, or indeed positive. Like Townley (1998), we prefer to see such activities as being potentially both positive/productive and negative/repressive at one and the same time. With regard to this point, the ontological stance of our analysis is to regard any notion of the essential self as being socially constructed via semiosis. In the above case, CBMD provides a rich set of discursive resources with which to construct such notions of the managerial self. However, it is these very acts of construction that render our selves vulnerable to manipulation in the interests of others. And when one's sense of self becomes linked so closely to notions of performative development and self-maximizing enterprise, this at best marginalizes and at worst closes off alternative identities or 'ways of being', at least for the purposes of progression or even survival within the organization. There is no little irony in such findings at a time when so much attention (or perhaps lip-service) is being paid to the importance of diversity within organizations.

The gender/culture issues we have briefly touched upon provide no more than a starting point for analysis of such matters. As such, we hope that our brief synopsis will encourage further use of CDA in researching the less obvious interests being served by MD. And we would suggest, for example, that the degree to which MD might work, inadvertently or otherwise, to produce conformity, elitism, exclusion and discrimination alongside any stated desire to promote diversity, inclusion and equality of opportunity, provides rich and fertile ground for the application of CDA.

Key learning points

- By typically portraying MD as a politically neutral means of building knowledge, skills and abilities, mainstream functionalist analyses tend to take the 'M' in MD for granted. They do so by treating the manager as a self-evident entity needing only to be 'developed' for the mutual benefit of individual and organization.
- In contrast to this, CDA helps us appreciate MD's role in constructing the very subjectivities upon which notions of development might actually depend.
- This opens the door towards an appreciation of power dynamics within MD, particularly with regard to how historically situated (e.g. culturally-specific and gendered) notions of management come to be taken for granted as naturally occurring 'norms'.
- This is turn provides a means to appreciate how MD can serve as a repressive form of regulation and control as well as (and at the same time as) a more productive and emancipatory avenue towards self construction and development.
- CDA treats language as a focus of study in its own right as opposed to a neutral means of representing an objectively pre-existing world. As such, the concern is somewhat removed from any functionalist one of linking MD to performance at the individual, organizational or societal level of analysis.
- We do not argue, however, that positivist/functionalist analyses of MD are without merit. Our argument is simply that this is only one concern amongst many legitimate alternatives.

Appendices

Appendix 3.1: Glossary of CDA terms

(Non-exhaustive, and sourced from Fairclough (1992) except where stated.)

Term	Explanation
Genre	A way of using language associated with some particular form of social activity, examples being the genres, of interview; of advertising; or of a textbook (Fairclough and Hardy, 1997). Genres within a text constitute tools that agents can use for interpretation, thus motivating them to use such texts by incorporating them into their own actions and texts (Phillips *et al.*, 2004).
Ideational function	Serves to represent and construct reality using different textual processes. These can be actional (incorporating agency), mental (incorporating cognitions, e.g. beliefs, recollections, etc.), or relational (incorporating statements of being). Scrutinizing the ideational function of a text helps to appreciate the political/ideological significance of nominalization and metaphor (see below).
Interpersonal function	Serves to project and negotiate identity and social relationships via textual choices that include those of mood and modality (see below).
Metaphor	Serves to construct reality by structuring thoughts, knowledge, beliefs and actions in particular ways. Scrutinizing the use of metaphor in texts provides a means to gain insight into the ideological and political processes operating therein, including those of hegemonic struggle.
Modality	An aspect of interpersonal functioning. Refers to the strength of commitment or affinity with propositions in the text. Unmoderated or 'objectivist' forms of modality often imply a form of power.
Mood	An aspect of interpersonal functioning. The overall mood of a text can be gauged by assessing the extent to which it uses declaratives, questions or commands.
Nominalization	Occurs via the use of nouns as opposed to actional forms. Heavily nominalized texts can have ideological significance in that they mask processes of agency and strengthen presuppositions, thus increasing the likelihood that assumptions will be taken for granted or regarded as fact (Fairclough and Hardy, 1997).
Presupposition	An aspect of intertextuality. Relates to aspects in a text the meaning/significance of which are taken by the text's producer to be evident or given, frequently because they are assumed (correctly or otherwise) to have been dealt with in some previous text. Presuppositions can be sincere

but they can also be used manipulatively, as they are often difficult to challenge due partly to their opaqueness. They can also serve to place the consumer of texts in certain subject positions (by assuming prior textual experience), thus contributing to the ideological constitution of subjects.

Subject position	An identity that is constructed and made relevant by specific ways of talking. Just as such ways of talking can vary within and between conversations, so too do the identities of the speakers (Edley, 2001). The concept provides a means of analysing how agents are variously positioned and subjectified, by others and by themselves, in the course of discursive interaction. Examining processes by which subject positions are offered, taken up and/or resisted can provide insight into motives and interests served by such interaction (Billig, 2001).
Textual function	Relates to the ways in which the text is bound together (and linked to the external context) using terms such as 'and', 'but', 'yet', etc. Textual functioning can vary in its degree of complexity. Complex functioning is often indicative of argumentative style (which in turn invites counter-argument), whereas simple functioning indicates a more descriptive style, which invites less counter-argument. Simple functioning also presupposes the making of logical linkages by a knowing audience, thus setting up subject positions for that audience to adopt.

Appendix 3.2: Transcription convention

[. . .]	Material deliberately omitted
[text]	Added clarificatory information
text	Emphasis added by the authors during transcription
(text)	Interjections by interviewer
text	Words uttered with added emphasis or volume
text. . .	Audible gap of short duration (less than 1 second)

Notes

1 Fairclough (2001) uses the term 'semiosis' to cover not just written or spoken language but also body language, visual images or any other form of signifying. Although not addressed further herein, like Fairclough, we consider all such semiotic material to be legitimate objects of scrutiny within CDA.

2 The word 'text' should be taken to mean here both instances of written and spoken material, whether or not the latter has been transcribed into written form.

3 Indeed, many of the ideas that we present in this chapter are more fully explored in Finch-Lees *et al.* (2005a) Reproduced here by permission of Sage Publications Ltd (© The Tavistock Institute, London, 2005).

4 The term 'data construction' (Alvesson and Deetz, 2000) is preferred to the more common one of 'data collection'. The former term more adequately

reflects the underlying ontological and epistemological assumptions of a study such as this, which considers the researcher to be taking an active role, along with participants, in processes of social construction. We lay no claim, therefore, to be merely collecting objectively pre-existent data.

5 The 'CapCo Way' is an umbrella term that covers the capabilities approach to MD within the organization, along with a number of other related business processes.

References

Althusser, L. (1971) 'Ideology and ideological state apparatuses', in Althusser, L. (ed.), *Lenin and Philosophy and Other Essays*, London: New Left Books.

Alvesson, M. and Deetz, S. (2000) *Doing Critical Management Research*, London: Sage.

Alvesson, M. and Karreman, D. (2000) 'Varieties of discourse: on the study of organizations through discourse analysis', *Human Relations*, 53(9): 1125–49.

Alvesson, M. and Willmott, H. (2002) 'Identity regulation as organizational control: producing the appropriate individual', *Journal of Management Studies*, 39(5): 619–44.

Antonacopoulou, E. and Fitzgerald, L. (1996) 'Reframing competency in management development', *Human Resource Management Journal*, 6(1): 27–48.

Bakhtin, M. (1986) *Speech Genres and Other Late Essays* (Emerson, C. and Holquist, M., eds; trans. V.W. McGee), Austin, TX: University of Texas Press.

Billig, M. (2001) 'Discursive, rhetorical & ideological messages', in Wetherell, M., Taylor, S. and Yates, S.J. (eds), *Discourse Theory & Practice*, London: Sage.

Clarke, M. (1999) 'Management development as a game of meaningless outcomes', *Human Resource Management Journal*, 9(2): 38–49.

Covaleski, M., Dirsmith, M., Heian, J. and Samuel, S. (1998) 'The calculated and the avowed: techniques of discipline and struggles over identity in big six public accounting firms', *Administrative Science Quarterly*, 43: 293–327.

Dick, P. and Cassell, C. (2002) 'Barriers to managing diversity in a UK constabulary: the role of discourse', *Journal of Management Studies*, 39(7): 953–76.

DTI (2001) *UK Competitiveness Indicators*, 2nd edn, London: Department for Industry.

du Gay, P., Salaman, G. and Rees, B. (1996) 'The conduct of management and the management of conduct: contemporary managerial discourse and the constitution of the 'competent' manager', *Journal of Management Studies*, 33(3): 263–82.

Edley, N. (2001) 'Analysing masculinity: interpretative repertoires, ideological dilemmas and subject positions', in Wetherell, M., Taylor, S. and Yates, S.J. (eds), *Discourse as Data: A Guide for Analysis*, London: Sage.

Fairclough, N. (1992) *Discourse and Social Change*, Cambridge: Polity Press.

Fairclough, N. (1995) *Critical Discourse Analysis*, London: Longman.

Fairclough, N. (2001) 'The discourse of New Labour: critical discourse analysis', in Wetherell, M., Taylor, S. and Yates, S.J. (eds), *Discourse as Data: A Guide for Analysis*, London: Sage.

Fairclough, N. (2003) *Analysing Discourse: Textual Analysis for Social Research*, London: Routledge.

Fairclough, N. (2005) 'Discourse analysis in organizational studies: the case for critical realism', *Organization Studies*, 26(6): 915–39.

Fairclough, N. and Hardy, G. (1997) 'Management learning as discourse', in Burgoyne, J. and Reynolds, M. (eds), *Management Learning: Integrating Perspectives in Theory and Practice*, London: Sage.

Finch-Lees, T., Mabey, C. and Liefooghe, A. (2005a) ' "In the name of capability": A critical discursive evaluation of competency-based management development', *Human Relations*, 58(9): 1185–222.

Finch-Lees, T., Mabey, C. and Liefooghe, A. (2005b) 'Management development as a gendered order of discourse', in *Academy of Management Conference*, Honolulu, 5–10 August.

Fournier, V. (1998) 'Stories of development and exploitation: militant voices in enterprise culture', *Organization*, 5(1): 55–80.

Fowler, R. and Kress, G. (1979) 'Critical linguistics', in Fowler, R., Hodge, G., Kress, G. and Trew, T. (eds), *Language and Control*, London: Routledge.

Gramsci, A. (1971) *Selections from the Prison Notebooks*, London: Lawrence and Wishart.

Halliday, M.A.K. (1978) *Language as Social Semiotic*, London: Edward Arnold.

Harvey, D. (1996) *Justice, Nature and the Geography of Difference*, Oxford: Blackwell.

Kamoche, K. (2000) 'Developing managers: the functional, the symbolic, the sacred and the profane', *Organization Studies*, 21(4): 747–74.

Mabey, C. and Gooderham, P. (2005) 'The impact of management development on perceptions of organizational performance in European firms', *European Management Review*, 2(2): 131–42.

Mabey, C. and Ramirez, M. (2004) *Developing Managers: A European Perspective*, London: Chartered Management Institute.

Mama, A. (1995) *Beyond the Masks: Gender, Race and Subjectivity*, London: Routledge.

Meyer, M. (2001) 'Between theory, method, and politics: positioning of the approaches to CDA', in Wodak, R. and Meyer, M. (eds), *Methods of Critical Discourse Analysis*, London: Sage.

Newton, T. (1998) 'Theorizing subjectivity in organizations: the failure of Foucauldian studies?', *Organization Studies*, 19(3): 415–47.

Phillips, N., Lawrence, T.B. and Hardy, C. (2004) 'Discourse and institutions', *Academy of Management Review*, 29(4): 635–52.

Potter, J. and Wetherell, M. (1987) *Discourse and Social Psychology: Beyond Attitudes and Behaviour*, London: Sage.

Reed, M. (2000) 'The limits of discourse analysis in organizational analysis', *Organization*, 7(3): 524–30.

Townley, B. (1994) *Reframing Human Resource Management: Power, Ethics and the Subject at Work*, London: Sage.

Townley, B. (1998) 'Beyond good and evil: depth and division in the management of human resources', in McKinlay, A. and Starkey, K. (eds), *Foucault, Management and Organization Theory*, London: Sage.

Willmott, H. (1993) 'Strength is ignorance; slavery is freedom: managing culture in modern organizations', *Journal of Management Studies*, 30(4): 515–52.

Winterton, J. and Winterton, R. (1999) *Developing Managerial Competence*, London: Routledge.

Wodak, R. and Meyer, M. (eds) (2001) *Methods of Critical Discourse Analysis*, London: Sage.

4 Strategic management development

Paul Brown

Objectives

The objectives of this chapter are:

- to provide an overview from the literature of perceived best practice in strategic management development (SMD);
- to describe conceptual frameworks which are supported by empirical evidence, and provide a theoretical underpinning for SMD.

Theoretical context

Definition of strategic management development

For the purposes of this chapter, SMD is defined as:

> Management development interventions which are intended to enhance the strategic capability and corporate performance of an organization.

This infers a collective approach to management development through a conscious process, which has probably been initiated or stimulated at corporate level, but can encompass both formal and informal activities.

Existing conceptual frameworks

The tensions between organizational and personal objectives in MD were recognized by Woodall and Winstanley (1998) in their model of the integration and differentiation which, they said, needed to be balanced. Differentiated MD was compatible with self-development and people's future careers and, being left to individual initiative, it was a bottom-up process which enabled choice to suit the individual's personality, own situation and learning style. In contrast, integrated MD was described as being compatible with both organizational development and the objectives of the business strategy, was proactively planned from the top and had a uniformity of objectives; these characteristics make it consistent with the concept of SMD.

Patching (1998) provided a model which combined the purpose of MD, either *success through change* or *success through alignment* (with current systems, culture and job roles), and different levels of *specificity to the organization* (high or low).

Where the purpose was success through change, the programme was either Transformational (high specificity to the organization) or Exploratory (low specificity). Where the purpose was success through alignment, the programme was either developing Specific Capabilities (high specificity) or Generic (low specificity).

Transformational MD will probably aim to gain competitive advantage and is driven by the management vision and corporate strategy, and is thus a form of SMD. Exploratory MD often aims to achieve innovation and learning through experimentation. It may be driven by entrepreneurial thinking, and could help to develop strategic management capabilities. Generic activities develop the knowledge, skills and attitudes which seem necessary for managers in almost any kind of organization. Arguably, because they are not unique they do not contribute to strategic advantage. Specific capabilities are those which are required in one particular organization, and help to defend the competitive position. As such, they may have strategic value.

Strategic human resource management (SHRM)

It can be argued that for SMD to be effective it should be one component of a bigger SHRM philosophy. This would provide vertical linkages connecting management development to SHRM and business strategy, and horizontal linkages to coherently connect SMD to other HR policies and systems such as appraisal and reward. Such links would be mutually reinforcing.

Research into the ways that HR strategies connect with and support business strategies has demonstrated that MD is one dimension of SHRM where this connection is most evident (Tyson, 1995; Gratton *et al.*, 1999). Gratton's study of eight large UK high-performing companies found that the emphasis tended to be on high-flyer leadership development programmes, and the connection with business strategy was less evident in lower-level MD initiatives. Nevertheless, Stiles (1999), another member of the Gratton team, found that middle managers were involved in strategic change processes – in cross-functional teams; in informal networks which gave feedback to senior management; and acting as champions for change. He highlighted that in a dynamic environment, the MD processes should not be bureaucratic or rigid. If competency frameworks and training programmes were too narrowly defined, they would be less appropriate than broader developmental approaches. Competencies had to be generic enough to be stretched to suit changing conditions: emphasizing teamwork, creativity, flexibility and leadership, while still giving some structure to the fast-changing nature of the work setting. Training and development programmes become less formal with more emphasis on personal development and learning, development centres, creativity workshops, teamwork, coaching and counselling.

Best practice SMD

Thinking on SMD has been heavily influenced by practitioner accounts, frequently case-study based: typical of this is Hussey (1996). First, the organizational needs are analysed, with an emphasis on the strategic drivers (e.g. expansion into Europe). This indicates competencies or skills for which there is a new or expanded need (e.g. market planning), and the current levels of these competencies are audited. The MD 'gap' is identified and the current MD activities are audited to examine what is being done to close the gap. Finally, new MD plans can be drawn up to meet the identified needs.

Temporal (1990: 4) provided a more dynamic view of MD:

> a continuous process of many activities, events and experiences that never actually ceases ... (it) is an integral part of management work ... (which) necessitates constant readjustment in accordance with the changing needs of the business ... (and) involves people working together to identify problems and developing means of solving them.

Temporal saw MD complementing rigid formal structures by adding informal flexible interactions, which lead to greater organizational learning, and placed emphasis on strategic projects, entrepreneurship opportunities and other real work activities.

Bolt (1993) emphasized the strategic *role* of executive development programmes – many CEOs in the USA had recognized them as an important tool for helping achieve their strategic agenda. Often such a programme sprang directly from their own vision, and they participated in the entire programme to demonstrate their commitment. Involving executives in formulating and shaping the vision and strategy increased quality, understanding, commitment and ownership. Seibert *et al.* (1995) stressed that programmes should include the implementation of business strategy.

Boshyk (2000) described the use of project teams to tackle strategic problems, where the main objective was the development of participants rather than acting as a task force. The key elements in this approach included active involvement and support of senior executives, action learning on real business issues and leadership development through teamwork and coaching, as well as training in group-working, problem-solving skills and more functional business topics. An example was the General Electric programme (Mercer, 2000), which covered four weeks, of which around two-and-a-half weeks were spent on the project work, report writing and presentation. There were also sessions for reflection, and analysis of the team process. In some cases – especially where the team is responsible for implementation – the duration can be much longer. For example, at Motorola (Hansen, 2000), projects have lasted from four months to five years, using up to 25 per cent of team members' time. Each project was selected and defined by the main Board, and represented a major corporate issue that crossed all Motorola businesses and functions. The project team was large, normally 20–25 executives representing a wide cross-section of the corporation, and was empowered to take many actions, with perhaps only 20 per cent – the high-level ones – requiring approval by the Board.

Michael's (1993) survey of 11 large US high-tech firms found that their executive development programmes tended to tap into deliberate aspects of strategy – more needed to be done to explore ways of tapping into the emergent components of strategy formulation and implementation. He also advocated that portions of these programmes should be pushed down the hierarchy to help with succession and create a critical mass of people who possess a similar vocabulary and culture.

A consistent picture emerges of some of the features of successful SMD, especially in dynamic situations. The value of strategic projects facilitated through networking and action learning, and of broad competencies (which contribute to strategic advantage), is seen. The involvement of middle managers, the potential contribution by SMD to strategy formulation and implementation, and the need for a driving vision and commitment from the most senior management are also important.

Evaluating SMD

Seibert *et al.* (1995) surveyed 22 US companies and found evidence of weak links between business strategy and MD strategy. This they attributed to three factors. First, the Human Resource Development (HRD) functions had been inwardly focused, rather than outwardly focused on the 'customer' (i.e. senior line management) and the business environment. Second, the HRD function devised rigid systematic plans which were not responsive to the rapidly changing business strategies and environment. Third, there was a false dichotomy between developing individuals and conducting business, which were seen as respectively the work of HRD and line management. This did not facilitate natural connections between business strategy and executive development. To overcome this, strategic project systems could be used and would foster the growth of meta-skills, i.e. skills for developing and deploying situation-specific skills. The relevance of meta-skills was also highlighted by

Osbaldeston (1997) as a way of dealing with the pace and unpredictability of change.

Some of the problems of integrating SMD with formal planning systems were highlighted by Hirsch and Reilly (1998, 1999), who looked at skills planning over an 18-month period in IBM, NatWest and The Post Office. They found that the biggest changes affecting skills needs were not documented in the corporate plan. In practice, strategic needs were generated by specific change projects or high-level messages from senior managers (about big issues or vision and values). The problem with the formal corporate (or business) plans was that they often didn't say very much about people. Even when organizational capabilities (or core competencies) were identified it was difficult to link them directly with skills, though easier at management level than other levels.

Evidence that, to be effective, SMD must be complemented by a commitment to strategic planning activities was provided by Newkirk-Moore and Bracker (1998). They correlated the financial performance of 152 small US banks with the levels of both commitment to the strategic planning process and the frequency of strategic planning training. The banks which had embedded the concepts of strategic planning into their culture were described as having a *strategic commitment* to the planning process. They had continuous monitoring, communication and evaluation activities which kept strategic planning on the agenda for the whole organization. In contrast, other banks either had no recognizable planning activity or had a short-term and *prescriptive commitment* to it – often failing to manage the implementation process, for example. The study found that there was a significantly higher return on equity for those banks which had *both* a strategic commitment to planning *and* provided regular strategic management training.

New conceptual frameworks for MD

A framework which could help as a guide to the types of MD intervention that may be most appropriate has been proposed as a matrix (Figure 4.1), mapping organization and individual development against the nature of the business environment (Brown, 2003).

The matrix proposes that in more dynamic and complex conditions there is greater emphasis on the process aspects of SMD because of a need for greater team-working and networking. Learning at the individual level will often be a collaborative activity involving small teams and action learning. Meta-competencies will be required to give individuals adaptability and flexibility. There is also a requirement for new technical/professional knowledge which may be met through self-development, since it is not possible for all such learning to be pre-planned at the organizational level (because of the complexity of the business and/or the speed of change). At the organizational level, the MD is steered by broad concepts of vision, values

Nature of environment

	Static/slow changing	Dynamic
FOCUS OF MD — *Organization*	Planned programmes, linked to business objectives Formal methods Detailed competency framework Concerned with strategy implementation and context Mainly directed at senior managers	Driven by vision, values and core competencies Change Initiatives, projects and experimentation Performance management systems Broad competency framework Senior and middle manager involvement Concerned with strategy formulation and implementation
Individual	Selection from internal menu of competency-based modules External programmes for generic needs Whole person development	Development of meta-competencies Leadership and teamworking skills Networking and action learning Self-development New technical knowledge

Figure 4.1 How the business environment influences MD.

and core competencies, and driven by organization-wide change initiatives and systems. Competency frameworks will be broad and dynamic, emphasizing teamwork, creativity, flexibility, leadership and change management.

In more simple/static conditions, a greater degree of centralized planning is possible, and learning can be planned in a more detailed way. There will probably be greater reliance on formal MD methods, as these can be planned to suit needs. The organization is likely to be more bureaucratic and to place less recognition on informal learning. Whole-person development may be encouraged through organization-led initiatives such as outdoor MD. SMD will be more concerned with strategy implementation than formulation, and middle managers are less likely to have an active part.

The factors identified in the literature as *drivers* of successful SMD can be contrasted with factors acting as *barriers*, to produce a third conceptual framework (see Table 4.1) (Brown, 2003).

This framework can be used as a diagnostic instrument when evaluating an SMD programme, and provides guidance on good practice when designing a new programme. A simplified presentation of the key requirements for successful SMD, emphasizing how each requirement builds on the others, is shown in Figure 4.2.

Table 4.1 Drivers and barriers for SMD

Driver	Barrier
Planned (or deliberate) strategy	Emergent strategy
High commitment to strategic planning	Low commitment to HR strategic planning
MD coherent with strategy and objectives	Fragmented MD responses to strategic issues
MD seen as lever for transformational change	Short-termism of business; failure to invest in long-term development
Good linkage between line and HRD management	Inward-looking HR departments
Championship of CEO, vision for MD communicated	Lack of emphasis on HR in corporate strategy
Analysis of MD needs derived from strategies	Difficulty translating strategic issues into MD interventions
Identifying organization-specific core competencies, and meta-competencies	Mindset of managers, emphasizing individual effectiveness; narrowly defined competency frameworks
Responsive MD and flexible competencies to meet dynamics of strategy	Rigid plans of HR; static or retrospective nature of competencies
MD through projects, on-the-job methods, integrated with management work	MD divorced from real issues and implementation
Supportive learning environment	Learning organization ideals difficult to achieve in practice

The research context

Case-study research was undertaken in six UK organizations (Brown, 2005). In the first of these, a medium-sized university college, the study was longitudinal and based on the design and implementation of a senior management development programme (SMDP).

This pilot case study generated a causal network showing how strategic management capability may be developed, and a hypothetical life-cycle typology of SMD levels. These two conceptual models were tested in the five further organizations which displayed varying levels of commitment to strategic management (based on the concepts of Newkirk-Moore and Bracker, 1998), as identified in a postal questionnaire. Data were collected through interviews and the analysis of company documentation.

The university college study

The inductive methods used in the pilot study included participant observation, interviews with delegates and directors, and the study of internal

Figure 4.2 Key requirements for successful SMD.

documentation (Brown, 2004). After a long period of little change, the college was undergoing reorganization in response to the more turbulent environment it was facing. The aims of the MD programme were to meet the individual learning needs of managers – especially in their new roles – and to develop their capacity to lead and cope with change, most specifically that associated with the reorganization.

The programme was multi-stranded, as in Figure 4.3 – the asterisked strands being voluntary. It was envisaged that the performance and development review system, already in place, would be used to set and monitor individual managers' development objectives.

The design of the SMDP emphasized job-related skills for managers, supporting both the implementation of a new organization structure and the rather vague notions of a desired culture change. The programme was not promoted as having a high strategic emphasis, and at first the participants did not accord high priority to the strategic aspects of the programme.

A need for discussion and revision of the corporate strategy emerged from the one-day workshops that came to be known as strategy conferences. The strategy was being questioned by participants, and the directors realized that a useful forum for discussing it had been created. The exact role of the strategy conferences was, however, ambiguous. Were they just a discussion forum, or should they be closer to a decision-making body, debating specific proposals and making recommendations which the directors could then endorse as strategy? There was an awareness that power shifts were taking place, and this would take some time to resolve.

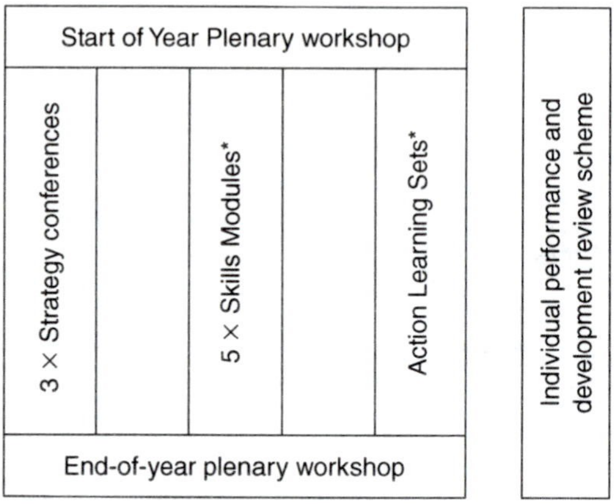

Figure 4.3 Senior management development programme (university college).

Nevertheless, the senior managers were debating strategy more than they had ever done before. A common language and understanding was being established. What is more, this new commitment to strategic thinking was stimulating new strategic processes, including biennial planning conferences. Another important benefit emerging in the first year of the programme was the strengthened networking, mutual support and bonding between participants. There was also a breaking down of barriers with the directors – with better communication and understanding evolving.

The apparent benefits emerging from the first year of the programme were threefold. First, some participants reported that their job skills had been enhanced. Second, a much strengthened commitment to strategic thinking had emerged, and had stimulated a major review of strategic direction. Third, useful communication, support and networking mechanisms had been established.

Clearly there were also external forces at play – the government's agenda for higher education being the most important. In response to this there had been signs of new emergent strategies in the institution, but this had not constituted a radical rethinking of mission, and a gap (strategic drift) had emerged between environmental change and institutional strategy. One manifestation of strategic drift was the growing problem of balancing the institution's budget. Whilst these budget shortfalls led to short-term operational cuts, they also demanded a more comprehensive review of medium- and long-term objectives and activity. The strategy conferences provided one forum through which these issues could be considered.

It seemed that some movement was being made towards establishing a new strategic direction though lacking full definition and consensus. Participants recognized that there was an increasing need for strategic

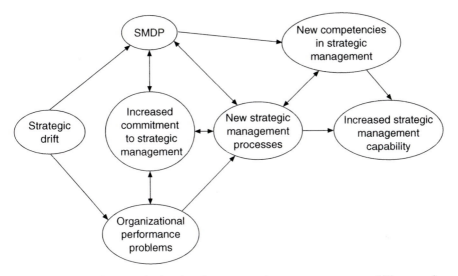

Figure 4.4 Causal network showing how strategic management capability may be developed.

leadership, complemented by organizational systems and competencies. Since the organization did not have mature, embedded processes for strategic management, it appears that it was necessary to develop both a commitment to strategic management, and competencies in formulating strategy and implementing change. The SMDP made an important contribution to this process by creating a common language for strategic management and embedding strategy in the management processes. Over time, the SMDP and the new management processes were leading to improved strategic management capability; a proposed model for this is shown in the causal network, Figure 4.4.

This causal network is probably most pertinent in situations where commitment to, and capabilities in, strategic management are low. Organizations with a low commitment to strategic management may be in a slow-changing environment, or in one which has recently experienced an increase from low to higher levels of dynamism and/or complexity. As the level of environmental turbulence (dynamism and complexity) increases, it is likely that the organization will need to move to higher levels of commitment to strategic management. Strategic drift leads to organizational performance problems, which also act as a trigger for change.

It was also concluded that the methods employed in SMD are likely to be most successful when they complement both the level of commitment to strategic management in the organization and the perceived needs of the participants. The indication was that the multi-strand design enabled the organization to meet a number of objectives, and that this 'mixed-menu' approach was helpful in maintaining energy and interest levels amongst participants.

From these ideas a generalizable hypothesis was developed by induction:

> The objectives and design of a strategic management development programme need to match the organization's level of commitment to strategic management and the degree of maturity of its strategic management processes and competencies, in order that the programme can be effective in enhancing the strategic capability and corporate performance of the organization.

The matching of strategic management commitment to the design of the SMDP will promote the development of strategic management capability. This matching might, over time, evolve through a number of stages, schematically shown in Table 4.2. The pilot case study illustrated how the university college was moving from Level 1 to Level 2. The more speculative propositions of Levels 3 and 4 draw in part from the ideas of Tuckman (1965), Gluck *et al.* (1982) and Newkirk-Moore and Bracker (1998).

Testing of the models: further case-study research

In the remaining five case studies another variable, strategy-making mode (Hart, 1992), was to emerge as important. Hart defined five strategy-making modes, which are summarized in Table 4.3. Different modes may be combined in any one organization, but there are likely to be one or two dominant modes.

To illustrate how the analysis of data helped identify strategy-making modes and position a company and its SMDP in the levels of Table 4.2, the findings for one company will be outlined.

Case study – Company A

Strategic planning in Company A is well developed with clearly documented five-year plans, at corporate and divisional level, which are revised annually. Corporate plans are produced by a central strategy team reporting to the chief executive. Each divisional plan is produced by the divisional senior management team (including the general managers of business units), which includes someone with specific responsibility for strategy. The strategy-making process has a strong upward thrust from divisions and a demand for entrepreneurship at business-unit level, exhibiting features of Hart's *Rational* and *Generative* modes. There are systems to support the strategic management process – an annual resource

Table 4.2 SMD typology

Commitment to strategic management	Organizational features	Role of SMDP
Low (level 1)	Strategy 'stuck' except for low levels of emergent/ incremental change Strategic drift Little participation in strategy-making Change projects rare/ poorly handled	Introduce knowledge and language of strategic management Exploratory discussions on strategic direction 'Forming' stage of team-building amongst senior managers (Tuckman, 1965) Mutual support role for participants
Emerging (level 2)	Experimentation with mechanisms for strategic debate and decision-making New language of strategic management Greater participation Dissatisfaction with current strategy Uncertainty over strategic direction	Forum for discussing proposals and recommending strategies Confronting issues: 'storming' stage of team-building (Tuckman, 1965) Recognition of need for strategic management competencies
Developed (level 3)	Embedding of mechanisms for strategic debate and decision-making Consensus on strategic direction can be achieved Systems and processes adapted to facilitate strategic management	Competencies in strategic management defined and being developed Cascading of organizational strategy to managers' own units 'Norming' stage of team-building (Tuckman, 1965)
Mature (level 4)	High commitment to strategic management evident through culture and systems Continuous review of high-level strategies Effective implementation of strategy	Strategic implementation through project teams and cascading of change projects Succession planning and cascade development of strategic management competencies 'Performing' stage of team-building (Tuckman, 1965)

Table 4.3 Hart's strategy-making modes

Command	Deliberate strategies are designed by a strong individual leader (possibly supported by a few top managers), and implemented by others
Symbolic	Top management creates a clear and compelling vision, which gives meaning to the organization's activities
Rational	Detailed written plans are created through upward sharing of data and a high level of information processing and analysis
Transactive	Strategy-making involves interaction and learning based on cross-functional communication, feedback and dialogue with stakeholders
Generative	New strategies emerge as a result of the championing of ideas within the organization

plan is linked to the strategic plan (though it does not strongly incorporate HR planning apart from senior management succession planning and 'talent spotting'). There are also statements of mission, values and key strengths. Communication of strategy is good at corporate and business-unit levels, but less so at divisional level.

These organizational features provide evidence of progression to the highest level of Commitment to Strategic Management (CSM) in Table 4.2. The features of Level 3, such as the embedding of systems for strategic debate and decision-making, and systems and processes to facilitate strategic management, have been seen to exist. Indicative of Level 4, there is a continuous (annual) strategic review, and a high commitment to strategic management is apparent from – for example – the central strategic planning team and the divisional senior managers who have particular responsibility for strategic management. The company has reported impressive growth and strong and improving financial results – evidence of the effective implementation of strategy.

The core senior management development programme is targeted at those newly appointed to the senior management team of a business unit. Formal training inputs are phased to cover strategic management, implementation and control. Simultaneously, each delegate works on a strategic plan for his/her own business unit, which is then presented to the sponsoring senior management team. This strategic planning project is mainly a learning process, but usually contains ideas that are capable of being adopted. However, because delegates are relatively new in post they may experience difficulties in getting a platform or having the authority to take some of the ideas forward. To help encourage the implementation of ideas, there is a review after four to five months. There is no formal link between the project and the annual performance appraisal process. One of the benefits of the programme is in bringing delegates together from different parts of the company, and some of the best projects have looked at harnessing capabilities from other parts of the company to create a new business opportunity.

This programme uses real strategic business issues as learning vehicles, and does sometimes produce direct business benefits from the projects. Whilst the interaction between delegates is a key element, this is not formalized within the structure of the programme – greater group involvement in the project work could be beneficial. Also, greater linkages with the performance appraisal system might help provide support for the development and implementation of ideas.

Another programme, attracting 400 middle managers, is clearly aligned to one of the main elements of the company's strategy. The emphasis is on developing behavioural skills associated with building strategic partnerships with clients, change management and entrepreneurship. It is intended to break down internal barriers so that all of the company's capability can be brought to bear on any particular client's needs. Learning networks, line-manager mentors and personal learning contracts are used. Participants work on live business issues with inter-module assignments, and are encouraged on residential modules to experiment with new behaviour in a safe environment.

When mapped against the SMDP dimension of Table 4.2, the requirements of Level 3 are seen to have been met. The defining and developing of strategic management competencies (such as strategic partnership skills), and the cascading of organizational strategy to managers' own units are evidenced. However, the interventions described on the core programme are mostly concerned with learning rather than real strategy implementation. Where real strategy implementation is attempted, it is somewhat disconnected from the mainstream strategic management process and does not carry the full support of other senior managers and directors. Nevertheless, this programme does have a strong strategic focus, and strategic management competencies are being cascaded within the organization – for example, through the line manager's coaching/mentoring role. Also, the company's MD programmes do clearly support succession planning. Thus a number of the hypothesized conditions for Level 4 are met. Overall the programmes have some strong strategic roles, and advance beyond Level 3, though not fully meeting the Level 4 role of SMDP. The evaluation of the programmes indicated that they were successfully contributing to strategic capability.

Analysis

Table 4.4 analyses possible objectives for management development programmes (derived from literature review), subdividing them into those with a strategic emphasis and those with a more functional or operational emphasis. It was evident from the questionnaire and interview analysis that some of the senior management development programmes did not have a

Table 4.4 Classification of objectives in SMDP

Strategic	Functional
Developing abilities in strategic management	Improving current job performance
Developing entrepreneurial behaviour	Developing managers to handle a bigger job
Encouraging innovation and creativity	Identifying high-flyers for succession planning
Helping formulate or refine corporate strategy	Preparing managers for lateral moves
Helping the organization achieve its strategic objectives	Developing leadership ability
Communicating and clarifying corporate strategy	Building teamwork and networks
Shaping and modifying a culture	
Creating a common purpose	
Developing abilities to manage change	
Creating a cadre of change agents	

strong strategic focus. This concept was operationalized as the SMD score (maximum 4.0) derived from questionnaire results to reflect the extent to which *strategic* objectives for the MD programme were set and achieved. The Functional Management Development score (maximum 4.0) measured the extent to which *functional/operational* objectives were set and achieved.

Table 4.5 shows the results for each of these variables. The data indicate that for organizations B and C the programme was not designed to have a strong strategic effect, and this was supported by the interview data. For B, a division of a larger corporation, the programme (which was organized at group level) was not deemed to be very successful and did not have a direct strategic linkage to the division. In C, each manager had an individually tailored development plan and there was little group activity. The diversity of individual programmes meant that there was no common strategic focus in management development activities, and there was more emphasis on job performance and succession planning. The other four organizations all scored above the midpoint on the scale for strategic objectives. However, only in the cases of D and F were the strategic scores higher than the functional scores, indicating that even A and E were apparently placing greater emphasis on the functional objectives of their programmes.

From the qualitative evaluation of the programmes (as illustrated with organization A) it was concluded that those of A, E and F were contributing to the development of strategic capability in the organization, but this was much less apparent in B, C and D.

Table 4.5 Overall summary of results

Organization and sector	Strategic management development score	Functional management development score	Strategy-making modes	Commitment to strategic management level	SMDP level	SMDP enhances strategic capability
A Engineering services	2.6	2.8	Rational Generative	4	3/4	✓
B Defence systems	1.7	1.8	Rational	4	1	✗
C Financial services	1.7	2.3	Command Rational	4?	1	✗
D Retailing	3.0	2.2	Command Rational	4	2	✗
E Telecoms	2.6	3.2	Rational	2	2	✓
F Higher education	2.4	2.0	Symbolic, Rational	1/2	1/2	✓

Hypothesis testing

Table 4.5 provides a basis for testing the main hypothesis, by examining the relationship between each organization's commitment to strategic management (CSM level) and the design of its strategic management development programme (SMDP level).

It has been seen that, in the cases of two organizations (B and C), the senior management development programmes do not have strong strategic aims. In the case of B, this seems to be tolerated because the slow-changing environment in which it operates has not provided sufficient stimulus to move to a more strategic form of MD (as reflected in the low SMD score of 1.7). Thus, there is mismatch between CSM and SMDP levels (shown as Level 4 and Level 1 respectively). The SMDP is not considered to be very effective, and would probably benefit from further development to a higher level on the typology. This is consistent with the hypothesis – that is, because of the mismatch between CSM and SMDP levels the programme is not effective in enhancing strategic capability.

In the case of C, the organization apparently has a high CSM level and aspects of Level 4 were seen. However, because the dominant strategy-making mode is *Command* there is little participation by managers in the strategy formulation process. This aspect is, therefore, also absent from the SMDP, which was judged to be at Level 1. The programme does not have prominent strategic management aims and does not enhance strategic capability. This situation may be acceptable because although the organization's environment is dynamic, it is not especially complex. There is not a strong international dimension, and the organization's activities are focused in financial services rather than being diversified. Therefore, the executive directors may be able to monitor environmental trends and competitive action and make the key strategic decisions needed.

The *Command* strategy-making style is also exhibited by D. Again, it was found that the senior management development programme does not contribute significantly to strategy formulation; although there is a high commitment to strategic management (Level 4) this is not reflected in the SMDP. Like C, D has apparently been able to prosper under a Command mode (and in both cases this is accompanied by elements of the Rational strategy-making mode). D also has a relatively simple environment, uncomplicated by diversification and with few international considerations. Where D does differ from C is in a desire to see some change in the strategy-making mode. There are demands for senior managers to be more innovative, and for better change management. This is moving the organization to more *Generative* and *Transactive* modes. To support this, the SMDP has a greater strategic emphasis, at least in its intent – as demonstrated by an emphasis on vision and strategic awareness in the programme, and a high SMD score. However, the SMDP design does not connect closely with the strategic objectives and business development processes of the organization, and only very limited progress has been made in widening the strategic thinking capability in the organization. Difficulty had been experienced in making managers more innovative, deriving from the historical command culture which demanded compliance rather than creativity. The new strategy-making modes are far from embedded and the level of SMD in the typology is low (Level 2), still largely reflecting the Command mode, and the hypothesis is supported.

The other three organizations all demonstrate a fit between the CSM level in the organization and the SMDP level, and the SMDP enhances strategic capability thus supporting the hypothesis. Overall, therefore, the hypothesis is supported in all six cases. Also, it has been seen that where there is a strong element of the Command strategy-making mode in the organization, the strategic aspects (especially strategy formulation) of the management development programme are inhibited.

Conclusions

The research has demonstrated that to be effective, the design of strategic management development programmes should be contingent on the maturity of strategic commitment and capability in the organization and the dominant strategy-making mode. The four-level typology helps in understanding this relationship, and demonstrates how the role of SMD can evolve. SMD is not the only determinant of strategic capability, and a causal network mapping some of the important variables has been proposed and supported by the case study work. Given the small sample size, it is necessary to be cautious about the representativeness of the organizations studied and the generalizability of the findings.

The research has yielded new conceptual frameworks which can be applied sensitively to other organizations. The four-level typology and causal network might be used to inform the analysis and planning of management development, helping in the diagnosis of organizational needs and in the design of more effective strategic management development interventions.

Key learning points

- The key requirements for successful SMD include high organizational commitment to strategic management, strategic goals for MD that are championed by the CEO, a strategic competency framework, and the integration of MD with real management work.
- Whilst normative models of 'best practice' in SMD are useful for practitioners, the design of effective programmes is also contingent on the maturity of strategic management in the organization and the dominant strategy-making modes.
- Strategic management capability can be developed through SMD, but

is also dependent on the organizational commitment to strategic management and the experiential learning gained whilst developing and implementing strategic management processes. SMD can facilitate this learning through the deployment of strategic project teams.

- The four-level typology models the relationship between SMD design and the maturity of strategic management in the organization, and is, therefore, a conceptual aid to designers of SMD programmes.

References

Bolt, J. (1993) 'Achieving the CEO's agenda: education for executives', *Management Review*, May: 44–9.

Boshyk, Y. (2000) *Business Driven Action Learning*, Basingstoke: Macmillan.

Brown, P. (2003) 'Seeking success through strategic management development', *Journal of European Industrial Training*, 27(6): 292–303.

Brown, P. (2004) 'Strategic capability development in the higher education sector', *International Journal of Educational Management*, 18(7): 436–45.

Brown, P. (2005) 'The evolving role of strategic management development', *Journal of Management Development*, 24(3): 209–22.

Gluck, F., Kaufman, S. and Walleck, A. (1982) 'The four phases of strategic management', *Journal of Business Strategy*, Winter: 9–21.

Gratton, L., Hope Hailey, V., Stiles, P. and Truss, C. (eds) (1999) *Strategic Human Resource Management*, Oxford: Oxford University Press.

Hansen, K.H. (2000) 'Motorola: combining business projects with learning projects', in Boshyk, Y. (ed.), *Business Driven Action Learning*, Basingstoke: Macmillan.

Hart, S. (1992) 'An integrative framework for strategy-making processes', *Academy of Management Review*, 17(2): 327–51.

Hirsch, W. and Reilly, P. (1998) 'Skills planning', *People Management*, 9 July: 38–41.

Hirsch, W. and Reilly, P. (1999) 'Planning for skills', Paper presented at the Strategic Planning Society Seminar, London, 18 March.

Hussey, D. (1996) *Business-Driven Human Resource Management*, Chichester: Wiley.

Meldrum, M. and Atkinson, S. (1998) 'Meta-abilities and the implementation of strategy', *Journal of Management Development*, 17(8): 564–75.

Mercer, S. (2000) 'General Electric's executive action learning programmes', in Boshyk, Y. (ed.), *Business Driven Action Learning*, Basingstoke: Macmillan.

Michael, J. (1993) 'Aligning executive training with strategy', *Executive Development*, 6(1): 10–13.

Newkirk-Moore, S. and Bracker, J. (1998) 'Strategic management training and commitment to planning: critical partners in stimulating firm performance', *International Journal of Training and Development*, 2(2): 82–90.

Osbaldeston, M. (1997) 'From business schools to learning centres', *Re-designing Management Development in the New Europe*, Luxembourg: European Training Foundation, Office for Official Publications of the European Communities.

Patching, K. (1998) *Management and Organization Development*, London: Macmillan.

Siebert, K., Hall, D. and Kram, K. (1995) 'Strengthening the weak link in strategic executive development: integrating individual development and global business strategy', *Human Resource Management*, 34(4): 549–67.

Stiles, P. (1999) 'Transformation at the leading edge', in Gratton, L., Hope Hailey, V., Stiles, P. and Truss, C. (eds), *Strategic Human Resource Management*, Oxford: Oxford University Press.

Temporal, P. (1990) 'Linking management development to the corporate future – the role of the professional', *Journal of Management Development*, 9(5): 7–17.

Tuckman, B. (1965) 'Development sequence in small groups', *Psychological Bulletin*, 63: 384–99.

Tyson, S. (1995) *Strategic Prospects for HRM*, London: Institute of Personnel and Development.

Woodhall, J. and Winstanley, D. (1998) *Management Development: Strategy and Practice*, Oxford: Basil Blackwell.

5 Management development for unemployed managers

The South Yorkshire 'Management Update Programme'

Geoff Chivers

Objectives

This chapter is concerned with analysing human resource development issues surrounding regional economic decline and its consequences for managers in terms of large-scale unemployment. Much learning can come from studying HRD interventions to support workers facing very adverse circumstances. A great deal of tax-payers' money is commonly diverted to support interventional programmes such as retraining of unemployed workers. However, such research into these programmes as is carried out tends to be quantitative in nature, and broad brush in terms of bracketing unemployed workers of many kinds together.

The focus of the chapter is to explore what can be learnt from a programme of research into the type of urgent retraining for unemployed managers which has been supported by the UK Government in modern times, and ways in which development for managers in employment sectors in decline might be addressed. Learning points from the research are directed at those determining policies and funding regimes for retraining the unemployed, at those who provide the training, and at managers themselves.

The 'Management Update Programme'

Introduction to the training initiative

In the chapter I will be looking back at an initiative to address a rapid rise in the unemployment of experienced managers and professionals which took place in the South Yorkshire region in the late 1980s and early 1990s. During this period unemployment in general surged upward in the South Yorkshire, North-East Derbyshire and North Nottinghamshire areas, due to a collapse of traditional industries, particularly the coal and steel industries (Halstead and Wright, 1995).

Traditional service industries in the region were in no way exempt from financial difficulties in this period. Hundreds of thousands of people moving from employment to unemployment are in no position to buy non-essentials, and the retail, leisure, tourism and hospitality industries began to suffer economically. Again, the response was to lay off staff in a bid to survive.

One of the Conservative Government's responses nationally and regionally was to introduce a portfolio of training programmes for the unemployed. These were initially focused primarily on the young unemployed. However, it gradually became clear that many older workers with considerable work experience, who had been made redundant in such concentrated numbers in regions of declining industry, could not find any employment, so government retraining schemes for this category of the unemployed were opened up (Lange, 1998).

The focus of retraining courses initially tended to be on relatively basic skills, not least how to apply for jobs in the modern era. However, such retraining courses did not take account of the fact that the collapse of whole industries was leading to increasing levels of unemployment of managers in those industries, and of professionals and technologists. There is no doubt that the realization that the ranks of the unemployed in South Yorkshire included ever-increasing numbers of experienced, and previously successful, managers – and even well-qualified professionals – came as something of a shock to regional agencies charged with implementing central government policies in regard to retraining of the unemployed.

Young managers and professionals had the option of moving to another less affected region to find work. However, older managers and professionals were much more embedded in the region, indeed in their local areas, by such considerations as their children's schooling, partner's local employment and ownership of their homes, to say nothing of family and friendship networks in the region. As redundancy payments began to peter out, such managers were becoming increasingly desperate (Kaufman, 1982). The responsibility for doing something to help locally and regionally fell substantially onto staff of the Sheffield Training and Enterprise Council (TEC) under the government's Employment Training (ET) Programme, and in 1993 these staff conducted a survey to determine the best way to proceed.

Initiation of the training programme

At the time when the Sheffield TEC approached me at the University of Sheffield, in the late summer of 1993, the unemployment rate in Sheffield was estimated to be around 12 per cent and up to 18 per cent in Rotherham. The unemployment rate of managers and professionals in the region was estimated to be running at more than 4 per cent in Sheffield, and higher elsewhere in the region. Equally worrying was the survey finding that 42 per cent of the unemployed had been out of work for more than 12 months. Amongst these long-term unemployed were to be found considerable numbers, certainly many hundreds, of experienced managers and professionals.

Given the considerable experience of these managers, to say nothing of their qualification levels, the standard retraining courses for the unemployed being mounted with Sheffield TEC funding in the local further education colleges, and via private-sector training providers, were deemed inappropriate to meet their needs.

The approach by the TEC to myself as Professor of Continuing Education at the University was not entirely surprising, as The Continuing Vocational Education group of staff that I led within the Division of Adult Continuing Education had a prior successful track record in the field.

Our experience in the 1980s in running courses for unemployed managers had demonstrated that they were highly motivated, brought with them many valuable skills, and contributed workplace wisdom derived from years of work experience. The experience of unemployment had seriously damaged moral in many cases (Westwood, 1980), and there was always much to be done to build up self-confidence, to inform course members of new career openings, and to help them to see how their existing abilities, topped up with more or less continuing education and training, could lead them towards these career openings. As well as raising their general self-belief, in many cases there was a great need to achieve a change of attitude towards themselves, and what they could be capable of achieving in future careers, possibly very different to their past careers. We had found from these earlier pilot courses that many of the managers were able to secure employment at an acceptable level during or soon after the course, while others obtained work placements or were at least sufficiently motivated to start applying for jobs or consider more extended study at higher education level.

Thus, when approached by staff of Sheffield TEC, I was in listening mode, although concerned about the financial basis of any operation in the unemployment retraining field, and aware of the extent of the challenge where long-term unemployed managers were concerned.

The TEC staff explained that its own 'Sheffield Labour Market and Skills Shortage Survey' for 1993 had shown that there was little scope for the local re-employment of displaced managers from collapsing traditional industries, and from the 'de-layering' of the larger service sector organizations, unless these managers undertook high-level retraining. Thus, in planning the 1993–1994 financial year programme the TEC had prioritized funding for high-level retraining courses for unemployed managers and professionals, or supervisory-level staff who aspired to management posts.

The funding had been found from the 'Adult Training for Work' budget, a substantial part of the TEC's total funding from the then Employment Department. It had been decided that the funding would be offered for 12-week courses, payment being largely related to so called 'positive outcomes', in line with their 'Training for Work' programmes. Positive outcomes in this case would be a course pass possibly at an appropriate level for entry into employment, or entry into higher education, with two such payments for a learner passing the course and subsequently taking up employment within 13 weeks, or going on to higher education.

The levels of payment for these outcomes, together with the much smaller sums available for weekly training per head, did offer a prospect of financial viability, provided sufficient numbers of participants passed the course and some then moved into employment rapidly. We did not feel happy about the 'positive outcomes' approach to funding, which would put the course team and the course members under pressure from the outset. There was also much angst about the importance of maintaining course assessment standards, set by ourselves for a University award, given that much of the essential funding would be secured only if large numbers of course members were awarded passes.

Nevertheless, we decided to generate a proposal for scrutiny by the University's senior management, as much as for the TEC managers concerned (Chivers, 1993). We scrutinized the TEC's reports and other intelligence available to us concerning what sort of 12-week retraining programme would offer the best prospects of career re-entry, possibly following a more extended study programme at higher education level.

The 'Management Update Programme' proposal

We proposed that the 12-week course should be set at initial undergraduate level, but the Employment Department was wary of this billing, and all stakeholders finally compromised on a 'Certificate of Access to Higher Education', which would be awarded by the University. Any course member passing the course at an 'access' level of achievement would receive this certificate, and the University would be paid for the 'positive outcome'.

Under some pressure from the TEC, we proposed a three-week general introductory programme after which course members would choose between four options for the remaining nine weeks of the programme. The options proposed were:

- manufacturing management
- service sector management
- information technology management
- technology management and technology transfer.

The TEC was keen on the initial, general three-week programme aimed at careers guidance, and job-seeking skills development. We saw the need for this in the course team, but would have preferred to integrate this content with the management knowledge and skills development throughout the 12-week programme. We knew that a large number of course members would need to be recruited to generate the economies of scale required to make the programme viable financially. At the same time, we believed that the heterogeneous nature of the student body, and the clearly differentiated sectors where jobs would be available, necessitated course study options. The four options, chosen to meet the market needs for managers as far as we could determine, as well as reflecting the expected orientations of course members, would enable us to produce manageable option group sizes from a training and coaching viewpoint.

A target number of 60 initial participants was proposed, given that some might be expected to drop out at a very early stage. We calculated that if most of the rest passed the course and at least 15 obtained jobs (either during the course or within 13 weeks after the course end), then the programme would be financially viable. A better 'positive outcomes' situation would then enable us to generate some surplus funding to reduce the risks on future similar courses, and to spend on improved equipment and facilities for the course.

On this basis the proposal for the course went forward to Sheffield TEC, which after some delay supported the proposal in full. Unfortunately the delay, caused by having to seek Employment Department approval, led to the course having to be organized on a rushed basis so that it could be substantially offered before the end of the 1993–1994 financial year, to use up the TEC finances allocated to it in that year.

Build-up to the first course

The course programme had to be advertised in the regional press over the Christmas period 1993 – the worst time to receive applications and arrange pre-entry interviews. However, we received a large number of enquiries from these advertisements, and from local TEC publicity aimed at the unemployed. Meanwhile, we had to recruit an overall course coordinator, appoint short-term part-time tutors (with an eye to the nine-week options), and find a venue for the 12 weeks, which could accommodate up to 60 or more course members and offer 'break out' rooms for the option sessions.

The core staff was soon recruited and set to work organizing timetables, including identifying many specialist speakers for the high-level content envisaged. Many of those interviewed to come on the course seemed suitable and were evidently keen to give it a try. We were able to offer a very small weekly attendance fee and cover the costs of travel to attend, and childcare costs for the 12 weeks involved.

Due to the rush to start the course, the final course numbers settled at 43 in total, which put considerable pressure on us to achieve a high proportion of 'conversions' into 'positive outcomes'. Few of these course members were interested in the 'Technology management and technology transfer' option, so elements of this were integrated into either the 'Manufacturing management' or the 'Information technology management' options. It seemed that the engineers and technologists recruited were keen to move out of this type of work completely, even though there was a regional demand for highly qualified technical staff. We realized that the 'macho' nature of most of the collapsing industries meant that their redundant managers would be largely male. In fact only five women were recruited, which was much as we expected, but was nevertheless concerning. It seemed additionally that women managers were not willing to remain unemployed for long, and if necessary were willing to move into – probably back into – clerical and semi-skilled jobs rather than remain out of work.

Start of the course

The course started on the scheduled day, approached apprehensively by the course team due to the rush to get it off the ground. Despite our cheery greetings some course members were clearly very nervous, others generally depressed at having to come on a course for the unemployed, and many rather cynical about what the course could do for them. Our efforts to cover a wide range of career options, education options, and issues about adult learning (especially learning skills) turned out to be a mistake. Even though we were sure that all these areas of knowledge and skills would be essential for progression with their later studies, and for job re-entry, the course members were not convinced. Our early efforts to get them to identify their strengths and opportunities, their prior learning from work and from life experience, and generally to treat them as adults who could manage their own learning, were misguided. Thus, our plan from the outset to teach the course from the front of the class in the morning, and encourage them to work and learn in tutor-less groups, or individually, in the afternoon proved inappropriate. This was despite course members needing to conduct large amounts of individual preparation for course-work assignments, and a major project of their choice.

As soon as the afternoon session started, with no close direction by tutors, course members stopped working and turned to social discussion or reading popular newspapers. We had to accept that, after so long out of work, the course members needed close-up continuous direction until such time as their self-confidence and self-discipline built up sufficiently for them to take control of their own learning.

The option groups which we had gone to so much trouble to organize proved a great worry to many course members. A minority was clear from the outset which option they favoured, but others remained undecided until the last moment, despite extensive tutor counselling. Many felt that they wanted to take some sessions from each of the three options. There was also dissatisfaction from all students that none of the three options offered specific training in hands-on computing skills. It became apparent that at job interviews prospective managers were being quizzed about their computer skills, and many had little or no competence. The small number of younger course members could give satisfactory responses, but most older course members had no hands-on expertise. They felt that their job prospects would be enhanced if we were to include hands-on computer training. As a result, special efforts were made to set up a computer suite and provide coaching support at very short notice – another unexpected cost to the course.

By general consensus the course programme 'took off' at the beginning of week three, when we offered a week of general management development sessions, via a mix of taught classes and work with open learning materials. While some course members found the theoretical and conceptual content hard to digest, others were excited to realize that there were actually theories and conceptual frameworks to explain and support all they had observed and experienced as workers and managers.

By week four, when the option sessions started, the now smaller groups were starting to become very lively and interactive. Successful completion of a formative assignment on management theory and practice, based on week-three learning, greatly enhanced learners' enthusiasm. They began to look like post-experience management and professional learners, and we began to believe that this high-risk gamble could really pay off for all concerned.

We were surprised by the enormous gaps in knowledge and skills of these managers, a good many of whom were graduates, to say nothing of their often narrow outlook and unfounded prejudices. Course topics such as equal opportunities at work, occupational health and safety management, and environmental risk management were challenged as a pointless waste of time by some course members, a reflection on the 'macho' and old-fashioned culture which had done so much to discredit so called 'rust belt' industries in the region.

On the other hand, we were often embarrassed by the high academic quality of some of the assignments and reports, which equated to at least final-year undergraduate level, or even postgraduate-level work. Our Certificate of Access to Higher Education could hardly do justice to such achievement. We agreed that, where warranted, a letter explaining the high-level performance of particular candidates would be attached to their certificates. Our thoughts were already turning to securing accreditation for the course programme at undergraduate level one under the UK national Credit Accumulation and Transfer Scheme (CATS), hopefully for 40 credits (equivalent to one term of full time study for conventional undergraduates). This was subsequently achieved.

All students, except one of the early job achievers, completed all the course work so that 42 could go forward to the relevant University Examination Board. They all passed, allowing us to claim 42 positive outcome payments from Sheffield TEC. The next big question was whether our retrained managers would now be able to find suitable jobs. We promised to go on helping them, and encouraging them to help each other.

Issues arising from the pilot course and subsequent changes

Sheffield TEC staff made it clear that they saw our programme as very successful, and were keen to see it continue with further cohorts, if similar students with the need for such management retraining were located in the region. For our part, we were also pleased, and felt that we were moving up a steep learning curve. However some key issues needed to be addressed.

It was extremely important for us to be sure that most if not all our course members from the pilot would either gain a job that they valued directly as a result of the course, or at least improve their employability or prospects for entry into higher or further education. Fortunately, within weeks of the course finishing, more and more course members reported that they had secured employment. In fact, 11 managed to find work within 13 weeks after the course ended. This meant that we could claim 11 positive job outcome payments from the TEC (paid out at a somewhat higher rate than for passing the course as an outcome). Our follow-up work on this cohort subsequently showed that a further 12 found work more than 13 weeks after the course ended but before 26 weeks had passed. A further two found work beyond this period, and six went into higher education in the following autumn (giving us six more positive outcome payments). This left us with ten of our course attendees without jobs or higher education entry. However, many of those went on to part-time study and voluntary work at a level they would not have considered before undertaking the course.

Despite this considerable success in terms of outcomes, the pilot course had generated numerous problems. Running three option programmes for nine weeks was costly relative to the funding return from Sheffield TEC, even if there were many positive outcome payments. We had found that even after the options were underway, some course members were still havering as to whether they had chosen the appropriate option. Certainly, there was continuing lobbying from course members to opt out of sessions on their own options so as to take sessions on another option. Furthermore, the separation into options was counter to the teamwork which the course was intended to foster. The pilot course also revealed the severe lack of computer awareness, let alone basic computing skills, amongst older participants. This was an important issue to be addressed in the follow-on courses.

The second and subsequent 'Management Update Programme' courses

For the second course we recruited a similarly heterogeneous cohort of participants to the pilot course, but took the decision to keep them in one group for the whole length of the course. We did away with the 'front loading' of careers and study skills sessions in the early weeks, and integrated these topics into the length of the course. We placed greater emphasis on the service sector management topics, given that this sector offered the best job prospects in the region for the foreseeable future. We introduced practical computing as a compulsory element of the course.

Participants found this training and the University's computer facilities empowering. They found the information technology sessions as equally worthwhile as the management and business sessions in terms of improving job prospects. In light of this finding, we arranged for the participants of each cohort to sustain their University computer access for three months after the end of their course. This both enabled participants to go on improving their computer skills, and helped them with their job search and applications for posts.

Description and analysis of research context

Although the funding for the retraining programme did not include any element for research into its development and outcome, an essentially action research approach was adopted by the tutor team. Documents were filed for subsequent analysis, including the project proposal, correspondence with Sheffield TEC, minutes of meetings, syllabus drafts, notes of interviews with prospective students, course handouts, student assignments, reports to Sheffield TEC, etc.

Prospective trainees were interviewed in some depth prior to entry to the programme. Those selected to come onto the programme were interviewed in-depth three weeks after start-up, and exit interviews were arranged for those leaving the programme early.

Course-review forms were completed by all trainees at the end of the training programme, which covered the relevance and quality of the programme, and particularly its strengths and weaknesses from the trainee's viewpoint.

Qualitative data in terms of programme documents, interview transcripts and student assignments were analysed by myself as Programme Director, and validated by feedback to the tutor team. Quantitative data were collected and analysed by the Programme Manager as part of his responsibilities in terms of generating reports to Sheffield TEC and myself. These data included the number of trainees in each cohort, the number of early dropouts, the numbers finding a job during the life of the programme, the numbers successfully completing the programme, and the numbers finding jobs within 13 weeks of the end of the programme.

Analysis and evaluation of main findings

The analysis of the research data obtained was most readily undertaken in terms of the issues involved in working with Sheffield TEC, and in terms of the qualitative and quantitative outcomes of the programme.

The issues involved in working with Sheffield TEC were identified from document analysis. The qualitative and quantitative outcomes of the programme were identified from programme document analysis, interview transcripts, and the formal reports to Sheffield TEC generated at specified intervals over the whole life of the Management Update Programme.

Working with Sheffield TEC

Apart from the problems with negotiating the initial contract on an urgent basis, the partnership with Sheffield TEC presented numerous ongoing concerns. The first was the amount of paperwork which had to pass through both parties in order to get the programmed started, and which persisted through its life. For example, the TEC quality audit was 148 pages long, divided into nine sections, each containing an average 15 questions which one had to score one's organization against. The questions were almost entirely designed for the TEC's traditional contractors for Youth Training programmes. Consequently, many were totally inappropriate for an organization such as the University.

Furthermore, while the University and the course team were concerned with the course content in terms of relevance, clarity, ease of progression, teaching excellence and assessment standards, the TEC's main interest was in terms of the number of participants per cohort, and how many training weeks the programme could deliver. With no options now offered, we were concerned to keep the numbers of participants down to ensure individual learning support at all stages. We also wished to offer a course which was long enough to benefit the participants in terms of upgrading skills on an intensive basis, and giving them the best chance to find employment. The TEC in contrast was constrained by government targets, which were measured in terms of numbers of trainees, training weeks and job outcomes.

The outcome payments offered were also a constant cause of concern to the University team. The competition for management posts in the region at this time was intense, and it was really too much to expect that most course members would be in post just 13 weeks after their course ended. Our course members were often being required to attend a series of interviews for one post, sometimes three or four spread out over a month or more. If a post were offered and accepted just after the end of the 13-week cut off period, we received no output payment.

The quality of our course did not seem to be recognized by the TEC. While we pressed for an increase in the meagre payment for training weeks per delegate delivered, the TEC actually cut this from £36 per delegate week on the pilot course to £22 per delegate for subsequent courses.

Quantitative and qualitative outcomes of the programme

The management update programme was finally closed down in 1997, three years after its start-up. In this time 275 delegates took part in the course (Okpara, 1997). The average pass rate was over 80 per cent, with most of those not completing leaving early for jobs, and only ten recruits failing the course as such.

Around 20 per cent of delegates left the course early to take up jobs, and some of these people actually finished off outstanding assignments and achieved the course pass. A further 30 per cent went on to obtain a job within the 13-week qualifying period, and ten others went into higher education.

This meant that over 40 per cent of those attending the course did not secure a job within the qualifying period for a positive outcome payment. Given the lack of incentive for past course members to notify the course team if they subsequently obtained employment, and given the work pressures on our team, no comprehensive account of what happened to these delegates in the following 12 months can be offered. We do know that some of these delegates did ultimately find employment, and we believe that most of them did so.

The short-term benefits to the course members during the time they were on the course became rapidly clear to us. Many of them came on the course at a very low point in terms of motivation and self-esteem. Within weeks, the attitudes of nearly all course members changed to enthusiasm and expectation of better times ahead. In addition to the skills, knowledge and qualifications obtained, delegates found that the programme benefited them in the affective domain. For many of them it was the first time in a long time that they were entering into well-organized, demanding working days, in a cheery group environment. They were surrounded by people who shared their problems and faced the same challenges. They were led by tutors who showed great concern for their welfare as well as their learning and their job applications. The course members were able to help each other in all kinds of ways, and take a pride in doing so. Self-confidence increased as course members performed well in class, and received positive feedback on assignments, and usually good grades. Even those receiving poorer grades initially received much support and encouragement, and were able to improve their assignment and project work later on.

The networking between course members was very effective, and we know that some have remained close friends to today, around a decade after they came on the course. The majority of those who found work have done so at similar levels to those encountered before becoming unemployed. This points to the fact that employers were taking advantage of both the experience of these older workers and their recent management updating.

Financially, the programme had to fight throughout its life to stay in modest surplus, and finally closed with a small deficit. By this stage recruitment was becoming increasingly difficult, and the management unemployment crisis was beginning to abate in the region around Sheffield as the economic position slowly brightened.

Interpretations and conclusions

We were rather shocked by the depths to which many of the unemployed managers we recruited had sunk, given their earlier achievements in work, education and life generally. There is no doubt that strenuous efforts need to be made to support managers and professionals threatened with unemployment, before they are redundant. Appropriate careers advice needs to be offered, together with updating of knowledge and skills in regard to searching for new jobs and applying for them. We found many of our participants had unrealistic expectations of posts they should be able to gain, together with poorly prepared CVs, weak interview techniques and a general inability to grasp what was involved in seeking out and gaining management-level posts in the environment of modern business.

We were similarly taken aback by how out of date some managers were in terms of their knowledge and skills. This was especially exemplified in the information technology area, but applied across the board. Often managers were up to date, but only in a very narrow field. Indeed, many saw themselves as specialist managers with experience only in a single industrial or commercial sector. They were often weak at identifying and acknowledging their generic management skills which could be built on to find work in growing sectors of the economy.

Few had gained qualifications in modern times – indeed, some seemed to have taken no opportunities to undertake updating training or retraining while in management employment. Their confidence in their ability to learn in new areas at all was often weak, and it took much patience from course tutors to build up their self-belief in this regard.

In regard to the financial inducements to training providers to organize programmes for unemployed managers, the positive outcomes payment approach suffered by our programme is very undesirable. This is especially so where the course provider is also organizing the assessment of learning, and awarding the qualification which gains the outcome payment for passing the course. The dangers in terms of lowering standards to ensure high pass rates are obvious in this case. However, under any such payment system, involving any training provider, the stress this positive outcomes approach creates for course tutors, assessors and learners is excessive and unwarranted. There are many accepted methods for assuring the quality of a course which are much less stressful.

Paying at the highest level of positive outcome for a job gained while the course is running is not an appropriate method to reward the course organizers either. This can only encourage them to focus all out on finding jobs for course members as soon as possible, to the detriment of learning anything on the course which could keep them in employment subsequently, and to the detriment of the quality of job gained. In our case, we could have tried to push course members out into low-quality jobs just to get the positive payment, instead of working with them to get them back into a job appropriate to their managerial experience and skills.

The rush to get our programme started was detrimental to it, and was entirely caused by the lack of planning by the funders. When a region is hit by large-scale redundancies, the highly qualified and skilled, and the experienced senior and middle managers, are hit as hard initially as the unskilled, poorly qualified 'shop floor' workers. Those hardest hit will be 'time served' managers who have spent most of their career in one area of management, in one work sector (often in one firm). If these managers have out-of-date qualifications and skills, with little or no evidence of learning achievements in modern times, they are likely to be particularly hard hit.

The risks I was forced to take financially throughout, and in terms of starting the programme on such an urgent basis, were doubtless unreasonable and should have been unnecessary. We had to cope with a lot of emotional stress as well as long hours, because of the funding methodology and the expectations that participants placed on us to turn their lives around.

Key learning points

We gained deep insights into what causes managers and professionals to become long-term unemployed. My own learning was extended considerably in terms of understanding how little other government-funded agencies really understood about the higher education sector in the UK. I also learned that for many civil servants, the over-riding concern is to please political masters and to meet their agendas and targets, however inappropriate these might be in terms of national, regional, local or personal needs. Our programme was seen as part of 'the numbers game' in terms of reducing the unemployment statistics. Signing up for our programme took managers off the unemployment statistics for six months, and our task was seen as to keep them from being counted as unemployed again at all costs. Universities need to undertake more dialogue with Learning and Skills Councils to ensure a better understanding in the future of the strengths and limitations of higher education as a vocational training provider.

I believe that those determining policies and funding regimes for retraining the unemployed need direct experience of such retraining work, involving direct contact with individuals who have gone through substantial periods of unemployment and many job application rejections. Modest government funding released for retraining while managers facing redundancy are still in employment would be much more effective than throwing large sums of money into trying to retrain long-term unemployed managers. The funding for retraining programmes for unemployed managers should not in future be based on so called 'positive outcomes' in terms of full qualifications gained in a matter of months, or in terms of jobs obtained. Many managers in the UK are under-qualified in management, and retraining during periods of unemployment should be linked to longer-term learning programmes leading to nationally recognized qualifications. Experienced and successful managers should not be put under pressure while on these programmes, to take low-level jobs, unsuited to their talents, simply to release funding to trainers, or to meet government targets to reduce unemployment. Appropriate careers guidance for managers should be offered over an extended period, with help regarding preparation of job applications and practice interviews.

Managers themselves should be strongly encouraged to undertake vocational learning while in employment. This should be broadly based, and include a focus on practical skills development, and advice on learning and possible future career directions.

Reflective practice interviews with appropriate human resource development professionals should be encouraged (Chivers, 2003). More research funding needs to be made available for qualitative research in the field, and especially for longitudinal research of the type we would have wished to carry out for this Management Update Programme.

References

Chivers, G.E. (1993) *Proposal to Sheffield TEC for a Twelve Week Course Programme Funded under the Training for Adults Scheme*, Sheffield: University of Sheffield Division of Adult Continuing Education.

Chivers, G.E. (2003) 'Utilising reflective practice interviews in professional developments', *Journal of European Industrial Training*, 27(1): 5–15.

Halstead, J. and Wright, P. (1995) *Confronting Industrial Demise – The Employment and Unemployment Experience of Miners and Their Families in South Yorkshire and North East Derbyshire*, Sheffield: University of Sheffield Division of Adult Continuing Education.

Kaufman, H.G. (1982) *Professionals in Search of Work – Coping with the Stress of Job Loss and Unemployment*, London: John Wiley.

Lange, L. (ed.) (1998) *Unemployment in Theory and Practice*, Cheltenham: Edward Elgar.

Okpara, A.I. (1997) *Management Update Programme Report*, Sheffield: University of Sheffield Division of Adult Continuing Education.

Westwood, S. (1980) 'Life stress in long term unemployment', *Policy Studies*, 5(4): 31–49.

Part II

Comparative insights

Introduction

In this second part of the book we are essentially concerned with what might be learned about MD research and practice through the lens of 'comparative insight'. Hence, each of the four chapters that follow depicts some form of comparative MD study or practice. In Chapter 6, Françoise Le Deist, Annie Dutech, Alain Klarsfield and Jonathan Winterton draw on the results of a Leonardo da Vinci project investigating management development in seven countries – Denmark, France, Germany, Norway, Romania, Spain and the UK (Chapter 3 of this volume discusses the UK strand of this project). The chapter seeks to interpret the meaning and nature of management development in France, using the results from the other six countries as comparisons. Conclusions identify the specificities of management development in France to explain the French approach, while highlighting what are thought to be the most significant findings and the differences in the other countries involved in the study. In drawing out the lessons, the chapter also shows that the main issues concern the relatively high level of education of those entering management in France and the relatively low link between management development and organizational strategy.

In setting out a case for research-informed and evidence-based management development, in Chapter 7 Bob Hamlin discusses a programme of collaborative research in managerial and leadership effectiveness as part of an HRD Professional Partnership study within a major department of the British Civil Service. Comparing the work of various writers, the author also makes the case for using interchangeably the terms 'manager' and 'leader' and 'management' and 'leadership', and for the decision to adopt an integrative approach to using both the 'management' and 'leadership' literatures for the purpose of the research reported in the chapter. He argues that the chapter will likely highlight the relevancy and importance to MD practitioners of using 'best evidence' derived from good research for the purpose of enhancing their professional expertise and practice. The notion of MD practitioners and MD scholars engaging jointly in 'partnership research' is also explored.

The notion of MD 'partnership research' is also developed in Chapter 8, where Lyn Stansfield and Jim Stewart explore a stakeholder approach to the study of management education – most of which, they argue, is conducted from a specific viewpoint, such as benefit to the organization or a particular group or individual. Taking a stakeholder approach means that a phenomenon may be viewed from a range of differing perspectives simultaneously. The stakeholder approach, its use in empirical research and its theoretical underpinnings and background are described, and a new model of the key stakeholders in management education is presented based on case-study evidence from research conducted in a manufacturing organization headquartered in mainland Europe and a service organization operating in the UK. The authors conclude with a discussion of the implications of the stakeholder approach as a research tool within the field of management education.

In common with Chapter 7, the final chapter in this second part of the book (Chapter 9) also illustrates the relevance of research-informed and evidence-based leadership development. In this chapter, Claire Ponsford and Graham Borley review the rationale for Panasonic UK (PUK) developing its own future leaders rather than looking for replacements on the open market. The theoretical context of the chapter considers the arguments for and against developing leadership potential internally. The research is based on a case study relating to PUK's Future Leadership programme, in which the authors present interview data from current and prospective leadership programme candidates and an analysis of programme costs and effectiveness weighed against the perceived risk of the programme failing to effectively address leadership succession management in PUK. The term 'succession management' is defined, and points of interest include the cross-cultural leadership dilemmas facing PUK as the UK arm of a Japanese multinational organization.

Summary

On comparing the individual studies featured in the four chapters in this second part of the book, the following themes emerge:

- Comparative studies are helpful in understanding MD in a particular cultural context, as the similarities and differences between the cases studied serve to bring the specificity of MD in the focal context into sharper relief.
- There *is* a case to be made for using interchangeably the terms 'manager' and 'leader' and 'management' and 'leadership'.
- The outcomes of MD research and practice can be significantly

extended and enriched through the adoption a multi-perspective approach, such as 'partnership research' or a 'stakeholder approach'.

- MD can be accomplished in novel and innovative ways, and does not have to be stuck in traditional approaches and models.
- HRD/MD practitioners should increasingly adopt research-informed and evidence-based approaches to their professional practice.

6 Management training and development in France

Will elitism give way to strategic development?

Françoise Le Deist, Annie Dutech, Alain Klarsfeld and Jonathan Winterton

Drawing on the results of a Leonardo da Vinci project investigating management training and development (MTD) in seven countries (Denmark, France, Germany, Norway, Romania, Spain and the UK), this chapter seeks to interpret the nature and meaning of MTD in France, in comparison with the other six countries. In each country, 100 enterprises were surveyed and telephone interviews conducted with the HR manager (or other responsible for MTD) and a line manager that had benefited from MTD initiatives. In the second phase, ten companies were selected for in-depth case study in each country. Chapter 3 provides an account of the UK strand of this research.

Theoretical context

The research began from the premise that organizational differences in HRD, and by extension MTD, are influenced by national contextual factors such as culture and systems of vocational training (Brewster and Bournois, 1991).

The survey was concerned mainly to identify the key characteristics of MTD in the 100 companies in each country and to compare the views of HR managers with line managers. As in the other countries, ten case studies were undertaken in organizations selected to capture a range of sizes of enterprises and different sectors of economic activity. The enterprises were selected from the list of those known to be practising MTD compiled during the first, quantitative, phase of the project. In each of the cases studied, face-to-face interviews were conducted with at least three managers, including one with responsibility for HRM or MTD. The interview guides used were developed from common schedules agreed as part of the case-study protocol for the project. The case reports were validated with the organizations concerned, which were asked whether they wished to remain anonymous (as they did in four of the ten cases). The four-frame model developed by Bolman and Deal (1997) was used as a framework for analysis to investigate beyond the rhetoric of the formal structural and HR frameworks the political and symbolic meanings of MTD within organizations.

Research context

The cultural context of management in France is extremely important and includes the tendency towards *dirigiste* public policies with little impact, the effect of profound organizational changes on management mentality, the benefits and drawbacks of a 'high-flying' education system (*Grandes Écoles, enseignement supérieur*, highly qualified *cadres*) and the difficulties of the current economic climate. These conditions define a very particular context in which management development takes place in France, and must be understood before any attempt is made to interpret the findings.

In France the very notion of 'manager' is problematic, having a wide and rather vague meaning approaching a generic term for any 'non-administrative employee' or technician. The notion of *cadre* is not only unique to France, but also extremely difficult to define and relate to other European traditions (see Boltanski, 1982; Groux, 1984). From the root *encadrement*, managers are considered to be the 'frame' (*cadre*) of the organization for which they work. Whereas most European countries distinguish between 'managed workers' and 'managers', official statistics in France divide the labour market into statutory categories and, since the reduction of working time in 2002, the law distinguishes three types of *cadres*:

- *Cadres-dirigeants* (directing managers) are managers with a high level of responsibility; they are highly independent in terms of work organization and deployment of time and are autonomous decision-makers. Their functions are regulated by article L 212-15-1 of the French Labour Code.
- *Cadres autonomes* (autonomous managers) are managers who work the standard hours of their organization with a degree of flexibility but less autonomy than the *cadres dirigeants*, often having both budgetary and human resource responsibility. Their functions are regulated by article L 212-15-2 of the French Labour Code.
- *Cadres intégrés* (integrated managers) are managers who adhere strictly to collective working hours and have no budgetary responsibility but can be considered team leaders. Their functions are regulated by article L 212-15-3 of the French Labour Code.

According to official statistics, 82 per cent of cadres have a managerial function and 66 per cent are responsible for teams of fewer than 20 workers. Half of these cadres manage other cadres (APEC, 2002). However, 26 per cent of cadres also coordinate temporary external subcontracting teams. Management in France cannot, therefore, be considered as purely hierarchical, despite the importance of hierarchy. The results of APEC's survey (APEC, 2002) provide a useful overview of French managers' perceptions of their role. Excluding top managers, Table 6.1 shows the differences in the two other types of *cadres*: 'team leaders', who manage internal human resources, and 'expert managers', who tend to be more innovative and to have more power.

The confusion around the definition of 'management' in France is also related to the state's attitude towards development. The framework for all continuing vocational training derives from the Grenelle Agreements, which followed widespread unrest in support of reforms in May 1968. These agreements invited the social partners to open *interprofessionnel* (inter-occupational, national-level) negotiation on this subject. Following the inter-occupational agreement of 9 July 1970 on training and professional development, the law of 16 July 1971 established the defining principles obliging companies to provide vocational training, including initial training of new entrants and continuous training for adults already employed. According to this law, 'professional continuous training must be part of permanent education allowing for the adaptation of workers to

Table 6.1 Managers' perceptions of their role

Word cited	Percentage of respondents	Characteristics
Organize	68	Production managers, experienced managers
Plan/anticipate	43	IT managers
Manage a team	38	Top managers, commercial managers, IT managers, older managers
Create and innovate	34	Research and development managers, IT managers, young managers
Control	30	Accounts and top managers
Decide	26	Top managers
Propose/suggest	26	Research and development managers, IT, personnel and communication managers
Represent the Board of Directors	18	Accounts and personnel managers

Source: Agence Pour l'Emploi des Cadres, *Cadroscope 2002*, Paris: APEC.

Note
Managers could use more than one term, hence the sum of percentages is greater than 100.

technical changes and conditions of work and to contribute to their cultural, economic and social development'. The law now requires employers to spend 1.6 per cent of total wages and salaries on vocational training of employees every year (or pay the equivalent in additional taxes). The proportion of training that must be dedicated to different categories of employees is not prescribed, leaving the employer to determine the balance of MTD and other vocational training. Perceived as another tax, employers often spent the bulk of the training budget on *cadres* (Barsoux and Lawrence, 1994; Géhin and Jobert, 2001) using MTD as a reward mechanism (Dany and Livian, 1995). Such practice has moderated as enterprises have adopted a more strategic approach to HRD (Dany and Livian, 2002), particularly with competence-based development (Defélix *et al.*, 2001; MEDEF, 2002).

Faced with inadequate government action, the employers' association MEDEF (*Mouvement des Entreprises de France*) actively campaigned to promote continuing training using a competence-based approach that is more comprehensive than the largely functional competence approach of the UK (Delamare Le Deist and Winterton, 2005). Since the end of the 1990s MEDEF has been working with companies towards a 'dynamic of transformation', significantly in cooperation with trade unions. The social partners have put in place different networks of consulting companies and have also created Observatories of Good Practices for MTD, at regional, national and international levels. Triggered by recent and projected demographic changes, these initiatives are concerned with the renewal of qualified managers. With the retirement of 755,000 'baby-boomer' managers (26 per cent of the managerial workforce) between 2001 and 2010, the renewal of the management population is seen as problematic. While such a proportion retiring over ten years is not extraordinary if the average manager has a working life of 40 years, MEDEF is actively trying to change employers' attitudes towards MTD for both younger and older (45 to 55 years) managers. The social partners highlight transfer of competences as key to the future of good management in the *Refondation Sociale* programme, which reiterates Ishikawa's emphasis on management as optimizing means, resources, methods, terrain and human resources. The limitations of this approach are also becoming evident as most of the resources to be optimized by management are nowadays immaterial, such as information, external image, brand names, competences, knowledge and ideas (MEDEF, 2003). Employers and government recognize the changing skills needs of managers, but little has been done to alter the dependence on initial education for training new managers.

Despite the relatively poor performance of French schools according to the PISA studies, initial education for managers is of a high standard, and this may act as a brake on MTD at enterprise level. Historically, the universities rejected vocationally-oriented applied subjects (except medicine and law) and focused on a classical curriculum of theoretical sciences and philosophy. To educate managers, engineers and the military, a system of *Grandes Écoles* was established along the lines of the *École Polytechnique* founded in 1793 following the Revolution. Lacking the state finance enjoyed by the universities, the *Grandes Écoles* were fee-paying and ultimately became highly selective, in the case of the *Écoles Supérieures de Commerce* taking only the top students who have passed the *classes préparatoires* at a particular level following two years of post-baccalaureate study. While the business schools have a reputation of developing very bright, dynamic young managers, they are neither easily affordable nor accessible, and Gordon (1993: 88) questioned whether such an elitist management education system was producing 'the right calibre of flexible, international manager, capable of responding quickly enough to shorter product life cycles'. Since then, the international accreditation processes EQUIS, AACSB and AMBA have effected major changes in the top schools, notably in relation to internationalization and research, but flexibility and responsiveness are not embedded in the curricula. The public universities are slowly developing departments of management, but they are unselective, under-resourced, and generally offer nothing approaching the educational experience of the *Grandes Écoles*.

As Tregaskis and Dany (1996: 23) note: 'the main way to have access to executive positions (i.e. *cadre*) in big companies is to come from a *Grande École* or hold at least a Master's degree, which has considerable impact on in-company management training'. Similarly, despite recent innovations with respect to accreditation of prior learning (*validation des acquis professionnels*), work experience has little recognition in comparison with initial education of managers, and this can also explain the relative underdevelopment of MTD in France. Ten years ago it was claimed that more young graduates were recruited to executive positions in France than in any other EU member state (Tregaskis and Dany, 1996: 24), and this may still be the case. Recent statistics from APEC (*Agence pour l'Emploi des Cadres*) show that the total number of *cadres* recruited was 111,000 in 1996 and peaked at 190,200 in 2001, falling to 147,900 in 2004. The number of *cadres* created through promotion also peaked in 2001 at around 50,000, and by 2004 had fallen to 45,800. APEC estimated that in February 2005 there were some 3.02 million *cadres* in post in 2004, compared with 2.28 million in 1994 – a growth of 32 per cent.

In recent years, MEDEF has argued that companies need to develop MTD at plant level urgently if they are to play an important part in the new competitive economy (MEDEF, 2003). MEDEF stresses that the key to understanding the role of the manager lies in the relationship between management of competences and access to new markets, using Hamel and Prahalad's (1995) conceptualization. MEDEF suggest that this new order for MTD should be established with the involvement of the unions. Since the *Accord Interprofessionnel* of 20 September 2003, the social partners have increasingly advocated an expansion of formal and informal vocational training and the role of social dialogue in determining arrangements.

The economic climate was highly favourable in the early 1990s (although not on a par with the 1960s, when France's growth outpaced Germany's), but national growth slowed towards the end of the decade and was seriously retarded with the downturn of world trade in 2001. Global slowdown had important repercussions on foreign investment, with a survey in 2002 suggesting that 43 per cent of American investors, representing the majority of foreign investors for France, were planning to delocalize (Ernst and Young, 2002). The terrorist attacks on the USA on 11 September 2001 and the fall of the new technologies sector contributed to this economic degradation, but so too did the anticipated enlargement of the EU, the greater fiscal attractiveness of Ireland and the UK and repeated efforts from Sweden, Germany and Belgium to attract foreign investment. The situation was further exacerbated by France's opposition to the US-led war of aggression on Iraq, which prompted withdrawal of American investment and a boycott of French products. To tackle the challenge of global competition French enterprises need MTD to raise competitiveness, but the fiscal, legal and administrative environment is far from conducive. France still suffers from excessive taxation, high non-wage labour costs and inflexibility in employment law, discouraging employers from investing further in vocational training as a whole.

Analysis and evaluation of main findings

The research findings are presented below, first in relation to the survey and then in relation to the case studies before offering a thematic interpretation across the whole study.

Results of the survey

In the following account, each figure in square brackets represents the entire sample of all the European countries covered, while the preceding figure relates to the French sample. Of the 100 [700] firms surveyed, 34 [34.4] per cent were in manufacturing or process industries, 35 [44.5] per cent were in the service sector and 31 [21.1] per cent were in transport and distribution, the objective having been one-third in each sector, excluding public enterprises and multinationals of overseas origin. In terms of number of employees, the mean size was 3,446 [2,504] and the median 251 [250], with a range from 22 [7] to 295,000 [340,000] employees.

In summary, it appears that in France MTD is perceived as less 'strategic' than in the rest of Europe. Our findings also suggest tension between an emphasis on development and an alternative of identifying potential, the latter being prevalent in France. Table 6.2 shows that

Table 6.2 Mean scores for perceived clarity of strategy, involvement of the **HR** function in strategy formulation and link between strategy and **HRM**

	HR respondents France	LM respondents France	HR respondents Europe	LM respondents Europe
Clarity of strategy	3.75	3.65	4.21	3.98
HR role in strategy formulation	2.77	2.54	3.44	3.06
Link between organization strategy and **HRM**	2.91	2.57	3.70	3.32
HRM perceived as source of competitive advantage	3.29	2.91	3.60	3.39

Note
Scores are based on a Likert scale ranging from 1 to 5.

organizational strategy appeared less clear and the HR function was perceived as less involved in France for both for HR and line managers. The perceived link between organizational strategy and HRM also appears weaker in France, and HRM is less likely to be seen as a source of competitive advantage.

Similarly, while 42 per cent of the HR managers surveyed in France reported having a policy on MTD, for the European sample as a whole the percentage was 47.8 per cent – yet, as Table 6.3 shows, French managers spend substantially less time on MTD activities in the French companies than do managers in companies in other European countries, by a factor of almost two according to the HR respondents.

Taking together all the items considered to reflect the importance attached to MTD (systematic evaluation, priority given to MTD, planned priority given to future MTD, MTD linked to business strategy, responsibility of organization towards MTD, responsibility towards career progression of managers), Table 6.4 shows that French firms in the sample score lower than the rest of the European sample.

Table 6.3 Development effort in days, French and European sample

	French sample	European sample
Days in MTD per manager (HR respondent)	6.54	12.88
Days in MTD per manager (LM respondent)	7.24	10.48

Table 6.4 Perceived importance of management development, French and European sample

	French sample	European sample
Systematic evaluation	2.86	3.10
Priority to management development	3.28	3.63
Planned priority to management development	3.07	3.58
Link with business strategy	2.80	3.65
Organizational responsibility towards management development	3.65	3.77
Organizational responsibility towards career progression	3.25	3.33

Note
Scores are based on a Likert scale ranging from 1 to 5.

Table 6.5 Career and development planning item scores, HR respondents

	French sample	*European sample*
Long-term management development	3.45	3.81
Use of internal promotion	4.12	4.11
Planned retention of manager	3.48	4.04
Planned hiring at senior positions	3.02	3.40
Development targeted for specific positions	3.08	3.48
Development of potential competence	3.41	3.66
Career planning	52%	60%
Identification of 'high potential' managers	77%	56.3%

Note
Scores are based on a Likert scale ranging from 1 to 5, or percentage of valid responses.

French HR managers generally reported a lower commitment to long-term career management than their counterparts in the other countries covered by the survey (with a comparable difference apparent between the line managers). Table 6.5 shows that related items (retention of managers, career planning, planned recruitment of senior managers, the development of potential competence), systematically display lower scores in France than in the other countries, except for the use of internal promotions. However, a far higher proportion of French firms appear to identify 'high potential' managers.

Case studies

This part of the analysis explores how and why management training and development is implemented in the French cases studied. After summarizing the scope and scale of MTD, the perceived strengths of MTD, including its impact on performance and problems encountered, are considered and the links between MTD and organizational strategy are explored.

The cases studied were as follows:

- DP (anonymous), the French division of a large pharmaceutical corporation
- Aswo, a small retail company selling electronic and household appliances
- AA (anonymous), a company providing private health and life assurance
- Leclerc Hypermarket La Part Dieu
- IA (anonymous), a small printing company
- CC (anonymous), a small business trading components for aerospace and agriculture

- Aciéries, a medium-sized company transforming steel products
- Nutrition et Santé, the French market leader in dietetic health products
- Access Industrie, a company renting equipment for maintenance work
- Ecocert, an enterprise specializing in the control and certification of organic produce.

When asked about the type of MTD implemented during the previous three years, respondents identified a range of initiatives that demonstrated a broad scope of activities contributing to the development of managerial competence. These included, in order of the most cited:

- team management or team-building, sometimes involving communication and appraisal techniques;
- communication skills, in some cases including presentation and negotiation skills;
- company-specific training in issues such as structure, philosophy, strategy, role in the organization and knowledge of the product range;
- training in managing people, including HRM techniques such as appraisal and coaching skills, and leadership skills for top managers;
- problem-solving, trouble-shooting and conflict management, sometimes including managing relationships with trade-union representatives;
- various specific management techniques, such as organization and time-management and, in one case, analysis and development of work processes.

In terms of scale, the specific MTD initiatives cited were in most cases part of a company-wide MTD programme through which all managers pass. In two cases the programme was reserved for senior managers or 'high flyers', and in one case they represented a menu of distinct activities in which managers could participate if they wished. In most cases the MTD was delivered by an external training provider or via the HRD department or equivalent, although in one case job rotation was also used for MTD and another was an exception to the French approach, where MTD was exclusively informal, experiential on-the-job training using shadowing and mentoring.

Views on what represented effectiveness of MTD varied with context. In most cases, positive individual impacts on performance were provided as examples of 'what worked' in terms of MTD. In other cases, respondents offered a more collective view of what worked in terms of positive organizational impacts, such as establishing a common culture or vision in the management team and ensuring common management practice through developing competence and understanding among managers.

Three of the cases where individual impacts of MTD were highlighted were identified as having relatively weak links between MTD and organizational strategy, whereas in all three cases with strong links between strategy and MTD, positive organizational impacts were reported. While this provides some support for the idea that MTD must be driven by organizational strategy to have impacts beyond the individual level, it is also interesting to note that in two cases where no such link was explicitly identified (AA and Leclerc), organizational impacts were also nevertheless reported.

The survey provided little or no information on the impact of MTD on performance, but the case studies illustrate the complex interaction between development and performance as well as the difficulties of attributing causality. In all cases, respondents reported performance improvements associated with MTD, but with varying degrees of precision. In five cases, clear performance improvements were justified in terms of monitoring or evaluation of outcomes. In the other five cases, performance improvements were assumed or envisaged rather than demonstrated, amounting to an 'act of faith' approach that MTD contributes to enhanced performance. In two cases, there was no formal evaluation of MTD and no link was apparent between MTD and performance.

In the cases studied, respondents identified a range of problems and difficulties encountered with MTD initiatives, including some (such as increased divisions between managers and increased stress), arising directly from MTD. Other problems stemmed from the absence of a formal HRM or HRD policy, which was linked to inadequate means of measuring the effectiveness of MTD. One of the major themes in discussions was the difficulty of establishing a clear link between MTD and the competences needed to support the organization's strategy. The survey suggested that links between MTD and organizational strategy were underdeveloped in France; HRD strategy was less clear to French respondents, and the involvement of HRM was perceived as less significant. HR managers as well as managers in France regard HRM and MTD as less important sources of competitive advantage than do their counterparts elsewhere in Europe.

The case studies provide a somewhat different picture. In three of the cases studied a link between organizational strategy and MTD was explicitly identified, and in two others such a link was implicit. In Aswo, the MTD initiative was centred on training all managers in key principles that would impact on the company's strategy and management of workers, in particular in relation to the company philosophy that 'growth should be a consequence of careful attention given to the client base rather than an objective *per se*'. While this might be considered to demonstrate a link between organizational strategy and MTD, in this case the HR manager specifically noted the absence of such a relationship as a weakness of the MTD policy. In three cases, no relationship between development and strategy was reported (although this does not mean it was absent, only that respondents did not express the link). Finally, in Access Industrie the *absence* of a link between MTD and organizational strategy was explicitly recognized and attributed to the managing director's philosophy and paternalistic management style. In place of a planned and organized programme for MTD, the managing director thought managers 'have to learn on the job ... [and] must train and perfect themselves by themselves as they are faced with day-to-day reality. They should learn from different experiences in order to develop a set of managerial competences.'

Interpretations and conclusions

These conclusions seek to identify the specificities of MTD in France and to explain the French approach, highlighting the most significant findings and differences from the other countries involved in the study.

Ten years ago, using data from a Cranfield Survey, Tregaskis and Dany (1996: 26) found that French organizations spent 3.83 per cent of the annual wages and salaries bill on training and development (over twice the legal requirement then and now) compared with 1.71 per cent for UK organizations. French managers and employees also spent more time in training and development (four and two days, respectively) compared with their UK equivalents (three days and one-and-a-half days, respectively). Concluding that the French organizations manifested a higher commitment to training than the UK organizations, Tregaskis and Dany noted major differences in the methods of training needs analysis employed. Whereas in the UK the primary method was performance appraisal and employee demand the least important, in France the primary method was line-manager demand, followed by employee demand. French organizations were more likely to have annual development reviews and to place greater emphasis on 'high-flyer' schemes than UK organizations, but less likely to have formal career plans and slightly less likely to use performance evaluation (Tregaskis and Dany, 1996: 28). They also noted the tendency in France to distinguish performance evaluation from development reviews, which were frequently (and mistakenly) conflated in the UK.

Our survey results strike a chord with many of these earlier findings. First, while expenditure on MTD is slightly higher in France than for the rest of the European sample, this is by a much smaller margin than was found ten years ago in comparison with the UK. Second, while the earlier study concluded that French organizations had a higher commitment to training and development, our survey suggests that for items considered to reflect the importance attached to MTD, French firms score *lower* than the rest of the European sample. Importantly, the perceived link between organizational strategy and HRM appears weaker in France, and HRM is less likely to be seen as a source of competitive advantage. The apparent paradox has already been noted that while French firms report a lower importance attached to MTD, absence of career management and, especially, a weak link between MTD and organizational strategy, they nonetheless appear to have a more *systematic* approach to MTD than do the firms in the rest of the European sample.

Key learning points

In drawing out the lessons, the main issues concern the relatively high level of education of new-entrant managers in France and the weak link between MTD and organizational strategy. Using the Bolman and Deal (1997) framework helped us to understand the nature of MTD from different vantage points.

The structural frame emphasizes formal roles and goals, processes and relationships, related to structural determinants of the organization's context. For MTD, the emphasis is on the link between development and strategy. The structural frame provided the major explanation of MTD in three cases. In Aswo, one MTD initiative to support the strategic initiative of adopting a focused differentiation strategy was designed with the assistance of the consultant who had helped the firm to shape its strategy at the beginning of the 1990s. Moreover, the strong link between management development and strategy observed in this case, which contrasts with the French sample, may be accounted for by the fact that neither the general manager nor the HR manager is French. Similarly, in Nutrition et Santé, there was an obvious link between the MTD strategy and the quest for performance, with the acquisition of management competences supporting economic objectives of enhanced productivity and efficiency. In Ecocert, the MTD initiative was driven by a wish to establish a link between individual performance and the performance of the enterprise, so the structural frame was an important explanatory perspective. In three other cases the structural frame was also very important, and in another three provided some insights into the MTD initiative, but such issues did not have a major explanatory role. Finally, in Access Industrie the structural frame highlighted the absence of structure; there is no formal link between development and performance, and managers are concerned by this absence of structure and the limited MTD.

The HR frame is more concerned with relations between individuals, groups and the organization, particularly formal HR systems and processes, but also informal social relations at work. For MTD, the emphasis is on opportunities for individual development. The HR frame provided the major explanation of MTD initiatives in only two cases. In Aswo, the senior management team encourages managers to initiate MTD activities themselves and, apart from a few compulsory training activities, most MTD is either proposed by the general manager and then accepted (or refused) by the individual manager, or initiated by employees (including managers) themselves. The policy is that the company is willing to pay for development, even in areas considered as non-strategic, therefore leaving room for emergent demands and needs. The only restriction on employee-initiated training is that it has to take place in the employee's own leisure time, rather than in company-paid working time. In Aciéries, changing the role and mission of managers demanded new competences, and the evaluation of MTD clearly shows that these competences were developed and performance targets achieved. Above all, this process enabled a revalorization of managers' functions, the legitimacy of which was seriously undermined by the old system. The HR frame was also an important perspective in understanding MTD in three other cases, and in another two cases it made a minor contribution to understanding MTD; in the remaining three cases, however, the HR frame was much less important in explaining MTD.

The political frame is concerned with the organization as a political arena, emphasizing power relations between groups and the reasons for alliances and struggles. In three cases, the political frame provided major insights into MTD initiatives. The political frame was important in explaining the role of MTD in Leclerc, a company directed by a charismatic Managing Director, but this never appears in interviewees' declarations because they strongly reflect the system's principles. In Aciéries, MTD challenges were important and much greater than simply providing purely technical competences. Similarly, in Nutrition et Santé, those selected for certain MTD activities have become an elite of 'high-potential managers', leading to feelings of marginalization among other managers. In two cases there were some political undertones to MTD, but in the remaining five cases the political frame added little or no understanding to MTD.

The symbolic frame explores motives and meanings, emphasizing the rituals of MTD within the organization and the attempts to change or reinforce a particular culture. In two cases the symbolic meaning of MTD seemed of paramount importance. In DP, corporate-led programmes hold a symbolic value for those invited to participate, since only three or four managers are involved every year out of the 60 present on site. Similarly, in Aswo, where the manager who was recently appointed to develop operations in Spain was perceived as having captured the essence of the initiative, MTD seemed to have an implicit symbolic function of identifying management potential. In six other cases there was also a strong symbolic element to MTD in relation to establishing, changing or reinforcing organizational culture, and in the two remaining cases the symbolic frame played a minor role in understanding MTD.

In conclusion, the first point to highlight is that the concept of 'manager' is problematic in France, where the major distinction is between *cadres* and other employees. The three levels of *cadres*, translated as 'directing managers', 'autonomous managers' and 'integrated managers', are defined in the French Labour Code, and therefore have statutory meaning and consequent implications for terms of employment. The second contextual point is that managers are largely a product of an elitist educational system, already well-qualified when appointed and therefore less likely to engage in MTD than their counterparts in countries like the UK, where the managerial workforce is under-qualified.

The case studies provide new insights into problems and difficulties associated with MTD initiatives, such as increased stress and increased divisions between managers. A major problem was the absence of a formal HRD, or even HRM, policy. This is consistent with the survey, which found that MTD in France is accorded less strategic importance than in other countries in the study. The absence of a clear link between MTD and the competences needed to support the organization's strategy was the difficulty most evident in the case studies.

Using the four frames proved a valuable way of surfacing a wider range of issues than might have been otherwise apparent. In three cases MTD could only be understood in its complexity by reference to all four frames, although in two MTD could be predominantly viewed as structural–political and in the third as HR–political. In each of the other cases, MTD was understood as having elements from two or three of the frames. In one MTD was seen as explicable in terms of structural, HR and symbolic issues, while in another it was understood as a structural, political and symbolic phenomenon. The explanation of MTD in a sixth case was mainly HR–political, in a seventh it was mainly structural–symbolic, while in an eighth it was more HR–symbolic. Finally, in the two remaining cases MTD was largely symbolic, with some minor structural explanations.

At the risk of over-simplifying, and with the usual caveats of generalization from a small number of cases, overall the case studies suggest a major role for symbolic explanations of MTD, followed by structural explanations, over and above HR or political perspectives. The most striking point about this is perhaps the apparent absence of a logic for MTD driven by HR concerns. Equally surprising, given the elitist *Grandes Écoles* education system and *dirigiste* traditions of French management, is the relatively minor importance attached to political perspectives. The fact that symbolic as well as structural interpretations have such currency probably reflects the importance of culture change in the MTD initiatives designed to support strategic objectives. The relative unimportance of HR perspectives is perhaps a consequence of the more strategic organization focus (as opposed individual development focus) of the MTD initiatives considered.

References

APEC (2002) *Cadroscope 2002*, Paris: Agence Pour l'Emploi des Cadres.
Barsoux, J.-L. and Lawrence, P. (1994) *Management in France*, London: Cassell Educational.

Bolman, L.G. and Deal, T.E. (1997) *Reframing Organizations: Artistry, Choice and Leadership*, San Francisco, CA: Jossey-Bass.

Boltanski, L. (1982) *Les Cadres: La Formation d'un Groupe Social*, Paris: Éditions de Minuit.

Brewster, C. and Bournoius, F. (1991) 'Human resource management: a European perspective', *Personnel Review*, 20(6): 4–14.

Dany, F. and Livian, Y.-F. (1995) *La Gestion des Cadres*, Paris: Vuibert.

Dany, F. and Livian, Y.-F. (2002) *La Nouvelle Gestion des Cadres: Employabilité, individualisation et vie au travail*, Paris: Vuibert.

Defélix, C., Martin, D. and Retour, D. (2001) 'La Gestion des Compétences entre concepts et applications', *Revue de Gestion des Ressources Humaines*, 39: 73–9.

Delamare Le Deist, F. and Winterton, J. (2005) 'What is competence?' *Human Resource Development International*, 8(1): 27–46.

Ernst and Young (2002) *Barometer 2002*.

Géhin, J-P. and Jobert, A. (2001) 'International briefing 8: Training and development in France', *International Journal of Training and Development*, 5(1): 81–93.

Gordon, C. (1993) 'The business culture in France', in Randlesome, C., Brierley, W., Bruton, K., Gordon, C. and King, P. (eds), *Business Cultures in Europe*, 2nd edn, Oxford: Butterworth-Heinemann, pp. 87–140.

Groux, C. (1984) *Les Cadres*, Paris: La Découverte.

Hamel, G. and Prahalad, C.K. (1995) *La Conquête du Future*, Paris: InterEditions.

MEDEF (2002) *Objectif Compétences: Des pratiques Européenne innovantes*, Paris: Mouvement des Entreprises de France.

MEDEF (2003) 'Compétences, Management et les Nouvelles Missions de l'Encadrement', *Cahier de Gestion* No. 66, Paris: Mouvement des Entreprises de France.

Tregaskis, O. and Dany, F. (1996) 'A comparison of HRD in France and the UK', *Journal of European Industrial Training*, 20(1): 20–30.

7 Towards evidence-based management development

Bob Hamlin

Objectives

The primary purpose of this chapter is twofold: first, to argue the case that human resource development (HRD) practitioners in general and management development (MD) practitioners in particular should increasingly adopt research-informed and evidence-based approaches to their professional practice; and second, to illustrate with a practical example how this might readily come about through the concept of HRD Professional Partnership research of the kind defined by Jacobs (1997) and advocated by Hamlin (2001a, 2002a). In so doing two assumptions have been made. First, that management development is a major component of the broad modern-day conceptualization of HRD, which places as much emphasis on organizational development as on people development (Delahaye and Smith, 1998). Second, that managerial leadership is a constituent part of the everyday task of most managers, as suggested by House and Aditya (1997) and demonstrated empirically by Russ-Eft *et al.* (1996). This latter assumption is further supported by the fact that many if not most managers in most organizations, as well as many modern-day management theorists, writers and researchers, use the terms 'manager' and 'leader', and 'management' and 'leadership', interchangeably (Barker, 2000; Alimo-Metcalfe and Lawler, 2001; Alvesson, 2002; Raelin, 2004). Consequently, much of the evidence used to support the arguments presented in this chapter is drawn not only from the management and management development literature, but also from the leadership and leadership development literature.

Theoretical context

The critical relevance of management development

Ever since the late 1980s, when the concept of HRD first emerged and gained currency in the UK as a field of study and practice, it has continued to evolve and expand way beyond its historical primary concern with securing an organization's skill base, to the point where it now incorporates a whole array of approaches to both individual and organizational learning. However, as Sambrook (2000) and Walton (2001) point out, there are many alternative discourses by which the domain has been and continues to be interpreted, understood and defined. McGoldrick *et al.* (2002) claim that the process of defining HRD by academics, researchers and practitioners is proving to be frustrating, elusive and confusing, with no single definition emerging, whilst McClean and McClean (2001) report that the understanding and meaning of HRD varies considerably from one country to another around the globe. By association, the same might be said about the concept of management development (MD), as can be inferred from the many different understandings and definitions of MD offered by various writers including, for example, Margerison (1991), Lees (1992), Mumford (1997), Burgoyne (1998) and Sadler (1998), as discussed by Mumford and Gold (2004). In light of the wide variations in focus and emphasis, it has been considered desirable by this author, drawing upon the thinking of McClagan and Suhadolnik (1989), Ruona and Lynham (1999), Stewart (1999) and Watkins (2000), to offer his own definition of MD in terms of its scope and purpose within the broader concept of HRD, as follows:

> Management development, being a component part of HRD, encompasses planned activities and processes designed to enhance organizational and individual learning, develop human potential, maximize organizational effectiveness and performance, and help bring about effective and beneficial change within and even beyond the boundaries of the organization.
>
> (Adapted from the definition of HRD previously offered by Hamlin, 2004a)

This definition gives recognition to the suggestion that management development is about engineering organizational change, pursuing quality, cost-reduction and profitability, structuring attitudes, contributing to the development of a learning organization, and assisting with self-development (Storey *et al.*, 1994), and rests on the three constructs posited by Chalofsky (2004) for HRD, namely people, learning and organization. These three constructs are inter-related, and the concept of change is embedded in all of them. The fact that the management of change is a critical responsibility of most managers at all levels of an organization suggests they should have a strong interest in MD and HRD. However, neither MD nor HRD register on the radar screens of many top managers and organizational leaders, or on the radar screens of managers in general (Gold *et al.*, 2003). Yet there is a compelling logic why all managers who strive for high or peak performance, from chief executive officers and managing directors through to first-line supervisory managers, should give MD and HRD a fair share of attention. All high-performing organizations are made up of high-performing groups, teams and individuals. However, high performance does not just happen on its own; it has to be made to happen, and in organizational contexts it is the management and individual managers who have the primary responsibility to make it happen. However, delivering consistent and sustainable high performance is easier said than done. Campbell *et al.* (2003) argue that individual differences in performance are a function of three interacting determinants, namely 'Declarative Knowledge' (DK), 'Procedural Knowledge/Skill' (PKS) and 'Motivation' (M), where ability is a key component of both DK and PKS. Similarly, Mullins (1993) suggests that high performance within organizational settings results from the function of two interacting factors, namely 'Ability' × 'Motivation'. Building on Mullin's suggestion, Hamlin (2004a) argues the result of this interaction is moderated by the positive or negative effects of a third factor – 'Environment' – and that all three factors comprise several components, as illustrated in the mental model below which he calls the 'High Performance Equation'.

$$\text{High Performance} = \int (\text{Ability} \times \text{Motivation}) \ \text{Environment}$$

Capability	*Confidence*	*Communication*
Cognition	*Commitment*	*Climate*
Competence	*Collaboration*	*Culture*
		Credibility

© R.G. Hamlin 2004

An explanation of each of the ten components can be found in Hamlin (2004a). This 'High Performance Equation', with its three factors and ten components, is simple to understand but much harder to apply. To keep the 'equation' up to date and in balance calls for a high order of managerial 'change agency' capability, cognition and competence. Unfortunately, literature suggests this is sadly lacking in the majority of companies, as evidenced by the fact that a large majority of organizational change and development (OCD) programmes fail (Hamlin, 2001b). Furthermore, many change initiatives fail badly with unintended and damaging consequences, as demonstrated by Marks (1994) in the USA and Worrall and Cooper (1997–2002) in the UK. Hamlin (2001b) has identified five root causes of failure on the part of managers in managing and facilitating organizational change and development programmes, as follows:

1   Managers not knowing the fundamental principles of change management;
2   Managers succumbing to the temptation of the 'quick fix' and 'simple solution';
3   Managers not fully appreciating the significance of the leadership and cultural aspects of change;

4   Managers not appreciating sufficiently the significance of the people issues;
5   Managers not knowing the critical contribution that the human resource development function can make to the management of change.

Regarding Failing (5), he claims that many managers often regard training and development as an undesirable drain on the scarce resources of the organization, a cost that can only be afforded when profits and funding are plentiful, rather than an investment that the organization can ill afford not to make even in the toughest of times, especially during periods of transformational change. Yet for managers to be in control of change, they must ensure they are in control of the knowledge, attitude and skill issues associated with change itself. This means giving sufficient time and attention to the 'soft' people-oriented MD and HRD aspects of the change management process. However, it is unlikely to come about whilst this failing and the other four OCD failings of managers continue to persist.

Unfortunately, these five failings are rarely given attention in management and leadership training and development programmes. Even if they are, few such programmes are likely to be that effective in bringing about change and improvement in managerial behaviour, competence and organizational performance. This is because, as various writers in the USA point out, the majority of formal management and leadership development programmes either fail or have only a limited effect (see Burke and Day, 1986; Lai, 1996; House and Aditya, 1997; Collins and Holton, 2004; McCall, 2004; Raelin, 2004). According to Fiedler (1996), the fact that we know very little about the processes of leadership and managerial training contributing to organizational performance is because hardly any meaningful, rigorous research has been carried out. Hence, as yet, little can be learned from the American management and leadership literature regarding what MD practitioners need to do to ensure that their management and leadership development programmes are effective. A similar situation exists in the UK where, despite massive investment by public and private sector organizations in leadership development initiatives, evidence suggests that these often fail (Alimo-Metcalfe and Alban-Metcalfe, 2003a, 2003b). That so much MD has had such limited impact, and the fact that many managers perceive it as of little use, should not be a surprise if, as Mumford (1997) argues, most managers do not see MD as part of their real world because much of what is taught in business schools and delivered by management trainers and developers is not based on the findings of empirical research. Similarly, Hamlin and Stewart (1998) have argued that much management training and development in the UK is not that effective or beneficial because it lacks a sound and sufficient empirical base. However, just as there is a dearth of management-development related empirical research, there is also a lack of relevant research into the everyday practical realities of effective and ineffective management at both an operational and strategic level. For example, Adler *et al.* (2004) refer to the challenges and opportunities facing management science, which continues to be too divorced from the world of management practice. Academic management research has been much criticized for being overly theoretical and abstract without sufficiently recognizing the problems and challenges facing the acting manager, and few research initiatives have been reported that actively seek to bridge the much talked about 'academy–industry' and 'research–practice' gaps. Yet such gaps do not exist to any significant extent in other professional fields, such as dentistry, medicine, pharmacy, law and engineering. Most of the empirical research relating to these particular professional fields of practice carried out by academic staff in universities is done with the clear intent to inform, shape and improve practice within the respective professions. Indeed, in the field of health care in general, professional practice informed by 'best evidence' derived from good research (i.e. evidence-based practice) has become firmly established worldwide, and is spreading into other fields outside health care with the establishment of initiatives for evidence-based practice in social care, criminal justice and education (Walshe and Rundell, 2001). If, progressively, evidence-based approaches to practice spread to most professions in the public, private and not-for-profit sectors, then MD practitioners and most other HRD professionals will need also to become evidence-based themselves. Consequently, the rest of this chapter discusses the issue of 'research-informed' and 'evidence-based' approaches to practice within the field, and how these concepts might progressively become a commonplace feature of professional MD practice.

Research-informed and evidence-based management development

As already mentioned, Hamlin (2001a, 2002a) suggests it is the absence of research-informed and evidence-based professional practice within the change management process that largely accounts for the failure of so many OCD and MD programmes. This is because those aspects of the management and organizational culture that can either enhance or impede transformational change are not sufficiently understood by managers at the outset of their change journey. Coupled with a lack of adequate change-agency skill, managers are unable to bring about successfully the changes they desire. This lack of competence helps to perpetuate the five OCD 'failings' of managers which, as Hamlin (2001b: 32–3) argues, turns into a vicious circle leading to:

> the organizational climate and management culture in many organizations not being conducive for trainers and developers to operate

strategically as internal change agents and as research informed or evidence-based HRD practitioners. This precludes the development of appropriate management development initiatives that might help managers to overcome their 'failings' concerning the management of change.

Furthermore, it leads to an absence of meaningful and rigorous MD research and management research to provide a sound and sufficient base of 'best evidence' to inform, shape and evaluate MD practice. This lack is a significant factor contributing to the perceived irrelevance and ineffectiveness of much management and leadership development and organization development, and needs to be addressed by MD practitioners and scholars exploring and engaging with the concepts of 'evidence-based' and 'research-informed' practice.

The meaning of 'evidence-based' practice has been strongly influenced by the development over the past ten years or so of the theory and practice of evidence-based medicine and evidence-based health care which, as already mentioned, are now well established worldwide. Since 1998 there have been various calls for evidence-based management (Axelsson, 1998; Stewart, 1998) and evidence based, or at least research-informed, MD and HRD practice (Leimbach and Baldwin, 1997; Russ Eft *et al.*, 1997; Swanson, 1997; Hamlin and Ash, 2000; Brewerton and Millward, 2001; Holton, 2004). In relation to the US context, Holton (2004) has called for a national movement as exists in the mental health sector to embed evidence-based approaches to practice throughout the HRD business, whilst in the UK Hamlin (2001a, 2002a) has strongly advocated for several years the benefits of evidence-based and research-informed HRD. However, MD practitioners will not be able to become evidence-based in their practice without the existence of a body of generalized 'best evidence' that has relevance to their context of application, or of practitioner instigated and/or sponsor commissioned programmes of specific practice-grounded internal research that focuses on the particular issues or problems that need to be addressed within their own organizations. As already mentioned, the field of MD and HRD lacks a sound and sufficient base of relevant and usable empirical research to support the concept of evidence-based practice. The same can be said about the field of management in general. For example, from his wide-ranging historical review of the management literature in search of strong empirical evidence to support the concept of evidence-based health-care management, a search that spanned more than 100 years of management research, Axelsson (1998) concluded few studies had produced empirical results that could be generalized beyond particular organizational settings. Furthermore, in many instances the research appeared to have been an end in itself, with little relevance for practical management. More recently, various concerns and criticisms have been expressed regarding the lack of relevance, utility and generalizability of most management and leadership research, and of the predominant use of quantitative research methods. These criticisms, which should be of concern to all MD and HRD practitioners as well as practising managers and management scholars, are explored further in the following section.

Concerns and criticisms of most management and leadership research

Concerns about the lack of relevance, utility and generalizability

As Adler *et al.* (2004: xix) argue, few management research initiatives have been reported that have 'actively sought to bridge the suggested "academy–industry" gap' or address the much talked about 'research–practice gap' which Starkey and Tempest (2004) claim is increasingly being debated in Europe. They suggest this also resonates with debates in the United States about the lack of relevance and utility of most academic management research, and about the limited impact management science has had on management practice (see Porter and McKibbin, 1988; Hambrick, 1994; Academy of Management, 2001; Das, 2003; Ghoshal, 2005; Bennis and O'Toole, 2005). We know a lot about the 'what' of management and leadership (i.e. the roles, functions, tasks and activities), but little about the 'how' of management practice. This is because staff in business schools tend to be more committed to the generation of knowledge about management rather than knowledge that generates better and more effective management in practice (Starkey and Tempest, 2004). Even when the latter type of research has been done, there has been very little agreement about what constitutes 'managerial effectiveness' and 'leadership effectiveness' (Luthans *et al.*, 1985; Martinko and Gardner, 1985, 1990; Luthans *et al.*, 1988; Cammock *et al*, 1995; Kim and Yukl, 1995; Willcocks, 1997; Conger, 1998; Van der Velde *et al.*, 1999; Barker, 2000; Shipper, 2000). Furthermore, a host of writers argue that managerial and leadership effectiveness is context-dependent, situation-specific and perspective-specific, and, therefore, research results cannot be generalized across different organizations and sectors (Burgoyne, 1990; Harrow and Willcocks, 1990; Willcocks, 1992; Raelin and Cooledge, 1995; Antonacopoulou and Fitzgerald, 1996; Cappelli and Crocker-Hefter, 1996; Flanagan and Spurgeon, 1996; Hayes *et al.*, 2000; Garavan and McGuire, 2001). Additionally, other writers argue that management and leadership are culture-specific and question the generalizability of findings obtained from US research to non-US cultures (Ayman, 1993; Smith and Bond, 1993; Triandis, 1993; Flanagan and Spurgeon, 1996; Peterson and Hunt, 1997; Holt, 1998; Hunter, 1998; Alban-Metcalfe and Alimo Metcalfe, 2001). Nevertheless, some researchers believe in the existence of the universally effective manager and universally effective leader, of universal indicators of managerial effectiveness, of generic managerial competencies, of generic leadership functions and universal effective supervisory leader behaviours, and of universal leadership styles (Bennett and Langford, 1983; Hamlin, 1988; Thompson *et al.*, 1996; Bass, 1997; House and Aditya, 1997). However, these beliefs are based more on compelling logic than on empirical evidence (House and Aditya, 1997), though recent research is beginning to support the views of these writers by producing evidence that demonstrates the 'universality' of management and leadership (Carl and Javidan, 2001; Russ-Eft and Brennan, 2001; Agut and Grau, 2002; Hamlin, 2004b, 2005; Walumbwa *et al.*, 2005).

Concerns about the use of quantitative research methods

In recent years there has been much criticism of the predominant use of quantitative research methods for researching managerial and leadership effectiveness, in particular the deployment of pre-determined survey-based questionnaires and instruments that have been generalized across a variety of contexts and consequently comprise broad terms that are relatively 'sterile' in the sense that a useful richness of detail is often missing. Hence, researchers end up measuring the presence and frequency of static terms, which generates results that have little perceived relevance to managers and leaders in their specific organizational contexts (Martinko and Gardner, 1990; Yukl *et al.*, 1990; Shipper, 1991; Yukl, 1994; Shipper and White, 1999; Alvesson, 2002). As Alvesson (2002: 97) recently concluded, 'much richer accounts than those typically produced are needed'. This echoes the calls of various other writers who advocate the use of qualitative research methods in this field of study and practice (Den Hartog *et al.*, 1997; Parry, 1998; Avolio *et al.*, 1999; Barker, 2000; Alvesson, 2002).

From the above brief review of current concerns and criticisms of most management and leadership research, and the very limited amount of generalized findings to be found at present in the literature, it should not be a surprise that the offerings of most trainers and developers regarding the 'how' of effective management and leadership tend to be based more on their own personal values, beliefs and experiences (or on the views of 'gurus' and/or prevailing 'fads and fashions') than on 'best evidence' derived from good research. This begs the question: how might 'evidence-based' approaches to practice become as commonplace in the field of MD and HRD as they are in the field of medicine and health care?

Research context

Towards evidence-based management development through HRD professional partnership research

Despite the various calls for research-informed and evidence-based MD and HRD practice, only limited progress has been made to date. Nevertheless, the experience of the author suggests that an efficient and effective means for MD and HRD practitioners to become evidence-based is through HRD Professional Partnership research of the kind defined by Jacobs (1997) and advocated by Hamlin (2001a, 2002a). In this type of 'partnership research', universities and organizations engage in a collaborative partnership wherein HRD (MD) scholars and HRD (MD) practitioners jointly conduct a programme of collaborative research, but do so with their own mutually exclusive yet complementary goals. Maintaining the integrity of both sets of goals for the common good is considered important. Thus, there is a dual goal to improve the organization through the application of academically rigorous applied research, whilst at the same time advancing the HRD and MD field of unique knowledge. The research can be either practice-grounded internal research that reaches for external generalization, or relevant external generalized research that can be applied within the organization. Sufficient time is allowed to ensure that an adequate level of academic rigour and robustness is built into the research design, but in timescales that are realistic for the organization by enabling early, timely and optimal utilization of the gathered data and research findings. To date, only a few case histories of HRD Professional Partnership research have been reported in the literature. These include, for example, those of Holton *et al.* (1998) in the USA, and Hamlin *et al.* (1998), Hamlin (2002b) and Hamlin and Cooper (2005) in the UK. To illustrate this concept of 'partnership research' in action, there now follows a brief description of a programme of collaborative research on managerial and leadership effectiveness that the author undertook as part of an HRD Professional Partnership study within the Anglia Region of HM Customs and Excise – a major department of the British Civil Service. An overview is also given of the subsequent research-informed OD and MD initiatives that helped the Chief Executive Officer (CEO) to bring about strategic organizational change within his region, including significant changes in the management culture. The American Society of Training and Development (ASTD) has recognized this work as a good example of research-informed practice by awarding its 2005 ASTD Excellence in Research-to-Practice Award to the two key research partners in the 'Anglia' professional partnership (see Hamlin and Reidy, 2005).

The 'Anglia' professional partnership research study

Organizational context

At the time of his appointment as Regional Head of HM Customs and Excise (Anglia Region) the CEO (Dick Shepherd) found himself in a region which, while still productive, was working with a 'command and control' style of management in need of change to reflect a new environment in which year-on-year demands to deliver more for less were being made. Furthermore, the traditional Civil Service management style did not sit well with the changing managerial philosophy being articulated by the Department's Board of Management. Dick Shepherd concluded that a new cultural infra-structure was required, one comprising characteristics such as flexibility, risk-taking, enterprise, and innovation and change that would enable the organization to cope efficiently and effectively with the various change programmes likely to be imposed from above and those he would also be initiating. Furthermore, he believed strongly in the concept of empowering people and teams by giving them all the facts and encouraging them to develop their own solutions. However, this required team managers to provide the right type and styles of leadership and to create the right environment when acting both as team heads and team members. Having set out his expectations clearly, and having encouraged a more open style of management, he found that the changes were very slow to happen due to 'cultural lag' – a term Bate (1996) uses to describe the condition when culture is no longer relevant to the needs of the organization. To make further progress, Dick Shepherd realized he needed to understand better the organization's culture so as to know more accurately how best to change it. Hence, he appointed an organizational behaviourist as a research officer/OD consultant (Margaret Reidy) to carry out, in the first instance, internal management research. This included a major ethnographic longitudinal case study on cultural change designed to help inform, shape and measure the changes he wanted to bring about. In the main, the change programmes he initiated were successful in terms of the desired changes in organizational structure, systems and procedures. However, the desired changes in management culture were only partially achieved. Whereas some managers exhibited behaviours indicative of enlightened management values consistent with the requirements of the changing organization, a large proportion continued to exhibit the characteristic behaviours of a traditional 'rigid' bureaucracy.

Dick Shepherd decided he needed to further develop and strengthen the cultural infrastructure of the organization, particularly the management culture in order to make it more relevant. Although he was generally aware of the effective and ineffective managerial behaviours exhibited by his managers, he felt he had insufficient specific knowledge to be certain about those that were strategic to success or failure and which, therefore, needed either to be encouraged and promoted or discouraged and eliminated. He required some means of determining with greater insight and clarity of understanding those particular managerial behaviours that were most effective (and conversely least effective or ineffective) for managing successfully within what had become an organizational environment of constant change and uncertainty. In OD terms, he wanted to hold up a mirror to his managers and help them decide how to make meaningful change. Consequently, he commissioned Margaret Reidy to carry out an in-depth empirical research study into the criteria of managerial and leadership effectiveness, in collaboration with the author of this chapter who had a proven track record of success in this field of research. On the latter's suggestion it was decided that the collaborative partnership research should be carried out not only to meet the organizational needs, but also to achieve an academic goal of advancing the field of knowledge. The approach adopted for this researcher–practitioner partnership was in all respects equivalent to the HRD Professional Partnership concept advocated in the USA by Jacobs (1997), with Margaret Reidy acting as the MD practitioner and Bob Hamlin as the MD scholar.

Role of the MD practitioner and MD scholar

The proposed HRD Professional Partnership research into managerial and leadership effectiveness was unique for the organization in terms of its high level of academic rigour, using rigorous methodologies and techniques over a longer period of time than was normally allowed for internal inquiries. This gave the collaborative partners more time to research and analyse the organization in depth, rather than taking 'snapshots' of current issues whose underlying factors may have had hidden depths. Margaret Reidy and Bob Hamlin worked closely in partnership throughout the research programme. The research design was developed jointly, the gathered data were co-analysed and co-interpreted, the behavioural item questionnaires developed as part of the research process were co-created, and all of the research-related papers, from the preliminary to the final reports, were co-written. The subsequent research-to-practice initiatives, which included OD workshops and MD-related interventions based on the research findings, were also designed jointly. Additionally, a significant range of research conference papers, academic journal articles and reports in practitioner publications were subsequently co-authored. Details of these are given later in this chapter.

Research methodology

The research programme comprised two phases. Phase A focused on the management tasks of Higher Executive Officers (HEOs) and Executive Officers (EOs), who had significant managerial responsibilities within their respective roles. Phase B was based on the research findings obtained from Phase A, and focused on the leadership aspects of the management task only.

Phase A: Criteria of managerial effectiveness research

This phase comprised three stages as follows:

Stage 1

In this job analysis stage, statements of behaviour and behavioural dimensions that characterized effective and ineffective management were generated using the well-established critical incident technique (CIT) of Flanagan (1954) as applied by Latham *et al.* (1975) and Hamlin (1988). Over 130 people operating in HEO or EO grade roles were interviewed from 15 out of 21 offices geographically spread throughout the region. In total, over 1,200 critical incidents (CIs) were collected.

Stage 2

This stage concerned the creation and administration of a behavioural item questionnaire (BIQ) based on the Stage 1 findings. Those CIs that were ambiguous or complex with multiple facets of meaning were discarded. Only the CIs that were found to be the same as or similar to at least two others gathered from different divisions or offices of the organization were used. Most behavioural items were based on a cluster of critical incidents comprising a minimum of three 'nearly the same' CIs, with one being selected as a representative 'verbatim' statement of that particular critical behaviour. Certain clusters of 'different yet closely related' CIs were combined into condensed and composite BIs expressed in the researchers' words. The process ultimately led to the creation of a BIQ rating instrument comprised of 83 discrete behavioural items (43 positive and 40 negative) to which a Likert-type scale was attached (Likert, 1967). Prior to the BIQ being administered throughout the regional organization, it was first assessed for credibility.

Stage 3

The final stage involved establishing job dimensions and identifying criteria of managerial effectiveness through a process of reducing, classifying and grouping the effective and ineffective behavioural items into behavioural categories. Factor analysis was used to explore the relationships between the 83 behavioural items and to make sense of the large number of correlations between these variables. The 43 effective behavioural items comprising the BIQ were factored separately from the 40 ineffective items. This yielded statistically sound correlations resulting in extracted factors that were readily interpreted and categorized, and to which descriptive labels were attached. The resultant behavioural categories were found to be consistent with the findings of the ethnographic longitudinal research programme on cultural change that had been running in parallel. These factors provided the basis for identifying the criteria of managerial effectiveness applying in the organization.

Phase B: Criteria of leadership effectiveness research

A leadership effectiveness BIQ was compiled comprising 20 of the effective behavioural items selected from the managerial effectiveness BIQ. The statements were assessed for fit against other behavioural concepts of leadership behaviour used widely in the UK. The BIQ was developed and administered in two versions; one for managers and team leaders to 'peer rate' colleagues, and the other for team leaders to 'self-rate' themselves. Factor analysis was again used to reduce, classify and group the items into behavioural categories from which to identify positive criteria of leadership effectiveness and the leadership competencies.

Results

The positive and negative criteria of managerial effectiveness identified by the Phase A Study are as set out in Table 7.1. From these research findings it was concluded that the core managerial competencies required to be an effective manager within the organization were those determined by the behavioural underpinning of the six positive criteria.

The positive criteria of leadership effectiveness/leadership competencies identified by the Phase B Study are as set out in Table 7.2

Full details of the specific behaviours comprising each of the positive and negative criteria of managerial and leadership effectiveness can be found in Hamlin *et al.* (1998, 1999).

Table 7.1 Phase A research results

Positive criteria of managerial effectiveness	Negative criteria of managerial effectiveness
1 Empowerment/effective delegation and communicating widely	1 Tolerating poor performance and low standards
2 Active supportive leadership	2 Uncaring, self-serving management focus
3 Proactive management	3 Autocratic/dictatorial management (*lack of concern/ consideration for staff*)
4 Proactive team leadership	
5 Active development of others (*training, coaching and mentoring*)	4 Exhibiting gradist behaviour
6 Managing change	5 Narrow/parochial behaviour
	6 Resistance to change
	7 Lack of emotional control
	8 Manipulative behaviour
	9 Irrational management
	10 Entrenched management thinking

Table 7.2 Phase B research results

Positive criteria of leadership effectiveness (peer-rated)	Positive criteria of leadership effectiveness (self-rated)
I Empowering people; providing help and creating a supportive climate II Developing self; developing others and enabling involvement and participation of others in decision-making III Promoting open and honest communication and a corporate approach	I Empowering people and encouraging self-reliance in problem-solving and decision-making II Adopting a corporate approach and involving people in corporate issues III Building and developing effective teams; effective teamwork IV Providing sound, expert advice and professional support to people

Research-to-practice

Application of the 'Anglia' research findings

This section discusses the application of the research findings within 'Anglia', and the win:win benefits of the HRD Professional Partnership derived both by the collaborating organization and by the university respectively.

Benefits of the researcher–practitioner partnership to the organization

From the organizational perspective, the research results were used by the organization to inform and shape several organizational development and management development initiatives as follows.

Research-based organizational development initiatives

Part way through the CIT stage of the Phase A research programme, Dick Shepherd and Margaret Reidy used the preliminary research findings to create a research-based OD instrument that could be used at Dick's annual management conference. Its purpose was to get his managers to discuss and confront various persistent managerial behaviours associated with the traditional 'command and control' style of management, which were now inappropriate for managing effectively in the new emergent 'flexible' bureaucracy. Over 800 CIs were subjectively classified and clustered into eight categories of managerial behaviour, each comprising examples of effective and ineffective management. The OD instrument so constructed was used in syndicate workshops involving 16 groups of managers. Each group was given one category to consider in depth, and tasked to identify ways of increasing the effective and eliminating the ineffective managerial behaviours. All syndicate groups produced a wide range of ideas for change and improvement that were presented to the conference in plenary session. This approach elicited questions and resulted in intense debate on the floor. People felt secure because patently attributable CIs had been neutralized in the form of composite statements, and their identities had been rigorously protected during the CIT phase of the research; they also knew that to be included in the instrument every statement had to have had as a foundation at least three CIs. Therefore, anonymity assured the managers that no statement could be attributed to any one person. This encouraged and enabled the managers to speak out freely and to admit in open forum the problems of managerial and leadership effectiveness that did exist. As a direct outcome, managers were inspired to initiate a diverse range of OD and other HRD-related interventions based on the research findings.

Research-based management development initiatives

The managerial and leadership effectiveness research findings were also used to develop a number of 'self-analysis framework tools' to help bring about further change in the management culture of the organization, and to support people through the change process. Five were created, which focused upon the behavioural competencies of active supportive leadership, empowerment, training and development, mentoring, and coaching. By employing the concept of self-analysis, managers and team leaders were invited to gauge their own managerial/leadership styles against the behaviours comprising the framework tools. The 'leadership tool' was used as a supplementary document within the 360-degree performance appraisal system, and enabled managers to obtain feedback from their peers and/or team members without the risk of compromising their positions within the organization. A further development was the use of the 'self-analysis framework tools' as diagnostic and developmental instruments for a series of OD workshops designed to address various problem issues revealed by the managerial and leadership effectiveness research. These workshops focused on such issues as consultation and communication, gradism, cooperation within and across teams, corporate awareness and parochialism. All of the initiatives were highly successful in engaging the active interest and commitment of individuals to organizational change, particularly to the changes in management style and culture that Dick Shepherd considered essential for the future. The use of research-based OD and MD for the purpose of bringing about organizational change was particularly powerful. However, the perceived benefits and value have centred on the academic rigour and credentials of the internal research effort, the strict codes of anonymity and confidentiality that were applied, the sense of ownership of the data and the relevancy of the research.

Benefits of the researcher–practitioner partnership to the university

All parties, including the university, benefited from the research by virtue of its wide dissemination nationally and internationally in peer-reviewed academic journals including *Strategic Change* (Hamlin and Reidy, 1997), the *Journal of Applied Management Studies* (Hamlin *et al.*, 1997) and *HRDI* (Hamlin *et al.*, 1998), which are published in the UK, and *Management Development* (Hamlin *et al.*, 1999), which is published in the USA. Additionally, the work has been disseminated widely in the world of practice through four British Government sponsored public service publications targeted at top management and professional practitioners working in all parts of central government, transport, local government and the regions of the UK (see, for example, Reidy and Hamlin, 2003a, 2003b). Other HRD Professional Partnership research studies of managerial and leadership effectiveness have subsequently been carried out by the author in different types of organization, including two NHS Trust hospitals (Hamlin, 2002c, and Hamlin and Cooper, 2005), a communications service company (Hamlin and Bassi, 2006) and several other private sector companies.

Toward creating a body of generalized 'best-evidence' in support of evidence-based management development

As already mentioned, research into the issue of managerial and leadership effectiveness is sparse, and as yet a significant body of generalized 'best evidence' to support evidence-based MD practice does not exist. Not only has the number of studies been small but, as Kim and Yukl (1995) point out, different researchers have examined different sub-sets of behaviour. This has made it difficult to compare and contrast the results from one study with another in search of commonalities and generalized findings. Avolio *et al.* (1999) argue that weaknesses in research design have been the cause of such limitations on generalizing the findings in various studies. One example cited is that of the deployment of several different people to gather large volumes of data samples where there is no central control over the consistency of procedures utilized. To demonstrate the generalizability of findings, they conclude that what is called for are 'replica' studies that use common research designs and methods.

Hamlin (2004b) is one of the few researchers in recent decades who has specifically set out to demonstrate empirically the 'universality' of managerial and leadership effectiveness, and the existence of what House and Aditya (1997) refer to as 'generic leadership functions' and 'universal or near universal effective leader behaviors'. Hamlin and colleagues have carried out a cross-case analysis of the findings from three previous empirical factor analytic studies that conform closely with the call from Avolio *et al.* (1999) for 'replica' research featuring some form of 'central control'. The studies took place in three different types of organization in the UK public sector, namely a range of UK secondary schools, the Anglia Region of HM Customs and Excise (as already discussed above), and an NHS Trust hospital in the British National Health Service. A common research design and identical/near identical methods were used for these three studies. Each study was focused predominantly on middle and front-line managers, as opposed to top managers and organizational leaders who have been the focus of most management and leadership studies reported in the literature to date. In each case, as can be inferred from the details of the 'Anglia' study given above, a qualitative approach using CIT within a grounded theory mindset was used for the initial data collection, and a quantitative approach, namely factor analysis, was used for reducing and classifying the CIT data and identifying behavioural categories/criteria of effectiveness. The criteria of managerial and leadership effectiveness identified from these three studies, specific details of which can be found in Hamlin (1988, 1990, 2002b, 2002c) and Hamlin *et al.* (1998, 1999), were compared and contrasted at both the factorial and behavioural levels in search of commonalities and generalized findings revealed by the evidence of sameness, similarity and congruence of meaning. The method used was a variant of open coding applied inductively and deductively within a grounded theory mindset (Strauss and Corbin, 1990; Miles and Huberman, 1994; Flick, 2002). The criteria and underpinning behaviours found to be generalized to all three studies were extracted and grouped into a new set of composite behavioural clusters. These were then interpreted for meaning, given labels that accurately described the behavioural classification of the so derived 'generic' criteria, and then used to develop a 'generic' model of managerial and leadership effectiveness. Full details of this model can be found in Hamlin (2004b). In a subsequent study, Hamlin (2005) compared his UK-derived 'generic' model with the US-based Zenger Miller model of 'grass-roots' leadership, which had also been derived using CIT and factor analytic research methods (Russ-Eft *et al.*, 1996; Bergmann *et al.*, 1999). The primary purpose of this study was to search for commonalities across cultures in order to reveal evidence (if any) of the *functional* and *variform universality* of managerial leader effectiveness. This was achieved by contrasting the 'criteria/functions' of managerial and leadership effectiveness comprising his 'generic' model against the corresponding 'grass-roots' leadership 'strategies/competencies' comprising the Zenger Miller model. Overall, the comparative analysis revealed a very high degree of alignment, overlap, similarity and congruence of meaning. As Hamlin (2005) concludes, the extent of the commonalities between the two behavioural constructs, albeit slightly moderated by differences in the cultural environments, provides strong empirical support for the notion of the 'universality' of managerial and leadership effectiveness, and points towards the existence of generic managerial leadership functions and universal/near-universal effective manager and managerial leader behaviours, as postulated by House and Aditya (1999) and Bennis (1999). Hamlin's model has also been compared and contrasted with the criteria of managerial and leadership effectiveness resulting from a more recent HRD Professional Partnership replica study carried out within the British National Health Service, namely in collaboration with the Birmingham Women's Healthcare NHS Trust (BWHCT). These BWHCT findings have been found to be strongly generalized to the findings from Hamlin's earlier HRD Professional Partnership study carried out in another acute NHS Trust hospital (Hamlin and Cooper, 2005). The findings of the latter study are also strongly generalized to the NHS version of the 'New Model of Transformational Leadership' offered by Alban-Metcalfe and Alimo-Metcalfe (2001), as can be seen from the results of Hamlin's comparative analysis (Hamlin, 2002c). Overall, these various comparative analyses have revealed a significant and coherent 'body of knowledge' that could act as a frame of reference for dialogue and debate concerning current management and leadership practice, and as 'best evidence' in support of research-informed or evidence-based MD practice, particularly within health- and social-care settings and the wider public services. Early results from other replica studies in a number of UK private sector organizations indicate that many of the findings are held in common with the public sector findings discussed above (See Hamlin and Bassi, 2006).

Conclusion and key learning points

The 'Anglia' study is a good example of HRD Professional Partnership research of the kind advocated by Jacobs (1997). It illustrates well how rigorous, internal practice-grounded research can profoundly influence and enhance the impact of HRD practice within organizations, and thereby bridge the much talked about 'university–industry' and 'research–practice' gaps. HRD Professional Partnership research has resulted in OD and MD initiatives being developed that have been particularly effective and successful. As Dick Shepherd of 'Anglia' explained at the time, the research results that he and Margaret Reidy used to inform and shape the organization and management development interventions were of enormous value in bringing about the desired change in the management culture, and gave him the confidence and courage to proceed with the change programme (Hamlin et al., 1998; Reidy, 2001). The several HRD Professional Partnership research studies of Hamlin and his various HRD practitioner co-researchers have produced results that add significantly to a small but expanding body of generalized findings. Potentially, these could be used as 'best evidence' in support of research-informed and evidence-based management development. As evidence-based approaches to practice become more widely and firmly established in the professions of all sectors, including the management profession, it will become increasingly incumbent upon MD practitioners to be seen using relevant 'best evidence' to inform and shape their practice. Engaging with MD scholars in programmes of practice-grounded partnership research that focus upon current strategic issues is one way for MD practitioners to maximize their professional contribution to the achievement of managerial and organizational effectiveness, high/peak business performance and long-term sustainable organizational success. In light of his own experience, the author strongly commends the concept of HRD Professional Partnership research to all MD practitioners and MD scholars.

Acknowledgement

In writing this chapter the author has drawn heavily upon the ASTD 2005 Conference and Exposition proceedings paper (Hamlin and Reidy, 2005), which he co-authored with Margaret Reidy, his longstanding HRD practitioner partner in the 'Anglia' partnership research. He wishes also to acknowledge Dick Shepherd, who was the sponsor of this particular HRD Professional Partnership.

References

Academy of Management (2001) *Research Methods Division Special Call for Conference Papers on Practitioner and Practice Grounded Research*, Academy of Management Meeting, Washington, DC, August.

Adler, N., Shani, A.B. and Styre, A. (2004) *Collaborative Research in Organizations: Foundations for Learning, Change, and Theoretical Development*, London: Sage.

Agut, S. and Grau, R. (2002) 'Managerial competency needs and training requests: the case of the Spanish tourist industry', *Human Resource Development Quarterly*, 13(1): 31–51.

Alban-Metcalfe, R. and Alimo-Metcalfe, B. (2001) 'The development of a new transformational leadership questionnaire', *Journal of Occupational and Organizational Psychology*, 74(1): 1–23.

Alimo-Metcalfe, B. and Alban-Metcalfe, R.J. (2003a) 'Under the influence', *Public Sector Reform*, March: 31–5.

Alimo-Metcalfe, B. and Alban-Metcalfe, R.J. (2003b). 'Stamp of greatness', *Health Service Journal*, 113(5861): 28–32.

Alimo-Metcalfe, B. and Lawler, J. (2001) 'Leadership development in UK companies at the beginning of the twenty-first century: Lessons for the NHS?', *Journal of Management in Medicine*, 15(5): 387–404.

Alvesson, M. (2002) *Understanding Organizational Culture*, London: Sage.

Antonacoloulou, E.P. and Fitzgerald, L. (1996) 'Reframing competency in management education', *Human Resource Management Journal*, 6(1): 53–62.

Avolio, B.J., Bass, M.B. and Jung, D.I. (1999) 'Re-examining the components of transformational and transactional leadership using the Multifactor Leadership Questionnaire', *Journal of Occupational and Organizational Psychology (UK)*, 72(4): 441–63.

Axelsson, R. (1998) 'Towards an evidence based health care management', *International Journal of Health Planning and Management*, 13(4): 307–17.

Ayman, R. (1993) 'Leadership perception: the role of gender and culture', in Chemers, M.M. and Ayman, R. (eds), *Leadership Theory and Research*, San Diego, CA: Academic Press, pp. 137–66.

Barker, L. (2000) 'Effective leadership within hospice and specialist palliative care units', *Journal of Management in Medicine*, 14(5/6): 291–309.

Bass, B.M. (1997) 'Does the transactional–transformational leadership paradigm transcend organizational and national boundaries?', *American Psychologist*, 52(2): 130–9.

Bate, S.P. (1996). 'Towards a strategic framework for changing corporate culture', *Strategic Change*, 5: 27–42.

Bennett, R.D. and Langford, V. (1983) 'Managerial effectiveness', in Williams, A.P.A. (ed.), *Using Personnel Research*, Aldershot: Gower Press.

Bennis, W. (1999) 'The end of leadership: exemplary leadership is impossible without full inclusion, initiatives and co-operation of followers', *Organizational Dynamics*, 28(10): 71–80.

Bennis, W. and O'Toole, J. (2005) 'How business schools lost their way', *Harvard Business Review*, May: 1–9.

Bergmann, H., Hurson, K. and Russ-Eft, D. (1999) *Everyone a Leader: A Grassroots Model for the New Workplace*, New York: John Wiley & Sons.

Brewerton, P. and Millward, L. (2001) *Organizational Research Methods*, London: Sage.

Burgoyne, J. (1990) 'Doubts about competency', in Devine, M. (ed.), *The Photo Fit Manager*, London: Unwin, pp. 20–6.

Burgoyne, J. (1998) 'Management development for the individual and organization', *Personnel Management*, June: 40–4.

Burke, M.J. and Day, R.R. (1986) 'A cumulative study of the effectiveness of managerial training', *Journal of Applied Psychology*, 71: 232–45.

Cammock, P., Nilakant, V. and Dakin, S. (1995) 'Developing a lay model of managerial effectiveness: a social constructionist perspective', *Journal of Management Studies*, 32(4): 443–7.

Campbell, J.P., McCloy, R.A., Oppler, S.H. and Sager, C.E. (2003) 'A theory of performance', in Schmitt, N. and Borman, W.C. (eds), *Personnel Selection in Organizations*, San Francisco, CA: Jossey-Bass.

Capelli, P. and Crocker-Hefter, A. (1996) 'Distinctive human resources are a firm's core competencies', *Organizational Dynamics*, 28(2): 7–21.

Carl, D.E. and Javidan, M. (2001) 'Universality of charismatic leadership: a multi-nation study', Academy of management Conference, Washington, DC, August, Best Paper.

Chalofsky, N. (2004) 'Human and Organization Studies: the Discipline of HRD', in Egan, T. and Morris, M. (eds), *Proceedings of the Academy of Human Resource Development, Austin, Texas, March 2004*, Bowling Green, OH: Academy of Human Resource Development.

Collins, D.B. and Holton, E.F. (2004) 'The effectiveness of managerial leadership development programs: a meta-analysis of studies from 1982 to 2001', *Human Resource Development Quarterly*, 15(2): 217–48.

Conger, J.A. (1998) 'Qualitative research as the cornerstone methodology for understanding leadership', *Leadership Quarterly*, 9(1): 107–21.

Das, T.K. (2003) 'Managerial perceptions and the essence of the managerial world: what is an interloper business executive to make of the academic-researcher perceptions of managers?', *British Journal of Management*, 14(1): 23–32.

Delahaye, B. and Smith, B. (1998) 'The management development professional', in Prokopenko, J. (ed.), *Management Development: A Guide for the Profession*, Geneva, International Labour Office.

Den Hartog, D.N., Van Muijen, J.J. and Koopman, P.L. (1997) 'Transactional versus transformational leadership: an analysis of the MLQ', *Journal of Occupational and Organizational Psychology*, 70(1): 19–34.

Fiedler, F.E. (1996) 'Research on leadership selection and training: one view of the future', *Administrative Science Quarterly*, 41: 241–50.

Flanagan, H. and Spurgeon, P. (1996) *Public Sector Managerial Effectiveness: Theory and Practice in the National Health Service*, Buckingham: Open University Press.

Flanagan, J.C. (1954) 'The critical incident technique', *Psychological Bulletin*, 51(4): 327–58.

Flick, U. (2002) *An Introduction to Qualitative Research* (2nd edn), London: Sage.

Garavan, T. and McGuire, D. (2001) 'Competencies and workplace learning: some reflections on the rhetoric and the reality', *Journal of Workplace Learning*, 13(4): 144–63.

Ghoshal, S. (2005) 'Bad management theories are destroying good management practice', *Academy of Management Learning and Education*, 4(1): 75–91.

Gold, J., Rodgers, H. and Smith, V. (2003) 'What is the future for the human resource development professional? A UK perspective', *Human Resource Development International*, 6(4): 437–56.

Hambrick, D.A. (1994) 'Presidential Address: What if the academy actually mattered?', *Academy of Management Review*, 19: 11–16.

Hamlin, R.G. (1988) 'The criteria of managerial effectiveness within secondary schools', *Collected Original Resources in Education*, 12(1): 1–221. Published MPhil thesis.

Hamlin, R.G. (1990) 'The competent manager in secondary schools', *Educational Management and Administration*, 18(3): 3–10.

Hamlin, R.G. (2001a) 'Towards research-based organizational change and development', in Hamlin, R.G., Keep, J. and Ash, K. (eds), *Organizational Change and Development: A Reflective Guide for Managers, Trainers and Developers*, Harlow: FT Prentice Hall.

Hamlin, R.G. (2001b) 'A review and synthesis of context and practice', in Hamlin, R.G. Keep, J. and Ash, K. (eds), *Organizational Change and Development: A Reflective Guide for Managers, Trainers and Developers*, Harlow: FT Prentice Hall, pp. 283–96.

Hamlin, R.G. (2002a) 'Towards evidence-based HRD practice', in Stewart, J., McGoldrick, J. and Watson, S. (eds), *Understanding Human Resource Development: A Research-based Approach*, London: Routledge, pp. 93–121.

Hamlin, R.G. (2002b) 'In support of evidence-based management and research-informed HRD through HRD professional partnerships: an empirical and comparative study', *Human Resource Development International*, 5(4): 467–91.

Hamlin, R.G. (2002c) 'A study and comparative analysis of managerial and leadership effectiveness in the National Health Service: an empirical factor analytic study within an NHS Trust Hospital', *Health Services Management Research*, 15(4): 245–63.

Hamlin, R.G. (2004a) Toward evidence-based HRD: a personal journey of discovery and contribution. Inaugural Professorial Lecture, University of Wolverhampton 8th Public Lecture Programme, 8 December.

Hamlin, R.G. (2004b) 'In support of universalistic models of managerial and leadership effectiveness: implications for HRD research and practice', *Human Resource Development Quarterly*, 15(2): 189–215.

Hamlin, R.G. (2005) 'Toward universalistic modes of managerial leader effectiveness: a comparative study of recent British and American derived models of leadership', *Human Resource Development International*, 8(1): 5–25.

Hamlin, R.G. and Ash, K. (2000) 'Toward evidence-based organizational change and development', Paper presented at the NHS-P Research into Practice Conference, Birmingham, England, 13 January.

Hamlin, R.G. and Bassi, N. (2006) 'Behavioral indicators of manager and managerial leadership effectiveness: an example of HRD professional partnership research from the UK private sector', in Nafukho, F.M. and Hsin-Chih Chen (eds), *Proceedings of the 2006 AHRD International Research Conference, Ohio, February*, Bowling Green, OH: AHRD.

Hamlin, R.G. and Cooper, D.J. (2005) 'HRD professional partnerships for integrating research and practice: a case study example from the British National Health Service', in Morris, L.M. and Nafukho, F.M. (eds), Proceedings of the 2005 AHRD International Research Conference, Estes Park, Colorado, February.

Hamlin, R.G. and Reidy, M. (1997). 'Effecting change in management culture', *Strategic Change*, (6): 435–50.

Hamlin, R.G. and Reidy, M. (2005) 'Facilitating organizational change and development through professional researcher–practitioner partnerships', in Carliner, S. and Sugruc, B. (eds), *ASTD 2005 Research-to-Practice Conference Proceedings, Orlando, Florida, June*, Alexandria, VA: ASTD.

Hamlin, R.G. and Stewart, J. (1998) In support of evidence-based human resource development practice *Lancaster–Leeds Collaborative Conference: Emergent Fields in Management-Connecting Learning and Critique*, Leeds, July.

Hamlin, R.G., Reidy, M. and Stewart, J. (1997) 'Changing the management culture in one part of the British Civil Service through visionary leadership and strategically led research-based OD interventions', *Journal of Applied Management Studies*, 6(2): 233–51.

Hamlin, R.G., Reidy, M. and Stewart, J. (1998) 'Bridging the HRD research-practice gap through professional partnerships', *Human Resource Development International*, 1(3): 273–90.

Hamlin, R.G., Reidy, M. and Stewart, J. (1999) 'Effective management culture change through research-based management development: a British case study', *Management Development Forum Empire State College, State University of New York*, 2(1): 21–47.

Harrow, J. and Willcocks, L. (1990) 'Public Services Management: activities, initiatives and limits to hearing', *Journal of Management Studies*, 27(3): 281–304.

Hayes, J., Rose-Quirie, A. and Allinson, C.W. (2000) 'Senior managers' perceptions of the competencies they require for effective performance: implications for training and development', *Personnel Review*, 29(1): 48–56.

Holt, D.H. (1998) *International Management.*, Orlando, FL: Harcourt Brace and Company.

Holton, E.F. (2004) 'Implementing evidence-based practices: time for a national movement', *Human Resource Development Review*, 3(3): 187–8.

Holton, E.F., Redmann, D.H., Edwards, M.A. and Fairchild, M.E. (1998). 'Planning for the transition to performance consulting in municipal government', *Human Resource Development International*, 1(1): 35–55.

House, R.J. and Aditya, R.N. (1997) 'The social scientific study of leadership: quo Vadis?', *Journal of Management* 23(3): 409–65.

Hunter, D. (1998) 'Something soft for hard times', *Health Service Journal*, November: 20–1.

Jacobs, R.L. (1997) 'HRD professional partnerships for integrating HRD research and practice', in Swanson, R. and Holton III, E. (eds), *Human Resource Development Research Handbook: Linking Research and Practice*, San Francisco, CA: Berrett-Koehler, pp. 47–61.

Kim, H. and Yukl, G. (1995) 'Relationships of managerial effectiveness and advancement to self-reported and subordinate-reported leadership behaviors from the multiple-linkage model', *Leadership Quarterly*, 6(3): 361–77.

Lai, L.C. (1996) *A Meta-analysis of Research on the Effectiveness of Leadership Training Programs*. Unpublished doctoral dissertation, University of Winsconsin-Madison.

Latham, G.P., Wexley, K.N. and Rand, T.M. (1975) 'The relevance of behavioural criteria from the critical incident technique', *Canadian Journal of Behavioral Studies*, 7(4): 349–58.

Lees, S. (1992) 'Ten faces of management development', *Management Education and Development*, 23(2): 89–105.

Leimbach, M.P. and Baldwin, T.T. (1997) 'How research contributes to the HRD value chain', in Swanson, R. and Holton III, E. (eds), *Human Resource Development Research Handbook: Linking Research and Practice*, San Francisco, CA: Berrett-Koehler, pp. 21–46.

Likert, R. (1967) *The Human Organization*, New York, NY: McGraw-Hill.

Luthans, F., Rosencrantz, S. and Hennessey, H. (1985) 'What do successful managers really do? an observation study of managerial activities', *Journal of Applied Behavioral Sciences*, 21(3): 255–70.

Luthans, F., Welsh, D. and Taylor, L. (1988) 'A descriptive model of managerial effectiveness', *Group and Organization Studies*, 13(2): 148–62.

Margerison, C. (1991) *Making Management Development Work*, Maidenhead: McGraw-Hill.

Marks, M. (1994) *From Turmoil to Triumph: New Life after Mergers, Acquisitions and Downsizing*, New York, NY: Lexington.

Martinko, M.J. and Gardner, W.L. (1985) 'Beyond structured observation: methodological issues and new directions', *Academy of Management Review*, 10: 676–95.

Martinko, M.J. and Gardner, W.L. (1990) 'Structured observation of managerial work: a replication and synthesis', *Journal of Management Studies*, 27(3): 329–57.

McCall, M.W. (2004) 'Leadership development through experience', *Academy of Management Executive*, 18(3): 127–30.

McClagan, P. and Suhadolnik, D. (1989) *Models for HRD Practice: The Research Report*, Alexandria, VA: American Society for Training and Development.

McClean, G.N. and McClean, L.D. (2001) 'If we can't define HRD on one country, how can we define it in an international context', *Human Resource Development International*, 4(2): 313–26.

McGoldrick, J., Stewart, J.D. and Watson, S. (2002) *Understanding Human Resource Development; A Research-based Approach*, London: Sage.

Miles, M.B. and Huberman, A.M. (1994) *Qualitative Data Analysis*, Thousand Oak, CA: Sage.

Mullins, L.J. (1993) *Management and Organization Behaviour*, 3rd edn, London: Pitman.

Mumford, A. (1997) *Management Development: Strategies for Action*, London: Institute of Personnel and Development.

Mumford, A. and Gold, J. (2004) *Management Development: Strategies for Action*, London: CIPD.

Parry, K.W. (1998) 'Grounded theory and social process: a new direction for leadership research', *Leadership Quarterly*, 9(1): 85–105.

Peterson, M.F. and Hunt, J.G. (1997) 'International perspectives on international leadership', *Leadership Quarterly*, 8(3): 85–105.

Porter, L.W. and McKibbin, L.E. (1988). *Management Education and Development: Drift or Thrust into the 21st Century?* New York, NY: McGraw-Hill.

Raelin, J. (2004) 'Don't bother putting leadership into people', *Academy of Management Executive*, 18(3): 131–5.

Raelin, J. and Cooledge, A.S. (1995) 'From generic to organic competencies', *Human Resource Planning*, 18(3): 24–33.

Reidy, M. (2001) 'Managing organizational and cultural change in the Anglia executive unit of HM Customs & Excise', in Hamlin, B., Keep, J. and Ash, K. (eds), *Organizational Change and Development; A Reflective Guide for Managers, Trainers and Practitioners*, Harlow: FT Prentice Hall, pp. 156–62.

Reidy, M. and Hamlin, R.G. (2003a) 'Managerial and leadership effectiveness', *Public Service Review: Central Government*, Spring: 172–6.

Reidy, M. and Hamlin, R.G. (2003b) 'Creating and applying HR development tools', *Public Service Review: Transport, Local Government and the Regions*, Winter: 14–19.

Ruona, W.E.A. and Lynham, S. (1999) 'Toward a philosophical framework of thought and practice', in Kuchinke, K.B. (ed.), *Academy of Human Resource Development Proceedings*, Baton Rouge, LA: AHRD, pp. 206–15.

Russ-Eft, D. and Brennan, K. (2001) 'Leadership competencies: a study of leaders at every level in an organization', in Raven, J. and Stephenson, J. (eds), *Competence in the Learning Society*, New York, NY: Peter Lang, pp. 79–92.

Russ-Eft, D., Berrey, C., Hurson, K. and Brennan, K. (1996) 'Updating the meaning of leadership: a grass roots model for the new workplace', *An Essay from Zenger Miller, M2021* V.1.1 (7/96), Zenger Miller Inc., pp. 71–2.

Russ-Eft, D., Preskill, H. and Sleezer, C. (1997) *Human Resource Development Review: Research and Implications*, Thousands Oaks, CA: Sage.

Sadler, P. (1998) 'Concepts and components of management development', in Propokenko, J. (ed.), *Management Development: A Guide for the Profession*, Geneva: International Labour Office.

Sambrook, S. (2000) 'Talking of HRD', *Human Resource Development International*, 3(2): 159–78.

Shipper, F. (1991) 'Mastery and frequency of managerial behaviors relative to sub-unit effectiveness', *Human Relations*, 44(4): 371–88.

Shipper, F. (2000) 'A cross-cultural, multi-dimensional, nonlinear examination of managerial skills and effectiveness', Paper presented at the *Academy of Management Meeting*, Canada, August.

Shipper, F. and White, C.S. (1999) 'Mastery, frequency, and interaction of managerial behaviors to subunit effectiveness', *Human Relations*, 52(1): 49–66.

Smith, P.B. and Bond, M.H. (1993) *Social Psychology Across Cultures: Analysis and Perspectives*, Needham, MA: Allyn and Bacon.

Starkey, K. and Tempest, S. (2004) 'Researching our way to economic decline', in Adler, N., Shani, A.B. and Alexander, S. (eds), *Collaborative Research in Organizations: Foundations for Learning, Change, and Theoretical Development*, Thousand Oaks, CA: Sage, pp. 23–36.

Stewart, J. (1999) *Employee Development Practice*, London: FT Pitman.

Stewart, R. (1998) 'More art than science?', *Health Service Journal*, 26 March: 28–9.

Storey, J., Edwards, P. and Sissons, K. (1994) *Managers in the Making*, London: Sage.

Strauss, A.L. and Corbin, J. (1990) *Basics of Qualitative Research*, London: Sage.

Swanson, R.A. (1997) 'HRD research: don't go to work without it!', in Swanson, R.A. and Holton III, E.F. (eds), *Human Resource Development Research Handbook*, San Francisco, CA: Berrett-Koehler.

Thompson, J.E., Stuart, R. and Lindsay, P.R. (1996) 'The competence of top team members: a framework for successful performance', *Journal of Managerial Psychology*, 11(3): 48–67.

Triandis, C.H. (1993) 'The contingency model in cross-cultural perspective,' in Chemers, M.M. and Ayman, R. (eds), *Leadership Theory and Research Perspectives and Directions*, San Diego, CA: Academic Press, pp. 167–88.

Van der Velde, M.E.G., Jansen, G.W.E. and Vinkenburg, C.J. (1999) 'Managerial activities among top and middle managers: self versus other perceptions', *Journal of Applied Management Studies*, 8(2): 161–4.

Walshe, K. and Rundell, T.G. (2001) 'Evidence-based management: from theory to practice in healthcare', *The Millbank Quarterly*, 79(3): 429–57.

Walton, J. (2001) 'HRD: the power of definitions', in Aliago, O.A. (ed.), *AHRD 2001 Conference Proceedings*, Baton Rouge, LA: AHRD, pp. 1079–87.

Walumbwa, F.O., Orwa, B., Wang, P. and Lawler, J.J. (2005) 'Transformational leadership, organizational commitment, and job satisfaction: a comparative study of Kenyan and US financial firms', *Human Resource Development Quarterly*, 16(2): 235–56.

Watkins, K. (2000) 'Aims, roles and structures for human resource development', in Ruona, W.E.A. and Roth, G. (eds), *Advances in Developing Human Resources, Vol. 17. Philosophical Foundations of Human Resource Development Practice*, San Francisco, CA: Berret Koehler, pp. 54–9.

Willcocks, S.G. (1992) 'Managerial effectiveness and the public sector: a health service example', *International Journal of Public Administration*, 5(5): 4–10.

Willcocks, S.G. (1997) 'Managerial effectiveness in the NHS: a possible framework for considering the effectiveness of the clinical director', *Journal of Management in Medicine*, 1(3): 181–9.

Worrall, L. and Cooper, G.L. (1997–2002) *The Quality of Working Life Surveys 1997 to 2002: Surveying Managers' Changing Experiences*, London: Institute of Management.

Yukl, G. (1994) *Leadership in Organizations*, 3rd edn, Englewood Cliffs, NJ: Prentice-Hall.

Yukl, G., Wall, S. and Lepsinger, R. (1990) 'Preliminary report on validation of managerial practices survey', in Clark, K.E., Clark, M.B., and Albright, R.R. (eds), *Measures of Leadership*, West Orange, NJ: Leadership Library of America/UK Monograph Psychological Corporation Center, pp. 223–38.

8 A stakeholder approach to the study of management education

Lynda M. Stansfield and Jim Stewart

Introduction

There are many ways of approaching the study of management development from both theoretical and practical perspectives. While this supposed dichotomy itself might characterize two broad approaches, they are not in our view mutually exclusive. This chapter is based on a study of the design and implementation of two education-based and practical management development programmes which, as well as 'containing' theory as part of their content, were also informed by theory in their design and development. The review and evaluation of the programmes were also informed by a similar theoretical framework; that is, that of stakeholder theory. Our overall purpose, therefore, is to explore the utility of applying stakeholder theory to understanding decisions on management development and meeting associated purposes of judging effectiveness. One benefit of stakeholder theory is that the specification of 'effective' is inherently subjective and will vary depending on the interests of the different categories of parties involved, and so we are unlikely to have a universally accepted specification. That being the case, privileging the interests of one single category, which is usually the case with many perspectives on management development, is unlikely to provide a full understanding. Our objectives in this chapter can be summarized as follows:

- to describe two particular examples of qualification-based programmes
- to explore the validity and utility of applying stakeholder theory to understanding management development
- to describe and assess a set of related conceptual models of management education design and evaluation.

A theoretical perspective – what is 'stakeholder theory'?

Stakeholder theory is not new. As a concept, it originated in law, migrated to the field of strategic management, and today has a pivotal place in the study of business ethics. Stakeholder theory has strong roots in the study of corporate governance and the right to run organizations in the way that certain groups think fit. One school of thought is that shareholders, or stockholders, having a financial stake in a company, should have the last say on how that company should be run. As will be seen below, a view has developed that suggests that groups or individuals who do not necessarily have a financial investment in a company might have 'stakeholder' rights to affect the way in which the company is run. The application of this way of thinking beyond corporate governance to other aspects of organization theory has been influenced by the pluralist argument in the unitarist/pluralist dichotomy. A unitarist view of an organization proposes that the aims, goals and objectives of all who have an interest in that organization will be the same (for example, to make a profit, to serve customers, etc.). However, there is an argument that says that the traditional idea of a firm having only two groups of members, i.e. owners and employees, is outdated. In our more complex and sophisticated contemporary environment, power is now more equally distributed and management needs to be more consensual and based on partnership. This pluralist view asserts that organizations are made up of a collection of groups and individuals who have their own aims, goals and agendas that might not match those of the organization (for example, trades unions, employee groups, shareholders, etc.). Moreover, it may be argued that there are external parties whose views and interests also need to be taken into account when making decisions and taking managerial action. It is in this latter context that stakeholder theory can make a contribution. For example, Mintzberg (1983) used the stakeholder concept to assert that an organization must recognize various interest groups and take their needs and wants into account in a broad range of its activities.

Stakeholder theory has waxed and waned in popularity in the last 80 years. There was quite a vigorous debate in the 1930s between two notable academics of that time in the legal field, Berle and Dodd. Their arguments concerned a basic legal principle: whether or not those who put up the wherewithal for a business and bear the risk should be entitled to run it as they think fit (the shareholder value model), or whether or not they should have to take the views and wishes of others with no financial interests into account (the stakeholder model). Jennings (2002) reports on the way that Dodd identified two types of owner: those who have put capital into a business and those whose investment is in terms of 'cares and concerns'. Another key writer at this time was Gardiner Means, who added support to Dodd's position. Despite this initial enthusiasm, interest waned for some 20 years. The stakeholder approach then enjoyed some renewed popularity in the 1960s through the work of the Stanford Research Institute. This arose through the Institute's work into the benefits of taking a long-term view of the consequences of corporate conduct and considering the possible parties affected so as to take avoiding action (for example, in the case of breaching environmental regulations and avoiding pollution). The Stanford Research Institute called these parties 'stakeholders'. Again, little interest was shown in these ideas for the next 20 years or so until, in the 1980s, Freeman wrote a book called *Strategic Management: A Stakeholder Approach*. In this, Freeman (1984) used the stakeholder concept and applied it to issues of corporate governance and business ethics, both emerging 'hot topics' of the day. It was particularly applied to the buoyant mergers and acquisitions scene in the United States at the time to either support or oppose takeover bids. Stakeholder theory has now taken root in the UK vocabulary in a variety of different contexts – for example, in the debate around corporate social responsibility, in relation to not-for-profit sectors such as public services, and even in relation to state-encouraged pension schemes.

Stakeholder theory has been criticized on many fronts: for example, on the grounds of its lack of clarity of definition (see below); the fact that parties other than those who own companies can override the property rights of those who do; the argument that stakeholder rights can discourage organizational and individual investment; and the notion that it gives power to unenfranchised social classes, encouraging conflict (Jennings, 2002). Many of these arguments are persuasive. However, when the stakeholder approach is applied to research it makes methods available that are multi-vocal in the way they provide an opportunity to hear the voices of a number of different parties who impinge upon, and are impinged upon by, a particular experience. This, in our opinion, gives it a distinction over other research approaches that is particularly compelling.

'Stakeholder': some definitions

One of the major difficulties in stakeholder theory is the notion of a stakeholder itself. Just who or what can be called a 'stakeholder'? Stakeholders can be defined as those who have an interest of some sort or another (not necessarily financial) in the object of study. Stakeholders have been referred to as groups or individuals who either affect or are affected by organizations' attempts to realize their objectives (Freeman and Liedtka, 1997). Difficulties with defining the term 'stakeholder' have been identified (see, for example, Clarkson, 1995; Key, 1999). To illustrate the range of potential parties to the stakeholder relationship, Ellis and Dick (2003) have provided a far from exhaustive list of possible organizational stakeholders as follows:

- employee groups (on-site, off-site)
- owner groups (shareholders, institutional shareholders, founders)
- environmental concerns (local and national)
- customers (past, present and future)
- industry bodies, trade associations

- buyer groups (supply-chain co-ordinators)
- competitors/collaborators
- professional bodies (for example, legal/financial)
- local residents
- government legislative and regulatory bodies (local, national and international).

So, as we can see, the possibilities as to who or what should be taken into account as part of an organization's deliberations are wide and many. Therefore, one of the recent themes in the literature has been an attempt to clarify and categorize groups of potential stakeholders. Initially, stake-holder analysis (Mitroff, 1983) or stakeholder audits (Roberts and King, 1989) can be used to identify the groups and/or individuals who differ in their perspective on a particular issue. From this general analysis, individuals or groups can then be identified as 'being directly or indirectly affected by an organization's pursuit of its goals' (Stoner and Freeman, 1995: 63). Stakeholders can also be 'internal' or 'external' to an organization. Stoner and Freeman talk about external stakeholders as 'groups or individuals in an organization's external environment that affect the activities of an organization' (for example, trades unions, competitors, special-interest groups), and about internal stakeholders as 'groups or individuals, such as employees, that are not strictly part of an organization's environment but for whom an individual manager remains responsible' (Stoner and Freeman, 1995: 64). Stakeholder theory also presents us with a difficulty in that at first sight, all stakeholders might appear to have an 'equal' stake or say in what the organization does. Clearly in practice this is not the case, and this has led to a further set of categorizations on the basis of importance or strength of influence. For example, Frooman (1999), Jones (1995) and Clarkson (1995) talk about 'primary' stakeholders as being those without whose involvement the organization would not survive, and 'secondary' stakeholders as those who influence or affect, or are influenced or affected, but are not vital to its survival.

Stakeholder behaviour

So, how does being a stakeholder affect what we do in organizations? Despite fraught attempts in the literature to define what is and what is not behaviour, one aspect of it can be said to be the means by which we can operationalize our various roles and achieve our various goals in life. In order to do this, we can be said to operate on at least three levels: the cognitive, the affective and the behavioural. For example, being a parent involves a cognitive element (our perceptions of, motivation towards and expectations of the parent role), an affective element (our feelings and emotions about being a parent) and a behavioural element (what we do about putting our parental role into action). We would argue that, in

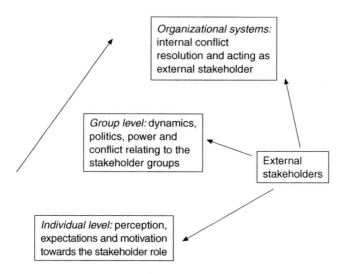

Figure 8.1 Levels of stakeholder behaviour analysis.

order to understand behaviour, we need to understand all of the elements. Likewise, we can analyse people's behaviour in organizations at three levels (Robbins, 1997). These levels are the individual level, the group level and the organizational system level. If we adapt this basic idea to reflect an application to stakeholder behaviour, we can construct the model shown in Figure 8.1.

The study of stakeholder theory at the individual level would involve individual and social psychology – for example, theories of motivation and perception, expectations and attitudes. Role theory is particularly important. In social psychology, the word 'role' usually applies to 'any pattern of behaviour involving certain rights, obligations and duties which an individual is expected, trained and, indeed, encouraged to perform in a given social situation' (*Penguin Dictionary of Psychology*). Being a stakeholder involves the adoption of a role – for example, in the field of management development, an individual may look upon his/her stake through the eyes of being a manager, as a 'lifetime learner', as a breadwinner, etc. Each of these roles will have different rights, obligations and expectations attached to them. Behaviours in organizations will differ according to the perceived stakeholding in the management development process – for example, as paymaster, as exemplary employer, as profit-maker, etc. Educational establishments' stakeholdings will differ according to their views about the roles they perform in society – for example, as a facilitator of learning, as guardian of academic standards, as gatekeeper for intellectual property, etc. An understanding of role theory is, therefore, essential when investigating the rights, obligations and expectations of parties to any social situation, for example, management development and management education. A particularly good example of stakeholder behaviour at the group and organizational level is that of political activity related to education (Burgoyne and Jackson, 1997). This describes management learning in organizations as an arena where conflicts relating to differing perspectives of purpose and values come together and become more entrenched, resolved, or more wide-spread. Looking at the nature of these interests and conflicts within a stake-holder framework is particularly useful, as doing so allows investigation in a pluralist manner with a degree of legitimacy not afforded by other theoretical and/or research approaches.

Application of stakeholder theory to management development

The stakeholder approach has already been applied successfully to studies in training and development, and the evaluation of management development initiatives (for example, Burgoyne, 1994; Mabey and Salaman, 1995; Thomson *et al.*, 2001). In particular, Chris Mabey in Thomson *et al.* (2001) draws our attention to the importance of adopting a pluralist stance to the study of management development. He argues that most of the literature on management development takes a unitarist or organizational perspective. That is only part of the picture. Mabey argues that there are clearly other parties to the development of managers, whose perspectives are largely under-represented in the literature. Working with his colleagues, Mabey has put forward a particularly compelling model that applies stake-holder theory to training and development (see, for example, the diagram in Mabey *et al.*, 1998: 381). In this model, Mabey identifies six primary stakeholders: senior managers as 'sponsors', business planners as 'clients', line managers as 'managers', individuals as 'participants', HRM staff as 'facilitators' and training specialists as 'providers'.

These stakeholders have different interests in the same phenomenon, which overlap in some respects but are largely in a 'central, negotiated territory with the power ... ebbing and flowing between the ... groupings within the organization' (Mabey *et al.*, 1998: 381).

Adopting a stakeholder approach to management education

Stakeholder theory can be a useful way in which to investigate the various dichotomies and issues in the field of management education, as it has developed a wide range of vocal and influential parties over the years with many different interests. Management education in the UK has been a major success story. Business schools as such originated in the United States, and did not take off in the UK until the late 1940s. Since then, demand for management education has blossomed. There are now around 130 business schools in the UK that offer postgraduate, post-experience programmes leading to qualifications in management. In part, the demand has been fuelled by the periodic publication of reports that are critical of the state of British management. For example, Constable and McCormick's report, *The Making of British Managers*, and Handy's report, *The Making of Managers*, both published in 1987, criticized management development in British organizations and called for more and better provision of management education and training. Responses in terms of increased activity were forthcoming from both employing organizations and the growing number of corporate education providers. There have been criticisms from some quarters about the varying quality of some of the programmes that came about as a result of the increased demand (Watson, 2001). Management education in the UK has largely developed via university business schools, and, because of this, development of programmes has been largely along knowledge-based lines. Business-school management qualifications usually have the status of degrees, or sub-degrees. The most typical award-bearing programmes in the UK are the CMS (Certificate in Management Studies), the DMS (Diploma in Management Studies) and the MBA (Master of Business Administration). There has long been a debate regarding the content of management education: should it be knowledge- or competence-based? Few programmes have traditionally involved substantive learning via workplace activity beyond academic assignments based around the students' own organizations or a host organization where students are not in employment at the same time as conducting their studies. Whilst the traditional approach has prevailed for many years, as Prince and Stewart (2000) observe, the ways in which management education is delivered in the future may be changing. Meister (1998) reports evidence from the United States that organizations want to become more involved in collaborations with universities in order to engage in effective corporate management education. We have seen developments along these lines in the US and the UK with the growth of corporate universities (Walton, 1999). Stewart (1999) asserts that organizations are becoming more sophisticated in specifying their management education requirements. Prince and Stewart (2000) suggest that partnerships between organizations and business schools are increasing. Whilst they talk about a two-way partnership between organization and business school, there is another, possibly even more powerful, partnership model. Management education programmes that involve three-way partnerships between the organization, the business school and an outside private provider add another dimension. This can bring a number of advantages to all parties and enhance the quality of the programme. If, however, we adopt a stakeholder approach, another party enters the arena: the participant. There is increasing evidence that participants on management education programmes are becoming more sophisticated in their role and demands as 'consumers', even when their programmes are sponsored by their employers. Stakeholder approaches imply expectations and responsibilities. In the context of management education, then, these relationships can be represented as a series of models.

Inspired by Mabey and colleagues' original concept, and for the purposes of illustrating these relationships, each of the principal stakeholder groups has been given a name as follows:

- *the Provider* – the party that designs, delivers and assesses the programme
- *the Commissioner* – the party that ultimately bears the financial cost of the programme and has vested interests in its effectiveness
- *the Consumer* – the party that goes through the programme itself
- *the Verifier* – the party that assures the quality of the programme and makes the award.

Four major variants of management education can be identified, although this does not exclude the possibility of variant others. First, there is the scenario where the participant pays for his or her own course and attends an 'open programme', for example a part-time MBA at a university. Second, there is the scenario where the participant is sponsored and attends an open programme. Third, there is a style of management education where the organization wishes to be involved in designing an in-house programme in conjunction with an academic provider. Lastly, there is the kind of programme where a commercial provider enters into a partnership with an academic institution to design and deliver an in-house corporate programme. These variants of management education programmes are represented diagrammatically in Figures 8.2 to 8.5. Each is briefly discussed.

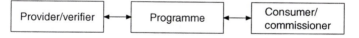

Figure 8.2 Self-funded/open programme model.

Figure 8.3 Sponsored/open programme model.

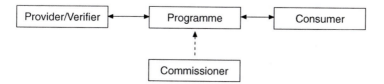

Figure 8.4 Two-way partnership model.

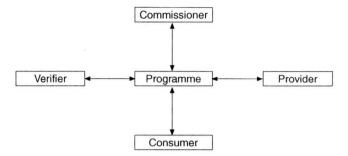

Figure 8.5 Three-way partnership model.

In the self-funded/open programme model (Figure 8.2), the main stakeholder groups are the university, which performs the roles of both Provider and Verifier, and the participant, who is both Consumer and Commissioner, paying his or her own fees. As it is an open programme, there will be participants from several sectors and organizations, therefore organizational input will be small – if indeed there is any at all.

In the sponsored/open programme model (Figure 8.3), organizations as fee-payers have a commissioning interest, but as this programme is open an organization is likely to have a weak relationship to the design and delivery. This may or may not involve feedback on participants' progress, dependent upon the Provider/Verifier's policy. Therefore, the relationship is likely to be one-way.

In the two-way partnership model (Figure 8.4), the role of the Commissioner is much strengthened. The organization has an important part to play in the design and sometimes even the delivery of the programme. It may well receive detailed feedback on how the course has gone, and in some situations on how participants have performed. The programme is tailored to the needs and circumstances of the organization. A criticism of this kind of model is that, by making these programmes focus on one organization, participants do not have the opportunity to learn from other organizations and/or sectors.

In the three-way partnership model (Figure 8.5), the roles of Provider and Verifier are separated. The university retains the role of Verifier, whilst another party takes up the role of Provider. The relationships of the organization and the participant are retained. Of course, the programme may not be completely designed and delivered by an outside provider. This model can also work in the case of a part provision by a third party.

From all this, it can be seen that in management education roles can be different and varied, making it an ideal field in which to apply a stakeholder approach.

A research context: the programmes

We now move on to examine the ideas discussed so far in application by outlining two experimental management education programmes, which provide the focus of our study. These follow the 'three-way partnership' model outlined in Figure 8.5.

For the last two years, colleagues at a UK university business school and a private provider have been developing a suite of in-house management education/development programmes leading to a university postgraduate Certificate and Diploma in Management based entirely in the organization and assessed by work-related means. A follow-on Masters level programme in Strategic Change Management has just been launched and has recruited a healthy cohort of students.

The management development programmes are a specially designed Certificate in Management (CiM) and Diploma in Management (DiM), which are recognized postgraduate programmes validated and awarded by a UK university. The CiM is a full postgraduate certificate, and the DiM is a postgraduate diploma that has equivalence to the Diploma in Management Studies. The way that the programmes have been set up is unusual in the higher education sector. They operate as the intellectual property of a private management development provider, which operates a franchise with the university to promote, develop, deliver and assess these programmes. Participants register as students of the university, but apart from the usual quality assurance procedures, including the submission of samples of assessed work to external examiners appointed by the university and the ultimate award of the qualification, the university itself has no direct involvement with the programmes.

The programmes have been run in a variety of different settings – for example, in an international manufacturing organization, a national trade association, and even with private individuals on an open programme basis. Two of these scenarios are presented below.

Method

Two of the provider's client organizations were used as case studies. The evidence came from several sources, based on a stakeholder approach to the evaluation of training and development (see above). We looked at four stakeholder parties: the Commissioner (the organization), the Provider (the consultancy), the Verifier (the partner academic institution) and the Consumer (participants).

For the Commissioner, data were gathered via feedback interviews with senior managers. For the Provider, an interview was conducted with the managing director, who was also the prime designer and deliverer of the management development programmes. For the Verifier, data were gathered via a series of meetings with a senior representative from the management department of the university. As far as the Consumers were concerned, data were obtained via two main sources: post-course evaluations and face-to-face interviews.

Case study 1: The manufacturing company

Organization X is a medium-sized manufacturing organization operating in the private sector in the north of England. It employs about 350 people in a range of capacities, including management, technical and shop-floor workers. The management development programme targeted junior to middle managers – those, in the opinion of the directors, 'with potential for senior management in the future'. Participants were invited by the directors to take part. All participants were interviewed and fully briefed by the Provider before signing up to the programme. The Provider had conducted two prior meetings with the main board directors, explaining and discussing the programme in detail and gathering enough information to customize and adapt the 'core' programme to suit the client's business needs.

Students went through the Certificate programme first. There was an initial group size of 12, and participants attended one day-long session every month for eight months. Following this programme, participants submitted their portfolios, which were assessed by the tutor and verified by a senior member of the university's management department academic staff. Successful participants were then awarded a university Certificate in Management. Those successful students who wanted to progress moved on to the Diploma programme.

Case study 2: The service organization

Organization Y is a service organization operating in the private sector. This is a national company, organized through regional offices with a headquarters in the north of England. It employs around 100 people, principally professionals and support staff. The management development programmes were at both Certificate and Diploma levels. The format of the programmes differed little to those designed for Organization X, apart from the fact that case studies and examples were slanted towards a service sector organization rather than a manufacturing one.

Around 30 students went through the Certificate programme. As in the case above, successful students wishing to progress went on to the diploma programme.

Results and discussion

It was found that there are significant advantages to be gained by all parties by adopting a collaborative approach. There are also some disadvantages.

For the *Commissioner*, the approach increases considerably the amount of influence and input that organizations have in respect of the management education programme. It gains the advantage that work-related projects can be used as the learning vehicle. Not only does its staff learn using real live issues; the issues themselves may well also become resolved as a result of the attention afforded to them. If the impact of the programmes on the organization's effectiveness is more overt in this way, then the organization may find it easier to evaluate the investment it has made, and politically the programme may well gain a greater degree of regard amongst the key organizational stakeholders than might otherwise be the case with open programmes. However, the use of a small Provider can mean that there may not be the same breadth of experience as there might be when using a conventional university business school or larger consultancy and there may not be effective back up in case of illness or inability to deliver the programmes.

For the *Consumer*, this approach may well give a way of using a style of learning that is more suited to the mature adult experienced manager. There is a greater degree of immediacy and relevance to learning that is work-related and work-based. The methods of assessment may well be better suited to adult learners, especially for those not experienced in more traditional methods such as examinations. The increased emphasis on personal lifetime development has proved to be particularly useful for mature adult learners. The portfolios have, for example, in many cases become 'living documents' that are regularly revisited, revised and utilized to facilitate future development.

For the *Verifier*, the main advantages seem to have been to provide ways of extending a traditional management education offering in a novel and innovative manner. In the particular cases studied here, the university received an income stream by way of a licence fee for very little academic and administrative time and effort. The Provider organized everything to do with the programme, including the marketing, apart from the essential quality control procedures. This is a very cost-effective way of delivering part of a business school's portfolio. It also makes staff with the right mix of academic and commercial skills available to it without the need to employ them directly.

For the *Provider*, the approach makes available a strand of business that would otherwise be unavailable to the commercial consulting community. Several people who have the necessary academic and commercial skills do not wish to be formally employed in an academic institution, but would like to do this kind of work. This approach enables them to do so. The principals of provider organizations have the freedom to market, design, deliver and assess the programmes in their own ways, without undue interference from academic bodies. However, they can avail themselves of necessary quality assurance processes to enable their programmes to have desirable and transferable qualifications attached to them. This is a very powerful marketing tool. One of the downsides, however, is that, if successful, small Providers may well be bought out by larger training organizations and the original aims, philosophies and intentions may well be lost.

The implications of what we have learned from these two case studies for future developments in management education are wide ranging. As we have seen, there are distinct advantages to all parties in the collaboration approach. This does not mean that there is now no place for traditional management education such as the MBA. Rather than seeing these programmes as direct competition to existing university-based management education, the authors see them as exciting niche products that can complement and inform traditionally taught programmes, and as a means of extending the portfolio of the conventional business school in a very cost-effective way.

Conclusion and learning points

We have limited the discussion of the research material generated in the study and the findings that can be drawn from them. However, it is clear that the stakeholder approach has the advantage that it can be both a theory and a method. Stakeholder mapping can be a useful tool for any and all of the parties to use when considering a management education initiative in the planning, design and delivery stages, and for the evaluation of programmes. The process can help to elicit important perceptions of key stakeholders from several perspectives, and their expectations, roles and responsibilities, providing a pluralistic framework to guide thinking and deliberation. This means that decisions and judgements are not limited to or exclusively determined by one set of interests. Application of stakeholder theory also, we would argue, opens up possibilities in relation to management education and management development more widely, as demonstrated by the two cases in our study. A further benefit of stakeholder theory is the potential it offers for resolving apparent and actual conflict between the different parties involved in management development.

The key learning point from our study is that management development can be accomplished in novel and innovative ways and does not have to be stuck in traditional approaches and models. A further learning point is that stakeholder theory has a lot to offer in the theory and practice of management development. Researchers will, we believe, benefit from applying the theory in analysing decision-making in relation to management development initiatives and also in evaluation studies. The latter will also be of benefit to practitioners. Moreover, using the theory will benefit practitioners in making decisions on, for example, design of programmes and, as applied to inform our conceptual models, selection of potential partners.

References

Burgoyne, J.G. (1994) 'Stakeholder Analysis', in Cassell, C. and Symon, G. (eds), *Qualitative Methods in Organizational Research*, London: Sage.

Burgoyne, J. and Jackson, B. (1997) 'The arena thesis: Management development as a pluralistic meeting point', in Burgoyne, J. and Reynolds, M. (eds), *Management Learning*, London: Sage.

Clarkson, M.B.E. (1995) 'A stakeholder framework for analyzing and evaluating corporate social performance', *Academy of Management Review*, 20: 92–117.

Constable, J. and McCormick, R. (1987) *The Making of British Managers*, London: BIM/CBI.

Ellis, S. and Dick, P. (2003) *Introduction to Organizational Behaviour*, London: McGraw-Hill.

Freeman, E. and Liedtka, J. (1997) 'Stakeholder capitalism and the value chain', *European Management Journal*, 15: 286–96.

Freeman, R.E. (1984) *Strategic Management: A Stakeholder Approach*, Marshfield, MA: Pitman.

Frooman, J. (1999) 'Stakeholder influence strategies', *Academy of Management Review*, 24: 191–205.

Handy, C. (1987) *The Making of Managers*, London: MSC/NEDO/BIM.

Jennings, M.M. (2002) 'Stakeholder theory: letting anyone who's interested run the business – no investment required' (available at: www.stthom.edu/cbs/conferences/marianne_jennings.html).

Jones, N. (1995) 'Supply chain management', *Brewer*, 81: 194.

Key, S. (1999) 'Toward a new theory of the firm: a critique of stakeholder "theory"', *Management Decision*, 37: 317–28.

Mabey, C. and Salaman, G. (1995) *Strategic Human Resource Management*, Oxford: Blackwell.

Mabey, C., Salaman, G. and Storey, J. (1998) *Human Resource Management: A Strategic Introduction*, Oxford: Blackwell.

Meister, J. (1998) *Corporate Universities: Lessons in Building a World-class Workforce*, New York: McGraw-Hill.

Mintzberg, H. (1983) *Power In and Around Organizations*, Englewood Cliffs, NJ: Prentice-Hall.

Mitroff, I. (1983) *Stakeholders of the Organizational Mind*, San Francisco, CA: Jossey-Bass.

Prince, C. and Stewart, J. (2000) 'The dynamics of the corporate education market and the role of business schools', *Journal of Management Development*, 19: 207–19.

Robbins, S.P. (1997) *Essentials of Organizational Behavior*, 5th edn, Upper Saddle River, NJ: Prentice-Hall.

Roberts, N.C. and King, P.J. (1989) 'The stakeholder audit goes public', *Organizational Dynamics*, Winter: 63–79.

Stewart, J. (1999) *Employee Development Practice*, London: FT Pitman Publishing.

Stoner, J.A.F. and Freeman, R.E. (1995) *Management*, Englewood Cliffs, NJ: Prentice-Hall.

Thomson, A., Mabey, C., Storey, J., Gray, C. and Iles, P. (2001) *Changing Patterns of Management Development*, Oxford: Blackwell.

Walton, J. (1999) *Strategic Human Resource Development*, Harlow: Pearson Education.

Watson, S. (2001) Keynote address at the Bradford University School of Management Re-naming Celebration, 22 June.

9 Raising future leaders

Claire Ponsford and Graham Borley

Introduction

The chapter reviews Panasonic UK's strategy of developing its own future leaders rather than looking for replacements on the open market. This strategy was pursued through the Panasonic UK (PUK) 'Future Leaders' project, the main objectives of which were:

- to investigate the extent of business and financial risk to PUK from significant perforations in its management structure as a result of losing key personnel and knowledge;
- to ascertain employee and management perceptions about managing succession;
- to consider the use of competency models as an approach of assessing managerial ability;
- to assess development programmes for future leaders;
- using this research, to make recommendations to PUK regarding the plan to manage leadership continuity in order to ensure that they have the future skills required for sustainability.

The theoretical context of the chapter considers the arguments for and against developing leadership potential internally. The research context is based on a case study relating to PUK's Future Leaders programme (a programme to develop people with leadership potential from within PUK), in which the authors present interview data from current and prospective leadership programme candidates and an analysis of programme costs and effectiveness weighed against the perceived risk of the programme failing to effectively address leadership succession management in PUK. The term 'succession management' will be defined, and points of interest may include the cross-cultural leadership dilemmas facing PUK as the UK arm of a Japanese multi-national organization.

Organizations are growing more acutely aware of the importance of retaining vital members of staff as they realize the substantial impact that demographic changes could have upon them. These changes are illustrated by an aging society, mass retirement of baby-boomers and an acute shortage of talent to take their place. This will dictate that, for many organizations, their future may be jeopardized if they do not attract, develop and retain the very best leaders. Failure to develop talent will force them to compete aggressively for talented staff in a decreasing market.

This is supported by the study conducted by McKinsey & Co. in 1997 (covering more than 120 companies and 13,000 executives), which suggested, 'the most imperative resource within an organization over the next 20 years will be talent' (www.Mckinsey.com). The survey exposed the 'war for talent' as a critical driver of performance, and demonstrated that the quality of people is vital to an organization if it wishes to gain a competitive advantage. As such, companies must take proactive steps to develop leadership talent from within and adopt strategies to take control of their human resourcing needs in the future, in order to compete and survive.

Organizational context

PUK is the local sales and logistics company of the large multi-national organization Matsushita Electrical Industrial Co Ltd. (MEI) of Japan, one of the world's largest consumer electronics manufacturers. Konosuke Matsushita founded MEI in 1918 in Osaka, Japan, at the age of 23, with just three employees. Working from home, he invented and produced the first product; a two-way socket. Over the years the organization has grown and diversified into new product markets, escalating the product range to currently comprise over 15,000 products being manufactured in over 40 different countries, employing 290,000 staff and accounting for £35 billion net sales worldwide.

PUK was established in 1972 in Slough, and began trading in its first year with just 34 staff, achieving a turnover of £6 million. Following substantial growth, PUK moved to a purpose-built site in Bracknell, Berkshire in 1989 – currently the UK headquarters for Business and Consumer Products and supported by a national distribution centre in Northampton. At the end of this financial year, PUK achieved record sales turnover of £850 million.

MEI has created a Basic Business Philosophy (BBP) that has become a major plank of its successful growth strategy. This includes value statements that firmly put people on the agenda – for example, 'we are committed to supporting, advising and developing all staff through line management to enable them to achieve their own and the Company's ongoing business objectives'. The BBP also commits to putting 'people before products' and supporting Konosuke Matsushita's company belief, developed in 1929, that 'progress and development can be realized only through the combined efforts and cooperation of each employee of our company' (Company Creed, Konosuke Matsushita, 1929). PUK had therefore already identified the importance of its people for organizational success. Nonetheless, up until the creation of the Future Leaders programme the organization (PUK) had no formal system in place proactively to ensure leadership continuity, and little effort had been made to ensure that, in the event of losing key leaders, the organization would not face gaping holes in its management structure.

In March 2004, a review took place that identified business critical job roles and highlighted successors with the competence to ensure continuity. The review assessed each role within the organization against a set of criteria that evaluated the financial risk to the organization if that role was left vacant; that is, roles that if vacated for a prolonged period would result in a significant negative impact on the operation of the business. The results of the business critical risk analysis determined a small number of business activities where PUK would be vulnerable if it lost role incumbents; that is, where there was little or no bench strength (i.e. ready-made replacements for key roles) or reserve competence. Interestingly, none of these were in management roles.

The business critical risk analysis, whilst seen as essential in assessing PUK's exposure and response to current risk, did not identify its future requirements. As such, a different process was thought necessary to provide the bench strength for future leadership roles; that is, to manage leadership continuity to ensure that PUK senior managers have the required skills to ensure business sustainability.

Theoretical context

Understanding succession management

The term 'succession management' is often confused with the traditional approach of replacement planning (sometimes known as the 'bus-stop' approach), or seen as a form of 'risk management that aims to reduce the risk of catastrophe by concentrating on pre-selecting back-up people for key positions' (Rothwell, 2001: 7). Neither should the term be confused with 'succession planning', which Hirsh (2000: 4) defines as 'a process by which one or more successors are identified for key posts'.

Succession management is a much more comprehensive process, with scope beyond succession planning and an aim to 'ensure the continued effective performance of an organization by making provision for the development and replacement of key people over time' (Rothwell, 2001: 6).

Approaches to succession management

The process of succession management is constantly evolving as a response to many changes in the workplace and 'rapidly changing business cultures where the future is uncertain' (IRS, 2002: 37). Succession planning has come a long way from just putting peoples' names in boxes on organization charts, and has had to adapt to unstable business environments with rapidly changing structures in order to succeed in the ever more competitive economic climate. Organizations are now developing 'transparent, cross-functional, flexible approaches that are focused on proactively developing individuals' (IRS, 2002: 37), and finding a balance between achieving the aspirations of the employees and those of the organization to ensure continuity in key positions.

Although, from the literature, it appears that there is no single, unique approach to succession management, it is possible to identify key themes and emerging practices that appear in the different approaches. These seem to fall into the general areas of either developing specific people for specific roles, or the 'talent pool' approach, which seeks to identify people with general potential and develop them for possible opportunities. The other major debate is about whether the process should be overt or covert. It seems that most modern thinking is moving towards an overt and inclusive approach, but it is still quite common for organizations to have a closed succession plan list of which very few people are aware; for example, PUK adopted this approach prior to the inception of the Future Leaders programme.

Focus on roles not jobs

Instead of identifying successors for specific posts, succession management is concerned with developing 'pools' of high-potential candidates who will be ready to assume leadership positions as and when required by the organization. By creating 'succession pools which develop groups of high-potential candidates for key positions in general' (Byham *et al.*, 2002: 17), organizations are able to move away from over-reliance on static replacement lists that target one or two handpicked people or 'back-ups' for specific jobs. This makes the difficult challenge faced by organizations of planning for roles that may not yet exist less problematic, as they are able to 'develop generic skills and competencies needed for a variety of roles rather than those required for specific posts' (IRS, 2000: 6).

Transparency

Historically, succession management in PUK was frequently an 'underground' process where senior managers kept private replacement lists and, rather than risk offending anyone, the organization adopted a philosophy of secrecy. The potential benefit to the organization was that they were able to keep their options open, especially as business conditions and the associated requirement for different types of skills to fill key vacancies changed. Hirsh (2000) suggests that openness about the succession planning process – to include the overt selection and development of individuals within that process – is critical for matters of staff motivation and retention. Rothwell (in Wells, 2003: 49) argues that superstars may leave the organization because they don't see a future for themselves – a perspective countered by Wells (2003: 49), who suggests that organizations need to consider how they manage individual expectations when sharing this information about who is included in the programme as 'star workers may stop performing because they believe a promotion is in the bag'.

The view taken at PUK was that the advantages of managing an open programme – for example, increased motivation and reduced staff turnover through opportunities for development/progression – should be a determinant of what was the best option for the company.

Contribute to the organization's strategic business plan

In order to remain competitive in fierce markets, organizations have constantly to rethink their business strategies. This inevitably impacts on the number of leadership positions and the skill set needed. Succession management can help an organization to 'align its business goals and its human capital needs by anticipating changes in management' (www.nature.com) and ensure that employee development within succession pools focuses on the skills and competencies necessary to meet business objectives. Rothwell (2001: 17) supports this view by suggesting that succession management should be 'integrated and supportive of such activities as organizational strategic plans, human resource plans and human resource development plans'.

Why manage succession?

> Businesses that don't take proactive steps to plan for future talent needs at all levels using their entire diverse workforce will face certain disruptions, heavy financial costs, and even disasters, when key employees retire or are lured away by competitors.
> (www.hubbardnhubbardinc.com/succession_planning.htm)

This indicates that the continued survival of an organization depends on having the right people in the right places at the right time. PUK's experience suggests that trying to find and attract leadership talent externally is proving ever more difficult. Even a simple analysis of the demographics in the UK workforce predicts that this will become more difficult over time as the average age of the workforce increases. This effect, combined with all the elements that work against an organization as they try to recruit leaders externally, makes succession management an advantageous strategy for a number of reasons.

Competition for talent

The business pressure for success will intensify competition for talent. Finding, attracting and retaining key talent with the right competencies will become more difficult over the next few years. The McKinsey study conducted in 1997 and found on their website (www.Mckinsey.com) high-lighted the colossal task that many organizations will face to attract talent as a shortfall in executive talent is exposed. Organizations that fail to think strategically about how succession is managed and 'delay addressing this critical issue may find the repercussions of a sudden employee loss disastrous' (www.execeptionalleadership.com).

Demographic changes

Demographic changes also provide organizations with another compelling reason for managing succession. With the 'baby boom' generation now facing retirement, 'there will be a significant shortage of qualified talent as subsequent generations are either too few in number or too inexperienced to fulfil the demand' (www.tdserver1.fnal.gov).

Loss of valuable workers

Fulmer and Conger (2004: 8) suggest that, without an effective succession management process, organizations could lose their knowledge workers, assigning them as 'those who carry their expertise between their ears'. These workers are vital to an organization, as they possess specialist know-ledge/brainpower that is unique and often cannot be transferred or repli-cated. A survey conducted by William Rothwell supports this theory (sent to 742 members of the Society for Human Resources Management, SHRM), indicating that the most important reason for succession manage-ment is to 'provide increased opportunities for high potential workers to improve retention of talented people' (Rothwell, 2001: 10).

Unanticipated loss

Succession management helps an organization to prepare for unexpected events. It is often difficult to plan for the unimaginable, but the sudden illness or death of critical employees can have disastrous effects on an organization and affect its ability to execute its business plan. Although it is not feasible to plan for every possible scenario – particularly for the loss of several key leaders at the same time – it is entirely realistic 'for organi-zations to take a close look at what is required to keep a business running if key executives suddenly depart' (Greengard, 2001: 34). Recent world events illustrate how important succession management is. When the World Trade Center and Pentagon attacks took place in September 2001, several companies had not only to confront the reality that key talent and brain power were gone forever, but that they also had to cope with gaping holes in their management structure.

The cost of not managing succession

Prior to 2002 the business need to plan for succession in PUK was reviewed, but there was no examination of the financial implications of not having individuals with the right skills and competencies ready to step into key positions. There are several factors to consider when calculating the cost of replacing a highly performing individual. The Chartered Institute of Personnel and Development (CIPD) uses four criteria to establish this outlay (www.cipd.co.uk):

- leaving costs – payroll and personnel administration;
- replacement costs – recruitment, interview time, replacement fees;
- transition costs – training expenditure, unproductive time whilst learning, induction;
- indirect costs – loss of customer service/satisfaction.

The CIPD Labour Turnover Survey 2003 (www.cipd.co.uk), which surveyed over 500 companies across industry sectors, estimates the replacement cost for managerial positions at approximately £7,000 per leaver. However, this figure is an average and takes no account of the lost productivity and impact on customer elements, which can be many times more than the cost of replacement.

Development Dimensions International (DDI), a research specialist organization, offers a more comprehensive approach to calculating the cost of filling open positions (www.ddiworld.com), suggesting that the factors in Table 9.1 should be included in the calculation.

This provides a reasonable checklist that could be used to determine the cost of replacing a staff member. There is no attempt to quantify the costs, but it clearly suggests an outlay beyond the cost of recruitment. However, it makes no attempt to quantify the loss of earning potential or

Table 9.1 Cost of filling open positions

Direct costs	Indirect costs
Advertising, employment agencies and job fairs	Time spent conducting recruitment and exit interviews
Screening applicants	Severance pay
Selection process	Lost productivity for staff and candidates
Travel costs	
Training costs	Costs of bringing new hires up to speed

damage to customer relations that could occur during the period when the new incumbent begins and is not performing at the same level of achievement in as someone proficient in the job.

Identifying talent

Identifying high-potential individuals is the foundation of any succession management programme. As a means of identifying talent historically, performance is frequently used, but this is of little use when attempting to determine potential for roles where the candidates have no experience. Organizations have learnt that this process is flawed because 'individuals with high performance outcomes at one level do not always repeat that high performance at the next level' (Fulmer and Conger, 2004: 45).

As a result, organizations have become more interested in assessing a person's potential for development, incorporating leadership competencies into their assessments to 'help clarify differences between outstanding and average performers' (Rothwell, 2001: 78).

Competency models

The use of competency models to identify future talent and leadership potential has emerged as a fundamental tactic for many succession management programmes.

Organizations that rely on an individual's current performance to identify talent for future leadership positions have found that they rarely proceed beyond a traditional approach of replacement planning. Rothwell (2001: 80) supports this idea, suggesting that competency modelling 'provides a newer way to identify characteristics linked to exemplary job performance than traditional approaches'.

Engaging competency models allows organizations to provide a fair and objective process against which individuals' future talent potential is assessed. The activity also conveys 'clear expectations for roles and for levels of performance to employees' (Fulmer and Conger, 2004: 49).

Research suggests that earlier competency models contained exhaustive lists of competencies; however, recently there has been a shift away from this. It could be argued that this shift derives from the work of Hamel and Prahalad, who introduced the concept of 'core competencies' in a *Harvard Business Review* article (Hamel and Prahalad, 1990: 71–91) which encourages organizations to simplify the number of competency dimensions to those core behaviours associated with successful leaders. The American Productivity and Quality Center's 2001 Study of best practice organizations (Fulmer and Conger, 2004: 51) found that their organizations 'begin with a core set of competencies – behaviours, mindsets and values that they believe should be shared company wide'.

Development tools for internal successors

For a succession management programme to be effective, an organization must have a process in place to replace critical role incumbents as vacancies occur. To prepare those individuals for promotion, an organization has an obligation to do more than merely identify high-potential employees. The American Productivity and Quality Center's 2001 Study of Best Practice Organizations (found in Fulmer and Conger, 2004: 80) found unanimous agreement that simply 'identifying high-potential employees is not enough'. It would seem that organizations that engage in a succession management programme should create developmental activities and development planning for high-potential employees that challenge and prepare them for future tests.

Research context

The main aim of the research discussed in the chapter was to investigate the business risk to PUK from losing key personnel and associated knowledge. A further aim was to explore possible approaches to managing succession that PUK could adopt to ensure leadership continuity. The research comprised four elements as outlined below:

1   *Survey:* a questionnaire was distributed to gather employee opinions about leadership development within PUK. Through analysis of the resultant data it was possible to discover employee attitudes to leadership development and their opinions regarding the design of the programme, and to discover any potential hostile or negative reactions to the process.
2   *Analysis of personnel database:* details of staff service, age profile and time to retirement within the team leader to director level grades were obtained via the personnel database. The data were used to assess potential business risk; that is, either current gaps or future loss of personnel and knowledge that would leave significant perforations in the management structure.
3   *Financial risk assessment:* using a combination of methodologies, it was possible to investigate the replacement cost of losing critical members of the organization. This provided an insight into the monetary risk to PUK, should it choose not to implement a succession management programme.
4   *Focus group meeting:* a meeting was held with the authors and four PUK top executives to ascertain their viewpoints associated with the selection and development of 'high flyers' within the organization. Other issues, concerns and criteria about the succession management programme were also discussed.

Analysis and evaluation of main findings

Staff survey

From 160 questionnaires distributed 100 were returned, giving a response rate of 60 per cent. The results are summarized below.

Attitudes towards a succession management programme

The results of the survey showed that the majority of employees (91 per cent) believe PUK should implement a succession management programme (see Figure 9.1). The general consensus showed that respondents favoured such a programme. They stated that a large company such as Panasonic, where the day-to-day running of the organization is largely dependent on the employees, should be proactively developing its staff to ensure that it can keep on running should employees leave.

The small number of respondents who thought that PUK should not have a succession management programme identified that the organization had effectively operated without one since being established in the UK, so questioned the relevance of implementing one now.

Benefits of a succession management process – to the organization

Of the respondents, 40 per cent recognized that by having a succession management process it was possible to ensure leadership continuity – consequently limiting the risk of large gaps in the management structure that could leave an organization operationally challenged. A further 17 per cent of employees believed that, by having a succession management programme, it would encourage the retention of effective leaders who possessed specialist, irreplaceable knowledge (see Figure 9.2).

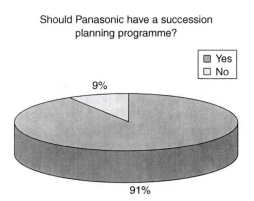

Should Panasonic have a succession planning programme?

■ Yes
□ No

9%

91%

Figure 9.1 Should PUK have a succession planning programme?

Benefits to Panasonic

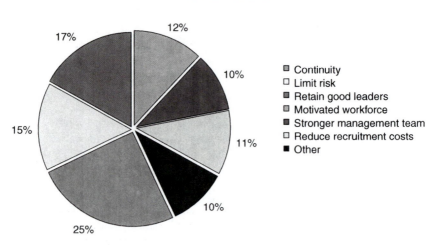

Figure 9.2 Benefits to PUK.

These findings suggest that employees were aware of the main reasons why succession management had become important for many organizations.

Benefits of a succession management process – to the individual

Figure 9.3 indicates that the majority of individuals (34 per cent) believed that career development is the main advantage of having a succession

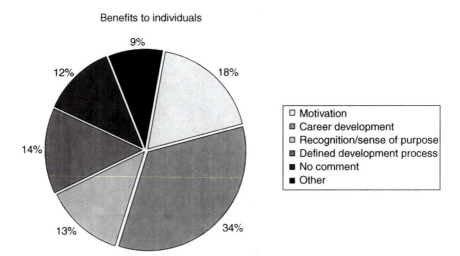

Figure 9.3 Benefits to individuals.

management process. Associated with this, 14 per cent of the respondents felt that a succession management process would provide them with a defined development process.

Of the respondents, 18 per cent felt that their motivation levels would increase with the implementation of a succession management process largely because it would recognize 'high potentials' and provide future direction and objectives to achieve.

Management recruitment

Of the respondents, 71 per cent favoured a combination of external recruitment and internal development to fill management positions within PUK (see Figure 9.4).

Of the 71 per cent of respondents who preferred this method, the majority felt that it enabled an importation of new ideas and different ways of working, whilst also giving promotional opportunities to internal staff. This implies that, if the organization were to implement a succession management programme and thus support the development of internal employees to fulfil management positions, they believed that external candidates should be considered when making appointment decisions.

Entry into the process

Figure 9.5 indicates that respondents would prefer an open management nomination as the method of entry into a succession management process.

The 9 per cent who suggested self-nomination into the process did recommend that the nomination should be evaluated and countersigned

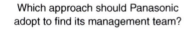

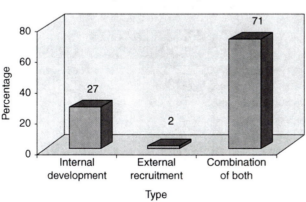

Figure 9.4 Approaches to finding management team.

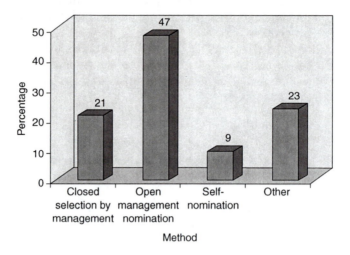

Figure 9.5 Candidate selection.

by the individual's line manager or by Personnel. However, a large percentage of respondents suggested that other methods of candidate selection should be considered.

Criteria for selection

It is evident from Figure 9.6 that the majority of respondents believed that the most important criterion in selecting individuals for the programme was 'current performance'. Although this contradicts some of the literature (for example, Fulmer and Conger (2004: 45) suggest that

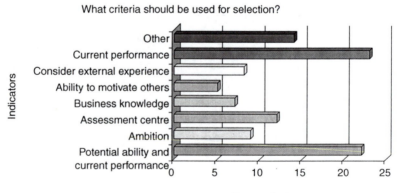

Figure 9.6 Selection criteria.

'individuals with high performance at one level do not always repeat that high performance at the next level'), it is clear that a large percentage of people (22 per cent), believed that an individual's performance is important in assessing his or her future managerial capability.

However, there are some issues – for example, numerous respondents believed that ambition and external experience should be considered as criteria for selection.

Development

Figure 9.7 illustrates that the majority of respondents (75 per cent) believed that development should take place before promotion, believing that this development should occur up to 12 months prior to the promotion.

However, respondents felt that external qualification programmes, management skills seminars, business briefings and assessment centres were all important development activities for these future leaders. Given the extent and range of these development activities, the suggested ideal development timeframe for this development (prior to promotion) may be unrealistic, especially when considered in the context of existing workloads and performance requirements.

Analysis of personnel data

Age profile statistics

PUK's labour force has a similar age profile to that of the general UK population between the ages of 25–54. Although Figure 9.8 shows a normal distribution between these boundaries, with a mean of around 38 years, it is concerning that 31 per cent of the workforce is aged between 45 and 60, compared with the national average of less than 25 per cent,

When should development occur for 'high flyers'?

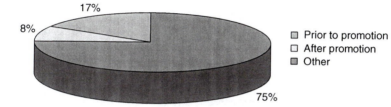

Prior to promotion
After promotion
Other

Figure 9.7 When should development occur?

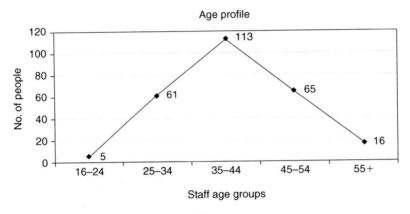

Figure 9.8 PUK's workforce age profile.

and that PUK has only 25 per cent of employees under the age of 35, com-pared with 39 per cent nationally (www.swo.org.uk).

There is a danger that the organization may become operationally chal-lenged as older employees with much experience leave the workforce in large numbers. Without adequate planning, this could put PUK in a situ-ation where its ability to achieve business objectives may be limited by having insufficient sufficient human resource with the required skill and experience.

Length of service

Figure 9.9 indicates an apparent imbalance in the length of service and experience held by staff.

There are 67 people (26 per cent of the work force) with less than three years' service, which is the period that most organizations believe that it takes an employee to achieve optimum performance level. The

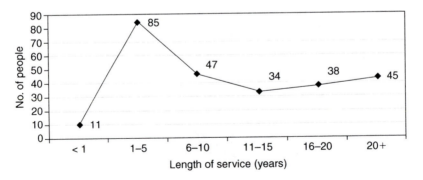

Figure 9.9 Length of service.

majority of the workforce has more than eight years' experience, and 45 per cent of the workforce has more than ten years' service.

This suggests that a significant number of PUK's workforce possess irreplaceable knowledge and skills acquired through lengthy periods of service. In order to sustain effective management, the organization would have to explore means of retaining these valuable workers and/or more effective ways of the organization capturing and sharing this vital knowledge.

Length of service and grade

Figure 9.10 indicates that average length of service increases with grade. This increase coincides with achievement of higher grade as the organization naturally promotes from within.

Time to retirement

Figure 9.11 indicates a disturbing situation for PUK, when, over a ten-year period, 20 per cent of employees are due to retire (assuming that all people will work to the company retirement age of 60 years).

By breaking down this information into grades (see Table 9.2), it was seen that the five main board directors were found in the group with an average of 26 years of experience, and are all due to retire in a five-year period. This illustrates a potentially disastrous situation for PUK, in that half of the organization's accumulated business experience in senior positions (Grade 7 and directors) is due to leave over a ten-year period. The position is more acute at the most senior level, where all the members of the main board (who have been together as a management team for more than 12 years) will retire over a three- to five-year period. This assumes, too, that this particular group will work until normal retirement age (60).

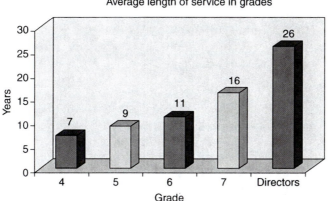

Figure 9.10 Average length of service.

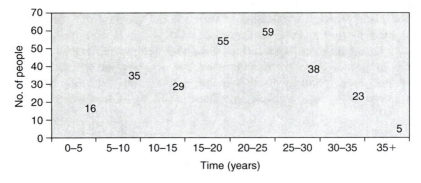

Figure 9.11 Time to retirement.

Of the 51 people retiring over a ten-year period, 32 (67 per cent) hold critical positions in the organization and possess an average of 18 years' business experience each.

Financial risk assessment

Using a combination of the methodologies provided by the DDI and the CIPD, it was possible to approximate the financial risk to PUK if a single director were to leave. All calculations are based on previous recruitment processes, and therefore the final cost is only an indication of the true outcome (see totals in Table 9.3). The calculation also fails to consider the loss of customer service/satisfaction incurred due to the departure of a director.

Table 9.3 illustrates the financial risk involved with losing a main board director. As five directors are due to leave over a five-year period, and without a succession management programme in place to ensure continuity of individual and organizational performance, PUK could face losing five times this amount – £865,805.25. It is therefore clear that such a programme is needed urgently.

Focus group

During a meeting with members of the board of directors, several decisions were made regarding the Future Leaders programme:

- The business and financial risk was too great to the organization not to implement a succession management programme.
- It was clear that the greatest risk was in the director and senior manager structure, where a high number of employees in this category were due to retire over a five-year period. This could create

Table 9.2 Time to retirement by grade

Time to retirement (years)	0–5					5–10					10–15					15–20				
Grade	4	5	6	7	D	4	5	6	7	D	4	5	6	7	D	4	5	6	7	D
No. of people	3	2	3	3	5	4	10	14	7	0	6	12	9	0	2	12	16	19	7	1
% Total	5	2	4	14	63	6	11	18	32	0	9	14	12	0	25	18	19	25	32	12

Time to retirement (years)	20–25					25–30					30–35					35+				
Grade	4	5	6	7	D	4	5	6	7	D	4	5	6	7	D	4	5	6	7	D
No. of people	14	22	19	4	0	11	16	10	1	0	14	6	3	0	0	2	3	0	0	0
% Total	22	26	25	18	0	16	18	12	4	0	21	7	4	0	0	3	3	0	0	0

Table 9.3 Analysis of financial risk of losing a director

Cost involved	Calculation	Total (£)
Administration costs (personnel and payroll)	5 hours × average hourly wage of admininistration team +2 hours personnel manager time for exit interview	97.43
CV screening	5 hours personnel manager time	128.20
Interview time (personnel director and HR manager)	14 hours × average personnel manager time and personnel director	1,023.08
Agency fee	25% (usual agency fee) × average director salary	23,125.00
Assessment centre (including manager time lost to run the day)	2 days × average salary of 3 senior executives and average salary of 1 personnel manager	865.38
Induction	5 hours × induction manager time	51.28
Loss of productivity	On average the position is left vacant for 2 months × average director salary	16,271.68
Lost productivity during period from replacement start to achieving full productivity	Figure taken from previous research at Panasonic (see Appendix 9.5 for explanation).	131,599.00
Overall total		173,161.05

problems at lower levels too if these exiting individuals were replaced from within the organization.

• It was felt that the selection process for the programme should emulate the process for applying for jobs in general in the organization, allowing individuals to nominate themselves for selection onto the programme.

• A strong emphasis was to be placed upon *potential* ability when selecting candidates, and the selection process must allow those previously overlooked to be reconsidered.

• A formal mentoring/coaching programme should be included in the programme.

• The programme MUST conform to the current Panasonic European high-potential development scheme, and not isolate recruitment for management positions to individuals within the programme.

Interpretations and conclusions

The financial evidence favouring the implementation of a succession management programme for executive grades in PUK was compelling, with the full cost of replacement of individuals being more than five times greater than the cost of their development. Even considering the possibility of poor selection choices or candidates leaving before posts are assumed, the return on investment was thought to justify the programme. It was thought too that the scheme would bring additional benefits, such as staff retention and increased motivation.

It was clear that PUK needed a flexible approach to succession management to ensure that replacements would be readily available to assume critically important positions and guarantee the continued effective performance of the organization.

Feedback from the survey of potential candidates and their line managers provided strong indications about how the programme was regarded and how it should be introduced and managed. For example, 94 per cent of the survey group felt that leadership skills could be developed, and 91 per cent believed that PUK should implement a succession management programme as soon as possible. Of the survey group, 69 per cent felt that entry into the programme should be overt – combining self-nomination with a management reference. When asked about the potential benefits of a succession management programme, 40 per cent suggested that the greatest advantage to the organization would be the opportunity to ensure leadership continuity; whilst 48 per cent believed that the largest benefit to individuals was the opportunity for career development. Survey group comments and suggestions were checked in the focus group meeting and found to be consistent with the thinking of the senior management team.

Key learning points

- It is important, when introducing a new programme such as the PUK Future Leaders initiative into an organization whose culture may be resistant to change, to undertake appropriate research such as that described in this chapter.
- The best succession management programme will fail if it is not fully understood and supported by both senior management and candidates within the organization.
- The review phase for the Panasonic Future Leaders succession management programme took almost a year. This may seem a long period, but it was felt essential to gain a thorough understanding of the needs of the organization and the requirements of the candidates if the programme was to be accepted as a vital part of the business environment.
- Programme content must be constructed to build candidates' expertise and chances for success in higher roles, as well as matching the organization's aspirations of its future leaders.
- A clear and transparent selection policy must be created to ensure that everyone in the organization believes that candidates are chosen

on merit. To this effect, PUK created a Future Leaders application process that was as rigorous as the organization's usual job application process. For example, a special behavioural application form was created, first sifting of applications was completed by an external occupational psychologist, short-listed candidates were interviewed, and a two-day residential leadership assessment centre was conducted.

- Great care has to be made to manage the aspirations of both the candidates and the organization. PUK gave a clear statement to all candidates before they applied that successful completion of the programme would not necessarily guarantee promotion. Future Leader graduates would be required to apply for vacancies, which would be open to the whole company. The message to both the candidates and the company, therefore, was that success of the programme would be judged on two criteria: (1) the improvement in performance in the candidate's current role; and (2) the number of candidates who successfully make the transition into higher roles.

References

Byham, W., Smith, A. and Paese, M. (2002) *Grow your Own Leaders*, Upper Saddle River, NJ: Prentice Hall.

Fulmer, M. and Conger, J. (2004) *Growing your Company's Leaders*, New York: AMACOM.

Greengard, S. (2001) 'Why succession planning can't wait', *Workforce*, 80(12).

Hamel, G. and Prahalad, C.K. (1990) 'The core competence of the corporation', *Harvard Business Review*, May–June, 34–6.

Hirsh, W. (2000) *Succession Planning Demystyfied*, Institute of Employment Studies.

IRS (2000) 'Making a success if succession planning', *Employment Review*, 718.

IRS (2002) 'The changing face of succession planning', *Employment Review*, 756.

Rothwell, W. (2001) *Effective Succession Planning*, 2nd edn, AMACOM.

Wells, S. (2003) 'Who's next?', *HR Magazine*, 48(11).

Websites

www.cipd.co.uk
www.Mckinsey.com
www.nature.com
www.hubbardnhubbardinc.com/succession_planning.htm
www.exceptionalleadership.com
www.tdserver1.fnal.gov
www.ddiworld.com
www.work911.com
www.swo.org.uk

Part III

Impact of management development

Introduction

We have named this third part of the book 'Impact of management development', as each chapter in some way provides an illustration of how MD can impact individuals, organizations and the external socio-economic landscape of a nation. In the chapters that follow, the nature and beneficiary/recipient of MD impact is mostly explicit; for example, Chapter 12 explores the effect of an MD programme on individual programme participants, the particular industry sector they work in and the country in which this sector operates. We would, however, encourage readers to extend their thinking beyond the obvious scope of a particular chapter and seek out possibilities of what might be termed as 'implicit impact'; that is, the potential effect of the piece of MD research or practice on other stakeholders, aspects or factors not specifically featured in the focal piece. An example of this is the potential impact of MD upon some of the ethical issues highlighted in the chapters in Part I of the book. There will, too, be specific examples of MD 'impact' in the chapters in the other three parts of the book. Although we will explore such linkages as part of our conclusions in Chapter 19, readers might want to develop their own theoretical frameworks of what MD might 'be' according the complexities and patterns that begin to emerge for them.

In Chapter 10, Karin Derksen, Paul Keursten and Jan Streumer report on a management development programme in a hospital in the Netherlands. They show how demographic and organizational changes have highlighted the need for this hospital to examine its management capability and competence, and the effect of MD upon the management behaviour and the organization itself. The chapter explores contemporary MD trends in the literature, reports on the prevailing effectiveness of MD in the hospital and shows how these results have been used to inform future MD programmes. The programme draws upon the principle of 'co-creation', which calls for a combination of organization, individual and collective learning and development techniques, and the involvement of programme stakeholders in their design and evaluation. A particularly interesting finding centres on managers' perceptions of the relationship between 'work' and 'learning'. A basic principle of the MD programme was that working and learning had to be integrated as much as possible, but the research reveals that managers seem to view 'work as being about working, and not about learning'. From this, the authors conclude that there is a need to ensure that a strong relationship between 'learning' and 'work' exists at the hospital – a conclusion they support with recommendations as to how this can be taken into account in the design of future programmes.

In the chapter that follows, Helen Francis and Norma D'Annunzio-Green examine the role of a leadership development programme in a large retail organization. They show how the programme, focused on generating 'emotional loyalty' amongst managers and their staff, has unleashed very high expectations of the future work and HRM policy environment, and thus, has shaped the 'psychological contract' of the trainees. Chapter 11 reflects on the literature concerning the psychological contract in HRM and emotion management, and draws upon a first phase of research into the leadership programme itself. Conclusions and key learning points indicate a 'wait and see' trial contract emerging in the minds of programme participants – a state which involves managers 'watching' for changes in their seniors' behaviours and in HR policy that might indicate a commitment to the contract as formed in the expectations unleashed by the training. The authors indicate that a second phase of research will seek to assess perceptions as to how far expectations have been met.

The impact of MD on women entrepreneurs in the small and medium-sized enterprise sector (SME) in Vietnam is the subject of Chapter 12 by Jaap Voeten. The chapter describes an MD programme and details how, with the help of tracer studies, the impact of this programme was researched by comparing test and control groups. Investigations set out to determine the effect of the training on the capability and standing of the women entrepreneurs, and also to establish how and to what extent management training impacts effective and efficient business operations. In the light of a preponderance of small entrepreneurial businesses in Vietnam – many of them run by women – the author reports how the MD programme was a recognition that improving the generally disadvantaged development position of these women entrepreneurs had the potential to both correct the gender imbalance in the provision of MD opportunities and also to accelerate general levels of activity in the Vietnamese economy. Four to six months after the training, findings indicate changes in business management practices, business performance and gender relations. From these findings, the author concludes that management training stimulates a change of management practice, business innovation and product upgrade, and increases productivity.

The SME sector also provides a context for the final chapter in this third part of the book, where, in Chapter 13, Hans-Werner Franz discusses a middle management training and development project in SMEs in Germany. In common with the point made in Chapter 10 about managers' perceptions of 'work' and 'learning' in the context of MD, Franz argues that many SME middle managers have become managers primarily due to their expertise in organizing technical and work processes, and that they have not learnt how to organize working and learning processes in an integrated way. Based on three years' experience of working with nine SMEs, the author reports the development of such an integrated approach to working and learning which engages a systemic learning organization approach of leadership by social construction instead of persuasion or coercion. The chapter traces how the project unfolds from its origins in a training needs analysis (TNA) to take the form of a self-sustained management learning network.

Summary

An emerging theme in this part of the book seems to be that MD has the potential to impact significantly a wide range of stakeholders and interested parties, both inside and outside of an organization. A corollary to this is could be that the nature of the impact (for example, beneficial, adverse, effective, off-target, etc.) depends on the rationale for initiating the MD programme, and the approach taken in its development and delivery. Another broad theme that seems to emerge from the chapters is that, conceptually and practically, MD evaluation (to determine impact) is complex and inherently difficult to design and enact. More specific points might include the following:

- The design and evaluation of MD based on the multi-faceted principle of 'co-creation' can be more potent than unilateral approaches.
- It may be easier to determine the impact on individuals than on collectives (for example, teams and the organization as a whole).
- The power and influence unleashed by certain types of MD/leadership development programmes may engender short-term benefit but deliver problematic outcomes for individuals and organizations in the longer term.
- MD can be more potent when 'working' and 'learning' are integrated, but this is something that is not naturally understood and seized upon by managers engaging in MD.
- There is a case to be made for using interchangeably the terms 'manager' and 'leader', and 'management' and 'leadership' (applied interchangeably in Chapter 11, seemingly without incurring confusion or lack of clarity).

- There is also a case to be made for making some distinction between 'management' and 'leadership' for purposes of improving the 'leadership' behaviours of 'managers' (Chapter 13 illustrates this with findings about what leadership 'means' to managers undergoing a leadership development programme).

10 Management by co-creation

Karin Derksen, Paul Keursten and Jan Streumer

Introduction

Over the last decade, the debate on the role of managers has been an issue of paramount importance. It has come to be widely acknowledged that management by planning and control is not enough in the information and knowledge era (see, for example, Drucker, 1999; Mintzberg, 2004). In this the twenty-first century, organizations are in need of inspiring leaders – managers who are able to take provocative decisions and lead radical change. This requires managers who can build and create. These competencies cannot be developed by merely 'following' a management development (MD) programme as consumers – digesting content and exercises prepared by others, and then translating these into one's own daily practice, with all the transfer problems we are only too familiar with. If managers are to be creators and leaders, they need to be in charge of their own learning, co-creators of their own development. The design of the learning process should be consistent with the objectives of learning and with what is required in day-to-day work.

Although the debate on and ideology of the co-creation approach to MD has grown, little has been written that is based on research in actual practice: can it really work? What does it take to make it work? What are the difficulties and dilemmas? We therefore started an elaborate case study, in which we designed and thoroughly evaluated an MD programme, based on co-creation and in which individual development and organizational development went hand in hand.

The case examined in this chapter describes how a hospital in the Netherlands attempted to implement its new mission statement, in which the requirements and needs of the recipients of care played a central role. This demanded an entirely different working method and organizational structure. The managers and potentials were the key figures in shaping this change. It turned out, however, that they did not possess or did not possess sufficiently the competencies that were necessary to carry this through. This was the reason for drawing up an MD programme. In this chapter, four issues will be examined:

1   *Theoretical frame:* what views on MD by co-creation and learning in organizations were used during the development and implementation of the MD programme?
2   *Research context:* what did the MD programme look like? How did we design the evaluation of this programme?
3   *Results:* what benefits has the MD programme produced for the hospital? What were the difficulties and dilemmas?
4   *Discussion:* what recommendations can be made. based on the experience gained from the MD programme? This relates to recommendations for a possible follow-up programme as well as to recommendations that could benefit others working in similar situations.

Theoretical framework: starting points for MD

The development of the MD programme was grounded in principles derived from the literature on management development and learning in organizations. These principles were made explicit and were elaborated, together with stakeholders in the hospital, as guidelines for the project (Derksen *et al.*, 2003). This proved to be very beneficial: the principles served as a means of communication and as a compass and reference point for reflection. During the process we worked with many people from both inside and outside the organization, and it was these starting points that guided all the activities and decision-making of everyone involved in the process. At the same time, they gave the hospital HRD professionals the opportunity to put into practice their ideas about learning and to show that they practised what they preached. The principles were as follows.

The organizational process of change is a learning process

The organizational change in the hospital was not a matter of merely implementing a blueprint, but was a learning process in itself. Such a process calls for combining organizational development, individual learning and collective learning; it is a process of co-development and interactive learning (Boonstra, 2004). Facilitating the process of change as a learning process means that thinking about and shaping the future are designed as learning activities, in which participants together structure the new organization and, at the same time, develop new competencies and behaviours.

By co-designing, experimenting and reflecting, managers were enabled to:

*   develop, together, a clearer, shared vision of the organization in the future (Keursten and Sprenger, 2004);
*   develop new knowledge, ideas and building blocks for the future by

thinking about and working together on such questions as: how will the hospital look in the future? What form will a client's visit take, and what role should professionals and managers play in that new organization?

Responsibility for and ownership of learning rests with the learner

Managers in an organization bear a great responsibility in their daily work. Here, they were the initiators of the 'new' hospital. In the MD process, managers need to be encouraged to exercise that responsibility and to assume the role of initiator too: they need to be co-creators (Wierdsma, 2004). By definition, learners own their own learning and choices: you cannot be taught, and you always have more than one option (Koestenbaum and Block, 2002). This calls for an approach that actively supports exercising this freedom and at the same time leaves the responsibility with the individual learners.

This point was operationalized as follows. At the start, participants were each given a self-diagnostic instrument, based on which they could formulate their own development ambitions. These were defined in terms of competencies and work results, and were then discussed with their supervisor. Participants then created their own MD programme, based on the ambitions and needs that were agreed upon. In all the learning activities, it was the manager's own contribution, questions and wishes that formed the starting point. Managers co-created their own MD, and almost every individual created his or her own mix and learning path. The importance of their responsibility was also stressed by organizing reviews of the learning process, and especially of the results of this learning, based on work-related evidence that the participants had gathered in their portfolios.

Working is learning

Managers tend to learn most from their work (van der Sluis, 2000; de Kleer *et al.*, 2002; Streumer, 2006): work is a powerful source of learning. The organizational change in the hospital provided the managers with many opportunities for development. In their day-to-day practice the managers were confronted with unexpected problems and complex questions, and these challenges formed the starting point for setting learning objectives and for each learning intervention: working instead of talking about work. In the first part of the MD programme, we used current daily challenges as a starting point for learning and developing new practices. In the second part, innovation projects on key elements of the organizational change provided the practical work-learning context.

In MD, managers were given the support to recognize the learning opportunities in their day-to-day practice and to use these effectively. This was important for the future, because organizational change is a permanent feature. The hospital may be on its way to becoming a new hospital, but there will never be a status quo.

Reflecting on critical dilemmas and tensions, as opposed to presenting the solution

Change and innovation often stem from situations in which existing routines and processes have reached their limits: more of the same will no longer work. These situations reveal themselves through growing tensions: more and more energy is expended, with ever-diminishing results. In such cases, new directions need to be found, and this often involves dealing with dilemmas: there is no single good solution, trade-offs need to be made or new positions developed (Hoebeke, 2004). One example of this is the tension between customer orientation and efficiency: both are clearly agreed, valuable principles, but how should one deal with situations where focusing on client needs calls for additional investment, while budgets have to be cut to reach financial targets?

The decisions made in these situations often have a major impact: they can either create or frustrate development and innovation. Here, the integration of competencies and true leadership is crucial and can be developed. We therefore deliberately brought to the fore such tensions and dilemmas from daily work in order to focus on the essentials of individual and organizational development. Reflection on and experimentation with these situations provide powerful learning opportunities. The challenge to rethink basic assumptions and beliefs supports double-loop learning, which is needed for organizational change (Argyris and Schön, 1996), and the skill to deal with dilemmas and tensions, the ability to find new viewpoints and approaches, are core competencies for managers. Learning to deal with dilemmas and tensions is thus a key element of MD.

Individually and together: learning as a social process of shared meaning and purpose

Individual managers will have their own unique learning needs. At the same time, the organization is attempting to change in a specific direction. This leads to some shared learning needs. MD needs to provide scope for individual and shared learning needs, which requires a flexible MD programme. It also calls for insight into individual and organizational MD results.

We took the view that learning is essentially a social process of constructing meaning and developing common directions and identity (Brown and Duguid, 1991; Lave and Wenger, 1991; Weick, 1991; Van Woerkom, 2003). The design of MD therefore needed to provide many opportunities for cooperation, exchange and challenge across departments and positions in the hospital.

Research context and intervention design

In this section, a description is given of the practical context of the case and the MD programme that was made to operationalize the principles outlined above. We will finish with a description of the methodology for evaluating the implementation and results of the MD programme.

Practical context: a hospital in transition

The population for this study consisted of managers (partly those already in the job, partly potentials in training) in a Dutch hospital. This was a medium-sized, regional hospital in the east of the Netherlands, serving both the local population and the surrounding district. Given the magnitude of the recent changes in the public health-care system in the Netherlands, the hospital aspired to be (from its mission statement):

> a modern, attractive and financially healthy hospital, providing excellent medical care geared to the needs of the regional population. This will result in as many people as possible in the region continuing to opt for care in our hospital.

The hospital realized that its mission statement required it to be quite different from the 'one-size-fits-all' hospital that it then was. Originally, the hospital was arranged around the specialists, instead of the clients. Clinical and outpatient care were kept strictly separate. In the new organization, the needs of the clients formed the starting point for the care that was to be provided; the organizational structure and the infrastructure had to be linked to this approach. This demanded a radically new method of working and of organizing things. HRD was recognized as being able to contribute to the changes needed, both in the attitudes and behaviour of employees and in the reform of the organizational structure (Bartlett and Kang, 2004). This process of change cannot simply be characterized as the implementation of a blueprint for the new organization. The problem is that such a blueprint (including all its product and process specifications) cannot be designed in advance, but rather the exact design of the new organization will develop gradually during this process of change.

It was widely acknowledged that managers were pivotal in this change. They endorsed the mission statement and their key role in the process of change, but were not always able to put this into practice, especially at the beginning of the process. The year 2000 saw the start of the development of an MD programme in which managers could learn their new role and, at the same time, shape the organization in the way desired.

Intervention design: the MD programme

The MD programme started with a working conference involving the hospital administration and the medical specialists, during which they translated the mission statement of the hospital into the future role of management.

Start-up

In the start-up phase, a number of issues were comprehensively discussed in a working conference by a group acting as a sounding board (Williams and Paauwe, 1999). What exactly is MD? Who owns MD? What should be learned and when, should there be artificial restraint or unchecked chaos, should MD be separate or integrated, and what difference does it make anyway? The answers to these questions served to formulate the guiding principles of MD in the hospital concerned; the mission statement and the strategic policy document of the hospital formed its basis.

The first step in designing the MD programme was to develop a joint vision of the hospital's future managers. The competency profiles for the managers concerned (operational and cluster managers) were drawn up using the input from a panel, coming from all layers of the hospital ($n = 60$). The competency profiles of the management team and the management board were then drawn up in a similar way. The activities that were carried out as part of this process were extremely helpful in clarifying and making concrete the rather vague image of the 'new hospital' that still existed at the time. The discussions also gave direction to the MD programme and helped the panel members to think along the same lines. MD was regarded by the members of the panel as a necessary process aimed at:

* building the new hospital together, and
* making managers competent to build the new hospital and preparing them for their future role.

After this, the participants were acquainted with the programme and were regularly helped in making the most effective choices to meet their personal development needs.

Assessment procedure

Participation in the MD programme was determined by an assessment procedure; all the current managers and interested potential candidates underwent an assessment, which was based on self-diagnosis. The instrument that was used for this was created on the basis of a competency profile that had been drawn up for 'new' managers. An initial dialogue with the participant's own manager, a fellow manager and an HRD professional followed. The participant only started on MD when all these people were confident of his or her ability to become the desired 'new' manager.

The initial dialogue resulted in a developmental agreement. MD participants had different developmental needs, according to their own strengths and weaknesses, and the MD programme gave them the ingredients to compile their own MD menu, based on these personal needs.

Halfway through the MD programme, individual participants had a dialogue with their own manager, a fellow manager and an HRD professional, who checked progress (based on a portfolio) and then made a new developmental agreement with each other. For a few managers, this moment resulted in ending their participation in the MD programme and making a career switch. At the end of the MD programme, progress was once again checked in a final assessment, resulting in a statement of either 'fit for the job' or 'not fit for the job' of 'new' manager.

Two phases

The MD programme consisted of two parts: in the first phase, personal development played a central role, and in the second, organizational development was at the forefront. The participants composed their own programme from a menu; in other words, they could make use of four forms of learning for developing their competencies. Each participant was given his or her own 'budget' that could be used to purchase parts of the MD programme.

In phase two (organizational development), participants were given the assignment of implementing a project plan aimed at achieving an organizational change in the hospital. The board of the hospital was a constituent part of the projects. One example of a project might have been: to realize collaboration between neurologists and cardiac and lung specialists that would lead to rapid – if possible, in one day – diagnosis and treatment advice for patients with vascular disease.

The projects for participants were selected on the following grounds: they should be valuable to the 'new' hospital, challenging for the MD participant, and should meet the learning needs of the MD participant.

In both parts, the menu was divided into:

1   *Coaching.* Participants were each offered personal coaching and were able to select their own coach from a coach 'pool'.
2   *Self-tuition.* Participants were offered readers and study guides for self-tuition on each of the MD themes.
3   *Learning teams, innovation teams.* Each participant joined a learning team of five participants all at the same management level. Learning teams gave their own interpretation and were supported in their learning process by a facilitator. Personal development was at the

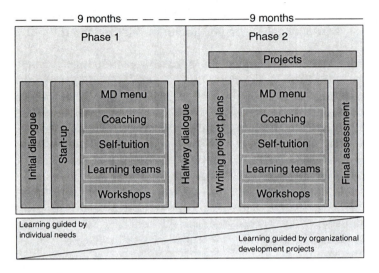

Figure 10.1 Design of MD programme.

forefront in phase one. In phase two, the learning teams became innovation teams. Participants helped each other to carry out an organizational development in phase two.

4 *Workshops.* In short workshops, participants learned and experimented with new meanings and behaviour. In each workshop, the participants' day-to-day practice formed the basis of the content. For phase one, a more or less standard programme for each workshop was developed. For phase two, only those themes were suggested that were in accordance with the intended organizational changes. When participants registered, the workshop was tailor-made for them, and very often an innovation team enrolled jointly for a workshop.

Analysis and evaluation

This section presents an overview of the main findings of our study. The main questions to be answered by our study were:

1 What benefits has the MD programme produced for the hospital?
2 What have been the effects of MD on the daily work of participants and on the organization?
3 What were the strong elements (things that worked well) and the weak elements (things that did not work well and had to be improved) of the MD programme?
4 What recommendations can be made, based on the experience gained from the MD programme?

The first three questions are dealt with in this section, and the fourth question (recommendations) is considered in the discussion and learning points sections.

Evaluation treatment

The hospital invested in the MD programme for more than two years. Almost 120 managers and potentials, divided into three groups, participated in MD. After the first group had finished the programme, the hospital board was keen to know the results of their investment in MD. Our evaluation concerns the first group of MD participants (52 managers).

To be able to evaluate the effects of MD on the working behaviour of the participants and to 'measure' its impact on the organization, it was decided to collect information by means of different instruments and to use different methods of information gathering (Phillips, 1997). The following mix of information sources and instruments was therefore made:

* A questionnaire for all 52 participants. The questionnaire consisted of six two-way questions, 16 ranking scales and six open-ended questions. The questionnaire collected background information on the participants (educational level, years of experience, etc.) and 'measured' the entry behaviour and behavioural changes in the managers as a result of the MD programme implemented. An example of the items is: 'I use at least 75 per cent of what I learned in the MD programme in my work'. The questionnaire was tested and revised before it was applied.
* Some structured interviews with five managers who were in charge directly of 29 and indirectly of 19 of the participants of the MD programme. The interviews consisted of two-way questions and open-ended questions. One example of the questions was: 'How many of the participants (percentage) you manage have become more result-oriented since the MD programme started?' Another example was: 'Do you think that the results of MD outweigh the costs?'
* Semi-structured interview with ten subordinates of MD programme participants. The questions included: 'What has your manager changed in his working routine in the last two years?' and 'In what kind of situations do you recognize this change?'.
* Four 'success case' interviews. These were interviews with a few 'extremes', meaning two participants who were of the opinion that they had learned a great deal and two who were of the opinion that they had learned nothing or very little from the MD programme.

All the answers were processed by means of SPSS, with the exception of the data resulting from the open-ended questions; these were processed by hand.

The overall effects of MD on the participants' day-to-day work

On the whole, it can be concluded that all the MD participants, their managers and subordinates were positive about the effects of the MD programme. The hospital board was also of the opinion that the programme had been successful. The skills that needed to be developed visibly increased in this period of nearly two years. Those skills were: exercising initiative and responsibility, being committed to the organization, being results-oriented, daring to be vulnerable, being willing to experiment with new and different ways of working, being entrepreneurial, and standing out from the rest.

The operational managers were more successful in achieving the goals of the MD programme than were their supervisors, the cluster managers. The board was positive about this result, because the developmental need of the operational managers was greater than that of the cluster managers (see also Derksen, 2004).

During the evaluation, nearly everyone mentioned that the MD programme had helped them in building internal networks. Looking beyond the borders of one's own section and working together with other sections in the hospital was an important result of the programme. This really did help the organization to change.

The strong and weak elements of the MD programme

Greater insight into the effects was gained by explicitly looking at the strong and the weak elements of the starting points and the MD programme.

Starting up

STRUCTURE

The first phase was very well structured. Participants were allowed to make their own selection from the MD menu. Workshop programmes were fleshed out by the trainers, using the participants' work experience. Learning in the workplace was structured by assignments coupled to the workshops. Participants were very active in phase one; they followed a great number of learning activities and developed rapidly. We mentioned above that the operational managers developed more than the cluster managers. This was partly because the cluster managers were already more experienced and had participated in more training programmes in the past. They had the idea that they already knew most of what they needed to know and were not always able to see what could be additionally learned about things they were already acquainted with.

In the second phase the participants had to develop their own learning interventions and ask for support, guided by the organizational change they had to achieve. This proved to be too difficult: the transition from phase one to phase two was too extreme.

Conclusion: The needs of the participants for a structured programme were underestimated. Next time it might be sensible to make a gradual change from an externally structured programme to a self-structured one.

COMPOSING YOUR OWN MD PROGRAMME

All the participants and their managers were very positive about the variety in the MD menu and the fact that they could make their own selection according to their personal needs. This resulted in very different MD programmes. Some participants chose to attend a lot of workshops; others only made use of personal coaching. This was a very strong element of the MD programme.

In making their own programme we had expected participants to make SMART (specific, measurable, attainable, relevant and time-bound) developmental agreements with their manager. At the start of MD this was difficult for both managers and participants, as they still had to become more results-oriented. However, halfway through the MD programme and at the end, they were better able to make SMART agreements with each other. A measurable developmental agreement also means that there will be a point of measurement. This was new in the hospital. Participants had to make their own portfolio as input for the halfway and final dialogue. At first it was received with a great deal of scepticism, but in the end it worked very well. It made talking about results much more objective, and provided the participant and his or her manager with greater insight.

Conclusion: Composing one's own MD programme is very successful. Learning to work with SMART developmental agreements and to judge the developmental results takes time. The facilitation of the process is a must; participants need time to grow.

EXPECTING NEW BEHAVIOUR

The MD participants needed new behaviour right from the start, but sometimes they had to learn it first. For example, in the beginning, during the initial dialogue, the managers of candidate participants had to give feedback and be clear about their expectations. This did not work well at the start. Some participants had been able to start on the MD programme only because their manager was not yet skilled enough to communicate clearly their – in general poor – opinion of the participant. In the halfway dialogue every manager had learned to communicate opinions clearly, and those participants who did not belong in the MD programme dropped out.

Conclusion: As programme-designers and facilitators, trust your choices and be patient. Communicate clearly what is happening, help in reflecting on the process and patterns and be a role model.

MD programme

PERSONAL COACHING

Most of the cluster managers made use of personal coaching. Participants were able to choose their own coach from a 'coach pool'. They were almost entirely positive about personal coaching: it gave them a greater insight into themselves, their ambitions, their strengths and their weaknesses. Hardly any of the operational managers made use of a personal coach. One argument we heard was: 'I don't have such a big problem that I need a personal coach'. Choosing one's own coach worked very well. The pool comprised external and internal coaches who were acquainted with the MD goals and agreements.

   Conclusion: Personal coaching is a worthwhile intervention in MD programmes. Choosing one's own coach works well. Next time we could do something about improving the image of personal coaching, or give everyone a personal coach without exception.

SELF-TUITION

For every MD theme, material for self-tuition was available. Many of the participants took note of parts of the material – especially beginners, who wanted to learn a lot, and the experienced managers, who thought they already knew it but wanted to check. Most popular were the practical self-tuition materials. Only a few participants were interested in more theoretical and background materials.

   Conclusion: Self-tuition added a useful way of learning to the MD menu. It is difficult to find out exactly what is appreciated by participants.

LEARNING TEAMS

It was easier for the operational managers to learn from each other in the learning teams than it was for some of the cluster managers. None of the operational managers saw the others as competitors, whereas the cluster managers sometimes did regard each other as rivals. This had a restraining influence in some learning teams on willingness to learn from each other.

   In the second phase, the learning teams became innovation teams. This did not work very well all the time. Teams were able to ask for external support, but only a few did so. It proved to be difficult for the teams to make it worthwhile for everyone. The participants chose to expend their energy on daily routine, and most of the innovation teams faded out.

Conclusion: Learning teams work well when participants do not see each other as competitors. The best results are made when the team is facilitated by an experienced process facilitator.

WORKSHOPS

All participants were very positive about the workshops, especially their practice orientation. At first participants chose far too many workshops, and found that this took up too much time and energy. After a while, every participant was able to make excellent choices that were appropriate to their learning needs.

Conclusion: Create workshops that are closely related to daily practice. Help participants to make choices whenever there are choices.

ORGANIZATIONAL CHANGE (SECOND PHASE)

In phase two, it was difficult to learn while working on an organizational change project. First of all, it took a very long time for the board to formulate the goals for the project: participants had to wait for a month or two before they could get started. This led to something of a vacuum in the MD programme. When participants were finally able to start on the project, it proved very difficult for them to combine work and learning: their focus was on work and not learning. They tended to pick up the projects in ways they already knew and were used to. Very often these ways had not worked in the past, but they had forgotten to take time for reflection and experimentation and to make use of the learning opportunities they had. This is connected with the self-structure we expected.

Conclusion: To make daily work a useful learning arena takes more than a challenging assignment and facilitating the participants using their initiative.

Discussion

This section examines the three tensions that appeared during the implementation of the innovation process. These were tensions that occurred as a result of a structure being either provided or not provided to the participants in the MD programme. In fact, this relates to the question of whether the call to be allowed to give direction to their own development always implies that participants have to be fully-fledged co-creators.

In the second place, it concerns the question of which configuration of workplace learning fits best into which phase of the innovation process. It also relates to the question of whether the participants do indeed recognize that they can learn through and during work.

Finally, we devoted attention to the friction caused by the difference between the speed at which the participating managers developed and the slow speed at which their environment reacted to the change in their behaviour.

A lack of structure produces tensions and lack of clarity!

As previously mentioned, the MD programme was a vehicle that supported the process of organizational development in the hospital. The watchword given to the organizational process was 'co-creation'. Broadly speaking, everyone knew what the objective of the process was, but the precise outlines still had to be mapped out together. Although the organization was eager to do this, at the same time this innovation approach produced tensions. The participants in the innovation process were not used to playing an active role in charting the course of change. A frequently heard reaction was: 'Just tell us first exactly what the innovation process involves and what you're trying to achieve by it'. There is thus clearly a conflict between the currently generally held 'philosophy' that, on the one hand, people themselves have to be able to choose and be able to give direction to their own development process, and, on the other hand, people's apparent need for clarity and direction. It is therefore not surprising that we were regularly bombarded with the following questions: 'What exactly is expected of me?' What should the portfolio look like?' 'What can I expect from the halfway dialogue?' We should therefore not be surprised that, if guidelines (for the portfolio, for instance) are provided by the project management, this will again lead to resistance and the participants will immediately feel they have been forced into a straitjacket.

A balance must thus be struck between freedom and using one's own initiative on the one hand, and direction and structure on the other.

Working is about work, and learning about learning

Another basic principle of the project was that working and learning had to be integrated as much as possible. This was tackled in a phased approach. In the first phase of the project, the participants stepped out of their everyday work with some regularity and were then, in a structured way, confronted with relatively large amounts of new knowledge by the trainer and facilitator. This knowledge was work-related. Under supervision, they reflected on their own progress in work and were given concrete ideas and tips about making use of what they had learned. They often practised applying this – also under supervision – and then returned to their day-to-day work practice. In phase two, conversely, the participants had to learn more directly in and from their work, and had to organize the learning process themselves. It became obvious that the participants' focus was very much on their work and hardly at all on learning in relation to work.

Conclusion: It could be concluded that work is about working and not about learning; the connection was hardly seen or made. Participants were barely able or entirely unable to distance themselves from their everyday routine which had proved ineffective. Participants allowed themselves insufficient space for reflection and experimentation. Does it take more than a challenging assignment and being presented with demand-driven learning opportunities for people to detach themselves from their everyday concerns?

Tensions as a result of having to display new behaviour at this early stage

One major problem encountered during the implementation of the project related to the fact that the development of the managers who were participating in the project was not running in parallel with the circumstances in which they had to apply their newly acquired behaviour. Their environment did not keep pace with the development that the managers were undergoing. This 'politics of different speeds' led to some friction. What was striking in this was that the managers participating in the project did not feel responsible for implementing changes in their environment: that was a task for others!

The following two examples give an impression of these tensions.

Calling each other to account and providing feedback is one of the competencies in the competency profiles for the managers who were participating in the programme. This was an area on which they would have to work very hard in the hospital in the months ahead. It appears that hospital managers tend to be very polite to each other and have difficulty in saying how matters really stand, but it is questionable whether that is really the case. Is there an explanation for this behaviour? One possible explanation can be found in the discrepancy that exists between what is generally proclaimed and the actual situation. On the one hand, the idea is propagated that there must be an open atmosphere, where everyone may express criticism and where providing feedback on each other's performance must be a very normal event. Conversely, however, the hierarchical relations do not as yet allow this desirable behaviour to be displayed. Giving uninvited feedback and assertively responding to this is perhaps not appreciated – or not yet – in broad layers of management. It was striking, for example, that during the learning activities that formed part of the MD programme, participants regularly complained about the lack of conditions for change. The participants felt that the MT and the management board were responsible for this, but managers did not directly call them to account on this. We noticed that this was happening increasingly often, yet only once did a learning team have an interview with the MT and the management board to make their dissatisfaction known.

A second example also provides an illustration. The learning activities in the MD programme were set up in such a way that managers learned on the basis of situations and issues from their working practice. It was important that participants both prepared for a learning activity and took part in it, even if they had a heavy workload that would seem to have priority. The success of a learning activity is, after all, largely determined by what people themselves make of it. Not turning up or not preparing sufficiently for the activity has a negative effect both on the participant and on others. During an interim evaluation that was carried out after three months, it appeared that the participants felt that the programme management did not demand enough commitment. Managers implicitly assumed that the supervisors of the workshops and learning team meetings would hold them accountable for their responsibilities, whereas the hospital, on the contrary, wanted to achieve a culture in which managers would call each other to account and act as an example to their employees. The programme management assumed responsibility for the managers, because we believe that changes in the behaviour of managers and in the organizational culture can only be achieved when these changes are expressed in both form and content in the learning programme (see also Schein, 1999). At the initial meeting of the second group of managers (we worked with three groups who started approximately six months after each other), we invited a number of participants from the first group to relate some of their experiences in the MD programme and to answer any questions. These participants emphasized to the newcomers – without this point having been prepared in advance – how vital it was to be well prepared. And that it was, above all, the participants themselves who determined how successful the learning activities would prove to be. They also pointed out that the MD programme had a great deal to offer, but only if the participants also put a lot into it. During the learning activities too it was striking that participants, certainly those in the learning teams, were more prepared to hold each other accountable for their responsibilities.

Key learning points

All in all, this shows that the co-creation of MD is not an easy process; it is complex. Whereas more traditional MD provides good learning opportunities from a clearly defined and thus dependably familiar programme, the co-creation of MD introduces the complexity of everyday life at almost full force. It is extremely important to be aware of this, and to determine explicitly whether this approach is feasible and preferable in the given situation. This can only be done by making the basic principles of co-creation explicit and discussing the consequences this may have on the approach to the MD programme with the participants, senior staff and the authority commissioning the programme. We hope that this chapter will provide a stimulus for others to design an MD programme together!

References

Argyris, C. and Schön, D. (1996) *Organizational learning II*, Reading, MA: Addison-Wesley.

Bartlett, R.B. and Kang, D. (2004) Training and organizational commitment among nurses following industry and organizational change', *New Zealand and the United States. Human Resource Development International*, 7(4): 423–40.

Boonstra, J.J. (2004) 'Conclusion: some reflections and perspectives on organizing, changing and learning', in Boonstra, J.J. (ed.), *Dynamics in Organizational Change and Learning*, Chichester: John Wiley & Sons, pp. 447–75.

Brown, J.S. and Duguid, P. (1991) 'Organizational learning and Communities of Practice: toward a unified view of learning, working and innovation', *Organizational Science*, 2(1): 47–57.

De Kleer, E., van Poelje, P.A.J., van den Berg, E., Singerling, E. and Brave, F. (2002) *Leren voor leiderschap. Een nieuwe kijk op managementontwikkeling* [Learning for Leadership. A New View on Management Development], Gorcum: Berenschot Fundatie.

Derksen, K. (2004) *Management development in het Deventer Ziekenhuis. Gids van je eigen ontwikkeling [Management Development in the Deventer Hospital. Guiding your own Development]*, Enschede: University of Twente.

Derksen, K., Geerdink, J. and Rondeel, M. (2003) 'Lerend vorm geven aan veranderingen: management development in het Deventer Ziekenhuis' [Learning to design changes: management development in the Deventer Hospital], *HRD Thema, Leren én veranderen: een nieuwe kijk op organisatieverandering*, 4(1): 37–48.

Drucker, P. (1999) *Management Challenges for the 21st Century*, New York: Harper Business.

Hoebeke, L. (2004) 'Dilemmas and paradoxes in organizing change processes', in Boonstra, J.J. (ed.), *Dynamics in Organizational Change and Learning*, Chichester: John Wiley & Sons, pp. 149–71.

Keursten, P. and Sprenger, C. (2004) 'Samen creëren van management development' [Co-creating management development], in *Opleiding en Ontwikkeling*, (17)3: 20–4.

Koestenbaum, P. and Block, P. (2002) *Freedom and Accountability at Work: Applying Philosophic Insight to the Rea*, San Francisco, LA: Jossey-Bass.

Lave, J. and Wenger, E. (1991) *Situated Learning: Legitimate Peripheral Participation*, Cambridge: Cambridge University Press.

Mintzberg, H. (2004) *Managers, not MBAs*, London: Pearson Education.

Philips, J.J. (1997) *Handbook of Training Evaluations and Measurement Methods*, 3rd edn, Houston, TX: Gulf Publishing Company.

Schein, E.H. (1999) *The Corporate Culture Survival Guide: Sense and Nonsense about Cultural Change*, San Francisco, LA: Jossey Bass.

Streumer, J.N. (2006) *Work-Related Learning*, Dordrecht: Springer.

Van der Sluis, E.C. (2000) 'Management learning and development' *Opleiding en Ontwikkeling*, 13(12): 40–2.

Van Woerkom, M. (2003) *Critical Reflection at Work*, Enschede: University of Twente (unpublished dissertation).

Weick, K.E. (1991) 'The nontraditional quality of organizational learning', *Organization Science*, 2: 116–24.

Wierdsma, A. (2004) 'Beyond implementation: co-creation in change and development', in Boonstra, J.J. (ed.), *Dynamics in Organizational Change and Learning*, Chichester: John Wiley & Sons, pp. 227–57.

Williams, R. and Paauwe, J. (1999) 'Een zevental vragen voor management development' [Seven questions for management development], in Paauwe, J. (ed.), *Management development: Grensoverschrijdende prespectieven [Management Development: Border Crossing Perspectives]*, Deventer: Kluwer.

11 The impact of emotion management training on the 'shifting sands' of the psychological contract

Helen Francis and Norma D'Annunzio-Green

Objectives

This chapter examines the role of a leadership development programme in signalling a new kind of psychological contract amongst a sample of managers in a large retail organization (ServCo) based on expectations of increased employee discretion and well-being. We show how the programme focused on generating what was termed as 'emotional loyalty' amongst managers and their staff, based on a move away from a task-oriented management style towards a more 'visionary' one that required managers successfully to manage emotions in themselves and others.

Respondents cited a range of leadership behaviours now expected of them, suggesting some ground rules for emotion displays. In what follows, we examine how communication of these new 'rules' through emotion management training, unleashed very high expectations about their future work environment. We show how managers displayed a willingness to believe that the leadership programme would, in time, lead to changes in HRM policy development that were congruent with the ideals expressed by the programme, and in this way illustrate the emergence of a 'trial' psychological contract (Grant, 1999).

Our case illustrates the dynamics of this 'wait and see' period, and concludes by raising questions about the impact of emotion management training upon managers' expectations and, therefore, perceptions about the state of the psychological contract. We conclude by pointing to the dangers of perceived contract breach, and invite more critical scrutiny of emotion management training than that provided in popular management texts.

Theoretical context

HRM and the psychological contract

The concept of the psychological contract has been widely used in the organizational psychology literature as a way of examining and exploring the changing employment relationship between the individual and the organization. Here, the employment relationship is viewed in more diffuse terms than that described by academics, who have traditionally drawn upon the systems model of industrial relations to focus on shifts in collective representations and the 'regulated exchange' between the state, management and employees (Sparrow, 1996: 76).[1]

Focusing upon the individual and subjective nature of the employment relationship, Rousseau (1994) has defined the psychological contract as 'the understandings people have, whether written or unwritten, regarding commitments made between themselves and their organization' (cited by Hiltrop, 1996: 36). Much of the research into the psychological contract has focused on the changing nature of such 'understandings', whether these are concerned with perceived promises, expectations or obligations, and how far such promises and obligations have been met (Atkinson, 2003).

Debate has also centred on whether the term should be treated as something that is essentially an individually based perception of the contract (formulated largely in the mind of the employee), or something that involves both employee *and* employer perceptions of reciprocity and exchange within the employment relationship (Guest, 1998). Analysts have typically focused on the employee perspective, although there is a growing body of literature in which the employer's perspective is treated as a legitimate basis for study (Guest, 2004). In this context, the psychological contract has been defined by Guest and Conway (2002a: 1) as:

> The perceptions of both parties to the employment relationship – organizational and individual – of the reciprocal promises and obligations implied in that relationship.

This definition rests on the idea that obligations can extend from the rather obvious ones, concerned with pay and safe working conditions, to less clear-cut 'promises' or 'expectations'. They will often be informal and imprecise: they may be inferred from actions or from what has happened in the past, as well as from statements made by the employer, for example during the recruitment process or in performance appraisals (Guest and Conway, 2002a, 2002b, 2002c, 2002d; Conway and Briner, 2004).

Building on the notion of exchange between employer and employee, Guest and colleagues' modelling of the psychological contract is based on the premise that more 'progressive' HR practices lead to a more positive 'state' of contract and improved employee/business performance (Guest and Conway, 2002a, 2002b, 2002c; Purcell *et al.*, 2003).[2]

Drawing on a range of case studies and survey work commissioned by the Chartered Institute of Personnel and Development, Guest (2004) argues that employers are increasingly seeking high levels of discretionary behaviour from their employees, consistent with a 'relational' psychological contract (Rousseau, 1990). This means moving away from a more 'transactional' relationship, based on a monetary exchange, to one in which employees are expected by their employer to work beyond the requirement of the job, or 'go the extra mile', in exchange for job security, financial rewards, and training and development. In this way, employees come to identify with the organization and there is a higher degree of mutual interdependence.

Assumptions underpinning the pursuit of relational psychological contracts are consistent with the idealized employment relationship denoted by high-commitment models of HRM (Storey, 1992; Guest, 1999). They are grounded in the idea that employees can (and are willing to) become self-managing and self-reliant in ways that act in the firm's interests and lead to improved employee/organizational performance (Landen, 2002). This notion of the self-reliant worker has led to increasing interest in use of emotion management techniques and development of 'emotional capital' at the workplace (Fineman, 2000; Gratton, 2003). Researchers disagree about the desirability of such normative controls – an issue that is highlighted in the following section.

Emotion management and the psychological contract

Organizations are increasingly demanding various forms of 'emotional labour', where employees are required to manage their feelings and behavioural displays of emotion to the benefit of the organization (Linstead and Fulop, 2004). Hochschild (1983) illustrates, for example, how emotion management is built into the job design and training of flight attendants and debt collectors, and Korczynski (2002) draws on a wide range of contemporary literature to show how emotional labour is increasingly built into front-line service work.

Less well understood is the application of emotion management across a wider range of occupations, including management positions (Turnbull, 1999; Kramer and Hess, 2002). Our research builds on this literature to explore managerial experiences of emotion management training in a large retail organization, and how this shaped managers' perceptions of the psychological contract. Earlier we pointed to connections that have been drawn between 'progressive' HR policies created to engender committed emotional labour, the psychological contract, and employee performance. It is in this context that models of effective leadership behaviours are increasingly rooted in the assumption that leaders will operate more effectively if they are better able to manage their own emotions and those of others (Humphreys, 2000).

Managers are being trained in the use of various toolkits to help them in their diagnosis of emotions and working out strategies for 'managing' emotions at the workplace, to the benefit of the individual, team and organization (see, for example, Goleman, 2000; Ashkanasy and Daus,

2002; Boyatzis and van Oosten, 2002). Kramer and Hess (2002) specify a range of general emotion management 'display rules' that could be incorporated into such training sessions, including ways in which employees are expected to mask negative emotions and to express emotions 'professionally'.

Critical studies of emotional labour have raised questions about the practicalities and ethics involved in attempts to 'commodify' and manage emotions in the workplace (see, for example, Hochschild, 1983; Sutton, 1991; Fineman, 2000; Gabriel and Griffiths, 2002; Korczynski, 2002). Attention has typically been drawn to the harmful effects of managerial imposition of 'feeling rules' on front-line workers – such as employee estrangement, alienation and customer abuse (Korczynski, 2002).

Less well researched are the perceived pleasures of emotional labour (Korczynski, 2002) and the broader range of emotion management rules that function to encourage community building and personal well-being, exemplified in Martin *et al.*'s (1998) account of 'bounded emotionality' at the Body Shop.

Research context

Throughout this chapter we take a social view of emotion in which it is accepted that emotions are culturally shaped and enacted through language, instead of viewing emotions as simply being 'in' people, having a life of their own (Fineman, 2000; Antonacopoulou and Gabriel, 2001).[3] From this position, the aims of our chapter are two-fold: first, to highlight the nature of emotion management training at ServCo, illustrating how this focused on maintaining relationships amongst co-workers and their managers and an improvement in employee well-being; second, to explore how these ground rules for emotion display shaped perceptions of the psychological contract amongst its participants.

We recognize the need to consider how emotion management could be used in ways that are damaging to the individual manager/employee, and this issue will be examined in further research work being undertaken by the authors. Here, we present initial findings from a two-phase project to illustrate how emotion management training unleashed very positive feelings and expectations amongst participants about increased employee autonomy, discretion and improved well-being, and how this process opened up the prospect of contract 'breach' or 'violation' amongst its participants (Robinson and Rousseau, 1994; Morrison and Robinson, 1997).

Morrison and Robinson describe a breach as a failure on the part of the organization to meet perceived obligations. This identification of unmet obligations may be relatively short-term (thereby allowing employees to return to their relatively stable psychological contract state), or alternatively it may develop into full violation that creates a deep emotional and affective state that involves a wide-range of responses (Pate *et al.*, 2003: 558).

Critical commentaries have questioned the impact of psychological breach on employee attitudes and behaviours, and conclude that contextual factors are key to understanding the psychological contract (Grant, 1999; Pate *et al.*, 2003; Guest, 2004). What is less evident in the management literature is the extent to which hyperbole and rhetoric surrounding such HRD interventions can specifically create unrealistic expectations and the inevitable sense of breach of contract when they are not met. Grant's (1999) analysis of the way in which expectations are influenced by management rhetoric provides us with a useful framework for exploring this dynamic within our case organization, and this is explained below.[4]

Methodology

This chapter draws on the first phase of our research within ServCo, which is a leading retailer employing over 170,000 people. Our research focuses on a leadership programme being introduced across all UK operations. The findings we present here are based on one regional grouping comprising 24 stores around the central belt of Scotland.[5]

The leadership programme was part of a corporate-wide culture change programme that involved a series of training workshops and events for all staff running from May to July 2003. In this chapter, our analysis draws upon documentary material and 21 in-depth interviews conducted over an eight-month period in 2003. This included interviews with the senior management team (three), a sample of store managers (seven out of 25) and a sample of HR managers at local store level (four). In addition, we conducted two focus groups with 16 regional HR managers from across the UK, and a few follow-up interviews. All respondents had attended the leadership programme between eight and 12 months prior to the interviews.

All interviews were tape-recorded with the permission of the participants, and fully transcribed. We eschewed a focus commonly found in the recent leadership studies on causal relationships between different types of leader behaviour and various outcomes (Bryman, 1999). Instead, we employed a data-driven inductive approach that is more concerned with process than content and structural issues, and with generating an understanding grounded in the perspectives of the participants (Strauss, 1987). This approach is consistent with treatment of the psychological contract as being socially constructed and multifaceted in nature, and the argument that conventional quantitative techniques may not be able adequately to capture their idiosyncratic and evolving nature (Conway and Briner, 2002; Atkinson, 2003).

Here, transcripts were reviewed line by line within a paragraph and coded according to emerging categories that indicated new 'display rules' for managers. This included appropriate and inappropriate displays of emotion, and the patterning of expectations around issues of employee health, well-being and work-life balance. Once complete, coded material was summarized and outlines placed into 'partially ordered' matrix displays that imposed minimal conceptual structure on the material displayed (Miles and Huberman, 1994). These included distilled data summaries and illustrative extracts that allowed for constant comparison and the analysis of any similarities and differences in participants' accounts. We also made use of secondary data in the form of relevant company training materials, reports and policy documents relating to the change programme and wider HRM practices.

Specifically, we draw upon Grant's (1999) framework to investigate managers' expectations prior to and after attending the programme, and how this was shaping their perceptions of the psychological contract. His framework borrows from expectancy theory in suggesting that the psychological contract is heavily influenced by our desired goals and outcomes, and that the expectation we have of achieving these influences our motivation and behaviour at work. Arguments are based on the idea that the employees' past/current work experiences, coupled with the rhetoric of HRM espoused by management, are key factors shaping employee perceptions of HRM and expectations of the contracts drawn up under it (Grant, 1999: 329). Positioning HRM policy/practice as an ideal, the rhetoric seeks to persuade employees to believe it is obtainable and will have a bearing on the extent to which employees allow their perceptions of past and current experiences ('reality' established in their minds) to affect their expectations.

Grant uses case-study evidence to illustrate this process of reality construction, and in doing so categorizes the psychological contract into four types: congruent, mismatched, partial or trial contracts. The *congruent* contract is one that appeals to the employee, and current HRM policies and practices are perceived to match with the rhetoric of HRM. The *mismatched* contract occurs where rhetoric has no appeal to the employees *and* does not match with their constructed reality. The partial contract is where only part of the rhetoric appeals and part of the employees' expectations have been met, and the *trial* contract is where employees 'buy in' to the contract on a 'wait and see' basis (Grant, 1999: 331). Here, employees are willing to accept that what is being promised under the rhetoric of HRM will take time to be realized.

Given that the congruent contract is an 'ideal' picture, Grant acknowledges that it is unlikely to be achieved, especially since organizational contexts are dynamic and change rapidly. Rather, movement is likely to occur between mismatched, partial and trial contracts, leading to unmet expectations and potential negative implications on individual motivation and organizational performance. Grant does not explore the dynamics of this process in depth, but Turnbull's exploratory study of culture change at

Aeroco plc usefully points to a range of behaviours amongst managers who displayed an 'openness' for change while looking for signs of shifts in the attitudes and behaviours of their seniors (Turnbull, 2001). Of particular significance was the watching and monitoring of each other's emotional and behavioural responses in shaping perceptions of the change programme.

Our application of this framework illustrates the role of the leadership programme in signalling a shift in contract from transactional to relational, and how the expectations it released opened up the prospect of 'contract violation'.[6]

Analysis and evaluation of main findings/results

Context and rationale

Over the last two years, ServCo has been rolling out a company-wide change programme with the overall objective being 'to put customer focus and development of people centre stage' (divisional HR manager). This has involved the introduction of a range of initiatives covering all aspects of the business, but of particular relevance here is the 'leadership stream', which is described as 'helping people to move from great management to great leadership' (ServCo company documentation, 2003).

While this has involved a range of development activities in areas such as coaching, personal development planning and HRM initiatives (such as absence management and 360-degree appraisal), one of the cornerstones was a four-day residential leadership programme attended by all senior and store managers, and regional HR managers. Aimed at developing managers' understanding of the practical differences between leadership and management, the programme focused on creation of behavioural change that was based on improving participants' self-awareness and self-management (physical and emotional), and an enhanced understanding of their ability to manage the emotions of others. This is illustrated in a visionary statement and programme objectives noted in Figure 11.1.

This emphasis on emotional loyalty and self-management is consistent with the concept of the 'new model' worker noted earlier (Landen, 2002), and pointed to a shift in the psychological contract from transactional to relational. Central to this shift was the creation of a 'visionary' leadership style that 'takes people with you', and 'motivates and inspires people by appealing to their needs, values and emotions so that they keep moving forward' (participant's workbook). In the next section, we focus on the emotional dimension of leadership style and the ground rules for emotion display that emerged from participants' accounts.

What will the future look like for us and our people?
- We need to attract and retain a more diverse and demanding workforce
- We need to focus on the needs of the individual:
  - ⇒ employees 'opt in' because participation (not promotion); drives commitment
  - ⇒ lifelong learning will be a key feature of work
  - ⇒ work/life balance will be a fundamental part of the employee offer (Participant's Pack)

By the end of the course you will
- ○ (. . .) have improved your self-awareness and know how to manage impacts on others
- ○ be able to choose your attitude in many different situations
- ○ be able to develop informal communication networks and have enhanced communication skills
- ○ improve understanding of how to take care of yourself to promote mental and physical well being
- ○ improve your personal capacity to lead and experience change

Figure 11.1 Leadership development programme: vision and learning objectives (Participant's Pack).

Emotion management and 'rules' for emotion display

Interview respondents explained how they were introduced to a range of tools that enabled them to both diagnose and manage emotions at the workplace. A number of ground rules for emotion displays emerged from these accounts that we have clustered under four broad headings, recognizing that these labels are our own particular constructions and that the 'rules' are not mutually exclusive: controlling negative emotions; personal disclosure of emotions; performance focused; and caring for others.

Consistent with extant research (Mumby and Putnam, 1992; Kramer and Hess, 2002), these ground rules had the potential to create more positive work relationships in that they focused on other people's emotional needs and not just the felt emotions of the individual, in order to function effectively in interpersonal relationships.

Controlling negative emotions

All respondents talked of ways in which they had been learning how to control 'negative' emotional expressions, particularly those that displayed what were described as 'angry', 'wound-up' and 'tense' behaviours. Learning processes focused on being able to control such emotions through the application of a process of 'clearing'. Participants typically drew upon the term 'in and out of the box' to describe how they enacted this process, drawing on instances where they experienced either a positive (out of the box) or negative (in the box) state of mind:

We learnt how to control our emotions more effectively and we used various tools to do this. For example, sometimes I would come in to a nightshift and go and sit in my office for an hour (or longer) before speaking to anyone – I was in the box. A technique such as going out into the car park and taking a brisk walk for five or ten minutes to clear my head and think about how I was feeling and why. And you can actually come back in and be energized and creative.

(Store manager)

[. . .] what I do tend to use a lot is the clearing process. It's definitely changed my attitude. It's made me a lot calmer, you know, it's just really. . ., at times I may have blown up, I've made myself think it's just childish, it's achieving absolutely nothing.

(Store manager)

I think that's the biggest benefit [of the programme], you know . . . what really annoys me is the store managers that think it's okay to act like spoilt kids when they're not happy with something. Now, you know, it's not okay to just behave how you feel. You need to, like, recognize the impact you have and behave like a *manager.*

(HR manager at store level)

Personal disclosure of emotions

A strong message from the programme was the requirement for managers to be 'more open about themselves' and to encourage their subordinates to do the same in order to build mutual understandings and foster 'emotional loyalty'. For those who tended to be more emotionally reserved, it meant pushing back the boundaries of what they previously felt as their private 'selves', emotions and feelings (such as guilt, anxiety), into the public arena with colleagues and their seniors. One store manager found this aspect of her training particularly challenging:

What I brought back from the whole programme, the biggest thing was to reveal more about myself to people in work. [. . .] in the store the relationship I have with the whole 170 people is very much a work one. You know, I never discussed home with them, I never really told them what I was doing at weekends or what my boyfriend was doing or anything. Most of the store didn't know if I was married, had a boyfriend or whatever.

(Store manager)

The revealing of personal feelings and motivations was seen to be dependent on trust that such disclosure would not disadvantage them, and the opening up of a new sense of personal choice was expressed by several participants. This is exemplified in comments from one HR manager describing her recent conversation with a store manager.

> One of them came back and he said to me 'you know., I no longer feel guilty about not wanting to be a Store Director'. By talking this through he had realized that he just wants a year away, [...] but his 'mind talk' was saying 'what would ServCo think of me?' And now he was able to trust his own instincts. But the biggest realization for him was that he had a *personal choice* about what he did next. And that is a big part of our job, coaching them though that. The company aren't telling them how to react – *they* choose.
>
> (Regional HR manager)

Performance focused

Another 'rule' for emotion display that emerged from our analysis of the talk about 'revealing oneself' was more explicitly performance focused, serving to meet store rather than individual goals. Here, managers were exhorted to encourage greater openness amongst staff in ways that would lead to enhanced emotional loyalty and the achievement of performance targets:

> People are far more open. . . . I had great success in my last store, you know, a particular member of the management team was not perform- ing, but, we never really got to the crux of the matter. But, by actually using the tools, you know, 'You're looking a bit tense there, how are you feeling?' We actually . . . just by using that, I could suddenly get a far greater result and actually find out something that we could actu- ally do to hopefully improve his performance.
>
> (Store manager)

Caring for others

Another rule that was linked to the emphasis placed on bounded emo- tions expressly focused on individual needs and well-being, and caring for others:

> I think the part about emotional loyalty was the biggest one, probably the second biggest was . . . we are trying to be leaders now rather than managers. In fact leadership is about small personal acts – not about big-man gestures or leading the store through enormous refit. It can just be about helping somebody who is struggling on the department for ten minutes. [...] helping somebody to carry something across to the garage because they're struggling.
>
> (Store manager)

[...] I'm far more receptive now, and recognize when people are emotionally flooded and am actually using the leadership tools to speak to them and find out what the issues are, how I can help, let them talk about it, and again also get to know them better as a person as well. [...] I tended previously in meetings to stick to business and expect everyone to be giving 100 per cent, feeling on top of the world, whereas now we'll have a meeting but we'll have open and honest sessions where the team can actually say 'I'm not comfortable about that, I've got too much work on, I think you're asking too much'.

(Store manager)

It is about you and your own personal feelings ... it was unlike any other ServCo course I'd been on [...]. You were talking about feelings, and things like that [pause] it was structured in a way that it wasn't just about the business. There was, you know, your own *personal* well-being. We had a sports psychologist in and he was showing you sort of um ... techniques to use if you're feeling lethargic and tired. [...] talked about nutrition, and sort of looking at the whole picture rather than just from a business point of view ... you know, do this, do this, do this.

(Store manager)

Raised expectations and emergence of a 'trial' psychological contract

As Grant observes, in attempting to shape expectations and therefore the psychological contract, 'the rhetoric of HRM has to contend with the influence of past and current experiences' (Grant, 1999: 333). Indeed, all respondents at ServCo referred to their past experiences of training, and one senior manager talked of 'initiative fatigue' being a problem in that change (and related training) initiatives often lost their impetus within the organization as new ones came 'on line'.

Yet little cynicism was expressed amongst respondents about ServCo's attempts to instigate widespread change in leadership behaviours. Rather, most managers interviewed[7] expressed high levels of enthusiasm about the nature and impact of the leadership programme upon their own behaviours and that of other managers. The holistic nature of the programme was perceived by many to be a key distinguishing feature, in that it was seen to have created a 'life skill' – something that can be applied at home as well as work. The group HR manager considered that this transferability of workplace training to home life would help sustain and 'keep it alive'.

I had not experienced anything like that before. It was quite revolutionary and it was the best course I've ever been on without question. And it's almost one of these life-changing type things, it was one of those things that really hit you quite hard.

(Store manager)

> Since LP I have changed my eating habits, get less wound up about things, and am more relaxed at home.
>
> (Store manager)

> I think my wife's seen me a wee bit calmer, not as tense about it, you know, about things.
>
> (Regional HR manager)

In this context, the programme led to a range of hopes and expectations and, therefore, a new kind of psychological contract that appeared to be based on a 'wait and see basis' (Grant, 1999). Here, managers were prepared to accept the ideal of HR projected by the leadership programme on a trial basis, allowing their employer time for HR policies and practices to materialize in line with a rhetoric which placed a premium on development of new leadership behaviours, employee well-being and a high-trust work environment. Those HR practices mentioned by respondents fell into three broad categories: flexible working practices, work–life balance, and health and well-being.

Flexible working practices

> Hopefully as my career progresses, my whole life is taken into account – things like mobility and shift patterns and [. . .] life-style changes, and that doesn't mean that you can never have a bigger store or progress more, it just means that you're going to work slightly differently perhaps to other people.
>
> (Store manager)

> It's very rare to get a job as part-time section manager, and certainly there are no part-time members of the senior team or store managers [. . .] I like to think that in five years time there would be some kind of job-sharing amongst store managers. I don't know if there will be but that is my hope; and that we would get more female store managers. We work 45–50 hours a week and it has to be full-time and you have to do your different shifts [. . .] But I'd like to think that you could make it so that you could have two part-time managers sharing a store.
>
> (Store manager)

Work–life balance

> It has made me realize that there is more to life than work, it's important to get the balance right.
>
> (Store manager)

Health and well-being

> I would love to see us take that next step to incorporate fitness and nutrition into stores as well. And I think we would see a huge difference, a lot of stores have space [. . .] it's just perhaps a small gymnasium, showers [. . .] It's being able to say it's 5.30 pm, perhaps my trading manager and myself go down to the gym for half an hour, an hour after work or something, and be able to discuss something maybe while we're in the gym.
>
> (Store manager)

Interpretations and conclusions

Honouring the deal?

While 'waiting' for the creation of HR practices noted above, respondents' accounts suggested that they were looking for some immediate evidence of culture change amongst managers and their seniors, to indicate they were honouring the 'deal'. For one HR manager, watching whether senior managers were ostensibly changing their own behaviours was an important factor in shaping whether or not store managers would fully embrace the ideas behind the leadership programme.

> The first people went through the programme last July so it is almost a year, but the last lot go in a couple of weeks and what you see is very much around 'well, is my boss demonstrating it?', they will watch. I mean we have a culture of when the store directors come into store they will walk around and have a look at what's going on and they [store managers] will notice if certain behaviours are evident or not as the case may be.
>
> (HR manager, store level)

Consistent with Turnbull's (2001) work noted earlier, this sense of watching and waiting was an important influence on managers' perceptions regarding whether or not the rhetoric was being met in practice. Such vigilance may lead to heightened feelings of disappointment where a sense of contract breach occurs (Robinson and Morrison, 2000), and the potential for this is illustrated in the following comments.

> [. . .] The company has opened up all these feelings and haven't really given as much support to these managers now they are back at work. You begin to ask yourself questions such as 'what would I do if I didn't work 70 hours per week?' And then you build up a picture of what you *could* do if you didn't do this and then the reality takes over and you don't have time so you then feel resentment towards the company.
>
> (Store manager)

I've got an example of a senior manager going to a new store. And the staff were so excited about him going and [...] he didn't speak to anybody apart from the store manager. And he just walked through the checkout, into the café, and off. And [...] I was tackled by all these managers who were saying 'what's going on ... that is not what we expected'. And actually they're right. He shouldn't have been there because he's not leading by example.

(HR manager, Group level)

At the course we talked a lot about improving our QWL, for example we were told that all managers should take four days off at Christmas. But how can we? We feel uncomfortable about this. We heard it at the course but we need to hear it *again* from our manager but it is not forthcoming. These are easy things to say in the course atmosphere when we are away from work. But the company made a real statement about this so it will be interesting to see if they carry it through because these things have the potential to make a difference.

(Store manager)

While these narratives suggested perceptions of breaches in psychological contract, these may be relatively short-term, as noted in Morrison and Robinson's (1997) work. Whether or not this would develop into full-blown feelings of contract violation would be dependent on a complex mix of macro- and micro-organizational factors (Robinson, 1996; Robinson and Morrison, 2000; Pate *et al.*, 2003). In our second phase of research we will explore senior managers' perceptions about difficulties they have faced in meeting expectations raised by the leadership programme, and which contextual factors are, in their eyes, shaping these difficulties.

The case study presented here provides an insight into the role of an emotion management training programme in structuring managers' expectations, and therefore, their psychological contract, with their employer.

We have shown how the organization sought to create new 'rules' about expressed emotions based on assumptions typical of this kind of leadership programme; that participants are able to learn how to remove unpredictable emotions and behaviours, in both themselves and their employees, thus ensuring improved interpersonal relations and employee performance (Goleman, 2000; Ashkanasy and Daus, 2002). Staff were also encouraged to engage in more open discussion of work-related and personal feelings that were not immediately in the interests of meeting organizational goals, but served to develop a wider community spirit.

Consistent with Grant's conceptual framework, the influence of past and present employment experiences were important factors shaping the appeal of an HR rhetoric which placed a premium on the development of 'visionary' leadership behaviours, employee well-being and a high-trust work environment. Managers, on the whole, expressed very positive reactions to the training they received, and drew on talk of past training and work experiences to emphasize the 'distinctiveness' of the programme, which had immediately obvious benefits to them in that it helped them develop 'life skills' that had the potential to enhance their physical and emotional well-being.

Key learning points

Managers' accounts suggested emergence of a 'wait and see' trial contract (Grant, 1999), which involved watching for changes in their seniors' behaviours and in the HRM policy environment in ways that would indicate that their employer had honoured the new 'deal'. Given the high expectations released by the training programme, there is a real danger of a gap emerging between the ideal shaping these expectations and managers' 'realities', which, Grant warns, is inevitable where seniors seek a 'congruent' contract. This factor raises questions about the need for human resource development practitioners to be fully aware of the likelihood of perceived contract breach in situations where training programmes are promoting idealized models of leadership that cannot be fully met in practice.

In this context, the enthusiasm with which such programmes tend to be delivered by trainers might be usefully tempered by building in opportunities for discussions between a *mix* of employer 'agents' – for example, line managers, trainers and course participants – about how new management ideals might be translated into practice in business environments that are constantly changing. On doing so, senior managers can constantly review and alter their rhetoric and idealized images of the employment relationship in more creative ways that take account of changing environments in which they find themselves, and of ongoing differences in the perceptions, needs and aspirations of their workforce. It means breaking out of traditional management perspectives that typically lock them into fixed frameworks (Morgan, 1997) and engaging in more critical reflection about the role of context (past and current) in shaping ongoing perceptions of the psychological contract.

A more critical stance could lead to a heightened awareness of the potential negative effects of emotion management that are not ordinarily considered by employers engaging in these techniques, and ways to reduce these. For example, it was noted earlier that one manager was somewhat cautious about the push for more intimate personal issues with co-workers, and this raises questions about the potentially harmful 'conformity pressures' of emotion management noted in Martin *et al.*'s study (1998) – for example, where people who prefer more impersonality and emotional reserve feel pressurized to express themselves in ways that are inauthentic to them.

Herriot argues that rhetorical persuasion in many organizations seldom meshes with employees' experience, which leads to mistrust and cynicism on the part of employees. He concludes that continual use of rhetoric of the kind we have noted here will result in a greater cynicism, which permits employees to 'play act the emotional responses that are expected of them' (Herriot, 2001: 321). Our findings at ServCo pointed to little cynicism amongst managers during the early stages of change, as they 'waited' for 'promises' to be realized. In our second phase of fieldwork we shall undertake follow-up interviews with our respondents to assess perceptions about how far their expectations have been met, whether the initial perceptions of contract breach continued or increased in intensity, and what effects, if any, this dynamic has on their attitudes and behaviours.

Notes

1 See Guest (2004) for an examination of recent economic, social and political trends shaping the changing employment relationship. He explains that the increasing focus placed by academics upon the employment relationship at the *individual level* has arisen from the steady decline in the traditional system of industrial relations in the UK based on collective representation, growth of individualism and HRM practices geared towards flexible and committed employees.

2 The *state* of the psychological contract, according to Guest and Conway, is concerned with perceptions about how far promises and obligations have been met, whether they are perceived to be fair, and whether there is trust that they will continue to be met (Guest and Conway, 1997, 2002a, 2002b, 2002c; Guest, 1998).

3 Research in this field has also led to debate about whether emotion should be treated as a psychological determinant or as something that is socially constructed. Researchers are increasingly placing emotion in a social and relational context, but, as Antonacopoulou and Gabriel explain, there has been a 'rapprochement' between these approaches, exemplified in Armstrong's (2000) work in which he 'does not deny the importance of the inner world but rather approaches it as open and accessible to social and organizational influences' (Antonacopoulou and Gabriel, 2001: 439).

4 See Francis (2002) for an in-depth case analysis of the role of rhetoric in constructing employees' perceptions of the 'reality' of HRM practice.

5 Within the UK, the business is divided into five divisions. The region that we report on here is one part of the wider UK North Division, which is made up of 11 regions each comprising 24 retail stores.

6 On presenting our findings we recognize that our choice of illustrative quotations reflects our own social constructions of the research material, and in this context our aim is to provide sufficient 'thick description' for readers to assess the appropriateness of our findings about HRD practice for their own settings (Miles and Huberman, 1994: 279; Alvesson and Deetz, 2000).

7 Average length of service amongst store managers was 13 years, and there was no apparent difference in responses between those with longer or shorter experience within the company.

References

Alvesson, M. and Deetz, S. (2000) *Doing Critical Management Research*, London: Sage.

Antonacopoulou, E.P. and Gabriel, Y. (2001) 'Emotion, learning and organizational change: towards an integration of psychoanalytic and other perspectives', *Journal of Organizational Change Management*, 14(5): 435–51.

Armstrong, D. (2000), as cited in Antonacopoulou, E.P. and Gabriel, Y. (2001) 'Emotion, learning and organizational change: towards an integration of psychoanalytic and other perspectives', *Journal of Organizational Change Management*, 14(5): 435–51

Ashkanasy, N.M. and Daus, C.S. (2002) 'Emotion in the workplace: the new challenge for managers', *Academy of Management Executive*, 16(1): 76–86.

Atkinson, C. (2003) 'Exploring the state of the psychological contract: the impact of research on outcomes', CIPD Professional Standards Conference, Keele University; abridged version in Atkinson, C. (2004) 'Why methods matter: researching the psychological contract', *Human Resources and Employment Review*, 2(2): 111–16.

Boyatzis, R.E. and Van Oosten, E. (2002) 'Developing emotionally intelligent organizations', Consortium for Research on Emotional Intelligence in Organizations, July, 1–9.

Bryman, A. (1999) 'Leadership in organizations', in Clegg, S.R., Hardy, C. and Nord, W.R. (eds), *A Handbook of Organizational Studies*, London: Sage.

Conway, N. and Briner, B. (2002) 'A daily diary study of affective responses to psychological contract breach and exceeded promises', *Journal of Organizational Behaviour*, 23: 287–302.

Conway, N. and Briner, R. (2004) 'Promises, promises', *People Management*, 25 November.

Fineman, S. (2000) 'Emotional arenas revisited', in Fineman, S. (ed.), *Emotion in Organizations*, London: Sage.

Francis, H. (2002) 'The power of "talk" in HRM-based change' *Personnel Review*, 31(4): 432–48.

Gabriel, Y. and Griffiths, D.S. (2002) 'Emotion, learning and organizing', *The Learning Organization*, 9(5): 214–21.

Goleman, D. (2000) *Working with Emotional Intelligence*, New York, NY: Bantam.

Grant, D. (1999) 'HRM, rhetoric and the psychological contract: a case "easier said than done"', *International Journal of Human Resource Management*, 10(2): 321–50.

Gratton, L. (2003) Leading the democratic enterprise, *Business Strategy Review*, 14(4): 512.

Guest, D. (1998) 'Is the psychological contract worth taking seriously'?, *Journal of Organizational Behaviour*, 19: 649–64.

Guest, D. (1999) 'Human resource management – the workers verdict', *Human Resource Management Journal*, 9(3): 5–25.

Guest, D. (2004) 'The psychology of the employment relationship: an analysis based on the psychological contract', *Applied Psychology: An International Review*, 53(4): 41–555.

Guest, D. and Conway, N. (1997) *Employee Motivation and the Psychological Contract*, London: CIPD.

Guest, D. and Conway, N. (2002a) 'Communicating the psychological contract: an employer perspective', *Human Resource Management Journal*, 12(2): 22–38.

Guest, D. and Conway, N. (2002b) *Organizational Change and the Psychological Contract*, CIPD Survey Report, London: CIPD.

Guest, D. and Conway, N. (2002c) *Pressure of Work and the Psychological Contract*, CIPD Survey Report, London: CIPD.

Guest, D. and Conway, N. (2002d) *Public and Private Sector Perspectives on the Psychological Contract*, London: CIPD.

Herriot, P. (2001) 'Future work and its emotional implications', in Payne, R.L. and Cooper, C.L. (eds), *Emotions at Work*, London: John Wiley & Sons.

Hiltrop, J.M. (1996) 'Managing the changing psychological contract', *Employee Relations*, 1(1): 36–49.

Hochschild, A.R. (1983) *The Managed Heart: Commercialization of Human Feeling*, Berkeley, CA: University of California Press.

Humphreys, R.H. (2000) 'The importance of job characteristics to emotional displays', in Ashkanasy, N.M., Hartel, C.E.J. and Zerbe, W.J. (eds), *Emotions in the Workplace: Theory, Research and Practice*, Westport, CT: Quorum, pp. 236–49.

Korczynski, M. (2002) *Human Resource Management in Service Work*, Basingstoke: Palgrave.

Kramer, M. and Hess, J.A. (2002) 'Communication rules for the display of emotions in organizational settings', *Management Communication Quarterly*, 16(1): 66–79.

Landen, M. (2002) 'Emotion management: dabbling in mystery – white witchcraft or black art'?, *Human Resource Development International*, 5(4): 507–21.

Linstead, S. and Fulop, L. (2004) 'Motivation and meaning', in Linstead, S., Fulop, L. and Lilley, S. (eds), *Management and Organization, A Critical Text*, London: Palgrave Macmillan.

Martin, J., Knopoff, K. and Beckman, C. (1998) 'An alternative to bureaucratic impersonality and emotional labour: bounded emotionality at the Body Shop', *Administrative Science Quarterly*, 43(2): 429–69.

Miles, B.M. and Huberman, A.M. (1994) *Qualitative Data Analysis: An Expanded Source Book*, London: Sage.

Morgan, G. (1997) *Images of Organizations*, London: Sage.

Morrison, E.W. and Robinson, S.L. (1997) 'When employees feel betrayed: a model of how psychological contract violation develops', *Academy of Management Review*, 22(1): 226–56.

Mumby, D.K. and Putnam, L. (1992) 'The politics of emotion: a feminist reading of bounded rationality', *Academy of Management Review*, 17: 465–85.

Pate, J., Martin, G. and McGoldrick, J. (2003) 'The impact of the psychological contract on employee attitudes and behaviour', *Employee Relations*, 25(6): 557–73.

Purcell, J., Kinnie, N., Hutchinson, S., Rayton, B. and Swart, J. (2003) *Understanding the People and Performance Link: Unlocking the Black Box*, Research Report, London: CIPD.

Robinson, S.L. (1996) 'Trust and breach of the psychological contract', *Administrative Science Quarterly*, 41.

Robinson, S.L. and Morrison, E.W. (2000) 'The Development of psychological contract breach and violation: a longitudinal study', *Journal of Organizational Behavior*, 21(5): 525–546.

Robinson, S.L. and Rousseau, D.M. (1994) 'Violating the psychological contract: not the exception but the norm', *Journal of Organizational Behavior*, 15(3): 245–59.

Rousseau, D.M. (1990) 'New hire perspectives of their own and employer obligations: a study of psychological contracts', *Employee Responsibility and Rights Journal,* 2: 121–39.

Rousseau, D.M. (1994) 'Two ways to change and keep the psychological contract: theory meets practice', *Executive Summary for the International Consortium for Executive Development Research,* Lausanne, Switzerland.

Sparrow, P.R. (1996) 'Transitions in the psychological contract: some evidence from the banking sector', *Human Resource Management Journal,* 6(4): 75–92.

Storey, J. (1992) *Developments in the Management of Human Resources,* Oxford, Blackwell Business.

Strauss, A.L. (1987) *Qualitative Analysis for Social Scientists,* Cambridge: Cambridge University Press.

Sutton, R.I. (1991) 'Maintaining norms about expressed emotions: the case of bill collectors', *Administrative Science Quarterly,* 36: 245–68.

Turnbull, S. (1999) 'Emotional labour in corporate change programmes', *Human Resource Development International,* 2(2): 125–46.

Turnbull, S. (2001) 'Corporate ideology – meanings and contradictions for middle managers', *British Journal of Management,* 12: 231–42.

12 Management development for women entrepreneurs in the small business sector of the Vietnamese economy

Jaap Voeten

Introduction and objectives

This chapter describes a management development programme conducted by Maastricht School of Management (MSM) that was aimed at women entrepreneurs in Vietnam. It details how the impact of the programme was researched with the help of tracer studies, and reports the main changes that had occurred in business management practices and performance and in gender relations four to six months after the management training.

MSM is a business school located in Maastricht, the Netherlands. It offers a variety of education and research programmes in the field of management development. The programmes range from MBA, DBA and PhD programmes for the international business community (mainly in economies in transition), via short tailor-made management courses and organizational development courses, to management consultancy for the public–private sector interface (public administrators, management education and research practitioners). Management development refers to the activities aimed at enhancing the ability of leaders, managers and entrepreneurs to plan, organize, lead and control projects, organizations or businesses and their staff, and at developing people's ability to manage within their organizational environment (Prokopenko, 1998).

Some of MSM's management development activities are embedded in broader institutional development programmes aimed at strengthening higher management education in developing countries. For many years MSM has been evolving into a globally networked management school, one that implements outreach education, research and technical assistance programmes overseas. MSM's institutional development outreach programmes comprise staff development, education and research programme formulation and implementation, infrastructure development, and the improvement of management operation and procedures.

The 'Training for Women in Micro and Small Enterprises in Vietnam, phase 2' (TWMSE2) project is an example of the management development initiatives undertaken by MSM. In the period 2001–2004, the project provided non-financial assistance to women entrepreneurs in Vietnam who own and manage a small business[1] by offering them management development in the form of management training. TWMSE2 incorporated a survey aimed at measuring the actual management development effects by comparing a group of women entrepreneurs that had undergone management development with a group that had not done so.

The overall objective of the management development practice in TWMSE2 was to improve women's disadvantaged position in Vietnam by promoting their entrepreneurship and supporting small businesses. It was assumed that management development facilitates business development, whether through promoting a more efficient way of operation or through facilitating business expansion. It is recognized that developing the small businesses run by women can provide an opportunity to accelerate general levels of economic activity and to promote a more equitable distribution of development benefits (Dignard and Havet, 1995), while also correcting gender imbalances.

Against this background, the immediate objectives of the TWMSE2 management development for women entrepreneurs were:

- to promote effective and efficient management practices among women entrepreneurs who own and manage a small business;
- to increase business performance in terms of sales and income, and stimulate employment generation;
- to improve the gender status of women who own and manage a small business.

The project was also aimed at obtaining knowledge about and experience in management development research by developing impact assessment methodologies to evaluate the effects, effectiveness and impact of management development. To that end, a survey was developed and carried out in parallel with the launch of management development activities for women entrepreneurs who own and manage a small business. The aim of the survey was to establish how and to what extent management training promotes effective business operation and development, and to ascertain its impact on the position of women entrepreneurs in Vietnam. It is important to understand this last point, since development interventions do not always serve both purposes at the same time.

Theoretical and organizational context

Management development is a rather broadly defined term encompassing various approaches. Prokopenko (1998) lists several approaches and components, such as management education and training, action learning, organizational development and management consulting. The distinction between education and training is not precisely defined. Programmes that deal with basic management disciplines, such as economics and psychology, and lead to a formal qualification (e.g. an MBA) could be grouped together under the heading 'management education'. Short courses that do not lead to such a qualification and focus on skills and techniques tend to be described as 'management training programmes'. Action learning can be seen as the middle ground between formal courses and learning from experience on the job. Management development also embraces the term organizational development, which is used to describe a planned process of organizational change designed to assist the organization or business in achieving its strategic goals.

In its outreach programmes overseas, MSM employs most of the above-mentioned approaches and components, combining education, research and technical assistance. For example, short management courses serve as input for MBA course-module development, research findings are used for education materials and case-study development, students in MBA programmes work on strategic research topics in their research papers, and beneficiaries from technical assistance and organizational development become equal partners in MSM's joint outreach management development. The components and approaches are thus closely interrelated and promote an effective and efficient design and delivery of the management development at MSM.

In the case of TWMSE2, women entrepreneurs underwent a three-day management training programme focused on business planning, marketing and financial management. The programme comprised a combination of lectures and interactive learning, such as case studies and the sharing of business experiences. The designers of the programme chose the subjects and methodology according to the training needs that had been identified some months earlier. TWMSE2 constituted a broader organizational development effort for the entrepreneurship development programme of the local intermediary organization, the Vietnam Women's Union. Several interrelated components were also incorporated, such as staff training, curriculum and management research programme development, policy development for entrepreneurship promotion, organizational and operations strengthening, and physical infrastructure building. However, this chapter discusses only the management training of women entrepreneurs in the small business sector.

Women entrepreneurs in the small business sector were chosen as the target group because small businesses are a major feature of the economic landscape in all developing countries, and in the last three decades the sector has been proposed as an alternative for achieving sustainable socio-economic development (Dignard and Havet, 1995). The choice was further supported by the neoliberal market paradigm in which the importance of small-scale growth-oriented enterprise development, based on the Western model of individualist entrepreneurship in order to increase the contribution to market-led economic growth, is underlined in private-sector development (Mayoux, 2003). As in many developing countries, the medium- and large-scale enterprise sectors offer limited new opportunities to the many who are seeking employment; governments and partners in development are increasingly looking to the informal and the small-scale sectors to generate new and sustainable employment opportunities (Harper and Finnegan, 1998). The contribution of small businesses to the creation of jobs and the alleviation of poverty has been recognized and proven in many developing counties.

Many Vietnamese women entrepreneurs run a small business; most of such businesses are in the informal sector, where women account for about half (and sometimes more) of the workforce of the entire sector.[2] In addition, the great majority of workers in women-owned and -managed micro- and small businesses are female. Both features have led to female entrepreneurship receiving increased attention. In addition, the field constitutes a cross-section of the main preoccupations of today's most influential approaches in international development – namely, gender and development, bottom-up strategies, privatization and entrepreneurship, and local capacity development (Dignard and Havet, 1995). The increasing profits and efficiency of women's businesses make a significant contribution to the growth of the economy as a whole (though especially to the small-scale sector, given the prominence of women in that sector). The main objective of developing women's entrepreneurship is to promote both dynamic small businesses that have growth potential, and the women who are most likely to be successful entrepreneurs, particularly in high-growth sectors of the economy (Mayoux, 2003).

In Vietnam, small businesses form a significant part of the rural and the urban informal sectors, and have been recognized as generators of income and providers of cheap goods and services. The importance of small businesses and the private sector, not least as a source of employment and income, is explicitly recognized in key policy documents of the Vietnamese Government in the past decade (Ronnas and Ramamurthy, 2001). With regard to the gender dimension of Vietnam's policy choices, the promotion of women's entrepreneurship has been articulated along two main lines of argumentation, namely gender equality and economic efficiency (Truong, 2002). Since the introduction of the *doi moi* ('renovation') policy[3] – which allows private enterprises to do business in all sectors of the economy – actors in the development field have provided a variety of services to promote women's entrepreneurship, of which TWMSE2 is but one example.

Despite the efforts to promote small businesses in Vietnam, management development agents lack information about the impact of management development, particularly in a broader context in the medium and long run (Harper and Finnegan, 1998). Moreover, many intermediary organizations involved in promoting small businesses are discovering the importance of impact assessment research in connection with practice.

Regarding gender, there is another reason for the lack of impact assessments: the practitioners' sense of urgency and the eagerness in practice have not been matched by research efforts. Many private-sector actors in the field of development and gender issues take for granted the need for management development for women, without differentiating categories of women entrepreneurs or looking at the longer-term effects. Subsequently, these approaches lead to the design of interventions that can produce results other than those intended.

Research context

The management training of women entrepreneurs in the small business sector, which formed part of the overall project's management development effort, was launched in parallel with research aimed at addressing the above-mentioned research questions related to (1) the change management practices of women entrepreneurs in the small business sector; (2) the positive effects on business results; and (3) how the observed changes relate to the changed gender status of women entrepreneurs resulting from the management training.

In 2001, 960 women entrepreneurs in 25 provinces in northern Vietnam underwent the lectured and interactive management training on business planning, marketing and financial management. Four to six months later, the survey team contacted a random selection of the women who had attended the course. At the same time, the team surveyed another sample of women entrepreneurs who were in the same economic, social and geographical context, using an identical questionnaire. Because of time constraints, it was not possible for the team to visit the entrepreneurs individually. It therefore carried out the survey by mail, even though it was recognized that this approach has its limitations. The questionnaire was worded as simply and clearly as possible in order to collect objective, reliable data.

Within three weeks, 102 women entrepreneurs who had undergone the training, and 43 who had not, returned the completed questionnaire. Most of the entrepreneurs in both groups were involved in one of four economic activities, namely trading (40.7 per cent), food/agro-processing (15.2 per cent), textile production/crafts (13.1 per cent), and food/refreshment shops (7.6 per cent). There was no significant difference in involvement in economic activities between those who had and those who had not undergone the training.

The survey team compared the data of both groups by applying a non-parametric chi-square test for nominal data and the Wilcoxon test for ordinal data (level of significance: $\alpha = 0.05$). It should be noted that a quarter of both groups reported that in recent years they had undergone some form of training or instruction on small business management, and that this gave both groups a comparable point of departure.

Analysis and evaluation of the main findings

Business management practices

Based on project surveys[4] that had been used to identify reliable and measurable indicators, the present survey used the following two key variables to observe changes in business management practices: (1) changes in actual management practices, in particular advanced financial records and new marketing techniques; and (2) the separation of business finances and family finances. Table 12.1 shows the changes in management practices in the test group and in the control group.

It shows that there are significant differences between the women entrepreneurs who had and those who had not received the management training, and that such training promotes a certain innovation in management practice. The data also show that around one third of the women entrepreneurs who had not received the training were seeking new management practices. Nevertheless, those who had undergone management development were more stimulated to do so.

With regard to financial record-keeping, the project baseline study shows that most (78.8 per cent) of the women entrepreneurs in the small business sector already kept some form of basic financial records (cash book, purchase book). The specific contribution of the management training has been the introduction of more advanced financial books, such as the transactions book, cash-flow book, invoice book, purchase journal, inventory book, stock book, outstanding debt book and salary records.

Another newly introduced management technique resulting from the management training is business planning combined with financial monitoring. This comprises longer-term business planning and the actual drawing up of the plan. Quality control and time management of entrepreneurs and employees were also mentioned, as was the introduction of human resources management techniques, such as a working time system.

Table 12.1 Changes in management practices that had occurred in the four to six months preceding the survey

Change in management practice	Share (%) of WEs* without TWMSE2 training	Share (%) of WEs with TWMSE2 training
Introduction of new management techniques	35.9 ($n = 39$)	84.0 ($n = 94$)
Introduction of advanced financial records	16.3 ($n = 43$)	44.1 ($n = 102$)
Introduction of new marketing techniques	27.5 ($n = 40$)	75.0 ($n = 96$)

Notes
* WEs = women entrepreneurs; $p = 0.000$, $p = 0.001$, $p = 0.000$ for all three variables.

With respect to marketing, there is an important difference between the trained and the untrained entrepreneurs: the share of women entrepreneurs who conduct marketing activities increased by 50 per cent after the TWMSE2 management training. A cross-check with the baseline data confirms this figure. The new marketing techniques mostly comprised advertising, the provision of extra services and after-sales, the better display of goods, the carrying out of market studies to assess the demand for certain products, product diversification, an improved service attitude towards customers, and a better balance between price and quality.

The change in the separation of business finances and family finances is a relevant indicator, since such a separation is an important step in the development and upgrading of a business venture. In this survey, a significant difference was established (chi-square test: $p = 0.000$): 54.8 per cent of the women entrepreneurs who did not receive the TWMSE2 training do not separate business and family finances, while 75.3 per cent of the women who had been trained were doing so four to six months after the programme. It is possible that this percentage increased in subsequent months. It is also possible that the separation of finances will increase in time as the entrepreneurs gain more experience with financial record-keeping, business planning and other related management techniques.

It thus appears that, in the TWMSE2 case, management development has had a positive effect on the business management practices of women entrepreneurs, in the sense that they better understand and separate internal financial processes and are better connected with their business environment.

Business results

Instead of carrying out an in-depth financial analysis of each individual business (obtaining reliable data would have been very time-consuming, as was the case in the TWMSE baseline surveys), the survey team evaluated four variables that reflect measurable changes in business results, namely: (1) whether or not an entrepreneur innovated or upgraded her product or service; (2) changes in sales volume; (3) changes in the number of paid employees; and (4) the development of personal income.

Table 12.2 shows the share of women entrepreneurs who had carried out a product or service upgrade/innovation during the four to six months preceding the survey.

The data show that the trained entrepreneurs performed more upgrading and innovation than did those who had not received the training. Although the difference is significant, the share of 48.8 per cent of women entrepreneurs who performed innovation without having received TWMSE2 training should not be underestimated. Such product or service upgrading ranges from change of design, production process or packaging, via increased quality while maintaining the same price, to the techno-

Table 12.2 Share of women entrepreneurs who had upgraded their product or service in the four to six months preceding the survey

	Share (%) of WEs* without TWMSE2 training	Share (%) of WEs with TWMSE2 training
Upgrade or innovation	48.8 ($n = 43$)	88.7 ($n = 97$)

Note
* WEs = women entrepreneurs: $p = 0.00$.

Table 12.3 Change in sales volume in the four to six months preceding the survey

Level of sales	Share (%) of WEs* without TWMSE2 training (n = 40)	Share (%) of WEs with TWMSE2 training (n = 99)
Decrease	7.5	2.0
No change	35.0	17.2
Modest increase (10–20%)	55.0	61.6
High increase (> 20%)	2.5	19.2
Total	100.0	100.0

Note
* WEs = women entrepreneurs: $p = 0.00$.

logical innovation of the production process (e.g. equipment and tools) and a broader range of products. Applying new management techniques and upgrading products was a first step; Table 12.3 shows the extent to which the women actually increased their sales volume as a result of the management development effort.

The trained women entrepreneurs achieved a larger sales increase than did the women entrepreneurs who had not received the training. Again, it should be noted that the entrepreneurs who had not received the training had performed quite well: 55 per cent reported a modest increase in sales volume. This observation reflects the favourable economic conditions for small-business growth in northern Vietnam. However, nearly one-fifth (19.2 per cent) of the trained women entrepreneurs had succeeded in achieving a large sales increase, while the figure for those who had not been trained was only 2.5 per cent.

Table 12.4 shows that the women entrepreneurs who had undergone the training hired more employees; however, the difference is statistically insignificant, implying that in the case of the project the direct employment generation effect of management training was not noticeable four to six months later. Nevertheless, there is an interesting difference between the two groups in the share of entrepreneurs who hired more than three employees.

Women entrepreneurs are reluctant to take on more employees for

Table 12.4 Change in the number of paid employees in the four to six months preceding the survey

	Share (%) of WEs* without TWMSE2 training (n = 37)	Share (%) of WEs with TWMSE2 training (n = 81)
Fewer employees	0.0	0.0
No change	83.8	71.6
Modest increase (1–3 employees)	13.5	16.0
Large increase (>3 employees)	2.7	12.4
Total	100.0	100.0

Note
* WEs = women entrepreneurs.

other reasons, too. The TWMSE2 baseline study established that only 36 per cent of women considered to be an entrepreneur aim at expanding their business, hiring more employees and having bigger workshops in order to achieve higher production, larger profits and more income. Another 33 per cent reported that they do not feel the need to hire more employees, as they aim to increase their income by increasing their productivity and efficiency. It was observed in the TWMSE surveys that women entrepreneurs who are engaged in other gender roles (e.g. reproductive and community management roles) want to increase efficiency and thus generate more income from the business while maintaining the same business size and the same number of employees.

Table 12.5 shows the personal income development of the two groups. There is a significant difference in the distribution of observed values: the trained women entrepreneurs achieved a significantly larger increase in income. It is worth mentioning that 12.2 per cent of the trained entrepreneurs generated 20 per cent more personal income after the training.

Table 12.5 Development of personal income in the four to six months preceding the survey

Change in income	Share (%) of WEs* without TWMSE2 training (n = 40)	Share (%) of WEs with TWMSE2 training (n = 98)
Decrease	2.5	4.1
No change	32.5	18.4
Slight increase (10–20%)	62.5	65.3
Large increase (>20%)	2.5	12.2
Total	100.0	100.0

Note
* WEs = women entrepreneurs.

In absolute terms, this percentage implies a personal income increase of approximately US$20–30 per month (assuming an average monthly income of US$100).

A review of the names of the entrepreneurs in the data revealed that the 12.4 per cent who had hired more than three extra employees (Table 12.4) and the 12.2 per cent who had generated much more income (Table 12.5) are the same group of individuals. These entrepreneurs obviously benefited the most from the management development provided by the project. It would be interesting to learn more about the common profile of these entrepreneurs and managers, as it would help to better target and set expectations and thus to maximize the effectiveness and efficiency of management development.

Impact on gender relations

The ultimate objective of TWMSE2 was to improve the disadvantaged position of women in Vietnam by promoting their entrepreneurship and supporting them in the development of micro- and small enterprises. To assess whether the project was successful, it is necessary carefully to evaluate both the improvement in the position of women, and the entrepreneurship promotion and management development, as there is a danger of focusing on management development and assuming that the position of women will be improved as a result of such development.

Apart from running a business, women in Vietnam are expected to assume a range of responsibilities in family and community life. In this respect, time is a critical factor for many women entrepreneurs. Table 12.6 shows the changes in the amount of time spent by those women entrepreneurs who achieved at least a 10 per cent growth in sales (Table 12.3).

Table 12.6 shows that the majority of these women entrepreneurs had

Table 12.6 Changes in working time in the four to six months preceding the survey

Hours worked per day	Share (%) of WEs* who had increased their sales by 10–20%	Share (%) of WEs who had increased their sales by > 20%
Fewer	8.7	–
No change	30.4	14.3
1 hour more	26.1	–
2 hours more	34.8	21.4
3 hours more	–	42.9
4 hours more	–	21.4
	100.0	100.0

Note
* WEs = women entrepreneurs.

been spending one or two hours more per day running their business; those who had achieved at least a 20 per cent increase in sales had been spending approximately three more hours per day running their business. Evaluating this change is not easy. At first, many would suggest that more working hours do not contribute to the improvement of a woman's position, since the extra hours put even more stress on her tight time schedule. On this point, however, further exploration is required, as spending less time running a business is not necessarily always the preference of a motivated entrepreneur. After all, fulfilling domestic and community responsibilities does not always match personal development ambitions or increase financial independence. Besides, domestic tasks could be assigned to others who are looking for employment, since the entrepreneur is generating more revenue, and thus benefiting both.

A second variable is the change in workload, since more work is seldom in line with the ultimate objective of improving the position of women in Vietnamese society through entrepreneurship development.

Table 12.7 shows the shares of the workload changes of those who had managed to increase sales volume by 10 per cent or more. Although the increase in workload was not quantified in exact terms, the table does show that roughly two-thirds of the trained women entrepreneurs had experienced an increase in workload as sales increased. Another one-third of the trained women entrepreneurs had managed to increase their sales with the same or a less heavy workload; this implies that they had increased the productivity of their business. The 5.6 per cent of the entrepreneurs who had achieved a large increase with a less heavy workload form an interesting group.

The whole trained group (i.e. the entrepreneurs whose business had grown and those whose business had not grown) was compared in order to establish whether there is a relation between sales volume change and workload change, since this is related to the issue of productivity increase. This comparison showed that a higher sales volume and a heavier workload do not imply an increase in productivity. The data do not show a significant correlation between sales volume change and workload change: the women entrepreneurs who had undergone management

Table 12.7 Change in daily workload in the four to six months preceding the survey

Change in daily workload	Share (%) of WEs* who had increased their sales by 10–20%	Share (%) of WEs who had increased their sales by >20%
Less heavy	1.6	5.6
No change	36.1	27.8
Heavier	62.3	66.7

Note
* WEs = women entrepreneurs.

development had increased their productivity. Although it is unlikely, this insignificant correlation might be caused by the fact that the women entrepreneurs whose business had not grown had experienced a heavier workload in the past as a result of other external factors.

A third, somewhat subjective, indicator that provides an insight into women's change of status is how they had experienced changes in their quality of life that were related to the growth of their business. Table 12.8 shows how those women entrepreneurs who had achieved a sales volume increase of 10 per cent or more (Table 12.3) rated their quality of life at the time of the survey compared with their quality of life four to six months before the survey.

Contrary to what might be expected from Tables 12.7 and 12.8 – which report more working hours and a heavier workload – the majority of women entrepreneurs whose business had grown said that they had had a better life since the TWMSE2 management training. One reason is that quality of life relates mostly to more income and to income security. Another reason might be the sense of satisfaction of being successful in business and having more control over management, despite a heavier workload and spending more time running the business.

There is also reason for cautious reflection, as 21.1 per cent of the entrepreneurs whose business had grown considerably reported that life had been easier and better in the past – and this is definitely not a positive development from a gender point of view. It is debatable whether using a questionnaire with mostly closed answers is a reliable way to address such subjective issues as perceived quality of life. This matter should be looked at more closely by means of, for instance, in-depth case studies.

Interpretations and conclusions

The TWMSE2 research and practice has provided insights into the effects of management development on management practices, business results

Table 12.8 Experienced change in the quality of life of the women entrepreneurs

	Share (%) of WEs* who had increased their sales by 10–20%	Share (%) of WEs who had increased their sales by >20%
Life was easier and better in the past	4.9	21.1
No change	18.0	10.5
Quality of life has improved since the training	77.0	68.4

Note
* WEs = women entrepreneurs.

and the gender status of women entrepreneurs and managers in the small-business sector in Vietnam.

Management development has a positive effect on the business management practices of women entrepreneurs in the sense that, as managers, they better understand and separate internal financial processes, and achieve a better connection with their business environment. In this, the most important contributing factors were the introduction of marketing techniques and the application of more advanced financial management techniques. The survey also confirmed that management development does not always result in business expansion and an increase in production, although it does stimulate innovation, the upgrading of products and an increase in productivity. The managers become more aware of the role and function of management.

Management development has a significant positive effect on the sales and income of small businesses within a relatively short period. However, no direct employment creation as a result of management development was observed. In fact, the employment creation effect is related to the growth orientation. The managers who pursue increased productivity and efficiency without expansion are not likely to hire more employees. Although the survey did not look at the creation of indirect employment, it is very possible that women entrepreneurs who achieve more growth hire more people to perform domestic work or supply services, or who free-time in some other way so that the entrepreneurs can spend it on running their business.

The survey provides a contradictory picture of increased workload and working time on the one hand, and a better quality of life and more control and decision-making with respect to their business on the other hand. Further exploration is required to understand how women entrepreneurs assess their quality of life as well, as control and decision-making.

Overall, it is important to be very careful in attributing too much credit to management development for expanding businesses in the case of Vietnam: the survey shows that, with or without management training, the small-business sector is growing in northern Vietnam. Current broader research into small businesses, such as sub-sector and value-chain analyses, could also identify whether or not small-business sectors have growth opportunities. If opportunities are limited as a result of external threats – such as competition or unfavourable policies – management development could help in identifying other business opportunities.

The management development programme comprised a training needs assessment and straightforward management training subjects, such as business planning, financial management and marketing. To what extent this experience is exactly replicable in other contexts and will produce similar outcomes is difficult to establish, because of the different external factors, the macro-economic situation, the cultural factors related to women's entrepreneurship, and the policy environment in countries in transition.

Key learning points

In order to gain a complete picture of the impact of management development programmes, the evaluation of the effects of management training is best carried out at various levels, since positive effects at one level do not imply positive effects at other levels. The levels considered could include the knowledge and skills acquired during management development, the actual application of such knowledge and skills, the effects on business operation and management, and the longer-term and broader impact on the target group's or the sector's interest as a whole. The last-named aspect could include whether management development is in line with personal context and ambitions. For women managers, this is of particular importance with respect to combining family life and a career in management.

Collecting reference data at various levels while conducting management development is required, since managers and their business may develop over time anyway. Or it might be the case that managers are confronted with limited development opportunities as a result of external threats, such as competition or unfavourable policies. Management development cannot address external threats: it only enables managers to deal with such threats. Identifying and evaluating what exactly the contribution is of the management development in what environmental context, will help in establishing the correct objectives, contents and expectations and will make the effort more effective and efficient.

In the case of Vietnam, it is possible to indicate the benefits of the management training for the target group in financial terms, as monthly incomes increased. Such quantifications, which are produced by implementing parallel research, could induce managers to enrol in fee-based training or to approach funding agencies to support programmes like these. Although simple quantifications might create overly high expectations, and other benefits may be invisible or come at a later point in time, no quantifications at all can mean that unrealistic benefits are automatically assumed. Parallel research helps to better establish and better meet the expectations, improving the overall quality of the management development provision.

Women managers respond differently to management development, depending on their ambitions and capabilities. The more homogenous the target group, the more focused a management development intervention can be with regard to establishing the objectives and contents and defining the methodology. Classifying managers according to their ambitions and development opportunities will produce more effective management development interventions.

Management development does not always result in higher productivity – that is, the production of more of the same products or services using same the production techniques and management procedures.

Particularly, women managers do not always have expansion in mind; instead, they want higher productivity and efficiency with the same time input, as this is the best way to combine business with family life. This case shows that management development encourages managers to reflect more on the function of management and on their role as managers, and subsequently to reorganize and innovate their business accordingly.

Notes

1 A 'small business' was defined as an enterprise with up to 50 employees in agriculture and off-farm related activities, trading, food and refreshment shops, food and agro-processing, manufacturing (textiles, footwear and leather, bricks, tiles and pottery, handicrafts) and other sectors/services.
2 A 'woman entrepreneur' was defined as a woman who has started a business, is actively involved in managing it, owns at least 50 percent of it, and has been in operation for a year or longer (Moore and Buttner, 1997).
3 In 1986, a new group of more liberal socialist party leaders within the Vietnamese Government launched reforms to help Vietnam out of its economic crisis: decentralization of state economic management, reliance on the private sector as an engine of economic growth, replacement of administrative measures by economic ones, and the adoption of a market-oriented monetary policy.
4 TWMSE2 carried out a baseline survey of women entrepreneurs in May–August 2001 and in October–November 2001.

References

Dignard, L. and Havet, J. (eds) (1995) *Women in Micro- and Small-Scale Enterprise Development*, Boulder, CO: Westview Press.

Harper, M. and Finnegan, G. (1998) *Value for Money?* London: Intermediate Technology Publications/International Labour Organisation.

Mayoux, L. (2003) *Jobs, Gender, and Small Enterprises: Getting the Policy Environment Right*, SEED Working Paper No. 15, Geneva: International Labour Organisation.

Moore, D.P. and Buttner, E.H. (1997) *Women Entrepreneurs: Moving Beyond the Glass Ceiling*, Thousand Oaks, CA: Sage.

Prokopenko, J. (1998) *Management Development – A Guide for the Profession*, Geneva: International Labour Office.

Ronnas, P. and Ramamurthy, B. (2001) *Entrepreneurship in Vietnam – Transformation and Dynamics*, Copenhagen, Nordic Institute of Asian Studies.

Truong, T.-D. (2002) *Gender and Enterprise Development in Vietnam under Doi Moi: Issues for Policy, Research and Training*, Working Paper 363, Den Haag: Institute of Social Studies.

13 Leading by learning

An integrated approach to middle management training

Hans-Werner Franz

Objectives

Middle managers (and higher) of small and medium-sized enterprises (SMEs) mostly have become managers primarily due to their technical competence. Many of them, depending on their qualifications, have learned to organize technical and work processes or how to manage financial transactions. However, many have not learned, at least not in a systematic way, how to organize the people who cooperate in doing this work, and many of them have not learned at all how to organize working and learning processes as an integrated approach of coping with continuously changing market, technological, organizational and social conditions. Normally, such managers in SMEs perform several functions, have little time, and their companies frequently cannot or do not want to afford systematic training for management and leadership. This chapter presents an integrated approach of (training for) leadership, working and learning in SMEs. It has been developed over a timespan of several years, and certain aspects of this approach have been applied in various contexts before.

Theoretical context

Theoretically and methodically, this integrated approach is based on a systemic organization theory and development approach, on constructivist learning theory and arrangements, and on an action learning approach integrated in a theory of the learning organization (for details of this, see Franz, 2003). All instruments used in the training have been developed against this theoretical background. A few basic assumptions of the integrated approach are now explored.

My fundamental hypothesis rests in the assumption that people, groups of people and organizations are interrelated self-referential systems who only learn from and in the context of challenges presented by new situations from outside the system. As we are dealing with intentional learning, the aim of the integrated approach can be defined as the enhancement of capability or competence to tackle and deal successfully with such challenges. In any case, it is the learner who decides what can be learned from a specific situation with the regard to its 'viability' (von Glasersfeld, 1998: 19). Arranging leadership learning thus means offering meaningful and ideally real learning opportunities providing possibilities of adapting the existing individual, group or company mindset by discovering or exploring partly or completely new and different ways of problem-solving, action strategies and methods; in other words, creating meaningful situations of experiential learning.

In such a setting, knowledge is considered to be an improvable resource rather than a truth, and learning is understood as a process of deconstructing and reconstructing existing knowledge, rather than instruction. An important means of arranging such learning processes consists of stimulating, developing and assisting communities of practice (Lave and Wenger, 1991; Wenger, 1998). In the example featured in this chapter, this occurs on several levels: among individuals representing companies, and among individuals representing departments within a company. Systems always strive for survival. Creating meaningful situations of learning, at least for companies, means going one step farther than the concept of communities of practices. In my own conceptualization of the 'learning organization', companies are considered to 'be' and the task of management is to lead them to become communities of performance. Hence, learning opportunities are considered to be meaningful if, in the view of the learners, the learning potential is perceived to be actually (or potentially) relevant in overcoming the reality of actual (or perceived) problems, deficiencies or workflow 'bottlenecks'.

When training is designed with these principles in mind, analytically conceived theoretical backgrounds may become foundations of normative thinking – an argument that underpins much of the discussion in the chapter.

Research context

The context for the chapter is a study of nine SMEs located around the German city of Bielefeld over the period 2000–2003. The research was based within the framework of the Opti.net project, co-funded by the European Social Fund (ESF), the Government of the Federal State of North Rhine Westphalia, and the nine SMEs themselves. What started as a 'project' in the year 2000 has now become a self-sustained network of active inter-company exchange and reflection on organization and human resources development, arguably representing a true community of practice.

Eight of the cases studied were medium-sized companies employing between 50 and 250 people; the remaining case was a large organization employing at the outset around 2,000 people, both inside and outside of

Germany. None of the cases studied had less than 50 employees. In contrast to small organizations (i.e. those with less than 50 employees), medium-sized enterprises are more likely to appoint someone to be responsible for continuing training, although this is hardly ever an exclusive role for such an individual. With one exception, an automobile outlet, all of the cases were manufacturers of products and product-related services, such as metal doors, baking ovens for large bakeries, laser-based computer to plate (CTP) machines, exposure and workflow machines and procedures, and ladies' high-class clothing. The organizations possessed varying levels of technological sophistication. The deployment of a training needs analysis (TNA) was used to gain access to the cases studied, since all felt the need to train their people for changed and rapidly changing requirements. To just highlight two examples:

- How will a world market leader in the development and production of laser-based CTP machines find somebody to train their front-end installation and service technicians, if the company cannot describe well which skills they need to learn? Most of these highly specialized technicians started as mechanics, they later learned to use computers, and now they must be able to adjust optical parameters of the CTP machines using mathematical models and laptops instead of adjusting screws on a trial and error basis.
- How will one of the German market leaders in fire-proof metal doors introduce statistical process control (to be used by the production team workers who are mechanics or specialized welders) without the benefit of detailed training needs analysis co-developed with these workers?

The Opti.net project used an innovative design specifically developed by Sozialforschungsstelle Dortmund (sfs) for use in practical, applied projects such as the one featured in this chapter. The project framework (see Figure 13.1) comprised four co-operating local networks organized by a local union-linked networking agency. Principle features of the networking structure were as follows:

- it was a newly built network of companies interested in systematic training needs analysis;
- it had a specialized network of systemic advisers who had previously collaborated sporadically, with sfs as the lead partner;
- it had a network of existing training providers who were willing to customize training according to the specific training needs as perceived by the companies and the advisers supporting them;
- facilitation and support (e.g. for building trust) was available via a network of local actors with an interest in the project, such as employers; union representatives; Chamber of Industry and Commerce; various enterprise associations, etc.

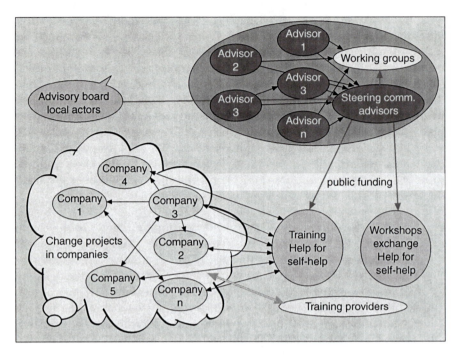

Figure 13.1 Networking structures.

The overall aim of the project was to qualify the companies and the training providers to carry out the complete TNA cycle, provide customized training and organization development, and enable the newly structured labour deployment to continue the training and development after the project was finished: essentially, to install a sustainable HRD and organization development system. Figure 13.2 shows the setting in which the project was structured.

The project was organized in learning spirals, and functioned on three levels of activity.

- *Level 1* provided common TNA training, organized by the advisers, the training providers and invited experts (see Curriculum, 2003), for one or more so-called Continuing Training Agents (CTAs) (in German: *Weiterbildungsbeauftragte*), from each of the companies. This included regular feedback and exchange between the CTAs on experience collected on Levels 2 and 3.
- *Level 2* consisted of TNA and/or organization development projects in the companies, with support from the CTAs, who immediately applied what they had learned on Level 1. These projects were implemented

in pilot departments chosen by the companies, and the CTAs received support by the advisers in order to help them make their first project a success. The specific training needs detected were developed into adapted training strategies, with support by advisers from the training-provider network. In some cases, these projects also detected training needs for middle and top management. Each of these projects led to Level 3.

- *Level 3* delivered specific tailor-made training courses, if necessary or possible organized for several companies to make delivery more cost-effective. These courses were carried out by specialists supplied by the training providers, some of whom were already involved in the development of customizing training materials and arrangements. In some cases, the in-house leadership training for managers was carried out by the advisers who also provided the TNA training (Level 1). Several special workshops were also organized to enable inter-company exchange processes between the management and works council representatives of the company network.

Evaluation of main findings on the project level

As can be seen from the project structure (see Figure 13.2) and the intense feedback relationship between the three activity levels of the project design (see also Figure 13.1), the TNA Curriculum (2003) developed for the CTA training, as well as the curricula developed within the company projects, follow a specific approach of 'doing by learning'. Everything learned is immediately applied in practical TNA and organization development

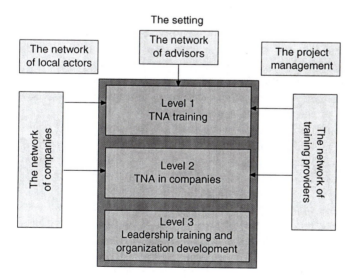

Figure 13.2 Project structure.

projects, and experience already collected can be discussed while learning and confronted with experience gained by other CTA in their own projects. All materials and instruments used in or developed for the project had to meet the same requirements laid down in the guidelines. They had to be fit for use in the change projects and, at the same time, fit for systematic learning of individuals and of groups – that is, the CTA learning group and the organizational units in the companies. Thus, learning beyond individual appropriation becomes and is organized as a collective, experience-based, practical process. Learning is therefore experienced as something immediately useful and as an opportunity for improvement by both the individual learners and by the organization as whole, making the prospect of continuing learning an attractive proposition.

Conceived as a practical approach to learning, the basics of human resource and organization development and the associated guidelines for organizing company-based continuing education and training (CVET) are formulated in a normative way – that is, reproducible as a set of guidelines for learning and doing on all three activity levels of the project.

Seven guidelines to company-based continuing training

1   *Company-based CVET should be based on a participative training needs analysis.* Training needs cannot be planned at a conference table; the employees of the respective work areas should actively participate in the assessment process. Their own view is as important as that of their superiors. All interventions must, therefore, consider the requirement of multiple perspectives.

2   *Company-based CVET must consider the requirements of all stakeholders.* On the one hand, the learning requirements expressed by the company must include an analysis of its situation and future strategy concerning the products and service provided by the respective working area; on the other hand, the requirements put forward by the employees are as important as those of the company. Human resource development is about meeting both sets of agendas.

3   *Company-based CVET should be planned along practical change processes.* TNA must become an integral part of technological or organizational change processes. Changes always lead to shifts in competence requirements. Thus, human resource development becomes a continuous task of change management.

4   *Company-based CVET should always relate to the work area and workplace.* Learning needs a perspective, an assumed application horizon and environment, it must make sense to the learners as well as to their colleagues in the context of the changes at the workplace. This includes the effective communication of these changes (see, guideline 1).

5   *Company-based CVET should be organized in teams.* TNA as well as the

learning processes leading to new competencies should be embedded in team structures. Common problems and change projects should be seen as team challenges, learning in teams as a way of solving or overcoming these problems jointly.

6   *Company-based CVET should be a continuous endeavour.* All change processes need also to be considered as shifts or changes in competence requirements. Continuous improvement means continuous learning. Learning is a way of improvement and self-improvement. The organization cannot improve without improving its people. This means that TNA is a continuous task and must become an integral part of management.

7   *Company-based CVET should be self-organized.* Understood as an integral part of management (at all levels) and of change processes, TNA and competence development must be (or become) an in-company function. A company striving to become, or perceiving itself, as a learning organization cannot outsource HRM. The arrangement of learning at work must become an integral function of management on all levels. In this sense, formal HRM/HRD departments serve to support HR as an integral function of management.

In-company training for middle management

The only large firm in the project network, a ladies' clothing manufacturer, has been selected as a case for further discussion in the chapter. At the beginning of the project the company had some 2,000 employees, although more than half of these worked in factories in Southern and Eastern Europe, in Northern Africa and in South East Asia – the German headquarters being only a design, development, distribution and service centre. All production has been relocated to countries with lower labour costs. The company has been growing constantly for 30 years; starting from a home workshop it has become one of the leading brands internationally in ladies' combination wear. When the training sequence for middle management started in October 2002, despite a critical market situation, the principal internal orientation still was the same as it had been for three decades: boost sales. Over the winter 2002–2003, for the first time, things started to deteriorate further. Since then, the company has lost some 400 employees, most of them in production.

The case context

The company is a corporation led by a CEO whose name is also the name of the company and the principal brand (one of four). He has been the founder and great entrepreneurial promoter of the company. Owing to the company's seemingly unlimited growth and success, his authoritarian and paternalistic style of leadership never seemed to be a structural

problem for the company. A young and more open-minded top management team was relatively successful in protecting the company from his
fiercest outbursts. Only few years ago, the personnel department was
extended from a recruitment centre and wage administration function
into something closer to a Human Resources Management function,
including a small organization-development task force. The three women
responsible for this department attended the Continuing Training Agent
(CTA) training of the Opti.net project, and as a result invited me to
develop and implement the first leadership training ever for the firm's
middle management.

The leadership training programme

Figure 13.3 outlines the detail of a leadership training programme that
was delivered to 40 middle managers in the case-study organization over
an eight-month period. The point made at the beginning of the chapter
about middle managers (that many have learned to organize technical
and work processes, but not learned that to organize such processes
means being responsible for organizing people working together in specific production or service processes) was true in the context of all of
these 40 departmental managers participating in the six-day programme.
The conception of 'organization' as organizing people is of particular
importance in a business where, each year, at least two complete design
collections for four different brands have to be developed and launched
in due time. As the company has rapidly grown, many of its middle managers have come from other companies in which leadership culture and
style have not been developed. Therefore, at the beginning of the training, all the 40 department managers stated that, on joining the case-study
company, they felt very much left to their own devices and ways of organ-

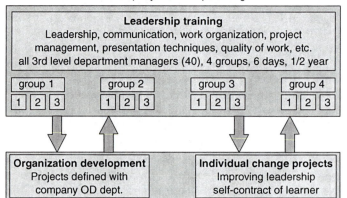

Figure 13.3 Leadership training.

izing things. However, they also claimed to have enjoyed a great deal of freedom to shape things in line with their own ideas and way of thinking.

Analysis of main training contents

What the managers learned

Summarizing the four six-day modules of leadership training in a few paragraphs is not easy. Therefore, I will focus on one main message to emerge from each of the modules.

MESSAGE/MODULE 1: ON MANAGEMENT AND LEADERSHIP

> Management means transforming the knowledge and competence of people into products and services useful to other people and profit for the company.

It is important to understand that organizations, above all, are purposeful cooperation of people and groups of competent people, certainly based on structures, rules and values, whereas in the perception of most managers the organization is a structure of rules and hierarchy – in other words, a 'vessel' containing people. Understanding that organizations only live through people and groups of people working together implies a completely different perspective on how to organize work. Leadership then means building common sense for common action, or building a community of performance.

MESSAGE/MODULE 2: ON COMMUNICATION

> Leadership, above all, means being responsible for successful communication. Communication in organizations means organizing common learning processes leading to common sense for common action.

Successful – that is, effective, result-oriented – communication means building shared models of action. Therefore, it is important to understand that individual people are likely to hold their own unique models of reality. For effective organization, people must share these models. Sharing models first of all means enabling people to participate in a dialogue with others in order to create and accept a number of shared models for common action. If a common action is successful, shared models become common sense. This process can also be described as a learning process of individual deconstruction and common reconstruction. Leadership means organizing learning processes for competent common action.

MESSAGE/MODULE 3: ON FACILITATING LEARNING AND PROJECT
MANAGEMENT

> Learning is a process of virtual deconstruction and reconstruction of
> reality. Organization development is a real process of deconstructing
> and reconstructing an organization. Both processes are inseparable in
> practice. Leadership means helping people to construct their indi-
> vidual and shared 'realities'.

Hence, leaders and managers need to acquire competence in how to facilitate learning and managing projects. Above all, they must learn how to
enable sensitive communication among their people leading to shared
(images of) models of future action through facilitated, result-oriented
debate and planning (in German, called 'Moderation'). Leaders and managers must learn how to help people be 'constructive', virtually and
practically.

MESSAGE/MODULE 4: ON QUALITY MANAGEMENT AND COMPETENCE

> Quality management does not mean management of quality, but
> quality of management. A fundamental feature of management com-
> petence lies in assuring that people under one's responsibility are
> competent to do their job. The quality of management competence
> strongly depends on the quality of competence management.

Here we are back at Message 1. Managers need to engage people
individually in conversations about their competence development
aims; both their own and those of the department. Regular (at least
annual) evaluation of performance and related training needs should
take place.

How the managers learned

It is self-evident that the arrangements of leadership learning within the
training course must correspond to what leaders learn about how to
arrange leadership as a learning process outside the course. The learning process on facilitating learning cannot be successful if it does not
apply the methods of facilitating learning itself. Many managers do not
do what they have learned in management courses unless they can use it
immediately, realizing and reflecting on the advantage of doing things
differently. Learning for practice has to be practical learning. Therefore,
in order to be effective the didactical concept had to imply two levels of
practice; practice within and outside the course. A further general rule
in adult education indicates that adults cannot be taught, but they can
learn.

PRACTICE WITHIN THE COURSE

During the whole training programme, the only PowerPoint presentations given were those of the trainees who had learned how to present the results of their projects professionally. Inputs by the trainer tended to be extended summaries of the thematic aspects and frameworks presented by the trainees. Initially, themes were derived in brainstorming sessions and then refined in practical work carried out in small groups of three, four or five, on cases and tasks which were mostly grounded in real work experiences and examples provided by the trainees themselves.

In the first instance, the brainstorming sessions helped to externalize the trainees' personal constructs, which were then visualized and displayed by means of images written on cards pinned to a wall. These images were mostly mind maps or other similar forms of systematic visual structures, which could then be discussed and reworked by all trainees within a particular group, thus leading to a construction of a new common image (shared model).

In the second round of small-group work, the trainees had to analyse and solve the same or very similar tasks, producing visualizations (written on cards and pinned to a wall). This experimental action helped trainees to practise this method of visualization and, at the same time, enabled a common image to be constructed by the group, which then had to be presented by one group representative. An interesting outcome of the group presentations was that the groups had solved the same task or problem in very different ways. Next, the small groups were invited to discuss their results in a plenary session. This helped to generate respect and tolerance, and the acceptance that there is more than one 'best' way. It also showed very effectively that broad participation is a worthwhile experience and pays valuable results.

Only at that point, and with explicit reference to the images and comments produced by the trainees, were general explications on the themes and methods used in the exercises given by the trainer.

Some examples of themes and discussion topics are:

- how to organize effective and fair participation;
- how to participate actively oneself;
- how to prepare and chair effective meetings and workshops;
- how to raise the degree of reliability of agreements and decisions taken in meetings;
- how to analyse an existing work organization, deconstruct and reconstruct it according to given objectives (the LEGO experience);
- how to combine this organization development task with training needs analysis;
- how to use analytical tools like decision analysis, Ishikawa diagrams, flow charts, task analysis, etc.

Later, when the practical projects (see the next section) had started, the trainees increasingly fed in their own examples and tasks for group work, thus discussing with critical colleagues a range of real problems that existed within their workplace.

A very important aspect of the programme highlighted by all trainees both during and at the end of the course was the relatively intense process of getting acquainted with colleagues (beyond the remit of 'small talk') from other parts of the organization and who were, therefore, outside of the scope of an individual's usual business processes. The programme also allowed for individuals' competence to be enriched through the sharing of experiences amongst colleagues who mostly had not known each other before the programme. As an integral part of the programme, the continual exchange on common issues also led to the development of a 'bottom-up corporate identity' among the 40 department (middle) managers, who numerically represented the largest cohort of managers in the organization.

PRACTICE OUTSIDE THE COURSE

In preparation for the course, the HRD and organization-development department was asked to suggest some organization-development projects of particular importance/relevance to either the departments represented by the trainees or the organization as a whole. As early as the second module the trainees were presented with these cross-cutting projects, which they could accept, reject or redefine, giving reasons as to their decisions. In doing so, trainees had to explain to each other what, in their view, was the essence of each project, and why they proposed to accept, reject or redefine each particular issue.

Having decided which project to work on, trainees then had until the next training meeting to plan and present results to the rest of the cohort. The projects were then officially registered as organization-development projects, and they received a budget and investment costs if needed. As 'project coordinator', each trainee could approach all departments impacted by the project. In each of the following training meetings the trainees had to present brief status reports, and when the projects were finished the trainees prepared and gave a presentation of the results, producing a critical assessment of goal attainment and process problems. Finally, new projects resulting from the first one had to be outlined and explained. One of the sayings coined during this experience was the phrase: 'Problems are projects' – that is to say, 'never approach your boss to tell him you have a problem, tell him you have an idea how to solve a problem'. Being 'bosses' themselves, the trainees' aim was also to teach their people to present their own ideas on how to solve perceived problems. It is not an exaggeration to say that critical departmental and organizational business processes have been re-engineered during the eight months of the training. The training and its outcomes have been jointly monitored by course participants and trainers, using methods, instruments and techniques explained or developed specifically during the training. Thus, the course became the largest organization-development measure ever implemented in the company without the (specific and expensive) assistance of a consultant.

A further practical tool used was the so called 'self-contract'. At the end of the first half of the first day's training, all participants received a 'to-do' chart which adopted the same structure as the to-do chart used for recording minutes of 'agreements' taken in meetings. The purpose of this chart was to note the small things learned during training from either colleagues or the trainer, and then relate them to perceived shortcomings or possible improvements of their own personal performance as a manager. At the end of each training day, trainees had to relate to their colleagues one of their ideas for personal improvement. At the beginning of the next training meeting, everybody gave a concise report (three minutes) on what he or she had done to tackle this personal development point. Each participant was encouraged to report systematically on the 'what?', 'how?', 'who?', 'when?' and 'completed' of their development point.

Some examples of personal improvement points engaged in this way were:

- how to analyse a perceived problem;
- how to focus, plan and organize a project;
- how to prepare and present project results (10–15 minutes) to an internal audience;
- how to prepare a meaningful presentation;
- how to use PowerPoint efficiently.

Conclusions and key learning points

The conclusions outlined here represent my own learning from the 'leading by learning' programme; it is appreciated that readers of this chapter will extract their own learning from what has been described and explained. Conclusions to be drawn from the project design as a whole across the nine organizations are few and brief. Training and organization development projects with a network structure constructed to be a community of practice provide interesting and meaningful perspectives of learning for companies, especially perhaps SMEs which normally are reticent regarding the time and money they afford for management and employee training. In particular, the possibility of customized training and the perspective of current exchange with other companies on similar issues and problems seem very attractive to these smaller companies, as is, of course, the sharing of training costs. Both aspects enhance (at least the expectations of) the viability of learning for better performance.

The same applies to the network of advisers who can create efficient mechanisms of sharing customers depending on the specific expertise needed in the individual case. Not only do they improve the range of expertise offered to the companies, they also enhance the range of mutual learning.

The network of training providers has also gained a completely new approach to customizing training provision to specific needs of customers who may not normally approach them.

The conclusions to be drawn from the bespoke leadership training programme in the larger organization (ladies' clothing manufacturer) are no less brief. How learning and training are conceived and how meaningful training conditions are arranged is decisive for their effectiveness or viability. The difference lies in providing opportunities to combine a learning situation with immediate usefulness to the learner and his or her (learning and/or working) community of performance.

It is possible to achieve far-reaching organizational change in companies with a practical leadership training approach based on immediate application under controlled conditions of methods and instruments learned.

Under certain conditions, as they have been created in the case described, training can be a useful contribution to successful community building in a performance-oriented organization. From the 40 initial beginners on the course only two left, for work-related reasons, and non-attendance was very low.

In parallel with the training programme featured in the chapter, the top managers of the four brand areas of the case-study company (that is, the immediate superiors of the 40 department managers) have been trained too, equally for the first time, by a well-renowned consulting company in a more traditional teaching and instructive way ('You tell us your problem, we tell you how to tackle it'). This programme had massive attendance problems. As our course had created a new participative approach to change management, and the department managers worked hand in hand in tackling change and development problems, their superiors had huge problems in keeping up with their dynamism and following the pace set by them. A further course is being planned to 'update' the brand managers to the level their department managers have achieved.

References

Curriculum (2003) *Curriculum zur Qualifizierung von Betrieblichen Weiterbildungsbeauftragten*, Bielefeld: Arbeit und Leben Bielefeld.

Franz, H.W. (2003) 'How organizations learn – a theory of learning and organizational development', in Nyhan, B., Cressey, P., Kelleher; M. and Poell, R. (eds), *Facing up to the Learning Organization Challenge*, vol. 2, *Selected writings*, Thessaloniki: CEDEFOP, pp. 50–72.

Lave, J. and Wenger, E. (1991) *Situated Learning: Legitimate Peripheral Participation*, Cambridge: Cambridge University Press.

von Glasersfeld, E. (1998) *Radikaler Konstruktivismus: Ideen, Ergebnisse, Probleme* [Radical Constructivism, A Way of Knowing and Learning], London: Falmer Press.

Wenger, E. (1998) *Communities of Practice. Learning, Meaning, and Identity*, Cambridge: Cambridge University Press.

Part IV

Aspects of management development

Introduction

The penultimate part of this book, entitled 'Aspects of management development', comprises five chapters, all of which introduce a particular facet of MD conceptualization and intervention. Several chapters in the book have already made a case for the involvement of 'stakeholders' and 'partners' in MD research, design, delivery and evaluation. In Chapter 14, Thomas Garavan and Alma McCarthy enter the 'MD stakeholder involvement' debate with a focus on 360-degree or multi-source feedback (MSF). Essentially, the chapter explores how managers experience and construct, through discourse, the contextual factors (in their work and work organization) that impact the effectiveness of MSF programmes. The authors argue that managers' discourse in this approach is not well understood, and that the majority of studies in MD focus on the prediction of acceptability and the evaluation of the effectiveness of the process as an intervention. The chapter reports on a study of 520 managers who participated in an MSF process in a financial services environment. The study gathered manager accounts of the context in which the process was implemented. It also investigated managers' accounts of attitudes towards personal development and participation in development post-feedback. The chapter outlines and explains the types of contextual issues that are relevant in implementing an MSF process for development purposes using discourse analysis. It explores how managers discoursed their development intentions, their attitudes to development and their ambiguities concerning the purposes of multi-source feedback. The study findings highlight the complexities involved in managers' responses to MSF and the contradictory reactions of managers to using MSF for development purposes. The chapter concludes with a discussion of the implications of the study findings for both the research and practice of MSF in an MD context.

In Chapter 15, Jill Palmer, Rosemary Hill and Jim Stewart link the concept of management development with that of commitment. As the authors suggest, the notion of commitment is complex and problematic. Arguably too, commitment could be perceived as either an input to or a consequence of the human condition embodied in the term 'emotional loyalty' as introduced by Francis and D'Annunzio-Green (Chapter 11, this volume). The juxtaposition of 'organizational commitment' and 'MD' as the focus of Chapter 15 is, perhaps, a further indication of the importance of taking into account the human condition in the design and delivery of MD and leadership development programmes. The chapter draws on a research project conducted in the UK operations of a major international vehicle manufacturer. The research took advantage of the introduction of an MD programme for supervisory level employees, which had competitive entry and which was designed to prepare participants for more senior roles. Through a review of previous studies, the chapter examines and explores the links that have, and can be, drawn between the two central concepts. The research design is fully explained, and the results presented and analysed. The chapter offers insights into the links between research and practice, and into the value and limitations of research-based practice as an approach to decision-making on investment in MD in organizations. It also provides a critique of the particular research design utilized in the study, and uses that as a base for providing advice and guidance on using research in professional practice.

Based on the premise that management learning and development has been largely focused around behaviourist and experiential traditions, in Chapter 16 Jeff Gold, Richard Thorpe and Robin Holt show how constructionist approaches to research can lead to the development of practical MD activity as well as to new insights into the development processes of the manager. In presenting this alternative perspective, the chapter develops the image of a manager as a practical author and demonstrates the ways in which constructionist views have practical use for managers. The authors introduce the 'Three Rs of Manager Learning' model, the basis of which is that managers need to be able to read a situation reflexively, write creatively about a situation as they see it, and reason authoritatively for the analysis they have made. The theoretical context of the authors' arguments and analysis is fully explored.

In Chapter 17, Kiran Trehan and Rod Shelton offer an examination of critical leadership development though an exploration of the interplay between leadership development and critical HRD. They begin with a brief examination of the basis of leadership power, and go on to reflect on how leadership has been defined and what theoretical approaches have been taken in its study. Inherent in this discussion is an analysis of leadership styles and effectiveness, and of supposed differences between management and leadership and between management and leadership behaviours. The authors posit an interesting thought that leadership itself is a discourse formed through patterns of communication and, as such, is likely to be a complex and mutable entity. They further imply that taking a critical, contingent perspective in leadership analysis may help avoid the application of overly rational and simplistic leadership development 'solutions'. The leads the authors to question what critical leadership development might look like. Conclusions and key learning points revolve around the potential choices, responsibilities and obstacles incurred by leadership educators and practitioners when pursuing a critical approach to leadership development.

In the last chapter in this final part of the book, Nadine Bristow focuses on research into the use of action learning (AL) in management development within the UK National Health Service (NHS). As a widely-used form of management development, a discussion of AL in Chapter 18 offers a sound theoretical and practical conclusion to the other chapters, many of which portray MD that is in some way grounded in AL principles. After outlining the initial research question and objectives, the author discusses the theoretical context of the research, served by a hypothesis that there is a need for diversity of learning styles within AL sets in order to achieve optimum set function and richness of discourse. A multi-method form of ethnographic research is described, which includes observation, interviews, personal construct development and discourse analysis. Analysis and evaluation of the main findings are provided in the form of a discussion with supporting interpretations and conclusions for the practical application of AL and organizational development. Key learning points are provided through excerpts from the author's reflective journal.

Summary

As well as highlighting topics already noted in Parts I, II and III of the book, Part IV identifies additional themes as follows:

- Multi-source feedback (MSF) as an MD approach.
- The importance of taking into consideration the context in which MD is designed and delivered.
- The role and impact of social constructionist approaches and discourse analysis in MD.
- The link between MD and commitment – does MD secure commitment and if so, commitment to what or to whom?
- The concept of the manager as a 'practical author' of his or her own development.
- The notion of critical leadership development to engage managers in a process of making connections between learning and work.
- The responsibility placed on management and leadership developers/practitioners involved in MD/leadership development design and intervention.
- The role and impact of action learning in change and leadership development.
- A conceptualization of 'leadership' as something distinct from 'management'.

14 Multi-source feedback and management development

Managers' discourse on context and development intentions

Thomas Garavan and Alma McCarthy

Objectives

This chapter explores how managers discourse the contextual factors (work and organizational) that impact on the effectiveness of multi-source feedback programmes. Managers' accounts of development intentions and attitudes following the multi-source feedback programme are also reviewed.

The objectives of this chapter are:

- to analyse contextual factors that impact the effectiveness of multi-source feedback when used for management development purposes;
- to evaluate the impact of multi-source feedback on managers' attitudes to development and development intentions;
- to describe and evaluate how managers discourse context and development intentions following participation in multi-source feedback;
- to examine the research and practice implications that emerge from the use of multi-source feedback in a management development context.

Theoretical context: the role of work context characteristics and multi-source feedback

Multi-source feedback (MSF) processes are commonplace in organizations today (Smither *et al.*, 2004). Multi-source feedback processes typically gather behavioural data from multiple raters (peers, direct reports, supervisors, self, and internal or external customers). This differentiates it from traditional performance appraisals systems, which concentrate on two sources at most. Some commentators are of the view that it is most effective in a management development context where the feedback is used to plan development initiatives rather than be used solely to evaluate past performance.

Contextual factors are important in explaining the participation of managers in development activity (Maurer and Tarulli, 1996; Tharenou,

2001). Context is complex, and operates at organizational, job and individual levels. It includes variables such as organizational structure and culture (Salaman and Butler, 1990; Lange *et al.*, 1999); perceptions of procedural fairness (Flint, 1999); management-development system factors (Garavan *et al.*, 1997); perceived social support (Noe and Wilk, 1993); time pressures and resource constraints (Sambrook and Stewart, 2000); and managerial role characteristics (Maurer *et al.*, 2002). It may also include various individual-level factors. These, however, are not the focus of this chapter.

Organizational structure and culture including support for development

Salaman and Butler (1990: 186) note that barriers to development may derive from 'an organization's structure and culture, from the way the organization is differentiated into specialisms, from pathologies of teamwork and from individuals themselves'. The most significant factors include the way in which power is exercised, and the behaviours that are rewarded and penalized in organizations. Mabey and Thompson (2000) found that a negative organization culture was the seventh most important factor of nine in discouraging participation in management development. Maurer *et al.* (2002) found that where an organization emphasizes skill development, managers are more likely to invest time and resources in management development. The degree to which the organization's culture promotes values concerned with learning and development explains attitudes to development and receptivity of feedback for development purposes.

Perceptions of procedural fairness

Multi-source feedback is designed to make managers aware of discrepancies between personal standards of performance and assessments made by other members of the organization. One of the more important issues determining the acceptance of multi-source feedback concerns its perceived fairness. Flint (1999) identifies four issues concerning how managers make assessments about the procedural fairness of multi-source feedback. These are voice opportunities at the time of feedback, the potential for managers to determine who performs the ratings, the opportunity of managers to express a voice on which dimensions are to be rated, and the opportunity to provide feedback on such ratings. The perceived accuracy of feedback influences managers' attitudes and behavioural reactions to feedback. Leventhal (1980) argues that perceptions of accuracy exert an important influence on perceptions of procedural justice. Greenberg (1987) found that feedback based on direct observations led to higher perceptions of fairness than did feedback made without observation. Lind and Tyler (1988) suggested that the positive impact of observations on fairness perceptions of feedback is due to enhanced perceptions of accuracy. The extent to which a manager believes feedback to be accurate is a critical determinant of his or her desire to improve in response to the feedback and to engage in development. O'Reilly and Anderson (1980), for example, found that managers' evaluations of the accuracy of feedback moderate the relationship between feedback, satisfaction with feedback, and intention to engage in development activity.

Management development system factors

This set of variables is defined as the extent to which an organization has in place policies, practices, roles and resources that are designed to facilitate management development (Garavan *et al.*, 1997). Multi-source feedback processes are of themselves insufficient to ensure that development takes place (Waldman *et al.*, 1998). Brutus and Derayeh (2002) highlight that multi-source feedback needs to be embedded in a development system that includes feedback mechanisms, development planning, specialized support and specific developmental resources. The lack of strategic alignment of the multi-source feedback process with other developmental activities is a major issue. Schneir *et al.* (1991) highlight that the lack of strategic alignment may include the absence of an appropriate competency model, inappropriate alignment with formal performance management processes, and the lack of follow-up such as development plans and development supports (for example, mentoring, coaching and formal training provision).

Perceived social support

Social support is defined as support from one's supervisors and peers. Social support is very important in explaining participation in development (Noe and Wilk, 1993; Maurer and Tarulli, 1996; Tharenou, 2001; Maurer *et al.*, 2002). Maurer *et al.* (2002) found social support to be important in predicting development attitudes and behaviour post-feedback. It was related to on-the-job development irrespective of the nature of the rating and the rating source. It was also related to off-the-job development. Tharenou (2001) found supervisory support to be the most significant dimension of social support and predicted participation in training and development. She speculated that supervisory influence may be due to the proximity to the manager's participation. Supervisors and managers encourage direct reports to participate in training and development; they help managers to develop skills and support the transfer of skills learnt during the training back on-the-job.

Physical, time-pressure and resource constraints

The extent to which managers experience physical pressures, time constraints and insufficient resources to participate in development is significant in explaining participation in development. Tharenou (2001) found that workload and time pressures did not predict participation in training and development. However, Maurer and Tarulli (1996) found that lack of time and/or resources provided by the organization might restrict a manager's involvement in development activities. Peters and O'Connor (1980) found that where organizations have few restrictions on opportunities for development, there will be greater levels of participation in development. Where managers perceive that the organization provides sufficient time and resources for development, it is positively related to manager attitude and development activities (London and Smither, 1995).

Role dimensions

A manager's current role will impact developmental behaviour and the perceived usefulness of feedback (Jagacinski, 1992). McCauley *et al.* (1994) have studied the developmental characteristics of managerial jobs. They found that particular characteristics included job novelty, non-routine activities, freedom to innovate, change opportunities, responsibility and visibility, opportunity for impact, and psychological pain and discomfort. Some jobs attach more importance to particular and specific skills. Managers may spend more time utilizing particular priority skills, and developmental efforts will likely be focused on skills that are critical for successful performance (Maurer *et al.*, 2002). Managers may not spend sufficient time developing skills that are considered less important to role performance (Spencer and Spencer, 1993). Managers may have limited insights concerning their current roles, either because they are new to the position or because they have limited role understanding and experience role ambiguity and/or conflict. These characteristics may undermine the developmental impact of feedback (Butler, 1987).

Managers who experience high job involvement, role ambiguity, vulnerability about performance outcomes, high levels of uncertainty and stress are more likely to seek and use feedback because they perceive the feedback to be of value (Ashford, 1986; Levy *et al.*, 1995). Some managerial roles have limited development potential because they involve little change in responsibilities and duties, they lack visibility, breadth and complexity, and there are insufficient interfaces (Ohlott, 1998).

Development attitudes and intentions

Multi-source feedback influences how managers perceive ownership of development (McEnrue, 1989; Wayne *et al.*, 1997), as well as their intention to participate in development. Managers differ in the degree to which they take ownership of development (Noe, 1986), the extent to which they initiate development or require it to be initiated by the organization (Birdi *et al.*, 1997). The typical development outcomes reported by managers include increased interest in learning in general, more self-actualization and increased self-confidence (Nordhaug, 1989). A multi-source feedback process may result in organizationally provided development activity but be less effective in changing individual attitudes to development. Smither *et al.* (2004) investigated the sharing of feedback and whether it leads to performance improvement over time, and found that it had a relatively small impact on performance improvement. Brutus *et al.* (1999) hypothesized that the impact of the rater source could be inferred from the developmental goals that managers set for themselves post-feedback. They found that feedback from subordinates had the most significant impact on developmental goal selection, followed by feedback from peers and then feedback by superiors. Overall, there is a lack of clarity concerning the impact of multi-source feedback on the development intentions of managers.

Therefore, a number of factors relating to the work context potentially impact on training and development participation by managers. The literature on multi-source feedback draws attention particularly to the six contextual factors reviewed above. The following sections of the chapter detail the research site characteristics and approach used to examine how these six contextual factors were understood by managers who participated in a multi-source feedback programme.

Research context and approach

The organizational context

The multi-source feedback programme explored in this study was introduced within a large financial services organization in the Republic of Ireland. The programme was adopted purely in the development context, and had no implications for evaluative decision-making.

The multi-source feedback programme

The MSF programme was rolled out at top management levels initially, and then introduced at middle and lower levels. Participants were either nominated to attend by their managers or asked their managers to nominate them. Participants were allowed to choose their own raters, and were required to have a minimum of eight raters complete the rating forms. The multi-source feedback formed part of a two-day leadership development programme, and a trained facilitator delivered the feedback to each participant on an individual basis. Participants were required to generate development plans based on the feedback received, and were encouraged to put the learning into action through follow-up training where needed. To facilitate those individuals who needed direction, a coaching/mentoring service was available to participants on an ongoing basis.

Method

The study described in this chapter is based on data collected from 520 managers who completed a multi-source feedback programme. A total of 778 managers completed the programme. They came from ten different managerial grades; all managers were included in the study, and we achieved a response rate of 67 per cent. We used a semi-structured questionnaire to gather the data, including open-ended questions asking respondents to give us accounts of their reactions to the multi-source feedback process that they had participated in. We did not direct respondents by providing themes or areas on which they should provide accounts, and the questions posed were non-directional in nature. Respondents volunteered to participate in the study on the understanding that all information provided would be kept confidential.

The accounts were transcripted and number-coded. The authors read the transcripts independently to achieve an overall sense of meaning. We adopted an analytical approach proposed by Potter and Wetherall (1987), which involves two closely related phases of a search for patterns in the data. The patterns can take the form of both variability (differences in the content of accounts) and consistency (the identification of features common to the accounts). We paid attention to the function that each account seemed to be achieving in the discourse context. Discourse analysis is appropriate to understand managers' reactions to multi-source feedback; it accounts for variability of human thought and avoids a problem in psychological research, that people tend to be inconsistent in their behaviour and opinions and adjust their responses according to perceptions of context. It abandons the positivist assumption that people can have a single attitude that can be represented through mutually exclusive response categories.

Demographic and human capital characteristics of our sample

Table 14.1 provides a summary of the demographic and human capital characteristics of our sample. Managers were aged between 27 and 59, with a mean age of 44 years (SD = 6.55). The mean length of time with the organization (organizational tenure) was 23.7 years (SD = 7.52), with a range of 2 to 40 years. The mean length of time in the current position (job tenure) was 4.7 years (SD = 4.67), with a range of one month to 26 years. Of the managers, 81 per cent were male and 19 per cent were female. We categorized managerial grade into three cohorts; senior management accounted for 8 per cent of respondents, middle managers accounted for 80 per cent of respondents and junior managers accounted

Table 14.1 Demographical and human capital characteristics of respondents

Variable	N	%	
Gender			
Male	422	81	
Female	96	19	
Managerial grade			
Senior management	43	8	
Middle management	417	80	
Junior management	60	12	
Educational qualifications			
Leaving Certificate	151	29	
Third-Level Certificate	49	9	
Diploma	137	26	
Bachelors Degree/Professional Qualification	113	22	
Masters/PhD	68	13	
	Mean	*SD*	*N*
Age (years)	43.6	6.55	511
Organizational tenure (years)	23.7	7.52	503
Job tenure (years)	4.7	4.67	460

for 12 per cent of respondents. Of the respondents, 29 per cent were educated to Leaving Certificate or equivalent, 9 per cent had completed a third-level certificate, 26 per cent a diploma-level qualification, 22 per cent a Bachelors degree or a professional accountancy qualification, and 13 per cent a Masters degree or higher.

Key findings

Work context factors were prominent in the discourse of managers regarding the multi-source feedback programme. Accounts indicated that context is particularly salient in explaining the perceived usefulness of a multi-source feedback process. The accounts reveal both positive and negative perceptions.

Perceptions of organizational cultural

One overriding discourse concerned the role of the organization's culture in inhibiting learning. Managers generally perceived that the organization's culture was not necessarily conducive to learning and development. One manager provided this extract:

> Of all the managers and senior managers in my department, no one spoke openly about the process. We need to see more action taken

at the top before the process really becomes effective. I also feel the priority is on getting people through rather than really making it work but I also appreciate that it is a two-way process.

The following account is representative of negative discourse regarding the organization's culture of learning:

While accepting that it's the individual's responsibility to follow through on the process, it has not become an integral part of the xxx culture or mind-set and is in danger of going the same way as previous efforts. xxx as an organization continues to be poor on the so-called soft issues and this stems from the fact that the A-type personalities continue to achieve positions of power and influence.

The discourse emphasized that the organization's culture was less effective in facilitating learning, in enabling change to happen and in supporting the development of managers.

Perceptions of procedural fairness

Managers' discourse featured particular observations concerning the procedural justice aspects of the feedback process utilized by the organization. Some of this discourse concerned the overall perceived fairness of the process. Other discourse focused on the perceived accuracy of the observations made by feedback givers. Managers had positive discourse concerning the perceived fairness of the overall process, as the following two extracts reveal:

It is as fair and informative as an instrument of this type can be. Perhaps more training/development opportunities should be available away from the day-to-day work environment to develop individual strengths and weaknesses as identified.

The process itself is excellent and fair and provides unexpected and useful insights into one's personality and work behaviours. My own work environment, however, meant that I did not have the most useful feedback, and continues to be one in which development is totally stifled. It is a most frustrating and stressful situation.

These extracts reveal that while managers considered the process to be fair, they considered the work situations to be delimiting. Other extracts reveal that managers had issues concerning the perceived fairness of managers and peers as raters. These two extracts highlight their concerns:

I believe my manager used the process to raise criticisms which were invalid and which he could not justify face-to-face. His feedback was not consistent with my peers and direct reports.

I was unfortunate in that some of my peers were not in the best position to judge my performance. I feel that the questionnaire should only be given to colleagues whom you deal with directly because I lacked this; I was forced to give the questionnaire to people outside that sphere, thus not giving a true picture.

Perceptions of effectiveness of management development systems

Multi-source feedback processes frequently fail owing to the lack of support systems post-feedback and the lack of integration with other management development and human resource management processes. This issue featured with significant consistency and intensity in the accounts provided by managers. The accounts were primarily negative and critical of the organization. A major theme concerned the perceived absence of systems and processes to enable follow-up development activities.

Managers' accounts emphasized the need to implement some form of goal setting process post-feedback. One manager articulated it this way:

I would suggest that an official in xxx Group HR is assigned to each person with a view to ensuring that action plans are matched to 360-degree goals following the initial session. This would ensure greater effectiveness of the programme. Greater visibility of support options available would also have encouraged managers to take further off-site action.

Another 'theme' related to the availability of training and development opportunities post-feedback. The following extract illustrates a frequently highlighted concern.

The 360-degree process is like an end in itself and not, as it should be, the beginning of a developmental process, supported by on-going training and developmental courses in line with the needs identified.

The availability of coaching and mentoring support were frequently mentioned in managers' accounts. For example, one manager highlighted that:

More proactive allocation of coaching would have been welcomed. Did not find counselling on 360-degree programme of any benefit.

Managers' accounts emphasize general follow-up systems. One manager was satisfied with the multi-source feedback process but had reservations about the general lack of follow-up. He commented:

While satisfied with the 360-process, there could possibly be a more structured follow up say every six months over the following two years to keep the process in the mind and to see for ourselves whether we are addressing the development needs highlighted.

Another manager espoused a similar viewpoint. He commented that:

The process is excellent. The time to follow up and develop it further is a problem ... Some individual assistance in this area would be of great benefit.

Perceived social support

Issues concerning social support from managers, peers and subordinates featured frequently in managers' accounts. Some managers' accounts revealed that a lack of social support from subordinates led in the first instance to negative ratings being provided. One manager commented about this issue in the following way:

It undermines your position amongst staff as when they are requested to complete a report, they perceive you as having a problem and complete it on that basis. Conditions of work do not lend themselves to a nice happy open work atmosphere.

Some managers' accounts revealed a perceived lack of general support and highlighted a multiplicity of support factors, which they perceived were absent:

While the idea and feedback were useful, and the company make an offer of support, the reality is that (a) time constraints (b) geographical location (c) lack of support/team (d) lip service by senior management and (e) no real follow-up by HR all lead to going back to the old way of doing things.

Even after numerous requests, I have been unable to sit down with my manager and discuss the feedback received.

One manager points to the important role that the line manager plays in the process and states:

xxx could not have done more to encourage and support me. Buy-in by my line manager is excellent, and this is crucial.

Role/task dimensions

Managers provided accounts of job characteristics, which either inhibited or facilitated development activities post-feedback. Managers in some cases provided accounts indicating that they had just changed roles and that they had insufficient learning time in their new roles to capitalize on the feedback.

> I am very satisfied with the 360 programme overall. However, I have recently moved roles and have developed (in a short time) the work relationship with direct reports. However, my new line operates at arm's length and my peers don't really know me, and we are also competing with each other.

One manager refers to the difficulty of extra role duties, given staff shortages:

> Management effectiveness is impaired by staff turnover, lack of skilled staff and difficulty in trying to provide quality customer service under these circumstances.

Another manager provided a more positive account.

> I found the 360 very helpful. I had moved into a new management role in a new area and I felt it validated my performance as an Assistant Manager. Overall, I feel I gained a lot of insight into my self and it gave me confidence.

And another manager states that:

> ...it articulates one's manager's priority attributes associated with the role.

Physical, time and resource difficulties

Managers provided accounts of external and internal pressures which acted as barriers to participation in management development post-feedback. These pressures primarily related to a lack of time. These extracts provide insights on perceptions of work pressures:

> I feel that work pressures mean that despite all the good feeling generated by 360, in very few cases can you learn or develop, as it's too busy and when you have to cut something, 'soft' things go first.

> I find that away from the work environment I am enthusiastic and energetic about the learning points from 360. However, back in the work environment the pressure and fire-fighting does not allow me the time or energy to put my learning into practice. This is despite fervent intentions to make it work.

Some managers' accounts focused on work pressures as a challenge rather than a barrier to participation:

> The process, including getting the feedback, presenting it and the course itself, are satisfactory. The problem lies with personal development thereafter and getting the time to devote to it, which is usually to the detriment of customer service or family/personal time or both.

Developmental attitudes, behaviour and activities

The way managers think about the process of development, developmental behaviours and intentions to participate in development activities are relevant issues in justifying investment by an organization in a multi-source feedback process. Managers' accounts revealed a number of themes illustrating how managers think about development and developmental actions.

Perceived ownership of and attitudes towards development

The accounts revealed that some managers espoused ownership of the development process and responsibility for driving development. However, despite these good intentions, they highlight that participation in development activities can be limited. For example:

> Good process to get an understanding of how others with whom we work/interact perceive us. The onus is on each of us to take corrective action. However, this can de deferred by most of us – being old habits. The 360 may then lose its effectiveness. I am aware that the onus is on us to follow through.

> The difficulty arose afterwards when it was up to the individual in putting into operation agreed action plans.

> I believe it to be a good process – follow-up developmental work is left very much to yourself, so prioritizing this vis-à-vis other priorities, can mean the developmental part receives inadequate attention. I accept that personal development is an individual responsibility; I would still like to see more interest on the organization's behalf.

Self-awareness/reflection

Change and learning post-feedback was understood primarily as a process of self-discovery. A number of dimensions of self-awareness and discovery were highlighted. These two extracts illustrate self-awareness and self-discovery dimensions:

The process is important for those people who fail to see how their actions impact on other people and/or who are genuinely blind to their [interpersonal] weaknesses.

Although I was aware of my strengths and weaknesses, I needed to have them confirmed and specified. The 360 helped me to 'stand outside' and have a good look at how I manage.

Some managers provided accounts of the MSF programme providing opportunity for reflection:

I found the process very useful. The time spent away from the office environment gave time to reflect on where I was going and my management style. I would be disappointed personally that I have not addressed some of the shortcomings highlighted during the process, which is primarily due to work pressures.

It is vitally important to take time out of the system and assess your management style, how you interact with peers and direct reports and how they perceive your management style. The process in my opinion sends one clear message of where improvements can be made, and identifies areas of self-development.

Understanding and clarity on development needs

Managers' accounts relating to development needs typically emphasized the role of the feedback in providing clarity on development needs and priority of these needs. One manager described it this way:

A useful exercise because it can highlight the difference between an individual's relationship with one's manager and direct reports and it clearly highlights areas of required attention.

Managers considered multi-source feedback to bean appropriate method to achieve an understanding of development needs. One manager articulated it this way:

Good view of how others see you. Highlights shortcomings. Safe environment to remedy issues of oneself. Facilitators help interpret issues that require action – this is necessary. Overall, a very good process.

Many managers' accounts highlighted the specific contribution of the multi-source process in clarifying the development needs that should be pursued:

> I thought the 360 programme was a very good developmental tool. It gave me the blueprint in terms of my development needs and also supported me in building on these needs.

Developmental actions

Accounts concerning development activity following the MSF programme were mixed. Some managers' accounts reveal that they pursued development activity post-feedback, while others indicated that they had undertaken very little or no development. One manager refers to improvements in ratings on a second iteration of MSF based on development efforts undertaken:

> Overall, I felt it was worthwhile. I have been on a second 360 programme and the comparisons of scores were interesting. Improvement shown in areas that I put in some effort.

Managers, in a small number of cases, provided accounts indicating that they had shared the multi-source results with their team as a basis to facilitate development:

> As a leader and department head, I give my own managers a copy of my assessment once I complete same, i.e. they know my views before they go on 360. I use it to convey transparency in my dealings and leadership approach.

However, a number of accounts reveal barriers to participation in development following the feedback. Lack of commitment post-feedback to initiate development is highlighted by the following comment:

> To be honest, I have not once opened the folder – not the right way to treat it I know, but that's the case. Certainly I have learned from the experience and will look back at the folder and notes at some stage.

> I would like to see much tighter follow-up accountability on individual action plans with a formal review built in with the line manager. I feel this is essential to ensure the programme is not seen as two/three days out of the system and then parked.

Some managers' accounts referred to actions that should have taken place within the wider organization but which they perceived did not happen due to lack of commitment at a management level:

> The process contributes nothing at all to remedying the HR management deficiencies of the organization. In particular, I think most

people would not be able to identify any change in the organization that has arisen on foot of this programme.

Implications and conclusions

This chapter addressed four key objectives. First, analysed the contextual factors that impact on the effectiveness of MSF when used in the development context. We focused on six dimensions of context: organizational structure and culture (including support for development); perceptions of procedural justice; management-development system characteristics; perceived social support for development; physical, time pressures and resource constraints; and manager job-role characteristics. The context of multi-source feedback is multifaceted. Context has the potential to facilitate or inhibit the effective implementation of a multi-source feedback process. It will impact how the purposes and intentions of feedback are understood by managers, and the level of commitment that managers will give to participation in development.

The second objective of the chapter was to review how MSF impacts attitudes towards development and development activity post-feedback. Four dimensions of attitudes and actions were considered important: (1) perceived ownership of and attitudes towards development; (2) self-awareness/reflection; (3) understanding and clarity of development needs; and (4) developmental actions. The accounts revealed something of the complexity and contradictions involved in discourses of reactions to multi-source feedback processes even amongst a relatively homogenous occupational grouping within a single organization.

The third objective was to describe and evaluate how managers discourse important context and development intentions and actions following an MSF programme in a large financial services organization. Several dimensions of the work context were considered important by managers. Managers' accounts emphasized social support post-feedback. Perceived social support was expected from supervisors, peers and subordinates. The role of the immediate manager was given particular prominence in the accounts of managers; managers expected this source to be motivational, to help identify learning opportunities, and to support learning and development initiatives. The immediate manager was considered more proximal and a key influence on both attitudes to and initiation of development activities. Where managers had the opportunity to meet with their direct report manager to discuss the feedback results, they were more likely to think positively about subsequent development activities. It also creates the expectation that participants should follow-through on agreed development initiatives. Managers reported that the use of multiple raters is a fair and just system of receiving performance feedback. Where there were concerns about fairness, it revolved largely around rater inopportunity to observe.

Negative accounts tended to focus on the perceived absence of appropriate management development systems, policies and processes to support the implementation of developmental actions agreed during the feedback process. There was also reference to the lack of a culture supportive of learning and development. The provision of resources to pursue development, and in particular the implementation of coaching and mentoring processes, was frequently highlighted as a development strategy that needed further investment. Where such resources were provided, managers provided more positive accounts of motivation to participate in development.

Managers' discourse on development intentions operated on a number of different levels; attitudinal, perceived ownership and commitment, self-awareness, reflection, and the initiation of development actions. Accounts emphasized awareness of development needs, awareness of priority development issues, and the espousal of positive attitudes and perceptions concerning personal ownership of management development. Specific development initiatives reported by managers included coaching and mentoring processes, formal training programmes, project-type activities and on-the-job learning. One of the key barriers to participation in development activity post-feedback was the lack of time and commitment. Managers referred to the inevitable lack of focus on development planning when faced with their roles and duties back on the job. One of the key positives emanating from the process was the enhanced level of self-awareness, as well as the opportunity to take time to reflect on personal development strengths and needs.

The fourth objective was to examine the research and practice implications that emerge from the use of MSF in a management development context, and this is discussed below.

Research implications

Recent research recognizes that managers' behavioural and attitudinal reactions and developmental intentions in respect of multi-source feedback depend on a number of factors unique to the workplace. Relevant aspects of context include organization culture, perceptions of procedural fairness, and characteristics of the organization's management development system. We highlight important insights concerning the diversity of judgements that managers make about the impact of context on multi-source feedback. We focused here specifically on work context; however, there are two further dimensions that also merit consideration. These are the motivational and self-efficacy characteristics of the manager, and the particular features of the actual feedback generated as well as the feedback programme itself. These issues are worthy of investigation using more qualitative approaches to capture the rich diversity of perceptions regarding such issues. The majority of research studies to date tend to use quantitative methodologies.

Implications for practice

Proponents of multi-source feedback argue that it is an indispensable management development tool that helps managers to increase their self-awareness of strengths and development needs. Furthermore, multi-source feedback allows organizations to improve the quality and effectiveness of their manager populations. This chapter suggests that it is best to think of multi-source feedback as part of a complex organizational context and management development system. As a result, the use of multi-source feedback influences, and is influenced by, other elements of the process and the wider context.

Organizations can enhance manager attitudes to multi-source feedback through careful attention to the cultural features of the organization, and in particular the extent to which the culture facilitates learning and development. A focus on the development of a learning culture raises important questions concerning higher human resource policy-making levels. Policy-makers should carefully assess whether the organization's culture is appropriate to sustain the feedback process. It is likely that where the culture is constructive, relationships are positive and high levels of trust prevail, feedback will be more constructive and perceived to be more accurate. It has a better chance of creating positive attitudes towards development. Organizations should consider the relationship that exists between managers and feedback providers (raters). Where there is little opportunity to observe the work and behaviour of ratees, it is likely that the quality of the feedback will be less useful.

Managers frequently reported that the immediate boss was not interested in the development issues that emerged from the feedback process. This finding suggests that organizations should spend time helping managers to understand the outcomes of the feedback, as well as developing their confidence and skills in conducting development discussions. The immediate manager is a key stakeholder in the implementation of a multi-source feedback process. Multi-source feedback will work best when it is integrated into the wider management development process.

We have yet to understand more fully how managers respond to context, and how these factors impact on development intentions. This greater understanding will ultimately aid organizational efforts to effectively incorporate leading-edge management development processes into the management of their human resources. A multi-source feedback system that is unsupported by other development initiatives is likely to fail. At a minimum, organizations need to implement a system of personal development planning. This will enable feedback to be translated into development needs and lead to the identification of specific development strategies. Development planning processes should involve the manager, who is encouraged to engage in development planning discussions with direct reports. Organizations should provide managers with resources in the form of alternative development options, sufficient time and psychological support to implement the plan. Managers have a critical role to play in facilitating or inhibiting development. A significant body of research supports the notion that many managers consider job experiences and tasks as a primary source of learning and development (Lombardo and Eichinger, 1989). Managers learn more from the challenges inherent in their jobs and from interactions at work than from formal development interventions. The characteristics of managers' jobs can restrict development opportunities, and this suggests that organizations should consider job assignments as development interventions. These may include job transactions, higher levels of responsibility, non-authority relationships and special projects. However, the extent to which such assignments are managed, as well as the guidance and support given to learners, will impact their effectiveness.

Key learning points

A number of key learning points emerge from our discussion in this chapter. Multi-source feedback is increasingly used by organizations as a management- or leadership-development strategy. It has a unique contribution to make to the development of managers due to its emphasis on multiple sources of feedback and the enhancement of self-awareness. Multi-source feedback systems are impacted by various characteristics of the organization. These include the culture of the organization, the perceived fairness of the multi-source process, the extent of social support provided to managers who participate in the process, and the development potential that exists in a manager's role. Multi-source feedback processes need to be designed as part of a wider management development process. They should be supported by individual and organizational-focused development planning processes in addition to appropriately selected development interventions.

References

Ashford, S. (1986) 'Feedback seeking in individual adaptation: a resource perspective', *Academy of Management Journal*, 29: 465–87.

Birdi, K., Allan, C. and Warr, P. (1997) 'Correlates and perceived outcomes of four types of employee development activity', *Journal of Applied Psychology*, 82: 845–57.

Brutus, S. and Derayeh, M. (2002) 'Multi-source assessment programs in organizations: an insider's perspective', *Human Resource Development Quarterly*, 13(2): 187–202.

Brutus, S., London, M. and Martineau, J. (1999) 'The impact of 360-degree feedback on planning for career development', *Journal of Management Development*, 18: 676–93.

Butler, R. (1987) 'Task-involving and ego-involving properties of evaluation:

effects of different feedback conditions on motivational perceptions, interest, and performance', *Journal of Educational Psychology*, 79(4): 474–82.

Flint, D. (1999) 'The role of organizational justice in multi-source performance appraisal: theory-based applications and directions for research', *Human Resource Management Review*, 9(1): 1–20.

Garavan, T., Morley, M. and Flynn, M. (1997) '360-degree feedback: its role in employee development', *Journal of Management Development*, 13(2&3): 134–48.

Greenberg, J. (1987) 'Using diaries to promote procedural justice in performance appraisals', *Social Justice Research*, 1: 219–34.

Jagacinski, C.M. (1992) *The Effects of Task Involvement and Ego Involvement on Achievement-related Cognitions and Behaviours*, Hillsdale, NJ: Lawrence Erlbaum Associates.

Lange, T., Ottens, M. and Taylor, A. (1999) 'SMEs and barriers to skills development: a Scottish perspective', *Journal of European Industrial Training*, 24(1): 5–11.

Leventhal, G.S. (1980) 'What should be done with equity theory? New approaches to the study of fairness in social relationship', in Gergen, K.J., Greenberg, M.S. and Willis, R.H. (eds), *Social Exchange: Advances in Theory and Research*, New York: Plenum Press, pp. 27–55.

Levy, P.E., Albright, M.D., Cawley, B.D. and Williams, J.R. (1995) 'Situational and individual determinants of feedback seeking: a closer look at the process', *Organizational Behaviour and Human Decision Processes*, 62: 23–37.

Lind, E.N. and Tyler, T.R. (1988) *The Social Psychology of Procedural Justice*, New York: Plenum Press.

Lombardo, M.M. and Eichinger, R.W. (1989) *Eighty-eight Assignments for Development in Place: Enhancing the Development Challenge of Existing Jobs*, Greenboro, NC: Centre for Creativity Leadership.

London, M. and Smither, J. (1995) 'Can multi-source feedback change perceptions of goal accomplishment, self-evaluations and performance-related outcomes? Theory-based applications and directions for research', *Personnel Psychology*, 48(4): 803–39.

Mabey, C. and Thompson, A. (2000) *Achieving Management Excellence*, London: Institute of Management.

Maurer, T. and Tarulli, B. (1996) 'Acceptance of peer/upward performance appraisal systems: role of work, context, factors and beliefs about managers' development capability', *Human Resource Management*, 35: 217–41.

Maurer, T., Mitchell, D. and Barbeite, F. (2002) 'Predictors of attitudes toward a 360-degree feedback system and involvement in post feedback management development activity', *Journal of Occupational and Organizational Psychology*, 75: 87–107.

McCauley, C.D., Ruderman, M.N., Ohlott, P.J. and Morrow, J.E. (1994) 'Assessing the developmental components of managerial jobs', *Journal of Applied Psychology*, 79(4): 544–60.

McEnrue, M.P. (1989) 'Self-development as a career management strategy', *Journal of Vocational Behaviour*, 34: 57–68.

Noe, R. (1986) 'Trainee's attributes and attitudes: neglected influences on training effectiveness', *Academy of Management Review*, 11: 736–49.

Noe, R. and Wilk, S. (1993) 'Investigation of factors that influence employee's participation in development activities', *Journal of Applied Psychology*, 78: 291–302.

Nordhaug, O. (1989) 'Reward functions of personnel training', *Human Relations*, 42: 373–88.

Ohlott, P.J. (1998) 'Job assignments' in McCauley, C.D., Moxley, R.S. and Van Velsor, E. (eds), *Handbook of Creative Leadership*, San Francisco, CA: Jossey-Bass.

O'Reilly, C. and Anderson, J. (1980) 'Trust and the communication of performance appraisal information: the effects of feedback on performance and job satisfaction', *Human Communication Research*, 6: 290–8.

Peters, L.H. and O'Connor, E.J. (1980) 'Situational constraints and work outcomes: the influences of a frequently overlooked construct', *Academy of Management Review*, 5(3): 391–7.

Potter, J. and Wetherall, M. (1987) *Discourse and Social Psychology: Beyond Attitudes and Behaviour*, London: Sage.

Salaman, G. and Butler, J. (1990) 'Why managers won't learn', *Management Education and Development*, 21(3): 183–91.

Sambrook, S. and Stewart, J. (2000) 'Factors influencing learning in European learning oriented organizations: issues for management', *Journal of European Industrial Training*, 24(2/3/4): 209–19.

Schneir, C.E., Shaw, D. and Beatty, R.W. (1991) 'Performance measurement and management: a new tool for strategy execution', *Human Resource Management*, 30: 279–301.

Smither, J.W., London, M. and Reilly, R.R. (2004) 'A meta-analysis of longitudinal studies of multi-source feedback', Paper presented at a Symposium titled 'Understanding the effectiveness of 360-degree feedback programmes', at the Nineteenth Annual Conference of the Society of Industrial and Organizational Psychology, Chicago, IL.

Spencer, L.M. and Spencer, S.M. (1993) *Competence at Work: Models for Superior Performance*, New York, NY: John Wiley & Sons.

Tharenou, P. (2001) 'The relationship of training motivation to participation in training and development', *Journal of Occupational and Organizational Psychology*, 74: 599–621.

Waldman, D., Atwater, L. and Antonioni, D. (1998) 'Has 360-degree feedback gone amok?' *Academy of Management Executive*, 12(2): 86–94.

Wayne, S.J., Shore, L.M. and Liden, R.C. (1997) 'Perceived organizational support and leader-member exchange: a social exchange perspective', *Academy of Management Journal*, 40: 82–111.

15 The dynamics of organizational commitment and management development

Jill Palmer, Rosemary Hill and Jim Stewart

Objectives and background

The aim of this chapter is to explore the links between management development (MD) and organizational commitment. First, the literature on organizational commitment is discussed. The chapter then proceeds with an account of research carried out in DaimlerChrysler UK Limited (DCUK) on its first MD programme for team leaders. The research design applied a widely held notion of organizational commitment as comprising three different types of commitment – Affective, Normative and Continuance – as based on the work of Meyer and Allen (1997). A conceptual framework linking management development, organizational commitment and job performance was developed, and a hypothesis formulated that management development has no impact on Affective or Normative commitment and has a negative impact on Continuance commitment.

Theoretical context

Problems with commitment

The notion of commitment has a number of problems. Three are of particular interest here. The first problem is the focus of commitment questionnaires regarding the individual's desire to stay in the organization. Reichers (1985) argues this means that the questions are similar to assessing the individual's intention to quit or stay and are therefore highly predictive of turnover. She argues that these questions may account for the high consistent relationship between commitment and turnover, and could be indicative of 'concept redundancy' (Morrow, 1983, in Reichers, 1985: 465). So while commitment is hypothesized to be highly related to turnover, it could in fact be that the measure of commitment used is actually a measure of turnover.

The second problem is the separation of Normative and Affective commitment. Most research either ignores Normative commitment altogether, or the findings show a strong link between Affective and

Normative commitment. A continuing question, therefore, is whether Normative commitment develops as a concept in its own right or is abandoned as a separate measure. The third problem is that literature views organizational commitment from a traditional rather than a processual viewpoint. When organization is viewed as a process which (re)constructs what is labelled 'an organization' rather than a monolithic structure, this calls into question whether there is something one can be committed to. In a sense, this is the point made by Reichers – although her work still derives from the traditional perspective. The research reported in the chapter highlights some of these problems through both the process and the results of an empirical study.

The current relevance of the concept of commitment

Yehuda Baruch (1998) argues that, in the light of business changes, the strength of organizational commitment as a leading concept in management and behavioural sciences is continuously decreasing. The reason for this, Baruch argues, is that at the core of commitment is the idea of mutuality. Employees will not be committed unless employers are similarly committed to them. However, employers' commitment is mostly overlooked in the equation. He argues that economic constraints and the development of technology have led employers to downsize, and this has had a damaging effect on organizational commitment because perceived organizational support is lost. Baruch tries to support this argument by producing evidence of weakening association between commitment and the traditional outcomes of commitment (employee retention, performance and absenteeism). However, if this weakening association is in evidence, then it does not support the argument that downsizing has reduced commitment, nor does it support the argument necessarily that commitment as a concept has decreasing importance. If downsizing has reduced commitment, then one would expect the link between employee retention, absenteeism and performance still to be there, but that there would be more employee turnover, more absenteeism and lower performance. If, however, the link has weakened then this merits further investigation, but downsizing cannot be said to have caused this weakening link without specific research on this point. Further, if downsizing is reducing organizational commitment, then it could be argued that the concept is as relevant as or even more relevant than ever. Despite the somewhat confused arguments, Baruch raises some important points. In particular, the link between employers' and employees' commitment merits further research, as does the impact of downsizing on organizational commitment.

The concept of commitment needing a fresh approach in the light of recent employee downsizing is taken up by Ulrich (2000). He argues that commitment can be measured by workforce productivity, employee retention and organizational climate. This approach once again confuses the outcomes of commitment with the measure of it. Notwithstanding this, Ulrich makes a strong argument that a new approach to developing employee commitment is required which takes account of individual circumstances and respects individuality. He refers to this as 'mass employee customization', and argues that traditional approaches to building commitment (such as job security and lifetime employment) are no longer appealing to new generations of employees. It is arguable also that because this approach is most likely to generate Continuance commitment, which has the least desirable outputs, it would not be an appealing strategy for organizations either, even if they were in a position to provide it.

The importance of generating commitment is stressed in the work of Gratton *et al.* (1999), who studied the human resource practices of eight leading-edge companies between 1993 and 1995. They find there are 'immense potential gains' (Gratton *et al.*, 1999: 206) from a highly committed and inspired workforce, but underline again the need to treat people as individuals and not resources. This is supported by Reichheld (seen in Mowday, 1998: 8), who argues (albeit for practising managers rather than the academic field) that loyal employees build customer loyalty and drive value-creation.

It would appear, therefore, that the message about commitment for the modern organization is the need to move away from traditional methods of building commitment through job security and towards methods that develop the individual. This would suggest the need for an approach that is inclusive to all employees and does not just develop the fast track. This approach is supported by Waterman and Waterman (1994), who take the notion of committed employees one stage further by introducing the concept of a 'career resilient workforce'. They argue for the need to develop a workforce that is dedicated to continuous learning and reinvention, with workers responsible for their own career management and committed to the company's success.

Iles (1997) supports the need to broaden development for all staff rather than just the chosen few on the fast track. He puts forward an alternative 'sustainable career development' view which draws on an environmental perspective, arguing that all human-resourcing decisions could be looked at from a sustainability perspective and that retaining sustainable competitive advantage should be the organization's goal. In this light, he argues that preoccupation with developing high-flyers while at the same time paying little attention to strategic labour management issues may not produce long-term economic benefit. This is especially the case when it is difficult to retain high-flyers in the organization.

Concepts and measurements of organizational commitment

The concepts of commitment which were developed during the 1970s and beyond echo the seminal work of Etzioni (1961) on compliance, which we will return to later in this chapter. In attempting to understand the meaning of commitment, the literature on the subject has taken two directions (Meyer and Allen, 1997). The first direction focuses on the nature of commitment and the different forms that it can take, while the second concentrates on the different entities that the employee could be committed to.

Suliman and Iles (2000) set out three main approaches that have been adopted to conceptualize organizational commitment:

1   *The Attitudinal Approach* adopted by Porter (in Suliman and Iles, 2000: 2) is one of the leading approaches, and describes commitment as:

> The relative strength of an individual's identification with and involvement in a particular organization.

Porter regarded this definition as having three components; acceptance of the organization's beliefs and values, a willingness to exert effort on behalf of the organization, and the desire to maintain organizational membership. He believed that these were factors that made up the one single definition. Mowday *et al.* (1979) used this concept when developing a 15-point measure of organizational commitment. Their research, over nine years and covering 2,500 employees in nine different organizations, became for many researchers the prominent way to measure commitment for many years.

2   *The Behavioural Approach* emphasizes investments ('side bets') an employee makes in the organization, for example to the pension fund and to friendships, which prevent the employee from leaving. This is described by Kanter (in Suliman and Iles, 2000: 2) as:

> profit associated with continued participation compared with the costs of leaving.

3   *The Normative Approach* considers the congruence between the employer's values and goals with that of the workers' own. Wiener (in Suliman and Iles, 2000: 2) defined this as:

> the totality of internalised Normative pressures to act in a way which meets the organisation's goals and objectives.

A multi-dimensional approach

Meyer and Allen (1997: 11) took each of these approaches, and argued that running through all of them is a common theme. They described this as:

a psychological state that characterises the employee's relationship with the organization and has implications for their decision to continue membership of the organisation.

Meyer and Allen further put forward a multi-dimensional approach to the measurement of commitment that takes each of the three strands set out above (Affective, Behavioural – which they label 'Continuance' – and Normative) and proposes separate measures for each which can be used in the same questionnaire. The also argue that researchers can gain by measuring each of the three strands of commitment and comparing the relative strength of each strand. The Meyer and Allen (1997) measurement of commitment is regarded by some researchers as a useful measurement tool, and so it was adapted for use in the research featured in the chapter.

It is now generally accepted that organizational commitment is a multi-dimensional concept (Suliman and Iles, 2000). However, there remains a question regarding whether it is right to recognize Normative commitment as a separate measure. Suliman and Iles' (2000) research suggests a weakness in the reliability of the Normative commitment measure. They argue that more research needs to be undertaken in this area in order to build a more robust measure of Normative commitment which takes account of the cultural characteristics of the measured. One aim of this present research is to compare each type of commitment score and, in particular, see if there is such a convergence between the score for Attitudinal commitment and Normative commitment that the concepts should either be treated as one or the Normative measure should be improved.

Back to Etzioni

It could be argued that, using Meyer and Allen's commitment measure, compliance commitment is really a reflection of Etzioni's fifth type of compliance relationship, with Normative commitment being the ninth type (Etzioni, 1961). Simply the language used by Etzioni seems to suggest a link between the two areas of work. Arguably, an alternative approach to the study of commitment is to regard it as a form of compliance and to measure the employee's involvement and relate that to the type of power being exerted.

If we follow Etzioni's argument, then in a factory environment where some element of coercion is being used on the workforce, Normative commitment scores should be low due to the fact that to combine coercive power with Normative power is very difficult.

Causes and effects of commitment

Iles and Forster (1996) conducted research on the impact of each type of commitment on health-service executives undertaking an executive development programme. They measured the three types of commitment before, during and after the programme. The development programme was designed to enhance personal flexibility. Iles and Forster argued that an attempt to increase flexibility was likely to reduce Continuance commitment (commitment due to the sense of having few alternatives or the high costs of leaving). This was supported by their research, as there was some evidence that the programme loosened Continuance commitment. Interestingly, there was no impact on Normative or Affective commitment from the programme. This may suggest that these types of commitment are not affected by executive development. It may also suggest the possibility mentioned earlier: that as Affective and Normative commitment react in the same way, they could be similar or the same concept and it is not correct to treat them separately.

That Affective commitment is not increased by development activities is further supported by the work of Sturges *et al.* (2001). They hypothesized that graduates who received more organizational career management (which could include training courses, mentoring and careers advice) were more likely to demonstrate Affective commitment towards their organization. However, the research failed to find evidence to support this. It did find strong evidence that a lack of organizational commitment would lead to people seeking to develop their careers outside of it. This confirms the close links between organizational commitment and intention to leave. Given this link, it would seem important to find the key that unlocks Affective commitment.

Orpen (1997) measured the effect of a formal mentoring programme over two years on each type of commitment, using the Meyer and Allen measurement. His hypothesis was that the programme would lead to higher commitment, and he found that to be the case. The weakness in the analysis is that Orpen appears to have taken each of Meyer and Allen's measures and developed an overall score. Given the view asserted above that Continuance and Affective commitment are very different indicators, it would seem difficult to draw conclusions from research that gives an overall score for both.

Meyer and Allen (1997) have broadly reviewed the research on the consequences of the three types of commitment upon employee retention, attendance and job performance. They suggest that all types of commitment are likely to be correlated positively with retention, but that only Affective and Normative commitment will be positively associated with job performance and attendance. They further argue that because Normative commitment derives from a feeling of obligation and duty towards the organization, the links with attendance and job performance will not be as strong as in Affective commitment, which derives from emotional attachment to the organization. The research in each of these areas is now considered.

Employee retention

Perhaps not unexpectedly, several researchers have found a negative correlation between commitment and both 'intention to leave' and 'actual turnover' (Allen and Meyer, 1996; Mathieu and Zajac, 1990; Tett and Meyer, 1993 – all in Meyer and Allen, 1997: 26). Further, this association has been found in all types of commitment, although it is strongest in Affective commitment. Meyer and Allen argue that if an organization's only goal is retention, then developing any type of commitment could achieve this goal.

Attendance

When considering the link between attendance and commitment it is important, if possible, to separate involuntary absence (due to sickness, for example) from voluntary absence (due to workers actively deciding not to attend when they otherwise could). Mathieu and Zajac (1990) found that attendance was positively associated with Affective commitment but did not separate voluntary and involuntary absence. Somers (1995, in Meyer and Allen, 1997: 27) found that suspicious absences were fewer in those with high Affective commitment. In contrast, attendance has not been found to be significantly related to Continuance commitment. No studies were found on the relationship between Normative commitment and attendance.

Job performance

In assessing the relationship between job performance and commitment, Meyer and Allen have divided performance into two areas: that of regular performance in role, and that of extra role performance (described as citizenship).

In relation to 'in role performance', the link to Affective commitment has not been conclusively demonstrated. There are studies which seem to have shown there to be a positive link (Meyer *et al.*, 1989, in Meyer and Allen, 1997: 29). However, in other studies (Williams and Anderson, 1991; Ganster and Dwyer, 1995 – both in Meyer and Allen, 1997: 29), Affective commitment and performance were not related. Orpen (2001), in his study of mentoring programmes, commitment and job performance, also failed to find a link between job performance and commitment. Meyer and Allen argue that a number of factors may impact on this result. These include the individual having adequate control over the performance outcome in question, and the extent to which the individual considers the task to be contributing positively to the organization. Also, Affectively committed employees may just not have the tools to undertake their role, either because they are not properly equipped or because they do not have the capability. Arguably, just because one is emotionally attached to an organization it does not mean that one is capable of fulfilling the role that one has been assigned.

What the research does establish is that there is no link between Continuance commitment and job performance. Again, not enough research has been undertaken on Normative commitment to show a conclusion.

When it comes to considering citizenship, then the link with Affective commitment is much clearer, with many studies finding a positive association (Gregersen, 1993; Moorman, 1993; Munene, 1995 – all in Meyer and Allen, 1997: 34). Meyer *et al.* (1993) also found a positive link between Normative commitment and citizenship, although, as suggested, this was weaker than for Affective commitment. As predicted, there was no link with Continuance commitment.

Research context

Conceptual framework and hypothesis

The conceptual framework (see Figure 15.1) underpinning the research links the concepts of management development, organizational commitment and job performance. The suggestions made in the framework are mostly supported by the literature already discussed.

Management development was conceptualized according to the definition by Woodall and Winstanley (1998: 5) as this was thought to be appropriate to the DCUK MD programme:

> Primarily orientated towards developing individuals in ways which are complimentary with the organization and its objectives and appropriate for meeting the individual's own career and development needs.

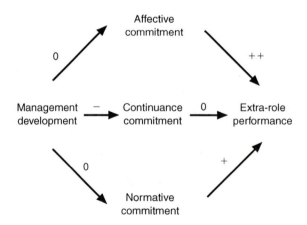

Figure 15.1 Conceptual framework.

As previously mentioned, the concepts of Affective, Continuance and Normative commitment are taken from Meyer and Allen (1997). The idea of extra role job performance is taken from Meyer and Allen, and conceptualized here as:

> Performance in areas outside of the specific role description which has a beneficial impact on the organization or the individual's co-workers in the work environment.

Arrows in Figure 15.1 indicate the association between the concepts. They are marked with either a single or double positive, a negative, or a zero. These arrows indicate the hypothesized level of impact that the concept to the left of the arrow has on the concept to the right of the arrow. So it is suggested that MD has zero impact on Affective or Normative commitment, and has a negative impact on Continuance commitment. Likewise, it appears that Affective commitment will have a strong positive impact on extra-role performance, with Normative commitment having a weaker but still positive impact; while Continuance commitment has zero impact on extra-role job performance.

The research focuses on the first part of the framework (the link between MD and the three types of organizational commitment) and investigates the impact of MD on organizational commitment. The research population was drawn from DCUK's cohort of team leaders.

DCUK's MD programme

In 2002, DCUK introduced an MD programme for 14 of its 233 team leaders, who were selected for development on the basis of their potential for promotion to a management position. This was DCUK's first MD programme for team leaders. These 14 individuals were studied along with a further group of 219 team leaders who did not participate in the DCUK MD programme. Line managers nominated team leaders, and a panel consisting of senior managers then made the final selection. In communications to team leaders it was made clear that the programme would be run annually, and those not selected one year would have the opportunity to participate the following year.

Survey method

A survey was used to compare the three types of commitment between the group selected for the first MD programme and the group not selected. The survey was adapted from Meyer and Allen's (1997) established survey instrument. The survey contained eight questions about Affective commitment, nine questions about Continuance commitment and six questions about Continuance commitment. Respondents were asked to score their responses on a Likert scale of seven items ranging from 'Strongly agree' to 'Strongly disagree'. The survey sought to investigate the following four items:

1   Whether within the two groups there were differences in the mean levels of Affective, Normative and Continuance commitment; that is, whether each type of commitment was displayed at the same level or whether each type displayed itself at different levels.
2   Whether there were differences in the mean levels of each type of commitment between each group.
3   Whether the hypothesis set out earlier – that management development has no effect on Affective commitment or Normative commitment but has a negative affect on Continuance commitment – was supported. The survey may support this hypothesis if levels of Affective and Normative commitment were the same across both groups and levels of Continuance commitment were lower in the management development group.
4   Whether there was evidence to suggest that the concepts of Normative commitment and Affective commitment are in fact the same or very similar. This would be supported if the survey across both groups showed Normative and Affective commitment at the same or similar levels.

Research findings and analysis

The response rate was very positive, with 100 per cent response from those participating in the MD programme and 70 per cent from those not on the programme. The positive response was, in part, attributed to the data collection method used, which was specifically designed to encourage response and ensure anonymity.

Mean scores were calculated for each type of commitment across each group. As the response from the second group surveyed represented a sample of the population, it was necessary then to carry out significance tests to determine whether the mean scores varied significantly from each other. Tests were carried out at 90 per cent, 95 per cent and 99 per cent confidence levels. Confidence at 99 per cent carries the most certainty that the difference is significant and the null hypothesis can be rejected. This is referred to as 'highly significant', while 90 per cent is significant but with less confidence attached to it.

Survey results are now considered against each of these factors in turn, but first it is worth considering the results overall.

Overall results

It is difficult to judge a DCUK commitment score in isolation from comparative data from another organization. However, given the seven-point

Likert scale where scores of 5, 6 and 7 relate to positive feelings of commitment – with 4 being neutral and 1, 2 and 3 being negative – it is reasonably safe to assume that any score above 4 (neutral) can be regarded as a positive level of commitment. Overall, the scores for Affective commitment were above 4.5 in both groups, while the score for Normative commitment was above 4 in the first management group and slightly below 4 in the other group. The Continuance commitment mean score was below 4 in both groups.

These scores can be directly compared to the work of Iles and Forster (1996), which used the Meyer and Allen commitment measure on a group of high potential senior managers within the National Health Service (NHS). In their study, which took place over two time periods, Affective commitment was scored slightly above 4; Normative commitment around 3.3, and Continuance commitment around 4. The difference between this result and DCUK's is surprising when one considers two factors. First, in relation to the seniority of the people surveyed, it might have been expected that Normative and Affective commitment would be higher in a group of senior managers than in a group of people below senior management level. DCUK's scores exceeded the NHS score even in the group which was not on the management development programme. Second, considering the nature of the organizations, it is perhaps surprising that Affective and Normative commitment (which measure emotional attachment to an organization and its values) appear higher at DCUK than in the NHS. One would have expected that many people work within the NHS because it is aligned with their values and beliefs, and that this would have been a lower score in a commercial private company.

The final surprise is that Continuance commitment is higher in the NHS than in DCUK. It seems highly likely that salaries and benefits at DCUK are higher than in the NHS, and yet, on the basis of this research, people find the costs of leaving the NHS greater than the costs of leaving DCUK.

Results are now considered in relation to the four specific items being investigated.

Item 1: Differences in mean levels of each commitment type within each group

For both groups, the highest type of commitment was Affective, followed by Normative and Continuance. The graphs at Figures 15.2 and 15.3 represent these results.

In the first management group, the mean scores were 5.0268, 4.3452 and 3.6349 respectively. As this represents the entire population, there is no requirement to carry out significance tests on the results. These results are referred to as a 'known mean'.

For the other group, the results were 4.6765, 3.8464 and 3.5218

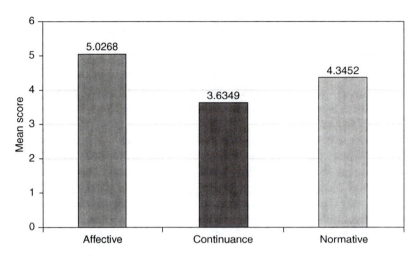

Figure 15.2 Team leaders on first MD programme in DCUK ($n = 14$).

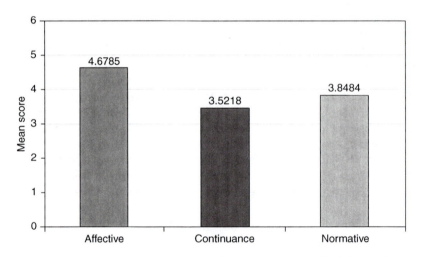

Figure 15.3 Team leaders not on first MD programme in DCUK ($n = 219$).

respectively. Differences between these scores were tested using a two-tailed test with the null hypothesis 'there is no difference between the two mean scores'. Tests were carried out at the 90, 95 and 99 per cent confidence levels. The results showed a significant difference between each type of commitment, with the highest level of significance attaching to the difference between Affective and Continuance, and Normative and Affective commitment. Table 15.1 demonstrates the results.

Although the results demonstrate positive levels of all types of commitment in all categories, it is notable that the highest level of commitment

Table 15.1 Difference between commitment scores

	Affective	Continuance	Significance
Mean	4.6765	3.5218	99%

	Continuance	Normative	Significance
Mean	3.5218	3.8464	95%

	Normative	Affective	Significance
Mean	3.8464	4.6765	90%

for both groups is Affective, whilst the lowest is Continuance. Given that those attending the first management programme were selected on the basis of their high performance in their current role and potential for progression within the company, one may have expected their Continuance commitment to be the lowest score. These people know they are regarded as high performers and are, therefore, likely to be less anxious about finding alternative work options outside of DCUK. However, it is notable in this group that Affective commitment is still higher than Normative commitment. Normative commitment measures the respondent's feeling of obligation to remain with an employer and, given that the respondents were in the middle of a costly management development programme being funded by the organization, one may have thought that this sense of commitment would outweigh all others. Turning to the other group, these individuals know that that they have not been selected for development and therefore that they are not the highest performers at their level in DCUK. They also know there is a group of peers who are more likely to be promoted than they are. In spite of this, they still score significantly higher on Affective commitment than Continuance commitment. One may have considered that these people were more likely to be staying with DCUK because of the good pension fund and job security while not feeling any sense of obligation or attachment to the values of the organization. From this survey, this does not appear to be the case.

The final part of the conceptual framework suggested that Affective commitment has a very positive effect on extra-role performance. This hypothesis would seem to be true on the basis of the literature on this subject (Meyer and Allen, 1997). While the survey conducted at DCUK did not seek to examine this hypothesis, the results are positive for the company, as Affective commitment is displayed more than any other category. The results also suggest that any negative impact brought about by introducing a development programme based on selection has not been sufficient to change people's attitude sufficiently for Continuance commitment to outweigh Affective commitment.

Item 2: Differences in mean level of each type commitment between the two groups

Figures 15.4, 15.5 and 15.6 show the mean level of each type of commitment for the two groups.

A directional one-tailed test was applied using the alternative hypothesis 'the mean levels of commitment in the non-management development

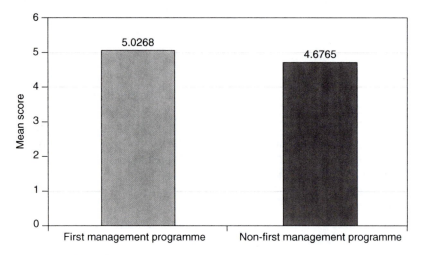

Figure 15.4 Affective commitment.

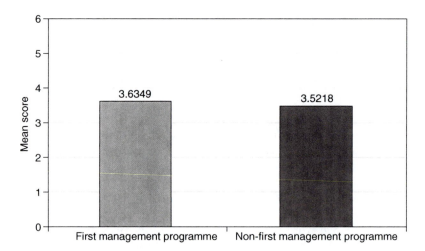

Figure 15.5 Continuance commitment.

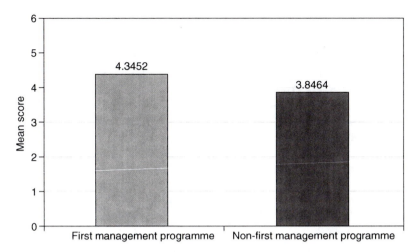

Figure 15.6 Normative commitment.

Table 15.2 Differences in organizational commitment between two groups

	First management programme	Non-first management programme	
Affective	5.0268	4.6765	95%
Continuance	3.6349	3.5218	Not significant
Normative	3.8464	4.3452	99%

group will be lower than the mean level of commitment in the management development group' to discover if the differences between the two groups were significant. The results are set out in Table 15.2.

As can be seen from the table, for Affective and Normative commitment the non-management development group's mean was lower than for those on the programme. For Affective commitment, this difference was highly significant. It is notable, however, that there is no significant difference between the two groups' mean scores on Continuance commitment.

It is worth comparing this result with the outcome of the published research reviewed earlier. Three studies were mentioned. First, Orpen (1997) considered the impact of a mentoring programme on commitment and found there to be a positive link. It was suggested that his research was questionable due to the way in which Meyer and Allen's (1997) measures were grouped together to produce one overall score. In Iles and Forster's (1996) research on NHS high-potential senior managers, it was found that developing this group had no impact on their Affective and Normative commitment but a negative impact on their

Continuance commitment. This research is the most directly comparable research to the DCUK survey, because it used the same measure and studied a group of individuals selected for development. It also measured a control group of individuals who were not developed, and found no difference in any measure of their commitment. The big difference between the research designs is that Iles and Forster's research measured the groups before and after development, while the DCUK research only measures one point in time around the middle of the programme. The final research considered was that of Sturges *et al.* (2001), who performed a longitudinal study of the first ten years of graduates' careers. They used a different measure of commitment devised by Cook and Wall (1980, in Sturges *et al.*, 2001: 5) and found there to be no link between commitment and planned career management (which included development activities). Potentially this research has the greatest validity, as it used the largest sample of data and considered graduates within five organizations.

On the face of it, then, the DCUK research is at odds with two of the pieces of research in this area, as it finds a greater level of Affective and Normative commitment within the group participating in the management development programme than in those not participating. There could be a number of reasons for this. First, it could be that the reason for higher commitment has nothing to do with the management development. One of the weaknesses of the research in the chapter is that it does not measure the commitment of the management development group before and after the development. It is, therefore, impossible to attribute the higher level of commitment to the development. High performers may, by their nature, be more committed, and this could be the reason for their selection for development and for this result. Another possible reason is the nature of the development being undertaken. The senior management programme measured in the NHS study (Iles and Forster, 1996) was specifically designed with the objective of exploring behavioural flexibility in order that the senior management team could address the major cultural change required by the NHS at that time. The outcome was that Affective and Normative commitment did not change but Continuance commitment was reduced. This may have been a desirable outcome, since Continuance commitment could be linked to less flexibility. Given the reported levels of Affective and Normative commitment, it could be argued, however, that reducing Continuance commitment alone would have the desired outcome.

The DCUK programme was not designed to address flexibility, but to prepare people for future management roles. The DCUK MD group members had no difference in their level of Continuance commitment than those in the non-development group. Unless Continuance commitment started out higher in the MD group before the development commenced (which would seem unlikely), then it is reasonable to assume that the programme had no impact on Continuance commitment. This is at odds with the NHS findings, but it could be that the NHS programme and the DCUK programme were designed to address different objectives, and therefore produced different outcomes on commitment.

From these findings, it could be suggested that it is impossible for development programmes to impact negatively on Continuance commitment while at the same time positively impacting on Normative and Affective commitment. It could be, therefore, that organizations have to carefully select the goals of their programmes with the impact on commitment in mind. The ideal outcome of reducing Continuance commitment while increasing Affective commitment may not be possible. Perhaps the key difference in these programmes is the employer's commitment to the employee. This would substantiate the argument put forward by Baruch (1998) for the need for mutuality in order to gain commitment (or at least Normative and Affective commitment). Perhaps development programmes which underline the employer's commitment to the employee could build Affective commitment, while programmes which seek to loosen the ties between the individual and the employer would not have that effect and may reduce Continuance commitment instead.

If we argue that different types of development programme have a different effect on commitment, then we call into question the validity of having one definition of MD. The one used here by Woodall and Winstanley (1998: 5), was that MD is:

> Primarily orientated towards developing individuals in ways which are complementary with the organization and its objectives and appropriate for meeting the individual's own career and development needs.

This is perhaps valid for the type of MD that includes the commitment of the employer to the employee. In fact, the mutuality of objectives is stressed in the definition. If, however, the development programme is designed to enhance flexibility and loosen ties to the organization, arguably this definition is not useful. An alternative conceptualization for this other type of development programme is required – possibly that MD is:

> Primarily orientated towards increasing behavioural and strategic flexibility in ways that benefit the organization and loosen ties between the organization and the individual.

We shall describe the first definition/conceptualization as 'MD1' and the second concept as 'MD2'.

Item 3: MD has no effect on Affective or Normative commitment, and a negative affect on Continuance commitment

This research does not support the hypothesis that MD has no effect on Affective and Normative commitment, and a negative effect in Continuance

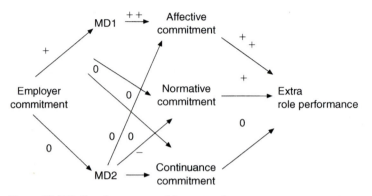

Figure 15.7 Refined conceptual framework.

commitment. It is not possible conclusively to reject it either, but on the basis of the results shown it would seem that the hypothesis is too simplistic an approach to the relationship between commitment and MD.

The significant differences in commitment between the two research groups do suggest that there may be a link between commitment and MD, and therefore the conceptual framework set out in the previous section still has some validity. A refinement of the conceptual framework (as shown at Figure 15.7) may, however, have more validity.

In this framework, the notion of employer commitment is introduced as another variable, and the suggestion that positive employer commitment will be associated with MD1, which in turn will have a positive impact on Affective and Normative commitment and a neutral effect in Continuance commitment, is made. On the other hand, MD2 has no positive employer commitment and reduces Continuance commitment, while Affective and Normative commitment remain neutral. The effect on extra-role performance remains unchanged.

Item 4: Normative and Affective commitment are the same or similar

The DCUK research does not conclusively support the argument that Normative and Affective commitment are the same. What is clear is that the difference between Continuance commitment and Affective commitment is greater than the difference between Normative commitment and, in fact, either of those two concepts.

However, on the basis of the DCUK research in the non-management population there was a more significant difference (99 per cent) between Normative and Affective commitment than there was between Normative and Continuance commitment (90 per cent). This could suggest a closer relationship between Normative and Continuance commitment than has emerged from the literature. Further research is required in this area to establish more about the attributes of Normative commitment.

Conclusions and learning points

Any conclusions based on this research are necessarily tentative. They arise from a single case and from a small population. There are additional limitations in the research design, such as the problem of causal direction, if any, of relationships between the variables and the related impact of prior factors on levels of commitment. Within that context, the following learning points are offered:

- The notion of commitment remains incompletely understood but seems still to have relevance in studying behaviour at work.
- Continuing relevance applies to managerial behaviour and the contribution of management development.
- Investment in management development may have either or both positive and negative impacts on the different forms of commitment. These potential relationships, though, require much more research to be fully understood.
- Notwithstanding the previous point, it does seem highly likely that management development programmes can be designed with different objectives in order to have specific impacts on the different forms of commitment. The idea of MD1 and MD2 presented in this chapter has some value for this purpose.
- Employer commitment is likely to be a significant variable in affecting employee commitment. Investment in MD can be an indicator of employer commitment.
- The conceptual framework developed for this project has been shown to have both validity and utility in researching the links between MD and commitment, and so will be of value in informing future research.

References

Baruch, Y. (1998) 'The rise and fall of organizational commitment', *Human Systems Management*, 17(2).

Cook, J. and Wall, T. (1980) 'New work attitude measures of trust, organizational commitment and personal need non-fulfilment', *Journal of Occupational Psychology*, 53.

Etzioni, A. (1961) *A Comparative Analysis of Complex Organizations*, New York: The Free Press.

Gratton, L., Hope-Hailey, V. Stiles, P. and Truss, C. (1999) *Strategic Human Resource Management*, 1st edn, New York: Oxford University Press.

Iles, P. (1997) 'Sustainable high-potential career development: a resource based view', *Career Development International*, 2(7).

Iles, P. and Forster, A. (1996) 'The changing relationships between work commitment, personal flexibility and employability: an evaluation of a field experiment in executive development', *Journal of Managerial Psychology*, 11(8).

Meyer, J.P. and Allen, N.J. (1997) *Commitment in the Workplace*, Thousand Oaks, CA: Sage.

Meyer, J.P., Allen, N.J. and Smith, C.A. (1993) 'Commitment to organizations and occupations: Extension and test of a three-component conceptualization', *Journal of Applied Psychology*, 78(4): 538–51.

Mowday, R.T. (1998) 'Reflections on the study and relevance of organizational commitment', *Human Resource Management Review*, 8(4).

Mowday, R.T., Steers, R.M. and Porter, L. (1979) 'The measurement of organizational commitment', *Journal of Vocational Behaviour*, 14.

Orpen, C. (1997) 'The effects of formal mentoring on employee work motivation, organizational commitment and job performance', *The Learning Organization*, 4(2): 53–60.

Reichers, A. (1985) 'A review and reconceptualisation of organizational commitment', *Academy of Management Review*, 10(3).

Stewart, J. (1999) *Employee Development Practice*, London: FT Pitman.

Sturges, J., Guest, D., Conway, N. and Mackenzie-Davey, K. (2001) 'What difference does it make?', *Academy of Management Proceedings*.

Suliman, A. and Iles, P. (2000) 'Is Continuance commitment beneficial to organizations? Commitment–performance relationships: a new look', *Journal of Managerial Psychology*, 15(5).

Ulrich, D. (2000) 'From e-business to e-HR', *Human Resource Planning Journal*, 23(2): 67–80.

Waterman, R.H. and Waterman, J.A. (1994) 'Towards a career resilient workforce', *Harvard Business Review*, 7(4).

Woodall, J. and Winstanley, D. (1998) *Management Development*, Oxford: Blackwell.

16 Writing, reading and reason

The 'Three Rs' of manager learning

Jeff Gold, Richard Thorpe and Robin Holt

Objectives

The objectives of this chapter are:

- to consider a practical application of a constructionist understanding of management development;
- to enhance the image of a manager as a 'practical author' in contrast to that of a 'scientist';
- to develop the view of manager learning as a process of being able to write about events reflect and understand critically so as to be able identify the possibilities for action and engage in reasoning that will lead to joint outcomes in a social context;
- to set out a range of practical approaches that managers can use to both make change and learn.

Introduction

This chapter illustrates how a constuctionist understanding of the management development process can have practical applications. Past contributors to the debate on management (Argyris, 1996; Eastman and Bailey, 1996) have criticized constuctionist perspectives as offering little in terms of practical relevance. Their view is that whilst they allow researchers to gain important insight into the influence of localized norms and prevailing patterns of behaviour, they do not offer managers solutions to their day-to-day problems. This chapter, therefore, seeks to challenge this view by illustrating how research in management development using constructionist approaches can lead to the development of practical understanding whilst at the same time offering new insights in management development and the behaviour of managers. It does this in two ways. First, it argues that constructionism does provide rational designs by which managers are able to 'test' their actions. Second, it shows how these designs can give managers insights into problems and issues that are *more effective* than those offered by science-based researchers as a result of them being the product of philosophically inspired creations of the managers themselves, as opposed to the potentially 'imprisoning' models updated from outside.

Theoretical context

To date, management learning and development has been largely focused on behaviourist and experiential traditions. Whilst these are undoubtedly important, such a rational scientific approach offers only a partial explanation of the process of development of a manager. This rational perspective highlights the importance of planning and the virtues of maintaining 'objectivity', it encourages the construction of testable hypotheses and links legitimacy with dispassionate, rational assessment (Holman and Thorpe, 2003). Looked at through this lens, managers operate in a 'transactional' way and are the arbiters of behavioural efficacy, whether this is of their own activity or of those they manage, and the standards are those of the market (MacIntyre, 1981: 29).

This view suggests that managers and research about management action follow what Shotter (1997) refers to as the 'way of theory' despite a persistent critique (Bernstein, 1983; Grey, 1999; Parker, 2002). Managers may fundamentally believe, and those that they manage come to expect, that they need to act like the mind of the organization, able to undertake a robust analysis of the organization and follow this with appropriate action. Further, they tend to think that this can be achieved through the adoption of some universal analytic approach (akin to software) that will remove the distortions of bias and prejudice.

However, from a social constructionist perspective, managers do not have separate 'minds' at all but are immersed in 'the vicissitudes of social processes' (Gergen, 1985: 268). From this perspective there is little possibility of separating thinking and doing, as everyone is immersed in the flux of everyday life and the authority of managerial instruction comes from living amidst, and learning about, the prodigious diversity of activities in which individuals find themselves (Hacker, 1997). The image that emerges from this recognition is that of a manager as a practical author (Cunliffe, 2001; Holman and Thorpe, 2003); that is, a person for whom organizational experience is less about the application of rationalized blueprints created from dispassionate, objective assessments but more about the creation of meaningful landscapes on which activity takes place into which others might join to help create a new reality. This image can be augmented by that of the 'philosopher-manager', argued for by Chia and Morgan (1996) on the basis that management education is narrowly concerned with social-economic activity and needs to be expanded to embrace 'the management of life in all its complexions' (1996: 41). So, in contrast to an emphasis on Argyris' generalized blueprints of identification and correction, managers should perhaps consider and 'challenge the mental abstractions which are confused for truth'.

In order to take this image of the manager as practical author further, we argue in this chapter that managers might benefit from the practice of what we term 'the Three Rs of Manager Learning'. Managers are often cast as rational problems-solvers with an ability to find answers that work. However (and perhaps just as frequently), they may be less successful than they wish. At such times, managers might gain benefit from a more critical examination of taken-for-granted assumptions and understandings. Our metaphor of the Three Rs indicates that managers must 'return to basics' of writing, reading and reasoning. First, managers must learn to *write* about situations so as to better understand them; second, they must interpret what they write by *reading* reflexively and third, they must learn to *reason* authoritatively for the interpretation they have made, offering a persuasive articulation of the situation as they see it so as to be able to offer the possibility of new practice that both engages and enables joint action. The notion of Three Rs has been inspired by the German philosopher, Hans-Georg Gadamer, along with his theory/method of critical hermeneutic questioning.

Gadamer's (1900–2002) principal work was *Truth and Method* (*Wahrheit und Methode*) (1989). In this text, he advances a theory of philosophical hermeneutics that places the practice of understanding as a central and universal feature of the world (Bernstein, 1983; Malpas *et al.*, 2002). In the first stage of the process, emphasis needs to be given to writing. Writing is the first stage in the development of reflection by managers and the means in which language and speaking can be detached. The action is for managers to produce a text so they can later understand and interpret it. The production of a text in this way brings the past into the present. However, as Gadamer identifies, while writing may be about personal feelings and emotions, the result is a detachment from 'everything psychological' (1989: 392), allowing a 'kind of self-alienation' (1989: 393). Through the act of writing, managers are able to give events a certain fixed view and, in so doing, separate intention from meaning (Bleicher, 1980). Thus, by reading the text new possibilities can become apparent.

The second stage is for managers to read what they have written. By reading, managers unify their understanding with interpretation. Writing, Gadamer suggests, is not 'an end in itself' (1989: 394) but a means to render an event or issue into a hermeneutical problem. Reading (or the understanding and interpretation of a text) is considered the primary hermeneutic task. By taking the effort to read the text via the medium of language, a manager works and is being worked within the hermeneutic circle. Here, a fusion of a manager's horizon between present understanding and past history and tradition takes place, and then managers can use those parts that provide meaning in a text to shed light on the whole. Crucially, such reading can only occur phenomenologically on the basis of a prejudicial pre-understanding, a tradition and a history. Reading hermeneutically and critically does not mean a return to the past, though, but it does mean there is an opportunity for managers to reveal how their understandings are historically dependent, perhaps malignantly, and thus move to develop new readings that will change and extend their horizon of meaning. Importantly, such readings feed practical possibilities through reasoning.

The third stage is one where the managers attempt to reason about their experiences of writing and reading. A manager's situatedness within a tradition removes the possibility or the idea of what Gadamer called 'an absolute reason' (1989: 276). Managers, therefore, reason by accepting how different views can be integrated and agreements reached in respect of particular issues being considered. This is not an easy process, and is one that requires an ongoing openness to voices and opinions of others (Arnswald, 2002). However, reasoning by arguing persuasively could be seen as the hallmark of an image of the manager as philosopher. On occasions where there is a failure to achieve agreement which can lead to joint action (Shotter, 1997; Holman and Thorpe, 2003), it becomes even more crucial for managers to both write and read afresh and for them to question their prejudices (Connolly, 2002). Further, if it is argued that the context of a manager's work resembles vague and disordered complexity composed of multiple voices pursuing multiple and competing purposes, then reasoning has to take on a different flavour compared to the more rational explanations of work life that employ a more scientific approach on the way of the 'way of theory'. There is little place here for structural equation models by which to guide managers. Instead (and following Toulmin (2001), managers need to tilt the balance towards what feels right and reasonable in particular situations.

In summary, the Three Rs describe the locus of an hermeneutic circle: writing, reading what is written, and reasoning on the consensual and disruptive effects noted, then considering the implications for action, followed by re-writing. This activity in its entirety gives substance to the idea of managers developing as practical authors. In the next section, we will explore how a group of managers undertook development through this process in two different organizations.

Research context

While managers may not necessarily see the value of conventional theory for their practice, the views of science and associated images of organizations as machines and biological/chemical organisms still informs the dominant discourse of what managers should do and how they should learn. Such views remain despite contrasting images that have emerged from studies of management practice (Watson, 1994; Cunliffe, 2001). To mitigate against an extreme reaction we adopted a collaborative approach, one in which, through conversation, opportunities were sought for linking diverse sets of interests (Gold *et al.*, 2000). We approached four managers in two different organizations where good relations were already established. Three managers came from a single organization, a fast-growing financial services company based in Skipton, North Yorkshire, England. The fourth manager came from a long-established, family-owned engineering company in Pudsey, Leeds. There were three males and one female involved. We arranged to meet with all participants at their workplaces. At the initial briefing session, only the basic idea of managers as practical authors was presented, with the requirement to learn the Three Rs. The basic simplicity of this requirement served to underpin the literary notion of authorship. Writing was already familiar, and reasoning required little further elucidation. However, the link to critical hermeneutics and the associated links to philosophy required more careful presentation. To do this, Figure 16.1 was employed.

A number of key features of hermeneutics were explained with reference to current events; these were:

- understanding and interpretation of events as complete;
- prejudice and pre-judgement connected to tradition and history;
- the notion that background understandings were both a help and a hindrance;
- the need to adopt an in-between in order to position to allow critique.

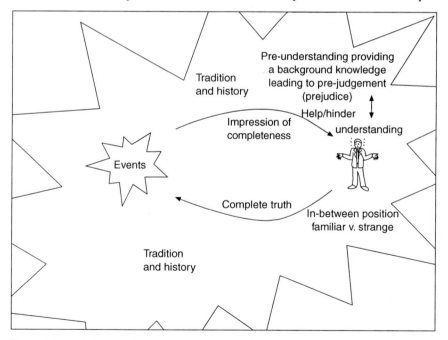

Figure 16.1 Briefing on the hermeneutical circle.

All managers practised a three-step process:

1   writing about an event;
2   using reading as a text to consider interpretation, prejudice, tradition and history;
3   considering possibilities that might lead to moving into particular situations.

Each manager agreed to keep a record of his or her use of the Three Rs over a period of ten weeks in the form of a mini-log or memo book, which could be easily maintained throughout the day. Agreement was reached to meet for a review after four weeks and then again after a ten-week gap to discuss findings.

Analysis and evaluation of main findings/results

The first review was held with the four managers after four weeks. Each manager was able to report back on progress (or difficulties) and share findings with the research team. In terms of the process, managers, as expected, had had most difficulty with the reading part, i.e. the working of the hermeneutic consciousness which seeks an illumination of how understanding of the writing occurs. However, all the managers were sufficiently positive about their participation to continue with the slight adjustment of giving more attention to how pre-understanding and prejudice links their understanding in language to a tradition. We now consider the findings from each manager after ten weeks.

Manager A

For Manager A, 14 events were recorded, of which 12 were seen as troubles, difficulties or uncertainties relating to 'the actions of others'. Such events were recorded with a range of negative views about the states of others relating to:

* not taking responsibility;
* not seeing a need for help;
* not backing decisions fully;
* not doing something;
* lacking motivation;
* not having the skills.

The use of negative encoding in his writing about events allowed Manager A to express his personal feelings and take an evaluative stance towards them. However, in taking a detached view of the events, particularly the actions and states of others, his prejudice had the effect of reducing others to mere objects, accepting knowledge from them as complete, fixed and unvarying. In reading his texts, Manager A had the opportunity to come to new understanding of others as being more human than at first thought.

For Manager A, reading 'took . . . a while to get used to' but '. . . has led to some interesting discoveries' with some 'clear patterns and recurring themes'. He was 'surprised' by the 'strong values' that were attached to his prejudices, which he also tended to 'conceal from others. A recurring theme was his prejudice 'about asking for and being given', which he linked to a civil service tradition of 'never asking for a job and never refusing one'. This was a finding that was affecting how he dealt with others. For example, R is member of his team. She is someone he finds 'difficult' but needs to 'get on board' in the development of a new design for a training module which fits 'the new structure'. His initial understanding was that 'she might not see the need to redesign'. His first reading of the text raised doubts and uncertainties: (1) is his categorization of R as difficult a hindering prejudice? (2) does the 'on-board' metaphor assume everyone has to be 'in the boat' and that 'R isn't'? (3) the assumption 'that there is a boat', which leads to (4) doubts about 'getting people to work in the desired structure'. This and other events led to a further hindrance concerning how he dealt with 'uncertainty' where he 'found it difficult to direct any [of his] thoughts to an external outcome'. A key finding was how this 'tendency is exacerbated by internalizing'. A short time later, the issue of R surfaced again. She had been 'reluctant to make any changes' to the module. He also saw the event as one where he should 'give her all the direct feedback'. His reading showed the hindering of his prejudice that R is 'difficult' and that this would affect how he delivers feedback and how he expects R to react (negatively), perpetuating a preference to do nothing. However, this tendency was identified as something that 'recurred on a fairly regular basis', a consequence of 'my deeper set prejudices'. His response was to 'convert . . . thoughts into actions', principally by finding ways to talk with others. With R, for example, the action was to 'balance the feedback' by focusing 'on the module and not the person'. He also recognized that his own action reduced 'levels of uncertainty' in himself and others, creating clarity where there had been vague feelings.

Manager B

Manager B felt the Three Rs framework helped her to recognize the influence of the 'baggage' that we carry with us and how it 'materially impacts how we relate to challenges, people and opportunities'. She identified nine events, eight of which were problematic. Of these, the most significant, in its being referred to in the context of other events, was her promotion. Notwithstanding her good performance assessment, she wrote of her feeling of distance from other senior managers (only one other member congratulated her) and how, in reading this, she began to doubt her abilities. In further reading she identified how her self-image had been negatively prejudiced by comments from a 'single source' in her past. Recognizing the 'crippling' effects of this prejudice – something in reading a later event she calls 'a small voice criticizing decisions and direction' – she began to reason by reframing her 'take' on this event. She found the prejudice 'disabling', manifest as it was in a heightened concern for the reputation of office. Evidence of this re-framing comes when she is surprised that as a director she was nevertheless invited to socialize with the IT team. She reasoned that she should not assume that her prejudice of deference and low self-esteem manifest in maintaining clear hierarchical divisions was extendible to others. The strangeness she might have felt inviting an 'outsider' into a social event cannot be imputed to others, for whom status may not necessarily be such a 'hang up'. She became aware of the voices of others. The IT team members were reasoned as other voices who saw the person first and status second, an attitude of 'openness' that could be learnt from when it came to building relations with her fellow senior managers.

This critical awareness of a felt need to re-frame her approach to business life was also experienced during a later event in which, under competition for organizational resources, she had conceded her 'position' to the benefit of others. Initial reading led her to think she had been too conciliatory. In further reading, she identified how this attitude was fed by a desire to be accepted and to avoid ridicule. These 'causes', however, are neither wholly determining, nor understandable in isolation. For example, she also talked about having learnt the importance of adopting accommodating roles from her experiences of family life, and how, unconsciously, this prejudice skewed decision-making in her business activities. Moreover, even where she was aware of anxiety concerning her unwillingness to be assertive and leader-like, she was not entirely enamoured of the identity of business leader to which she felt she was being impelled. The hermeneutic approach afforded Manager B the possibility of critically appraising the socially constructed roles she was playing out. For example, how she was able to learn from the different worldviews of people, and so by inference come to doubt her own worldview, was accompanied by a prevailing ethos informed by a distaste for 'spinning' and a general suspicion of pedalling 'good news' stories merely to motivate others. Manager B became aware that she often conceded points without fully articulating her own position, but equally remained critical of the specious charisma that characterizes many modern business leaders.

Manager C

Manager C recorded 29 events, a process he found 'enlightening' despite having a 'busy senior management role'. His writing focused on events that were mainly 'bothersome', ranging from those events that were of 'high' to those of 'slight' concern. Manager C, like others, found the reading for prejudices 'easier' once he 'got used to the exercise', eventually enabling him to 'drill down to my deepest thoughts/values' and the extent to which these hindered his performance. A pattern revealed in early events was the prejudice of 'being seen to work hard' and 'I have to do my best possible work at all times'. These views were linked to the importance of building 'credibility', 'taking pride in work', 'standing' and 'reputation and respect for my competence'. However, the reading revealed the way such values affected his feelings of 'nervousness' and 'guilt'. For example, 'needing quiet' to prepare, Manager C worried about working from home '*but* felt obliged to be at work' (original emphasis), or 'guilt over being off work with a back strain', stemming from a prejudice that 'you must not be ill'. Continued reading started to produce doubts and questions. For example, following nervousness about a 'good first impression' with directors, Manager C considers whether concern for reputation is a hindrance and a cause of his failure to relax.

Further doubts were surfaced about achieving 'perfectionism' and establishing 'self-sufficiency'. Again, such values were associated with 'nervousness' and 'apprehensiveness'. For example, an audit was seen as 'checking up on me', with auditors 'trying to pick fault'. Another concern came from unease that a 'new line manager' wanted weekly meetings, seen as interference with 'self-sufficiency and independence', both associated with 'signs of competence as a manager'. In reasoning about these readings, Manager C focused initially on 'asking for feedback' from others and from themselves. For example, one response to nervousness was to 'build on success' and 'practice positive self talk'. He reasoned that the audit could be instrumental in his becoming more proactive in turning intentions into action. It also provided the impetus to 'drill deeper' into prejudices. These principally centred on family upbringing, the influence of his father and valuing education, and the link of establishing credibility to build a career. Rather than constantly seeking to impress, his reasoning suggested he step into the 'in-between' and approach the next meeting 'as if the need is to share not impress'. This allowed him to begin to build more open and constructive relations with his colleagues. As with Managers A and B, the identification of prejudices involved both psychological and social influences, and the reasoning by which re-framing actions were undertaken was itself relational and specific to particular events.

Manager D

Manager D recorded 11 events which in one way or another related to aspects of communication or miscommunication. In one event, all staff had been invited to take part in a training course but Manager D registered surprise at the lack of interest. In reading, he considered that being 'invited' gave out the ambiguous and unintended message of attendance being an optional and unimportant decision. Reasoning created a determination to be clearer in general by asking others how his communication was perceived. In reading another event in which an employee's response to a direct question was 'I don't know', Manager D considered that the individual concerned was not confident to make decisions about the unknown. Reasoning meant Manager D felt he needed to help the individual make a decision by explaining more rather than labelling the individual 'feeble'.

Reading these events made Manager D aware of the different perspective people could have of the same message. This awareness was further heightened when reading his text describing the introduction of a new system of performance reviews and his detection of his employees' reluctance to embrace them. In yet another discussion with staff, Manager D noted how because he felt that there were potentially many opportunities for disagreement, he avoided them by suppressing his own prejudices in order to maintain the flow of communication and interaction.

Reasoning on these readings led Manager D to isolate the importance, as he saw it, of having a good rapport with employees. The action necessary for this was attempting to push his won prejudices into the background whilst encouraging others to be open about theirs. This was seen as an important device to resolve actual or potential conflict. As he did this, Manager D also became aware that rather than repressing his own prejudices it was probably better to talk openly about them, so as to approach others on a more 'equal' footing. This was also identified as a way of validating his prejudices, checking whether they were shared by others, and their potential effects on the business.

Conclusions

Gadamer (1989: 294) explained that the 'true locus of hermeneutics' is an in-between or intermediate position between what is familiar based on assumptions (or a 'fore-conception of completeness') and what is strange. For the four managers who collaborated in the study, the entry point for such a move was the identification of events from their experience in writing. As with other reflective tools, such a process can be of most benefit when facing difficulties, and it was clear that the managers faced these frequently. Thus, situations were seen, in varying degrees of difficulty, as 'bothersome', 'difficult' or lacking in essential attributes or dispositions, and assumptions made understood or seen as false or confusing. Managers, therefore, were principally writing about events from what Gadamer (1989: 354) referred to as their 'experience of negation' (*Erfahrung der Nichtigkeit*). For Gadamer, this is the distinguishing feature of a 'genuine' understanding of experience since it allows for the refutation of 'false generalizations' and the consideration of 'better knowledge' (1989: 353). It is, therefore, a dialectical but ongoing process in which experience is taken as both the prompt and the foundation for learning (Taylor, 2002).

The managers in this study demonstrated their willingness to embrace experience following our approach, without seeking recourse to generalized models of behaviour and response. As they worked through the exercise they acquired new understanding, becoming more experienced at engaging critically with their own 'fore-knowledge' and the ways this blends or contrasts with that of others. Following Gadamer, we suggest that an *experienced* manager is not someone who has perfected techniques or passed the exams to demonstrate command of theories, but rather one who is 'undogmatic' enough to be open to new even negative experiences.

The problematization of events allowed the managers to unify understanding with interpretation and so begin the hermeneutic process by reading the text prepared by writing. Initially, as we have indicated, the managers found this a rather difficult part of the process and, at the time of the first review, reading tended to focus on judgements made about themselves and others rather than considering how prejudice worked and connected to tradition. Thus, managers surfaced questions such as: 'Why others do not engage in a process?' 'Why do staff fear the unknown?' What are the 'real' reasons for poor responses to requests?' 'Why do I feel guilty about being ill?' There were also challenges to assumptions about 'the original way as the best way' or 'making snap judgements', and doubts such as 'why is my understanding different to my intention?', 'looking fundamentally at what I don't do' and judging reasons given by others as 'feeble'. At this review, we were able to prompt mangers to confront the prejudice that connected this situatedness within a tradition that provided a hindrance to understanding. In various ways, managers did begin to consider ('drilling down into') 'deeper set' and 'strong values' and reconsider the 'baggage' that feeds the 'little voice within' that sets understanding within 'a particular frame'. Much of their critique centred on upbringing, past education, training and work roles, and the influences of family. However, there was also a wider awareness of deeply embedded cultural assumptions relating to organizational hierarchies, commonly accepted images of leadership and unifying organization metaphors, and how careers are meant to develop.

One of the most interesting features of reading was the consideration of managers' own states and the states of others. Thus managers considered their own nervousness, guilt, uncertainties, feelings and perceptions, but particularly the states or dispositions of others. For example, in various events others were categorized as difficult, lacking motivation or lacking skills. These were the kind of categorizations that were challenged in reading, the managers becoming aware of how their own prejudices informed their view of others (and themselves) and how for these others different views of self became available. In this way, we believe they reflect how 'Being that can be understood is language' (Gadamer, 1989: 474); how their descriptions can create an image that whilst sensible was not universal. In addition, the managers became aware of how when we speak or write about the state or disposition of others in addition to our own, it is a view that is mediated by pre-understanding and prejudice. Gadamer (1989: 475) suggests:

> that which comes into language in not something that is pregiven before language; rather, the word gives it its own determinateness

As a consequence, the interpretation of someone as 'difficult', 'feeble' or 'lacking' in motivation, or of the self as 'weak' or 'risk-averse' are meanings that are made by the managers through language and, as a consequence, are potentially both challengeable and changeable by them. From a constructionist perspective, what emerged amongst the managers is not only an understanding of how richly textured and prejudicial are the array of human motivations to action, but also that these are always couched in their own terms. This understanding enables the manager to experience the 'dramatic impact' of hermeneutic reflection better than would the adoption of any external model of rational reflection.

It was this dramatic impact that allowed the managers to reflect on why others had failed to respond to invitations, messages or even basic instructions. The expectation here was that on such occasions there 'ought' to be a response to the requirements of management. This is not an untypical expectation of those in positions of management, and is a feature of the prevailing management identity in Western economies. However, what we see here are the dangers of theoretically informed understandings which cast other humans as objects of whom a complete explanation by managers is seen as being both desirable *and* entirely possible. Instead, what the managers in this study were to find was that such a conception was as debilitating as it was effective – what was experienced as a benefit in terms of validating rationalized decision-making (of the kind 'employees understand performance', or 'people respect hierarchy') was disabling when experiences were 'read'. What was consistently felt by all managers was a growing awareness of how, as leaders, they were expected to behave, and how these expectations on occasions clashed with their personal values. This meant the result of the managers having to constantly resolve or dissolve tensions by amending their values *from within* the established prejudices associated with leadership in business whilst maintaining a sense of integrity and identity.

Initially, reasoning for oneself provided such a 'resource for reframing'. Managers found understanding, clarity and certainty. One manager also emphasized the value of 'positive' self-talk. However, it was through reasoning with others that managers made the most progress. Eschewing formal methods, with their built-in assumptions for manipulation and control, in favour of more 'substantive arguments' (Toulmin, 2001) is, for us, the hallmark of the manager as a practical author. Whether it was relatively 'small' changes of habit through seeking, or giving feedback to more significant dealings, managers saw that there was more to be gained by conversation with others than through formalized and modelled approaches. This reflects Gadamer's (1989) insistence that the making of a meaning is dependent on at least two voices in relationship held in dialogue and characterized by openness to the opinions of others.

Key learning points

This chapter shows the results of a management learning project that sought to introduce managers to the ideas of critical hermeneutics based on the philosophy of Hans-Georg Gadamer. Crucial to this process was the contrast with more orderly presentations of how managers should conduct their practice, in line with the requirements of the 'way of theory'. However, to facilitate this move, and to develop the necessary trust between researchers and the managers, we provided a simple heuristic tool we entitled the Three Rs or writing, reading and reasoning. This enabled managers to begin the consideration of their 'ignorance' (Chia and Morgan, 1996: 41), challenging the various abstractions that can be confused for truth or, in Gadamer's terms, 'completeness'. Where such understanding flipped into misunderstanding, managers were invited to step into the in-between position between what is familiar and what is strange – what Gadamer called the 'true locus of hermeneutics' (1989: 294). The managers reported in this chapter seem to have accepted such an invitation, although not without trepidation and with resultant doubts, insecurities, self-blame and questions as long-held beliefs and assumptions were often surfaced. Managers became aware, perhaps for the first time, of their situatedness within a tradition, the fusion of present (mis)understanding with the past, where prejudice could be confronted. However, rather than produce further intentions that *do not* become behaviours, managers moved to reason, locally via talking and dealing with others. In this way, managers as practical authors find their primary purpose of co-constructing worlds with others.

References

Argyris, C. (1996) 'Actionable knowledge: intent versus actuality', *Journal of Applied Behavioral Science*, 32(4): 441–4.

Arnswald, U. (2002) 'On the uncertainty of uncertainty', in Malpas, J., Arnswald, U. and Ketscher, J. (eds), *Gadamer's Century*, Cambridge, MA: MIT Press, pp. 25–44.

Bernstein, R.J. (1983) *Beyond Objectivism and Relativism*, Oxford: Blackwell.

Bleicher, J. (1980) *Contemporary Hermeneutics*, London: Routledge.

Chia, R. and Morgan, S. (1996) 'Educating the philosopher-manager: de-signing the times', *Management Learning*, 27(1): 37–64.

Connolly, J.M. (2002) 'Applicatio and explicatio in Gadamer and Eckhart', in Malpas, J., Arnswald, U. and Ketscher, J. (eds), *Gadamer's Century*, Cambridge, MA: MIT Press, pp. 77–96.

Cunliffe, A. (2001) 'Managers as practical authors: reconstructing our understanding of management practice, *Journal of Management Studies*, 38(3): 351–71.

Eastman, W.N. and Bailey, J.R. (1996) 'Epistemology, action and rhetoric: past and present connections', *Journal of Applied Behavioral Science*, 32(4): 455–61.

Gadamer, H.-G. (1989) *Truth and Method*, 2nd rev. edn, trans. by J. Weinsheimer and D.G. Marshall, New York: Crossroad.

Gergen, K.J. (1985) 'The social constructionist movement in modern psychology', *American Psychologist*, 40(3): 266–75.

Gold, J., Hamblett, J. and Rix, M. (2000) 'Telling stories for managing change: a business/academic partnership', *Education Through Partnership*, 4(1): 36–46.

Grey, C. (1999) ' "We are all managers now"; "We always were": On the development and demise of management', *Journal of Management Studies*, 36(5): 561–85.

Hacker, P. (1997) *Wittgenstein: On Human Nature*, London: Phoenix.

Holman, D. and Thorpe, R. (eds) (2003) *Management and Language*, London: Sage.

MacIntyre, A. (1981) *After Virtue*, London: Duckworth.

Malpas, J., Arnswald, U. and Ketscher, J. (eds) (2002) *Gadamer's Century*, Cambridge, MA: MIT Press.

Parker, M. (2002) *Against Management*, Cambridge: Polity Press.

Shotter, J. (1997) 'Problems with the way of theory', available at: pubpages.unh.edu/~jds/Berlin_fin.htm, accessed 3 Jan 2000.

Taylor, C. (2002) 'Understanding the other', in Malpas, J., Arnswald, U. and Ketscher, J. (eds), *Gadamer's Century*, Cambridge, MA: MIT Press, pp. 279–97.

Toulmin, S. (2001) *Return to Reason*, Cambridge, MA: Harvard University Press.

Watson, T.J. (1994) *In Search of Management*, London: Routledge.

17 Leadership development
A critical examination

Kiran Trehan and Rod Shelton

Introduction

What is leadership, and how can theories about leadership be constructed and applied in the development process? This chapter aims to explore the interplay between leadership development and critical HRD. We begin by contemplating the power we attribute to leaders – especially when they are remote from us. We go on to reflect on the ways in which leadership has been defined, and to discuss some of the theoretical approaches that have been taken to the study of leadership. The next section looks at leadership development in terms of underlying theory and identifies how certain assumptions tend to lead to particular development practices. Finally, the chapter gives examples of critical perspectives on leadership development and notes some implications and learning points.

Suppose you are sitting in the office, and a friend passes by and says that the news on the grapevine is that the big boss is coming round sometime during the day. Now, without too much thought about it, write down your responses (see Gabriel, 2000). Leaders tend to have a significance in our lives, whether we feel positively or negatively towards them, that may be disproportionate to their human powers, to their interest in us, or to their control and power over the organization. It is as if we are prone to treating them as archetypical fathers and mothers. Their usual remoteness adds to their allure and mystique. Chance conversations, accidental proximity to them, can become memorable events for relating to friends as anecdotes. Frequently people seemed surprised by the humanity of the leader, but can just as quickly demonize them for their perceived arrogance. Leaders are the objects of our fantasies and fears, our projections and conflicts, in some cases, usually unacknowledged, left over from childhood. This psychoanalytically informed perspective on leadership is not a commonly discussed viewpoint in basic management texts, but it is a worthwhile one at times of uncertainty, when information is ambiguous, and when motivations to believe implicitly in someone are strong. It is as if we actually construct our idealized images of leaders and then react to the images as if they were real.

Defining leadership

Leadership, a perennial and universal topic of interest in history, politics, philosophy and literature, has been enjoying a period of renewed practical interest and critical attention. Making an attempt to define a term such as leadership can appear fruitless and misleading, since it might imply an unwarranted stability or singularity in the dynamic phenomena under discussion. Nonetheless, it may be worthwhile to indicate the degree of consensus that exists in some of the literature about leadership definitions.

Leadership definitions show, perhaps surprisingly, a measure of agreement; leadership is primarily explored as a social process, not confined to qualities of position or personality alone, so much as a dynamic, changing, phenomenon in a social organization. Leadership does tend to be attributed to a person, though it implies a role relationship with one or more followers. According to Naylor (1999: 523), 'Leadership is the process of influencing people towards achievement of organizational goals'. Senge (1996) states that 'Leadership is a phenomenon, not a position. It's absolutely nothing to do with hierarchy. Leaders are people who move ahead and who have some influence over others. They are not necessarily in any position of authority'.

Writers also define leadership by contrasting it with management. Naylor regards management as concerned with questions of choosing goals, solving problems, interpreting control signals and spotting development in the environment. 'Leadership provides inspiration, risk-taking, creativity, and change' (Naylor, 1999: 523). The manager is painted as using position power and working in ostensibly analytical rational mode, while the leader uses personal power, with a noticeable emotional content such as passion, inspiration, courage and imagination to enthuse people about a vision. We might contrast managers as seeking situations they can control, with leaders as seeking situations they can transform (Burns, 1978).

Definitions of this type are very helpful in focusing our attention on ways of making such concepts operational in organizations, but it is useful to see them as only a part of a wider theoretical apparatus. Definitions can appear absolute, when they are relative to the theory from which they are drawn. Theories ultimately serve purposes of explanation, utility, ideology, sense-making, etc., and can be seen to reflect the concerns of the age in which they are conceived.

Yukl defines leadership to include: influencing task objectives and strategies, influencing commitment and compliance in task behaviour to achieve these objectives, influencing group maintenance and identification, and influencing the culture of an organization (Yukl, 1989: 253, quoted in Alvesson and Deetz, 2001a). Of course, leadership implies followership in environments containing ever-increasing levels of hierarchy, specialization and complexity. The leader can be a figurehead of an organization (Mintzberg, 1973) who represents the organization to the outside world and is its formal connection and decision point. In the context of the business ecosystem, where businesses relate multilaterally across formal boundaries, the leader and follower roles may be changed towards a more flexible network.

Theories of leadership

Leadership has been studied from many viewpoints. These have produced a diverse analysis of development needs, which have in turn been associated with varied HRD policies and practices. Further the patterns that formed in this knowledge system over the latter part of the twentieth century are now seen to be in dynamic change as a result of the interplay of social, political, economic and technological factors influencing business behaviour today. The modern networked organization is very different in structure, function and culture from the classic bureaucratic form (Castells, 2000). It is a rapidly evolving hybrid, capable of being viewed simultaneously in a variety of ways (Boje, 1995).

Leadership has been seen in the past by social and organizational psychologists as a group or organizational phenomenon, as a set of role behaviours performed by an individual to influence others towards a goal (Conger and Kanungo, 1998: 38–9). Leadership is seen as a relational and attributional phenomenon in that it depends on the perceptions, decisions, behaviour and attributions of a number of followers (Beckhard, 1969). Leadership is studied in terms of its content (i.e. the behaviour and attributes of leaders and followers and the situation they are in at the time) and process (i.e. the use of different types of power and social influence). Finally, leader effectiveness can be evaluated by reference to follower attitudes, behaviour and satisfaction, and followers' acceptance of the leader.

Several thousand empirical studies have been conducted on leadership development and effectiveness (Grint, 1997) but, according to critics, most of the results are contradictory and inconclusive (Yukl, 1999, seen in Alvesson and Deetz, 2001a: 52). Part of the problem is dealing with leadership as an abstract concept capable of practical simplification, rather than as part of a complex social process. Fundamental to these issues are questions which explore what is meant by leadership and how it might be developed in both theory and practice. Sadler (2001) has identified the development of theory about leadership as a series of eras. The 'personality approach' explored those traits that could be measured and correlated in some way with performance figures. Occupational and organizational psychologists often work in a scientific tradition privileging statistical analysis, which can at times appear remote in some ways from experience and action. There are five big factors in modern personality theory, namely Openness to Experience, Conscientiousness, Extraversion, Agreeableness and Neuroticism. The Myers Briggs Type Indicator, a 16-factor model, talks more in terms of how a person with a certain personality type might lead (Briggs, Myers and McCaulley, 1985). Many consultancy psychology firms offer their own leadership personality scales. Assessment centres have often been used to select leaders on the basis of evidence of the predictive correlation between a profile and organizational success measures.

During the twentieth century, in America, leadership studies changed from being concerned with the biographies of great people, often male military leaders, to the psychological/behavioural orientation typical of research in the United States of America from the 1930s onwards. Some major works include the Ohio State Studies and the Michigan Studies (see Naylor, 1999). These models drew on empirical work with laboratory groups that observed the effect of changes in leadership style on groups of students doing laboratory tasks. Measures were taken of follower productivity and satisfaction. According to the model, leaders would be offered a prescription that they should involve employees more in decision-making to maximize both variables. Tannenbaum and Schmidt's article 'How do you choose a leadership style?', published in a *Harvard Business Review* of 1959, and Blake and Mouton's (1982) work with United Airlines, the Cockpit Grid, became the generalized Managerial Grid of production and people concerns. McGregor's (1960) Theory X and Y essentially contrasted task-centred leadership with relationship-centred leadership. Such models underpinned complex organizational interventions designed to change styles and improve effectiveness. Trainers advocated that leaders should have a high concern for both task and people. These models were rationalistic in that they proposed a choice of style in the pursuit of goals based on evidence, and tended to be perceived as universalistic in that they were taken to apply equally across cultures, sectors and individuals. They often focused on one or two main variables, and began to seem simplistic and mechanistic in the way they were often applied after training courses. Gradually these models were modified to include a contingent element.

Later versions, the 'situational' and 'contingency' approaches to leadership development, recognized that situations might vary and so require specific modifications in leadership approach. Groups mature over time, and become more capable of working effectively without the close supervision and structuring that leaders of new groups often feel compelled to provide (see Bion, 1968). Task simplicity or complexity, leader power over subordinates, leader–follower liking and situational requirements (e.g. for a quality decision or a quick decision) were shown to be related to certain styles. Thus, if the task were straightforward and the followers supported the leader, perhaps an autocratic style might work for a time; however, in more ambiguous circumstances, or where the leader's power was weaker, then a more involving style might be advised.

From the 1980s, when the speed of institutional change appeared to increase, a new school of thinking emerged called New Leadership (Goleman *et al.*, 2003). It advocated visionary and inspirational, charismatic and transformational roles for the leader, and offered empowerment for the worker/follower. Transactional styles, in which rewards were exchanged for performances, were regarded as insufficient in that they lacked the power to enthuse and inspire possessed by transformational leaders.

The charismatic leader (Conger and Kanungo, 1998) was required to offer a vision of the future and to enrol staff in an exciting mission with the support of skilled change agents. Drastic changes in performance were achieved in this approach, sometimes at the expense of labour relations, public satisfaction and morale. Contrasts were drawn between the inspirational–transformational leader, who engaged followers in sometimes quite vague projects to make the world or organization a better place, and the merely transactional leader, who got people to do things for the rewards they might obtain.

Transformational leadership development programmes – for example, as can be seen in the model by Alimo-Metcalfe and Alban-Metcalfe (2001) work on the basis that certain attributes can be statistically identified as being keys to success.

The factors in transformational leadership as defined by Alimo-Metcalfe and Alban-Metcalfe (2001) are as follows:

- Genuine concern for others – genuine interest in me as an individual develops my strengths.
- Political sensitivity and skills – sensitive to the political pressures that elected members face; understands the political dynamics of the leading group; can work with elected members to achieve results.
- Decisiveness, determination, self-confidence – decisive when required; prepared to take difficult decisions; self-confident; resilient to setbacks.
- Integrity; trustworthy, honest and open – makes it easy for me to admit mistakes; is trustworthy; delegates effectively; enables me to use my potential.
- Inspirational, networker and promoter – has a wide network of links to external environment; effectively promotes the work of the department/organization to the outside world; is able to communicate effectively the vision of the authority/department to the public/community.
- Accessible, approachable – accessible to staff at all levels; keeps in touch using face-to-face communication.
- Clarifies boundaries, involves others in decisions – defines boundaries of responsibility; involves staff when making decisions; keeps people informed of what is going on.

- Encourages critical and strategic thinking – encourages the questioning of traditional approaches to the job; encourages people to think of wholly new approaches/solutions to problems; encourages strategic rather than short-term thinking.

The authors recognized at the end of the article, as is normal, that the study has limitations given its narrow (public sector) sources. The article indicated differences between UK and USA views of leaders and leadership. UK leaders tend to be seen more as servants of the people they lead (but see Greenleaf, 1991), whereas USA leaders may be seen in more transactional terms. USA leaders inspire and act as role models, whilst UK leaders are seen more in terms of what they do for their people with regard to support and development.

By the 1990s, some popular attention turned to the more charismatic transformational leader, who has been defined as someone who transforms the outlook and behaviour of followers so that they move beyond their self-interests for the good of the group or society (House and Shamir, 1993; Bass, 1997). Such leaders have the ability:

- to communicate a vision of higher performance and the confidence in peoples' ability to reach it;
- to implement a vision, e.g. serving as a role model;
- to demonstrate a charismatic communication style.

Transformational leaders may emerge during times of change, growth or crisis.

Lists of leadership qualities are common, but typically fail to satisfy expectations fully, since the same qualities can be shared by non-leaders. Koontz and Weihrich (1988: 438), quoted by Bjerke (1999), list, for example, skills in using power, understanding different human motivations, being able to inspire others and being able to create a motivational climate.

Talk and writing about leadership might be considered to be problematic in itself – for example, as revealing an ideological or theoretical stance. A first step in organizational leadership is to classify what all the talk is trying to achieve. A local culture tacitly defines what is on the leadership agenda and may negatively exclude certain topics from conversation. The silent, unsaid or un-sayable may be as powerful in defining leadership–followership realities as that which is explicitly promoted.

The public has become skilled at deconstructing leadership speeches (see Fairclough, 2003), and at noticing how words are used with care to create rhetorical impressions. We are aware how words do things, create effects and have consequences, often unintended, when quoted out of context. Words are not the transparent glass through which we see the real world. Leadership itself is a discourse; it is a patterned form of communication with particular genres of speech and typical concerns. The key is to remain open to different readings of the leadership text, rather than to unwarranted optimism about their unproblematic substance. Leadership texts are often written in a popular style but employ subtle techniques to persuade their readers of the truth of their arguments – for example, selective quotation of positive cases.

These arguments suggest that whilst theories may seem technically sound, on analysis they can be shown to contain contradictions which to some extent can undermine their claims. This approach is informed by critical theorists. Critical theory seeks to highlight, nurture and promote the potential of human consciousness to reflect critically upon oppressive practices, and to facilitate the extension of domains of autonomy and responsibility (Alvesson and Willmott, 1998: 13).

Guba and Lincoln also emphasize outcomes, suggesting the aims of critical inquiry is the 'Critique and transformation of social, political, cultural, economic, and gender structures that contain and exploit humankind (Guba, 1994: 113).

Brookfield (1987, quoted in Alvesson and Deetz, 2001b: 8) defined the critical view as challenging assumptions of ordinary perceiving; conceiving and acting; recognizing influences on beliefs and actions; exploring alternatives that disrupt routines; and being appropriately sceptical about truth claims. Alvesson and Deetz 2001b: 50 et seq.) went on to provide several critical views on leadership theory. They noted the scepticism of reviewers such as Yukl (1989, in Alvesson and Deetz, 2001a) regarding the conceptual and empirical weaknesses in much of leadership theory. They pointed out how limited references to style can seem when applied uniformly to the very different social roles in which leadership might be enacted, and noted that the positivist approach tended to suppress variation in leadership concepts and practice in favour of an artificial universalism. Leadership is not in this view, a stable entity, but a complex and variable process, either not referring to the same material reality from one case to the next, or perhaps being better thought of as manner of speaking and writing about a social phenomenon at a certain time and place (i.e. a discourse). The critical view can be taken as a warning to avoid simplistic application of ideas to social situations, and to maintain a critical perspective.

Leadership development

How, then, does this affect how we see management development? If leadership can be reduced to uniform definitions and formulaic presentations such as those about successful styles, then it is reasonable to suppose that it can transmitted through culturally accepted processes to each successive generation of leaders, in similarly reliable and valid ways. However, if there are many definitions of leadership, and if each organization or social context has its unique character, then exploring the variations may be more important for management developers to encourage than the 'one right way' approach.

It has become almost routine to assert the importance of leadership development. This section explores literature on leadership and draws from current debates on how leadership might be theorized, before offering a critical perspective on the interplay between leadership and HRD. Rigg argues there has been a recent upsurge in enthusiasm for and investment in management and leadership development (Rigg and Richards, 2003). She argues that an exploration of the kinds of leadership capabilities organizations might require, whether or not they are distinctive and what approaches to leadership development might be most appropriate has followed belatedly.

The authors of some modern formulations of leadership development frameworks seek to include sufficiently broad parameters to allow for this complexity. In 2004 The NHS modernization programme contained a leadership model featuring a number of extra-personal aspects such as political astuteness, broad environmental scanning, empowering others, collaborative working, and intellectual flexibility. Notions of personal integrity also conveyed the possibility of working to ethical and moral standards, and perhaps to hold the organization to account.

When we come from a critical perspective to the question of management and leadership development for HRD, we are faced with a number of options: first, we can expand the theoretical range by including or adopting non-conventional views; second, we can relate methods of development to our theories of the leadership phenomenon. It is tempting to analyse this discussion and to formulate proposals for a technology of development to fit every theoretical position. This invites a repeat of the criticisms made by Alvesson and Deetz (2001a) indicated above. Instead, we will take the position that leadership and management development approaches can be questioned along the following lines.

How is the idea of development being used by the various groups in the debate – for example, by HR specialists, senior line executives, and the main body of managerial, professional, technical and administrative leaders? What are their tacit assumptions about growth and the desired outcomes of investment in it? In whose interest is the development that is proposed? How does the adopted development process work as a social process? For example, what outcomes does it create, and for whom? Are any of these undesirable for a stakeholder? For example, might some groups (e.g. non-graduates) be regarded by a company executive as not qualified to be part of the fast-track graduate recruitment scheme that is 'producing tomorrow's leaders'? How are implicit conflicts between the purported aims of the sponsors and the actors in the system played out in events that take place such as 'workshops'? What happens when someone questions the approach being taken to be development?

We could argue that critical HRD practitioners are employed to get the results desired by the owners of the system, such as the public, the customers and the shareholders, in effective, efficient and equitable ways. They must become skilled at breaking up traditional ways of doing things that have become ineffective, and capable of sufficient mental agility that they can produce new and useful innovation out of the mix of theories and practices available to them. They must have a grasp of what they can achieve by their own efforts and of what is better regarded as part of an ecological process of social change and evolution.

Critical leadership development

What might critical leadership development look like in practice? Reynolds (1997), drawing from ideas of Giroux (1991), introduces the concept of content-radical and method- or process-radical pedagogies.

Content radicals disseminate radical material (in the sense of critical theories and concepts) alternatives to technocratic management education. Typically, there is no challenge to the contradictions in power relationships between lecturers/institutions and students, and no focus on the power dynamics within the students' collectives.

Process radicals attempt to address power asymmetries of the traditional teacher/learner relationship – for example, by using experiential learning, negotiated syllabi, peer appraisal or action learning approaches. Reynolds argues that an approach which could be both content and process radical would have characteristics of questioning assumptions and analysing power relations, and a collective focus 'in the sense of acting in concert with others' (Reynolds, 1997: 316).

Thus, critical leadership development study engages managers in a process of drawing from critical perspectives to make connections between their learning and work experience, to understand and change interpersonal and organization behaviour. Learning from experience is also central to psychodynamic and systemic traditions, with their focus on development, insight and understanding. But what separates psychodynamic from other approaches is the idea of learning from unconscious phenomena. Trying to think about and apply such phenomena to leadership development is a complex and multidimensional task. Whilst insights and theoretical contributions (Rice, 1965; Bion, 1968; Miller, 1990; Armstrong, 1997; French and Vince, 1999; Gould *et al.*, 2004) have enabled us to explore leadership development, the question we wish to address is, what does this mean in practice? How can the interplay between critical HRD studies and psychoanalytic thought be expedited in leadership development? What outcomes can critical HRD studies and psychoanalytic thought have for leadership development? And how can the interplay between critical HRD and psychoanalytic processes be fulfilled in practice in the current climate, preoccupied by outcomes, business improvement and performance management, and where the processes of learning becomes a subsidiary activity?

The emerging nature of theory and practice in this area is leading to much reflection as to what constitutes critical leadership development. Vince (2001) proposes the notion that if it is to flourish, management development may have to get more complicated and start focusing on supporting the impact managers/leaders can have on organizing rather than on people development. Vince further argues that the political struggle in organizations in terms of practice is often represented in 'the reluctance managers have towards enacting their leadership openly and in public' (Vince, 2001: 1331). Thus it is crucial to the development process to examine the ways in which critical leadership development is able to unveil power relations and the emotional context within which they operate rather than to avoid them.

Trehan (2004) argues that a rationale for encouraging management developers to be critical lies in the realization of how powerful leaders now are in the world, yet how poorly traditional management education has prepared them for power and responsibility. Alvesson and Willmott (1998) argue that the practice of management has a dominant effect on the lives of an organization's employees, its customer's and wider society, extending even to the lives of unborn generations through the environmental impact of an organization's processes. Because of the rise of managers' social importance, French and Grey (1996: 2) reason that 'the management academy has, for better or worse, a crucial role in producing and reproducing the practices of management'.

The traditional view of management development has been a technocratic 'development of effective practitioners', as epitomized by the Constable and McCormick (1987) reports. Implicit within this tradition has been the presumption of management development knowledge and practice to be objective, apolitical and value-free. In 2004, the UK Department of Health issued a Knowledge and Skills Framework to shape the development of its many thousands of practitioners. This supposes that the framework and associated 'development' processes will work sufficiently in a complex and changing political environment.

Many writers have challenged the over-use of competences, and have argued the need to deconstruct the discourse of practice. Edwards (1997: 155), for example, writing on adult education, argued '"practice" is already informed by overt or covert discursive understandings and exercises of power'. Watson (1994: 2), writing on management, said 'managers themselves, however much they tend to scorn the very idea of theory, are inevitably theorists of a sort'. And Schein (1999: 97), writing on shared assumptions about nature, reality and truth says:

> A fundamental part of every culture is a set of assumptions about what is real, how one determines or discovers what is real . . . how members

of a group determine what is relevant information, how they interpret information, how they determine when they have enough of it to decide whether or not to act, and what action to take.

A rationale has been that it is no longer acceptable that management development educators allow managers to maintain the illusion that their choices and actions are without political consequences.

Applying critical ideas to leadership development means not just exploring assumptions of power and control, but also actively engaging in an examination of political and cultural processes affecting the development process. Willmott (1997: 175) argues that the challenge is:

> To envision and advance the development of discourses and practices that can facilitate the development of 'management' from a divisive technology of control into a collective means of emancipation.

In order to show the importance of power and psychodynamic perspectives to the study of leadership, it is necessary to examine the inseparability of power between academic disciplines and leadership practitioners. By conducting research, using the techniques of deconstruction, into the dominant and subjugated discourses in their organizations, leadership developers could gain far greater insight into the invisible workings of managing and organizing than is provided by other analyses of organizational workings. This could provide us with a powerful tool for understanding and influencing future 're-authoring' in the workplace.

Another consideration in reviewing the role of a leadership developer is the way in which they and their role can be inscribed and objectified by others in the organization. Lyotard (1979) provides the concept of 'the differend' to explain the difficulties in gaining acceptance for new ideas that fall outside of the accepted discourse. The differend is the term Lyotard uses to describe the shutting out of one player from a 'language game'. The concept of a language game is derived from Wittgenstein. This shutting-out phenomenon occurs where there are no agreed rules for the introduction of something new to the game. This could be a new rule, a new idea, principle or grievance. The differend is the impossibility of giving expression to an injustice as it is rendered invisible. This has implications for leadership practitioners trying to introduce new concepts and values to an organization.

Similarly, Reynolds (1999: 182) argues the function of management development should not be to help managers fit unquestioningly into the roles traditionally expected of them but to assist them in engaging with the social and moral issues inherent within existing management practice and to become more conscious of the ideological forces which constrain their actions.

The issues and dilemmas that have been highlighted are those that teachers and practitioners might identify for discussion even if they cannot be neatly or easily resolved. Equally, there is a role for tutors in supporting discussions of these issues when they are initiated by students. Where critical leadership in some form is practised, there is value in an open examination of what it entails. Within this context the importance of being a critically reflective practitioner becomes clear. As Burgoyne and Reynolds (1997: 2) argue, the critically reflective practitioners play an important role as 'they are aware that with every practical action they take they are fixing (temporarily) their belief and acting their current best working theory, but they realise that this may also be open to challenge and improvement'.

Processes of critical thinking in practice are rooted in reflection, either in the form of self-reflection or in the relationships between individuals, collectivities and society. For example, Carr and Kemmis (1986: 130) suggest that individuals 'reflect upon their own situations and change them through their own actions'. For Alvesson and Deetz (2001a):

> Critical Theory seeks to highlight, nurture and promote the potential of human consciousness to reflect critically upon such oppressive practices, and thereby facilitate the extension of domains of autonomy and responsibility.

Alongside the cognitive tools of analytical critique and application of critical theory, the methods of critical thinking borrow from psychoanalysis, using 'critical self-reflection as a means of bringing to consciousness those distortions in patients' self-formation processes which prevent a correct understanding of themselves and their actions' (Carr and Kemmis, 1986: 138).

For Collins (1991: 94), critical reflection describes the facility to:

> Put aside the natural attitude of their everyday life-world and adopt a sceptical approach towards taken-for-granted innovations 'necessary for progress', supposedly 'acceptable' impositions as the price of progress, and seemingly authoritative sources of information.

The implication of the above for leadership development is that it reveals the tensions, contradictions, emotions and power dynamics that inevitably exist in understanding leaders' lives. Critical leadership development as a pedagogical approach emerges when those dynamics are treated centrally as a site of learning about leadership.

McLaughlin and Thorpe (1993: 25) argue:

> At the level of their own expertise, managers undertaking critical reflection can come to know themselves and their organization

much better. In particular, they can become aware of the primacy of politics, both macro and micro, and the influence of power on decision making and non-decision-making, not to mention the 'mobilisation of bias'.

In Willmott's view 'To the extent that critical learning engages with the struggles of individual students and practitioners, it may also open up an appreciation of, and sensitivity towards, "darker" aspects of organizational life' (Willmott, 1997: 119).

What this analysis begins to indicate is that when we are thinking about critical leadership development, we need to recognize that power operates in areas which may be obscured by traditional theories and approaches. It is easy to see how individuals wishing to embark on leadership programmes might be forgiven for thinking that were they only to follow the formula set out for them they would succeed, were it not for the fact that organizations might be changing more rapidly, and in more complex ways than the aligned model could accommodate.

Many of the issues that we have explored are complex, and pose as many questions as they provide answers. The aim of this evaluation is not to offer a prescription but to stress the importance of actively exploring and working with the complexities and contradictions associated with leadership development.

Conclusions

In the debates previously presented we have reviewed and discussed various perspectives on leadership development and the challenges it presents in relation to management development. A number of conclusions can be distilled from the discussion.

First, critiques of the values, the purposes and approaches to management education and development have become well developed in recent years. At the same time, leadership has continued to be an area of academic debate and practitioner focus. Yet, whilst there are many potential areas of overlap between HRD, HRM and management development, they have been evolving as parallel discourses, with little attention accorded to exploiting their interconnections.

Second, the exploration of leadership from within the critical paradigm has highlighted that overcoming the functionalist representation of leadership cannot be achieved unless the field of management development applies a critical perspective to content as well as to method or process. This means encompassing the following, as outlined by Reynolds (1999):

- questioning the assumptions embodied in both theory and professional practice;

- foregrounding the processes of power and ideology subsumed within the social fabric of institutional structures, procedures and practices;
- confronting spurious claims of rationality and objectivity and revealing the sectional interests which can be concealed by them;
- working towards an emancipatory ideal – the realization of a more just society based on fairness and democracy.

Third, the theoretical debates presented have sought to emphasize the distinctive nature of critical leadership and to argue for its place in the professional activity of management development practice. Leadership development, whether in an educational institution or in organizations, can support people in an examination of the social and political processes within the workplace. Leadership practice is about moral issues and requires ethical consideration because, as Reed and Anthony (1992) argue, these are fundamentals upon which any organizational reality rests. It is also important for education and organizational practice to counter current preoccupations with instrumentalism and introduce methodologies which focus their attention to the moral, political and cultural aspects of leadership.

For leadership educators and leadership practitioners, adopting critical approaches is a choice and responsibility. As Kemmis argues:

> in reflection we choose, implicitly or explicitly, what to take for granted and what to treat as problematic in the relationships between our thoughts and action and the social order we inhabit. In reflection, we have a choice about whether to think and act in conformity with the patterns of communication, decision making and action in our society, or whether we will intervene at this historical moment on behalf of more rational communication, more just decision making and more fulfilling human and social action.
>
> (Kemmis, 1985: 148)

Key learning points

In addition to the conclusions, the following key learning points emerge. First, whilst critical approaches to leadership development may be appealing in theory, they are also fraught with difficulties and problematic consequences. Leaders and management developers may resist engagement in critical processes because to do so would be to question the organizational context in which they operate, and challenge traditional norms.

Second, leadership development may find it counter-cultural to the pressure to conform to organizational ideologies. However, in arguing for a more critical approach to leadership development we would concur with Reed and Anthony (1992: 610), who call teachers to account, insisting on their responsibility to 'recover their institutional and pedagogical nerve' in supporting managers in critical learning within their working environment, not withstanding the complexities and conflicts of interests which may surface.

Our third learning point concerns the developmental relation between leaders and managers. The literature indicates that both of these functions are better regarded as shared social processes, rather than residing in single persons – however charismatic. We draw the conclusion that followers need to be considered more deeply in development discussions. Team-development workshops and group sessions closely address this point, and skilled facilitators can do much to empower people to understand this better in day-to-day practice – for example, moving to more inter-dependence. Innovation provides further opportunities for leaders and followers to develop together. This opens the development agenda and offers space and time for it to succeed.

References

Alimo-Metcalfe, B. and Alban-Metcalfe, R. (2001) 'The development of a new transformational leadership questionnaire', *Journal of Occupational and Organizational Psychology*, 74(1): 1–27.

Alvesson, M. and Deetz, S. (2001a) *Doing Critical Management Research*, London: Sage.

Alvesson, M. and Deetz, S. (2001b) 'Critical theory and post modern approaches to organizational studies', in Clegg, S., Handy, C., and Nord, W. (eds), *Handbook of Organizational Studies*, Thousand Oaks, CA: Sage.

Alvesson, M. and Willmott, H. (1998) *Making Sense of Management: A Critical Introduction*, London: Sage.

Armstrong, D.C. (1997) 'The institution in the mind: reflections on the relationship of psychoanalysis to work with institutions', *Free Association*, 7(1: 41), 1–14.

Bass, B. (1997) 'Does the transactional–transformational leadership paradigm transcend organizational and national boundaries?', *American Psychologist*, 52: 130–9.

Beckhard, R. (1969) *Organization Development: Strategies and Models*, Reading, MA: Addison Wesley.

Bion, W.R. (1968) *Experiences in Groups*, London: Tavistock.

Bjerke, B. (1999) *Leadership and Culture: National Management Styles in the Global Economy*, Cheltenham: Edward Elgar.

Blake, R. and Mouton, J. (1982) *Cockpit Resource Management*, Denver, CO: United Airlines.

Boje, D. (1995) 'Stories of the storytelling organization: a postmodern analysis of Disney as "Tamara-land"', *Academy of Management Journal*, 38(4): 997–1035 (see cbae.nmsu.edu/~dboje/papers/, accessed 21 September 2005).

Briggs, Myers, I. and McCaulley, M. (1985) *Manual: A Guide to the Development and Use of the Myers Briggs Type Indicator*, Palo Alto, CA: Consulting Psychologists Press.

Burgoyne, J. and Reynolds, M. (1997) *Management Learning*, London: Sage.

Burns, J. (1978) *Leadership*, New York: Harper Row.

Carr, W. and Kemmis, S. (1986) *Becoming Critical: Knowing through Action Research*, London: Routledge.

Castells, M. (2000) *The Information Age: Economy, Society and Culture*, Vol. 1, *The Rise of the Network Society*, 2nd edn, Oxford: Blackwell.

Collins, M. (1991) *Adult Education as Vocation: A Critical Role for the Adult Educator in Today's Society*, London: Routledge.

Conger, J. and Kanungo, R. (1998) *Charismatic Leadership in Organizations*, London: Sage.

Constable, J. and McCormick, R. (1987) *The Making of British Managers: A report for the BIM*, London: BIM/CBI.

Edwards, R. (1997) *Contested Terrain, the Transformation of the Workplace in the Twentieth Century*, London: Heinemann.

Fairclough, N. (2003) *New Labour, New Language?* London: Routledge.

French, R. and Grey, C. (eds) (1996) *Rethinking Management Education*, London: Sage.

French, R. and Vince, R. (1999) *Group Relations: Management and Organization*, Oxford: Oxford University Press.

Gabriel, Y. (2000) *Story-telling in Organizations: Facts, Fictions and Fantasies*, Oxford: Oxford University Press, pp. 191 *et seq.*

Giroux, H. (1991) *Ideology, Culture and the Process of Schooling*, Philadelphia, PA: Temple University Press.

Goleman, D., Boyatzis, R. and McKee, A. (2003) *The New Leaders: Transforming the Art of Leadership into the Science of Results*, London: Little, Brown (Harvard Business School Press).

Gould, J., Stapley, L. and Stein, M. (2004) *Experiential Learning in Organizations. Application of the Tavistock Group Relations Approach*, London: H. Karnac.

Greenleaf, R. (1991) *Servant Leadership: A Journey into the Nature of Legitimate Power and Greatness*, Mahawah, NJ: Paulist Press.

Grint, K. (1997) *Fuzzy Management: Contemporary Ideas and Practices at Work*, Oxford: Oxford University Press.

Guba, E. (1994) 'Competing paradigms in qualitative research', in Denzin, N.K. and Lincoln, Y.S. (eds), *Handbook of Qualitative Research*, Thousand Oaks, CA: Sage., pp. 105–17.

House, R. and Shamir, B. (1993) 'Toward the integration of transformational, charismatic, and visionary theories', quoted in Conger, J. and Kanungo, R. (1998) *Charismatic Leadership in Organizations*, London: Sage.

Kemmis, S. (1985) 'Action research and the politics of reflection', in Bond, D., Keogh, R. and Walker, D. (eds), *Reflection: Turning Experience into Learning*, London: Kogan Page, pp. 139–63.

Koontz, H. and Weihrich, H. (1988) *Management*, 6th edn, New York, NY: Harper and Row.

Lyotard, J. (1979) 'La condition postmoderne: rapport su le savoir', in *Critique Les Editions de Minuit*, Paris: Critique les Editions de Minuit.

McGregor, D. (1960) *The Human Side of Enterprise*, London: Penguin.

McLaughlin, H. and Thorpe, R. (1993) 'Action learning: the problems facing a challenge to traditional management education and development', *British Journal of Management*, 4(1); 19–27.

Miller, E.J. (1990) 'Experiential learning in groups, the development of the Leicester Model', in Trist, E.L. and Murray, H. (ed.), *The Social Engagement of the Social Science: A Tavistock Anthropology*, London: Free Association Books.

Mintzberg, H. (1973) *The Nature of Managerial Work*, London: Prentice Hall.

Naylor, J. (1999) *Management*, London: FT Pitman.

NHS Leadership Qualities Framework: Technical Research Paper – Summary (2004), at http://www.nhsleadershipqualities.nhs.uk/docs/lib/Technical_Research_Paper_Summary.pdf, accessed 7 October 2005.

Reed, M. and Anthony, P. (1992) 'Professionalizing management and managing professionalization', *Journal of Management Studies*, 29: 591–613.

Reynolds, M. (1997) 'Towards a critical pedagogy', in Burgoyne, J. and Reynolds, M. (eds), *Management Learning*, London: Sage.

Reynolds, M. (1999) 'Critical reflection and management education: rehabilitating less hierarchical approaches', *Journal of Management Education*, 23: 537–53.

Rice, A.K. (1965) *Learning for Leadership: Interpersonal and Intergroup Relations*, London: Tavistock.

Rigg, C. and Richards, S. (2005) *Action Learning Leadership and Organizational Development in Public Services*, London: Routledge.

Sadler, P. (2001) 'Leadership and organizational learning, reading 18', in Dierkes, M., Berthonin, A., Child, J. and Nonaka, I. (eds), *Handbook of Organizational Learning and Knowledge*, Oxford: Oxford University Press.

Schein, E. (1999) *Process Consultation*, Reading, MA: Addison Wesley.

Senge, P. (1996) 'The poor suffering busters at the top', *Business Age*, 1, quoted in Naylor, J. (1999) *Management*, London: FT Pitman, p. 523.

Trehan, K. (2004) '"Who is not sleeping with whom? What's not being talked about in HRD?"', *Journal of European Industrial Training*, 28(1): 23–38.

Vince, R. (2001) 'Power and emotions in organizational learning', *Human Relations*, 54(10): 1325–51.

Watson, T. (1994) *In Search of Management*, London: Routledge.

Willmott, H. (1997) 'Critical management learning', in Burgoyne, J. and Reynolds, M. (eds), *Management Learning*, London: Sage.

Yukl, G. (1989) 'Managerial leadership: a review of theory and research', *Journal of Management*, 15(2): 251–89.

Yukl, G. (2001) 'Critical theory and post modern approaches to organizational studies', in Clegg, S., Handy, C. and Nord, W. (eds), *Handbook of Organizational Studies*, Thousand Oaks, CA: Sage.

18 Clinical leadership in the NHS

Evaluating change through action learning

Nadine Bristow

Objectives

Whilst undertaking a Doctorate in Business Administration, I embarked upon a number of separate, but linked, action research programmes. It was during one of these earlier research programmes into action learning and learning styles preference that a participant made this comment:

> When I first heard about action learning I thought, well this is going to be interesting, all sit around in a group and talk to each other but actually action learning is not about what you say, it's about the way you say it and watching the body language. It's not the words it's the interaction between people and groups, and if there is anything I have learned from action learning, it is the hidden messages and it's about how people want you to perceive these. It's games, I mean it's very serious games, but it is games.

Action learning is currently a widely used management development tool within the UK National Health Service (NHS). Action learning sets and their facilitators emphasize the use of questioning to assist personal reflection designed to aid critical insight to a member's experience, with the objective of maximizing learning from experience. The questions help the member to focus on areas where change is needed. As an experienced action learning facilitator, I was intrigued by the above comment. How important are the words versus body language? What kind of 'talk' during the set is most effective? If the talk is critical, then how can we measure its effectiveness in transforming managers and leaders through the process of action learning?

I developed two key questions to frame my subsequent research:

- Can action learning help to develop transformational leadership construct?
- Can personal construct and explanatory style be influenced by the questions put to them during an action learning programme?

As an ethnographic researcher utilizing a quantitative methodology, I developed a method of evaluating change as a result of participation in an action learning set. This has resulted in a series of recommendations for practitioners in the field on how to: (1) prepare themselves before, during and after an action learning set event; and (2) conduct both formative and summative evaluation of individual leadership development through action learning.

The purpose of this chapter is to show how I developed these recommendations and how they inform my own practice.

Theoretical context

Several theories informed my research. By mapping them onto each other I developed the model seen at Figure 18.1, and this formed the framework for my research. The theories were action learning, explanatory style, experiential learning theory, learning-style preference, transformational leadership and personal construct theory. A brief description of these follows.

Action learning

There are a number of schools of action learning. Marsick and O'Neil (1999) make specific reference to 'four faces of action learning' – Scientific, Experiential, Critical Reflection and Tacit. However, action learning can essentially been described as:

> a continuous process of learning and reflection supported by colleagues, with an intention of getting things done. Through action learning individuals learn with and from each other by working on real problems and reflecting on their own experiences.
>
> (McGill and Beaty, 1992: 21)

The process of eliciting, recording and testing validity of thoughts is facilitated through individual presentations on work-based problems within action learning set meetings, and subsequent critical questioning by colleagues. The personal action plan developed after the questioning is the platform for action back in the workplace.

Explanatory style

Explanatory style emerged as a way of explaining diversity in individuals' responses to events in their lives (Abramson *et al.*, 1978). Discourse plays a major role in the development of this style. Weiner (1986) suggests that when people are exposed to an external event in their lives, a common response is to ask why it happened. The various answers to this 'why?' set

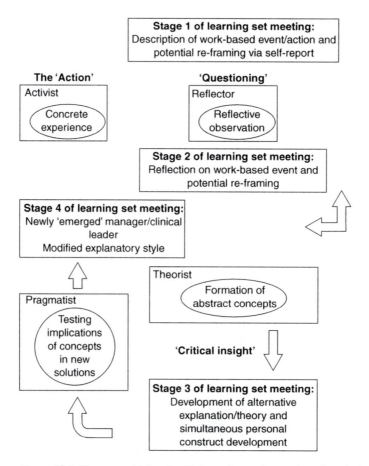

Figure 18.1 Honey and Mumford's learning-style typology in relation to Kolb's experiential learning cycle and Revan's model and process of action learning, depicting the development of explanatory style and personal construct.

the parameters for their perception of control and the possibility of subsequent action. If the causal explanation is stable – perceived as unchanging – then the inability to act is long-lasting. If unstable, then it is short-lived. If their explanation is global, then the inability to act manifests itself across a number of situations for that individual, but if it is specific then it is accurately circumscribed. Finally, if the attribution is internal then the individual's self-esteem may take a beating, but if external the self-esteem is left intact.

When individuals constantly blame external factors for their faults or when things go wrong, their opportunities to choose appropriate behaviours are limited. How managers explained their experiences in terms of attribution – and how this was elicited by participation in an action learning set – was a key factor in my research. Explanatory style became widely used when measures of these individual differences were developed, the first being the ASQ (Attributional Style Questionnaire), closely followed by CAVE (Content Analysis of Verbatim Explanation). The latter is a procedure for extracting statements about how people perceive 'why' something has happened from their 'talk'. The data are then rated along the explanatory style dimensions of internality, stability and globality.

Experiential learning theory

David Kolb's (1984) theory sets out a four-stage learning cycle in which immediate or concrete experiences provide a basis for observations and reflections. These are distilled into abstract concepts which can be actively tested. Kolb states that learning is 'needs driven'.

Learning-style preferences

Honey and Mumford (1982) presented a typology of preferred learning styles based upon the similar premise that learning is a cyclical process. They developed their typology on the basis that learning is such an automated and unconscious process that we often take it for granted and rarely attempt to teach individuals how to learn, but by becoming consciously aware of how we prefer to learn we can set about learning to become a better learner. Their typology is centred on: Activists, who involve themselves in new experiences; Reflectors who are cautious and thoughtful, preferring to consider issues; Theorists, who interpret their observations into their own cognitive models; and Pragmatists, who are keen to apply new ideas and see how something works in practice. Honey and Mumford are keen to emphasize that learning-style preference can change at will or via circumstance.

Transformational leadership

The Alimo-Metcalfe (Metcalfe and Alban-Metcalfe, 2000) model of transformational leadership infers that when managers or leaders are successful in achieving the task, they perceive this success as a team effort. When managers or leaders are unsuccessful in achieving a task, they should perceive this lack of achievement as their own personal responsibility, recognizing the difference between their accountability for the task and their team member's responsibility in the achievement of the task.

Personal construct theory

Kelly (1955) was the original proponent of the theory that we all make sense of the world in terms of the meaning that we apply to it, and that we all have the ability to select a new fresh meaning at any given point in our lives – we can 'construct' it and ourselves any way that we wish. We can potentially release ourselves from a negative relationship or event in our lives, for example, by reconstructing it and re-framing it in some way. Kelly recommended that we consider the implications for alternative constructions when considering the relationship between affect, cognition and action. Within his model we experiment with varying constructs at different times. We sometimes organize our constructs into groups and sub-groups allowing us the opportunity to view the same event in differing ways. This understanding helps managers to evolve and grow into their newly assigned roles.

My conceptualization of how personal construct development, explanatory style and action learning link in with previously mentioned models and theories of learning is demonstrated in Figure 18.1

The process and structure advocated in all of the action learning set meetings was a cyclical one based upon stages where each member took a turn to deliver a verbal problem-based presentation to their colleagues. The action learning presentations included detail of the context of the problem and actions undertaken to date; what they had said and what they had done to avoid or deal with the issue. The focus was, therefore, on description of managerial/leadership behaviours as well as their feelings and the actions of others where appropriate. The emphasis was upon the task and their role in it.

The second stage of each action learning set meeting was where each member took a turn in posing a question(s) to the member who presented his or her problem. The recipient had the choice as to whether to answer the question posed (in order to gain critical insight into an aspect of the problem) or to take the question away and reflect upon it. This stage of the process potentially enables the recipient to re-frame the problem, identify alternative solutions, gain confidence in risk-taking, gain motivation and subsequently go on to plan for the application of a solution (or combination of solutions) which have been considered during the round of questions.

The third stage of the cycle was where the presenter had time to consider the questions posed, reflect upon them, and in some instances go on to develop a revised or fresh perception of him- or herself, the situation, others, his or her action (or inaction) to date, etc.

The fourth and final stage is where the presenter makes a decision to test out this theory or concept via action so action planning is the focus within the learning set. This action then becomes the 'learning material' for that presenter's next learning set presentation.

My research was based upon the premise that explanatory style is a *cognitive* process rather than a personality trait. In my view, the action learning process and meeting model aided the development of 'appropriate' explanatory style and transformational management/leadership construct. Initially, the link I saw was firmly associated with the first stage of action learning – Stage 1, the description of work-based events. However, I recognized that Stage 2, the 'reflecting' stage was equally significant in the process of reframing.

According to Revans (1983), questions during Stage 1 are designed to be reflective and probing in order to encourage reflection on events to aid problem-solving. However, the questions *and the responses they evoke* may also aid the development of one's explanatory style and, therefore, perspective of the event, the environment and, just as importantly, one's own participation – all of which influence future leadership behaviour.

My research was to test how these theories mapped onto each other and illustrate the transformation process.

The research context

I audio-tape recorded 144 action learning set meetings during a 12-month period. A particular learning set was selected for detailed discourse analysis. This set was diverse in terms of gender and vocational background – one dietitian (female), one surgical theatre nurse (male), one prosthesis technician (male) and one occupational therapist (female).

The raw data analysed were the naturally occurring verbatim reports from action learning set meetings. The audio-recording of interactions as they happen has been termed 'real time' by Samra-Fredericks (1998). I applied the coding and analysis system developed by Peterson and colleagues (1983), known as CAVE (the content analysis of verbatim explanations) to measure participant's explanatory style following the application of Schulman *et al.*'s (1989) guidelines for extracting and rating spontaneous explanations.

In addition to this primary data collection, each entire piece of narrative provided by the individual participants was analysed for content. A coding system was developed for identifying specific content and evidence to show how individuals had embraced the concept of manager/leader within their own personal construct. When describing successful events, the manager/leader should frame the event as being undertaken by the use of 'we', 'the organization/department/team', 'us', 'our' and 'they' – essentially, any descriptor that implies plurality – for example, 'We hit our budget this year'.

However, the reverse should apply when describing a problem or unsuccessful event. This should be framed as 'I', 'my', 'me' – essentially, any descriptor that infers singularity, and in particular, use of the personal pronoun – for example, 'I misunderstood the impact of not meeting that deadline'.

Each piece of transcribed tape for these four learning set members was scrutinized for use of such language at 'Time 1'. This analysis was then repeated for the action learning set 'Time 2'. Every instance of use of such descriptors was scored with one point. The scores were then submitted for statistical analysis to identify whether the prevalence of a particular position was consistent or whether it had changed from Time 1 to Time 2 – perhaps indicating an emergence of the theme of leadership responsibility and accountability as time had progressed and with continued exposure to the action learning process.

I identified that by analysing the explanatory style of the participants at Time 1 (January) and then again ten months later at Time 2 (October), it would be possible to identify whether their styles had been influenced by the action learning process. The set met on a monthly basis. However, due to other external variables which may influence a shift during this timescale, I made an attempt further to isolate the influencing factor as the process of critical questioning in the action learning set meetings themselves. To do this, I analysed examples of narrative from both before and after the questioning process for each participant at both Time 1 and Time 2. The number of questions posed by fellow action learning set participants was also recorded to see whether there was an influence in the volume of questions posed.

I went on to analyse the discourse from each participant for the two time slots and then again for pre- and post-critical questioning, scanning for evidence of both positive and negative events. An event was defined as any stimulus that occurred in the individual's environment or within that individual (e.g. thoughts or feelings) that had a good or bad effect from the individual's point of view. Events could be mental (e.g. 'I was afraid'), social (e.g. 'I had a successful team meeting') or physical (e.g. 'I was working in the orthopaedic theatre'). I decided that selected events should be unambiguously good or bad from the participant's point of view, and may have occurred in the past, present or hypothetical future. Twenty events were selected for each participant; five negative and five positive from Time 1, and five negative and five positive from Time 2. This selection included enough information for me to rate all three causal dimensions.

During the first phase of identifying positive and negative events, these raw data were submitted for statistical analysis before the next stage of coding. The data for action learning set Time 2 were also collected in the same way. Once all of the 20 events and explanations for each participant were analysed and coded, a composite score was devised for each one. These scores were then submitted for statistical analysis aimed at identifying what the participants' explanatory styles were towards the start of the action learning programme, and again eight months later.

Analysis of main findings

Positive/negative descriptions and responses

The number of positive and negative comments made by the participants in both their individual presentations and during subsequent responses to questions was examined. In particular, any changes from Presentation 1 to Presentation 2 were examined for the effect of time and exposure to the action learning process.

Altogether, 91 positive comments were made in Presentation 1, increasing to 127 in Presentation 2. In Presentation 1, 113 negative comments were made, decreasing to 66 in Presentation 2. However, although the differences seem quite clear from the raw data, statistical analysis using a *t*-test (for related, ratio, data) to test whether the groups were significantly different did not produce significant results, and therefore, chance cannot be ruled out.

Learning style and positive/negative descriptions and responses

Statistical analysis found no significant findings when examining respondents' most dominant learning style and the number of positive or negative events described within the presentations or in response to questioning.

Personal pronouns and positive/negative descriptions and responses

The participants' discourse was coded to identify usage of personal pronouns in Presentation 1 and Presentation 2. This aided the analysis of leadership construct development at individual level. Each participant's use of personal pronouns was categorized into pronouns referring to the self or to others; for example, the category 'self' included pronouns such as 'me', 'I', 'mine' and 'my'. The category 'others' contained terms such as 'the Trust/the department', 'their/them', 'our/us' and 'we'.

The direction of change that was anticipated (if transformational leadership personal constructs had developed) was: first for an improvement in the number of positive comments to be attributed to the team ('others') and other external factors; and second, for negative comments to be attributed more internally ('self') following exposure to: (1) the process of action learning; (2) programmed knowledge; and (3) personal construct development as a clinical leaders/managers.

Again, there appeared to be some interesting changes – the positive comments seemed to be shifting in the right direction over time; however, statistical analysis of the data did not produce any significant results. Examination of the dimensions of explanatory style data showed that there had again been changes from Presentation 1 to Presentation 2. The total CPCN mean score for the sample group at Presentation 1 decreased from 2.05 to 0.40. This highlighted how, at group level, the learning set had become more pessimistic in their general attributions for negative events and more optimistic for positive events.

The lack of significant results indicated that exposure to the action learning process had not influenced results either substantially and/or consistently for all respondents. It was therefore difficult to draw any conclusions about any changes, as they had not been substantiated by statistical analysis and could thus have been due to 'chance'. However, when examining explanatory style, one significant finding was found in this data set. The statistics indicated that change had occurred with the overall group's perception – becoming increasingly likely to review their own behaviour and personal role in the occurrence of negative events within their workplace. Rather than attributing cause to someone or something external, they were attributing it to a combination of self and other.

It was clear that at group level there was an increase generally in the number of positive descriptions and responses provided and a decrease in the number of negative examples. Several factors may have been responsible for influencing this change. Perhaps the individuals felt more confident and optimistic in their roles as managers/clinical leaders? With a better developed personal construct, they may have felt empowered to act and/or perceive events in a different light. Alternatively, it may have been due to the organizational climate having changed in some way. Without specifically questioning participants about their perception of this change, I was not able to isolate the variables here. This was a prime example of where numbers alone were insufficient.

Generally speaking, the sample group had shown that gender was relevant in terms of pessimistic/optimistic outlook on work-based events. Females appeared to be much more optimistic than their male counterparts, but whether this was due to the effects of action learning it cannot be said. Neither gender nor levels of optimism/pessimism showed any correlation to preferred learning style.

When analysed at the individual level, personal pronoun usage demonstrated that, over time, half the group took less personal credit for work-based successes. Three-quarters of the group, however, perceived less personal responsibility for failures and problems too – counterbalancing this positive, anticipated shift in accountability and reasoning. This was the predominant measure within the study of personal construct development (explanatory style measure being the secondary), and so cannot be seen as conclusive evidence that action learning aids the development of transformational personal constructs.

At group level, the composite scores for explanations demonstrated that, generally, the participants had become more pessimistic in relation to negative events and more optimistic in relation to positive events. Therefore raw data showed that explanatory style had changed for the worse *and* for the better. I reflected upon the possibility that participants' explanatory styles may have remained relatively stable – possibly because, as Seligman *et al.* (1990) have concluded, it is a personality trait and therefore not open to change and development. Another potential explanation for this consistency may relate to the length of time that an individual has been involved within an action learning programme. It may have been that the interval between Time 1 and Time 2 was not long enough accurately to evaluate changes in explanatory style and their personal value system.

Festinger's (1957) theory of cognitive dissonance tries to account for how and why people try to achieve some degree of consistency in their value system and way of behaving. Some individual participants may have seen the process of re-framing events as inconsistent and therefore a direct attack on their judgement and, subsequently, their sense of who they are.

One statistically significant finding in relation to explanatory styles was that the group had become more personally responsible for the occurrence of negative events, partially supporting the hypothesis that participants had developed in one aspect of transformational leadership construct.

The challenges of discourse analysis

A key challenge associated with qualitative research is that it is mainly carried out with words, not numbers. Words have multiple interpretations, making them almost impossible to manipulate. This becomes even more difficult when one is analysing discourse by moving forwards and backwards in time as I did with content analysis at Time 1 versus Time 2. As words are more difficult and complex than numbers to analyse, trying to convert words into numbers can cause meaning to be lost. I was also concerned that all action learning presentations are stories and initially may be compelling and persuasive. To counteract this, I decided to transcribe the entire dialogue for particular participants during an entire set meeting to ensure that the sensational incidents were not the only ones addressed.

Any potential conflict in the way action learning participants frame their role and what they think and say in a set meeting may be due to the amount of public rhetorical activity that we all engage in. This may be due to what Watson (2001) identifies as the 'discourse of professionalism'. This can be used to hide or distance oneself from occupational insecurities – for example, 'Things never change around here...', 'This organization is stuck'. Action learning participants don't always say what they think or mean – they may say what they think is organizationally acceptable. I felt it important to be present during all the recorded meetings as the set facilitator so that any intermittent changes in set membership and subsequent dynamics could be controlled as far as possible – another variable. I developed relationships and an understanding over time of members' likely explanatory style, albeit informally via my own observation.

Recommendations

As an academic requirement, I needed to demonstrate my competence in utilizing a range of research methodologies in this research programme. The constraints of this ambitious personal goal led to a relatively narrow research focus in terms of the population studied. However, I did go on to draw much practical learning which has informed my work as a facilitator. It is this learning that I would like to share in the form of a series of practice-based recommendations which deal with each stage of the action learning process.

It is my personal view that action learning facilitators and others involved in transformational change evaluation would benefit from adopting the following model and process:

1   Pre-initial meeting preparation
2   Research-based tailored facilitation during the meeting using modified CAVE technique
3   Post-meeting discourse analysis, research and reflection (formative evaluation)
4   Preparation for subsequent learning set meetings
5   Post-meeting discourse analysis, research and reflection (summative evaluation).

Pre-meeting preparation

Pre-initial meeting preparation (initial evaluation) is important. My earlier research indicated that a diversity of learning styles in participants increased the quality of the learning. Therefore, these styles should be identified and made part of the selection process for the sets. This includes the preferred learning style of the facilitator. As a contingency, this initial preparation allows the facilitator to tailor his or her questions in the absence of a particular 'style'.

A shared concept of learning styles was in existence amongst the research sample group and was relatively 'typical'. However, the concept of action learning was much more 'fuzzy' and in fact quite different to my own – which, of course, then subsequently led to difficulties within the evaluative process for the programmes. I learnt that in order for action learning to be evaluated by participants effectively, they must be made aware of and understand the concept of the model and process being utilized – that is, scientific, experiential, critical reflection, or tacit.

The outcomes of action learning in terms of agreed constructs (e.g. transformational leadership) and associated discourse (e.g. 'I', 'we', 'you', 'us') need to be identified so that individual templates can be designed to facilitate the capture of the discourse. A codifier then needs to be appointed who has strong listening and concentration skills to populate the templates. This allows the facilitator to focus fully on ensuring that his or her interventions are 'tailored' to the needs of the set. A caveat may be that the codifier can be perceived by participants as too obtrusive. However, my experience is that participants become absorbed in the process and forget about such measures after a surprisingly short period of time. Alternatively, audio-tape or video may satisfy the need to record discourse, but of course coding is time-consuming. A codifier allows the benefit of the facilitator fully focusing on the group process.

First meeting

At the first meeting there will be initial data collection. Subsequently, post-meeting discourse analysis, research and reflection (formative evaluation) is carried out.

The facilitator should analyse the most recent data collected via discourse analysis and prepare 'tailored' questions designed to test development of the desired transformation against the agreed construct during the following learning set meeting.

Research-based tailored facilitation during the second and subsequent meetings using modified CAVE technique

During the meeting the facilitator poses 'tailored' questions to test whether a member is showing evidence of developing desired transformation against the agreed construct. Having done the above analysis before the meeting, the facilitator (as I did) can then probe various aspects of individuals transformation leadership construct with them where the data indicate there may be a gap. By doing this, I was using action research to inform my practice as a facilitator, thereby allowing me to adapt my own behaviours to maximize the learning for those respective participants.

If a 'learning style' is absent, the facilitator needs to identify this and then pose questions in the missing style or use a hypothetical style.

Post meeting discourse analysis, research and reflection (formative evaluation); preparation for subsequent learning set meetings

The facilitator must analyse the most recent data collected via discourse analysis and prepare further 'tailored' questions designed to test development of the desired transformation against the agreed construct. Using the templates allows faster coding of the 'talk'. The analysis of the changes can be fed back to the respective set participants to aid personal reflection and to show in a tangible way that they are learning more effective ways of leading.

Post-meeting discourse analysis, research and reflection (summative evaluation)

This provides feedback on overall trends, patterns and themes in the data which act as a platform for the action learning participants to put their action plan into practice in the workplace.

Conclusion

Ultimately, the research study – which set out to investigate the premise that action learning influences development of explanatory style – cannot be unilaterally supported with such a small sample group, but it did provide an interesting illustration of discourse analysis as a useful tool to aid practitioners and participants alike.

I believe that I have developed an evaluation process for measuring change and development in leadership through action learning via the application of discourse analysis. The methodology became simple (with practice) and could easily be modified to measure other aspects of personal development e.g.; examples of specific behaviours linked to an organizational competency model.

It was indicated earlier that action learning is a key organizational development tool within the NHS, and therefore significant resources are being invested. A way of analysing whether this investment has a return would be by using discourse analysis in order to identify changes in explanatory and explanatory style. These would indicate that, in their day-to-day jobs, managers and clinical leaders are putting into practice the lessons taken from their action learning sets.

For the future

In order to build further on this methodology I intend to 'replay' extracts from the discursive materials from Time 1 and Time 2 back to the relevant research participants as a tool to support reflection and analysis in explanatory style. I also see this model being helpful in analysing the effectiveness of coaching.

Acknowledgement

I wish to acknowledge the help and support of Denise Taylorson (Taylorson Associates) in the development of this chapter.

References

Abramson, L.Y., Seligman, M.E.P. and Teasdale, J.D. (1978) 'Learned helplessness in humans: critique and reformulation', *Journal of Abnormal Psychology*, 87: 49–74.

Festinger, L. (1957) 'A theory of cognitive dissonance', in Fisher, C. (2000), 'The Ethics of Inactivity: Human Resource Managers and Quietism', unpublished paper, Nottingham Trent University, p. 7.

Honey, P. and Mumford, A. (1982) *The Manual of Learning Styles*, Maidenhead: Honey.

Kelly, G.A. (1955) *The Psychology of Personal Constructs*, New York: Norton.

Kolb, D.A. (1984) *Experiential Learning: Experience as the Source of Learning and Development*, Englewood Cliffs, NJ: Prentice-Hall.

Marsick, V.J. and O'Neil, J. (1999) 'The many faces of action learning', *Management Learning*, 30(2): 159–76.

McGill, I. and Beaty, L. (1992) *Action Learning – A Guide for Professional, Management and Educational Development*, Kogan Page.

Metcalfe, B. and Alban-Metcalfe, R. (2000) 'Heaven can wait', *Health Service Journal*, October: 26–9.

Peterson, C., Luborksky, L. and Seligman, M.E.P. (1983) 'Attributions and depressive mood shifts: a case study using the symptom-content method', *Journal of Abnormal Psychology*, 94: 96–103.

Revans, R. (1983) *The ABC of Action Learning*, Bromley: Chartwell-Bratt (Publishing and Training) Ltd.

Samra-Fredericks, D. (1998) 'Conversation analysis', in Symon, G. and Cassell, C. (eds), *Qualitative Methods and Analysis in Organizational Research – a Practical Guide*.

Schulman, P., Castellon, C. and Seligman, M.E.P. (1989) 'Assessing explanatory style: the content analysis of verbatim explanations and the attributional style questionnaire', *Behavioural Research Therapy*, 27(5).

Seligman, M.E.P., Nolen-Hoeksema, S., Thornton, N. and Thornton, K.M. (1990) 'Explanatory style as a mechanism of disappointing athletic performance', *Psychological Science*, 1: 143–6.

Watson, T.J. (2001) 'Professionals at work? – Social scientists, occupational anxiety and discursive ingenuity among human resource specialists', in Whitehead, S. and Dent, M. (eds), *Managing Professional Identities*, London: Routledge.

Weiner, B. (1986) *An Attributional Theory of Motivation and Emotion*, New York: Springer-Verlag.

Part V
Editors' conclusion

19 Management development

The holy grail of HRD?

Rosemary Hill and Jim Stewart

Introduction

As stated in our introductory chapter, the overall purpose of the book is to advance knowledge and understanding of the concept of HRD and its professional practice. We also posited that, whilst being confident in the assertion that MD is intrinsic to HRD theory and practice, we do not adopt a singular or consistent understanding in the book of what MD might be. Rather, the thrust of this volume has been to explore and probe – widely and deeply – the conceptualization, scope and impact of MD, and how it is researched and practised. A further implicit aim of the book has been to examine the contribution that it makes to the overall concept of HRD and its professional practice. The main aim of this final chapter is to pull together key strands of the book in a way that both appreciates the richness of the contributions and yet yields some interesting themes and messages from within the inherent complexity.

Before discussing how we propose to do this, we offer the following thought, which is reflected in the title of this chapter. It is clear from a collective reading of the chapters that MD *could* be conceived as the 'holy grail' of HRD, as MD does not exist in any straightforward, readily identifiable or workable fashion; and yet, despite its nebulous and illusive nature, it is persistently and passionately pursued by academics, professional practitioners and managers alike in search of what 'it' might actually 'be'. Arguably, the book is an axiomatic testimony to this claim.

Thus, in order to capture a wide-ranging and integrated view of the field of MD, our conclusions from putting together this book, and from considering the overall picture it represents, have been conceptualized in the framework at Figure 19.1. In her foreword to the book, Monica Lee likens getting to grips with MD to 'octopus wrestling', and suggests the need for a good net to capture the octopus in. The framework is, perhaps, a sort of octopus-catching net!

Figure 19.1 indicates that we have drawn conclusions from three main sources: (1) from some of the common chapter elements (the theoretical context of MD, the methods and approaches used to research and practise

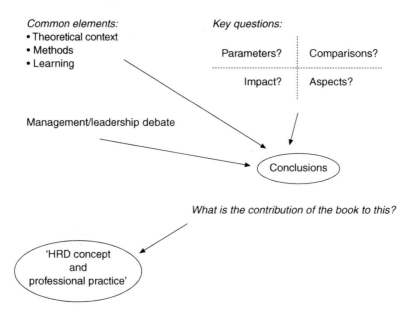

Figure 19.1 A conceptual framework for exploring MD.

MD, and the authors' key learning points); (2) from what the chapters have contributed to the management/leadership debate; and (3) from the four key questions introduced at the beginning of our introduction to the book in Chapter 1. We also speculate what the book may have contributed to the concept of HRD and its professional practice.

At this point, we would remind readers that the picture of MD we portray is neither exclusive nor exhaustive: inevitably it would be impossible to extract every theme or nuance from all of the chapters in the book, and there is a wealth of alternative pictures of MD to frame. We would therefore suggest that readers seek their own perspectives on 'octopus wrestling' and frameworks for netting one. The set of suggested activities at the end of the chapter is intended as a resource to assist this endeavour.

The theoretical context of management development

This section addresses the questions: '*What collectively might the chapters be telling us about the theoretical context of MD? Is an overall theoretical framework discernible?*'

Several theoretical context themes and contrasting perspectives can be traced in the book. We identify some of these in Table 19.1, and indicate the chapters in which they are exemplified. Again, we must stress that this is our interpretation of what may be some important components of an MD theoretical framework, and is in no way meant to be definitive. From our analysis, it would appear that several chapters adopt a pluralistic

Table *19.1* Some theoretical perspectives on MD

Themes	Chapters
Social constructionist (discursive) perspective	2, 3, 11, 13, 14, 16, 18
Rational/normative perspective	4, 5, 7, 9, 12, 15
Pluralistic/collaborative perspective	7, 8, 10, 13, 14, 18
Context-specific/contingent perspective	4, 5, 6, 12
Research-informed/evidence-based perspective	7, 9
'Working is learning' perspective	10, 13, 16, 17, 18

rather than a singular theoretical perspective – an observation that, perhaps, highlights both the broad-banded nature of our modelling in Figure 19.1 and also the complex patterning and interplay of MD theory derived in the chapters.

Several authors have grounded their work in a *social constructionist/ discursive perspective*. For example, Chapters 2 and 3, by Rigg, and Finch-Lees and Mabey, respectively, argue the case for managers being actively engaged in the construction of their development rather than merely being the object of development. In Chapter 11, Francis and D'Annunzio-Green focus on the individual and subjective nature of the employment relationship, and through their exposition of manager learning as a process of being able to write, reflect and critically understand events, Gold *et al.* (Chapter 16) add a further interesting dimension to this perspective.

By way of contrast, in Chapter 4 Brown leans more towards a *rational/normative perspective* through his analysis of strategic MD as an input to organization capability and performance. Similarly, Ponsford and Borley (Chapter 9) and Palmer *et al.* (Chapter 15) focus on the influence of MD on the performance capability and commitment of managers. Several contributors extol the virtue of a *pluralistic or collaborative perspective*. For instance, in Chapter 8 Stansfield and Stewart explore how stakeholder theory can be engaged to underpin MD research and practice in a pluralistic sense; and in Chapter 14 Garavan and McCarthy explain how the collaborative principles of multi-source feedback have been used as a theoretical context in their study of MD. These two examples, by Stansfield and Stewart, and Garavan and McCarthy, provide an interesting comparison to other chapters in the book where the research or practice does, perhaps, serve more a single than a multiple client or stakeholder interest.

Chivers' account of the South Yorkshire 'Management Update Programme' in Chapter 5 illustrates a relatively localized *context-specific/ contingent perspective* in terms of both geographical location and industry setting. By comparison, the studies featured in the two chapters by Le Deist *et al.* (Chapter 6) and Voeten (Chapter 12) are each theorized to the idiosyncrasies and contingencies of MD in a much wider context – that of a particular country, France and Vietnam respectively. Whilst the specific situation and set of contingent factors differs considerably in each of the examples mentioned here, the three chapters collectively offer a noteworthy insight into how context and contingency can significantly shape the way that MD is theorized, enabled and enacted.

Both Hamlin (Chapter 7) and Ponsford and Borley (Chapter 9) argue theoretically a *research-informed and evidence-based perspective*. They do so explicitly; the former in the context of an 'HRD Professional Partnership' research programme in a large civil service department, and the latter in the context of evidence-based practice in a multi-national organization. Even though just two chapters have been placed in Table 19.1 within the 'research-informed and evidence-based perspective', given the essential characteristics of this book, most (if not all) of the chapters could be categorized thus.

Given, too, the essential disposition of MD, a *'working is learning perspective'* can be identified in some guise in most, if not all, of the chapters. However, in Chapter 10 by Derksen *et al.*, and Chapter 13, by Franz, the notion of work and learning as inextricably entwined constituents of MD is an explicit focus. In Chapter 17, Trehan and Shelton examine leadership and its development from a critical perspective, one that encourages managers to make connections between learning and work. The exposition of action learning in the UK national health service by Bristow (Chapter 18) inevitably imparts a specific 'working is learning' perspective to MD research and practice.

So, is an overall theoretical context for MD discernible? Although it is really not possible to affirm this, two distinct typologies do seem apparent. One revolves around ideologies of learning, collaboration and constructionism; the other points to a more rationalist picture of MD theory that speaks to the strategic imperative, performance and sustainability of organizations. Seemingly, this presents a dichotomous position. However, the context in which MD is researched and practised, together with other design and delivery contingencies, will inevitably soften this framing.

MD research/practice methods and approaches

The book exhibits a fascinating assortment of innovative research and practice methods, ranging from large-scale surveys to single case studies, from long-term ethnographies to short-term studies, from programmes aimed at large homogenous groups to those designed for more discrete populations. As such, it is difficult to determine any clear methodological patterning and preference.

However, one thing does seem clear. In the book, there are several examples of research methods which are essentially 'reflections on practice' – designed to either evaluate the effectiveness of an MD programme or extract the learning from it. In this sense, we detect a blurring of the supposed separate activity streams of 'research' and 'practice', and from this conclude that much of what might be termed MD 'practice' could be construed as 'research', especially where a strong element of reflection and critical analysis is present in the design. An interesting illustration of this point is found in Chapter 5 – the account of the South Yorkshire Management Update Programme – whereby the impetus to reflect actively and critically on the wider learning from the programme was the writing of the story for this book, albeit some 15 years after the event. In the opening section of the chapter the author makes the case for studying HRD interventions in order to maximize learning, inform future practice and, potentially, influence national policy on how to support workers facing adverse circumstance. The research method in this case was relatively simple: to reflect upon and 'tell' the story of the practice – a methodological principle also prescribed by Gold *et al.* (Chapter 16). Who knows what contribution the knowledge gained in the South Yorkshire Management Update Programme could have made to alleviating adversity in similar, subsequent industry collapses had there, at the time of programme delivery, been a formal mechanism to encourage reflection upon the wider learning from it?

The book also exhibits an inspiring range of research and practice contexts, settings and situations, and what becomes apparent from reading across the chapters is that such factors of context and contingency have a profound influence on MD research and practice methods and approaches.

Key learning points

The following is a summary of some themes from the 'key learning points' sections of the book as a whole:

- There are many novel and innovative ways to research and practise MD. A corollary to this is that MD research and practice methods can be two sides of the same coin. For example, the evaluation of action learning using discourse analysis can help identify the extent to which managers and leaders are practising the lessons learned from working in action learning sets; and collaborative practice-grounded research partnerships can influence and enhance the impact and profile of MD, and HRD in general, in organizations
- There are both pros and cons in utilizing collaborative research and practice models. Benefits include the engagement of a wide range of 'clients' and stakeholders in activities such as professional research partnerships, multi-source feedback and co-created MD programmes, which can lead to a full and rich representation of the organization, groups and individuals in the study, design and delivery of MD. Potential pitfalls include the difficulty that some managers may have with a perceived lack of focus and structure in collaborative models and

partnerships. This situation may be exacerbated by a tendency for such methods to expose managers to the full force and complexity of everyday life in ways that they may not otherwise experience through normal managerial activity. Aligned to this thinking is that, whilst critical approaches to MD may be appealing in theory, they are fraught with difficulties and problematic consequences due to a reluctance on the part of managers to question and challenge operational norms and conventional ways of working and behaving

- The study and enactment of MD brings into focus the role that managers play and the influence and power that being a manager imbues. How 'qualified' are managers to operate effectively and ethically in such power plays? To what extent does MD explicitly acknowledge and address this issue?
- Creative constructionist approaches to MD can help managers find their own practical solutions to everyday problems as well as (or instead of?) facilitating longer-term behavioural change. When MD is seen (by the CEO and senior managers) to be of immediate and practical relevance and benefit to the organization, it is more likely to receive employer commitment and investment
- Whilst the notion of 'commitment' may not be completely understood, employer commitment is likely to have a significant impact on employee commitment. Whilst investment in MD may be an indicator of employer commitment to employees in general, it is also important that mutual commitment and expectations to/of MD itself are clarified and understood
- Misaligned or mishandled expectations of MD can lead to disaffected managers and a serious breach of their psychological contract with their employer
- The connection between 'working and learning' is a desirable characteristic of MD and should not be ignored or underestimated. However, the connection, and how to make it, is something that is not naturally understood and seized upon by managers engaging in MD

'Management' and 'leadership'

Only four of the chapters (Chapters 9, 13, 17 and 18) contains the terms 'leadership', 'leader' or 'leading' in the title. Does this mean then that these chapters connect exclusively with the concept of 'leadership' and distinguish clearly between 'leadership' and 'management'? Conversely does this mean that the other chapters, through the omission of 'leadership' in the titles, identify more with 'management' and exclude 'leadership' from their discussions? The short answer to both speculations is 'no'. We do not detect a particular theme, model or pattern emerging from the chapters that leads us to believe that management and leadership (and, by extension, management development and leadership development) have been explicitly or specifically defined as distinct, each from the other. We do, however, see some evidence of management and leadership being used interchangeably to mean one and the same – albeit mostly an implied rather than an explicit usage of the terms. One illustration of this is in Chapter 11, where the terms are applied interchangeably without specific rationalization and, seemingly, without incurring confusion or lack of clarity in the authors' arguments.

There are, of course, some interesting nuances and exceptions to the above generalizations. For example, in Chapter 17 the authors seem to identify more with the concept of leadership than management, reflecting from the literature that 'both these functions should be regarded as shared social processes, rather than residing in a single person'. Use of the word 'both' here may suggest that the authors differentiate between management and leadership, but even so this is an implicit distinction as they do not specifically explore the differentiation inferred. Discussions in Chapter 7 explicitly acknowledge the interchangeability of 'manager/management' and 'leader/leadership', arguing that 'managerial leadership is a constituent part of the everyday task of most managers'. In emphasizing the management competence of organizing people in leadership development, is the author of Chapter 13 making a distinction between management and leadership, or is he merely using the terms interchangeably? And in Chapter 4, where the focus is on strategic MD (SMD), could this, by implication, be construed as a focus on leadership development?

However, an overriding message from the chapters is that no concerted attempt has been made to define either the difference or the similarity between leadership and management, either theoretically or operationally. This leads us conclude that it may not really matter which term is used, but what may be important is the context in which these terms are engaged and the potential impact of their usage in a particular context or on a particular situation. For example, the study in Chapter 9 focuses on succession planning in the context of the need for the organization to raise future leaders – in effect, demonstrating a concern for enhancing the leadership capacity of the organization. Somehow it would seem inappropriate to speak of raising futures 'managers' in this context, as the organization clearly wants 'leaders' and, as this is a large multi-national private organization, it may be more politically astute to talk of leaders rather than managers in the context of succession planning and building organizational capability. Another illustration of using management and leadership in a specific context for particular effect can be found in Chapter 13, where the author makes a case for distinguishing between management and leadership for purposes of improving the 'leadership behaviours' of 'managers'.

Integration of key questions

In Chapter 1, we argued that the book addresses a number of questions about the conceptualization, scope, impact and delivery of MD. These are:

- What are the parameters of MD?
- What can we learn from comparative insights of MD?
- What is the impact of MD?
- What aspects of MD (techniques and approaches) are being engaged in MD research and practice?

To an extent, the summaries at the end of the four introductions to each part of the book have responded to these questions, and the foregoing discussion in this concluding chapter will have added to the learning from these summaries. In this section, we try to add value to what has already been said through an analysis of how the dimensions of MD used to structure this book ('parameters', 'insight', 'impact' and 'aspects') might be engaged in an exploratory model – exploratory in the sense that it can be used to facilitate an enquiry into MD.

An underlying assumption in Figure 19.2 is that MD is bounded by the parameters summarized at the end of Introduction to Part I – in the Figure, noted as 'Strategic', 'Practical', 'Global focus' and 'Individual focus'. A further assumption is that matters of 'impact', 'design' (aspects) and 'insight' are important components in the conceptualization and enactment of MD and the outcomes it needs to deliver to individuals and collectives.

The 'parameters of MD' are positioned as a set of four, paired 'cornerstones' with the connecting lines representing a continuum between each pairing. The vertical continuum assumes that MD will serve some predefined need in the organization, whether that be strategic (improving the performance capability of an organization, for instance) or practical (personal skills development, for example). As represented on the hori-

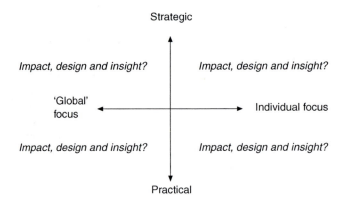

Figure 19.2 A way of understanding MD.

zontal continuum, the MD intervention will have a target audience which is likely to have primarily either **an individual** or a 'global' interest. We use the term 'global' here to mean a 'collective' – that is, a work team, a particular stakeholder group, an organization as a whole, an industry sector, a nation, a continent or, **used** in its literal sense, the world. Wherever an MD intervention sits on either continuum, a number of questions concerning the 'impact', 'design' and 'insight' of the intervention need to be explored. Some examples might be:

- What is the desired impact of this MD intervention?
- What is the best design for achieving the desired impact?
- What insights do we wish to gain?

Rephrased, these questions can be asked retrospectively in order to evaluate the effectiveness of a completed or ongoing MD project. The model at Figure 19.2 could therefore be utilized as either a design or evaluation model.

Conclusion and overall contribution of the book

Our intention in developing this book was to provide a comprehensive and up-to-date work on the state of MD research and practice. We believe that we have achieved this. The individual contributions jointly and severally represent a wealth of research and practice information and innovation. The framework at Figure 19.1 has proved to be a useful tool both for exploring the richness of the contributions and for capturing some important themes and messages. Ultimately, it has to be said, though, that we have probably found more questions than answers to the notion of what MD might 'be'. The diagnostic model at Figure 19.2 may provide a helpful resource, but it is certainly not intended as any kind of definitive model or tool. We do, however, hope that it will be used to promote thought and action amongst researchers and practitioners alike.

Turning the matter of what the book may have contributed to HRD theory and professional practice, it is evident that our search for the 'holy grail of HRD' has been rewarded with a number of important insights, many of which are exposed in this chapter. We are still confident in our initial assertion that MD is intrinsic to HRD theory and practice and, therefore, by extension, these insights into MD are also insights into HRD.

A particularly strong and notable theme from the book is the connection between 'learning and working', and the potential burden this may place on managers undergoing development if they incur confusion and dissonance in understanding and making the connection. This issue has significant bearing on HRD theory and professional practice, and the vital role that HRD professionals play in engaging line manager interest and commitment – not only in their own development, but in that of the people they lead and manage, their peers and the organization itself. If we look to the even wider field of HRM and the influence that the work of David Ulrich (Ulrich, 1997; Ulrich and Brockbank, 2005) has had on the way in which HR has been (re)organized in many private and public sector organizations over recent years, then HRD may too need to contemplate how it (re)organizes itself to work in innovative and engaging ways with managers in their development and the development of the organization. We suggest that much of this agenda would be concerned with helping to build management and leadership capacity and capability, in all areas and levels of the organization.

Some suggested activities

The following set of activities is offered as a resource for helping readers to consolidate their learning from the book and to further their own research and practice:

1   With reference to the framework at Figure 19.1:

  • Select one (or more) of the common elements of the book and analyse the chapters against this element(s).
  • What conclusions do you draw from the book about the 'management'/leadership' debate?
  • Identify some key questions of your own about MD. What answers to these questions can you find in the book?

2   Compare your findings and conclusions with those in the book. What are the similarities and differences? What meaning (specifically about MD) do you take from this analysis?

3   Identify some of your own key learning points from reading the book and from doing the activities at points (1) and (2), above. What specifically have you learned, and how could you/will you apply this learning in practice?

4   Use Figure 19.2 to critically analyse one (or more) of the chapters in the book. Given the nature of the MD intervention featured, what are your views about its conceptualization, methodology, delivery and outcome?

5   Use Figure 19.2 in the development of a piece of MD research or practice you currently plan to undertake, or use it to evaluate the appropriateness of a project you have worked on or are currently engaged in.

References

Ulrich, D. (1997) *Human Resource Champions: The Next Agenda for Adding Value and Delivering Results*, Cambridge, MA: Harvard Business School Press.
Ulrich, D. and Brockbank, W. (2005) *The HR Value Proposition*, Cambridge, MA: Harvard Business Press.

Index

Italic page numbers indicate illustrations and plates not included in the text page range.
References to notes are prefixed by n.
MD – management development
HRD – human resource development